10th Edition

ENGLISH FOR CAREERS

Business, Professional, and Technical

10th Edition

ENGLISH FOR CAREERS

Business, Professional, and Technical

Leila R. Smith

Roberta Moore

Prentice Hall
Upper Saddle River, New Jersey
Columbus, Ohio

Library of Congress Cataloging-in-Publication Data

Smith, Leila R.
  English for careers: business, professional, and technical / Leila R. Smith,
  Roberta Moore.— 10th ed., annotated instructor's ed.
     p. cm.
  Includes bibliographical references and index.
  ISBN 978–0–13–607200–3 (pbk. : alk. paper)
1. English language—Business English—Problems, exercises, etc. 2. English
language— Technical English—Problems, exercises, etc. I. Moore, Roberta,
II. Title.
PE1115.S62 2010
428.2'02465—dc22   2008045515

Editor in Chief: *Vernon Anthony*
Acquisitions Editor: *Gary Bauer*
Development Editor: *Linda Cupp*
Editorial Assistant: *Megan Heintz*
Production Coordination: *Nesbitt Graphics, Inc. and The Book Company*
Project Manager: *Christina Taylor*
AV Project Manager: *Janet Portisch*
Operations Specialist: *Pat Tonneman*
Art Director: *Diane L. Ernsberger*
Cover Designer: *Kellyn E. Donnelly*
Cover Image(s): *Getty*
Manager, Rights and Permissions: *Zina Arabia*
Image Permission Coordinator: *Annette Linder*
Director of Marketing: *David Gesell*
Marketing Manager: *Leigh Ann Sims*
Marketing Assistant: *Les Roberts*
Copyeditor: *Susan Gall*

This book was set in Melior by Nesbitt Graphics, Inc. and was printed and
bound by Courier-Kendallville. The cover was printed by Lehigh-Phoenix
Color/Hagerstown.

Pearson Education Ltd., London
Pearson Education Singapore Pte. Ltd.
Pearson Education Canada, Inc.
Pearson Education—Japan

Pearson Education Australia Pty. Limited
Pearson Education North Asia Ltd., Hong Kong
Pearson Educación de Mexico, S.A. de C.V.
Pearson Education Malaysia Pte. Ltd.

Prentice Hall
is an imprint of

www. pearsonhighered. com

10 9 8 7 6 5 4
ISBN-13: 978-0-13-502331-0
ISBN-10: 0-13-502331-9
(Annotated Instructor's Edition) ISBN-13: 978-0-13-607200-3
ISBN-10: 0-13-607200-3

To Seymour, Eric, Alice, Roberta, Nina Beth, Sheela Danielle, Sarala Rose, Sean Suresh, Jonathan
—Leila R. Smith

To Ivan, Alma, and Ben
—Roberta Moore

"A word fitly spoken is like apples of gold in settings of silver."
—The Bible

CONTENTS

CHAPTER 3 Writing Complete Sentences 51

Read, Recap, and Replay

CHAPTER 7   Mastering Verbs   132

Read, Recap, and Replay

CHAPTER 8 ## Mastering Adjectives and Adverbs   158

CHAPTER 11   Mastering the Fine Points of Punctuation 219

Read, Recap, and Replay

Communication skills are highly valued in today's job market. Writing and speaking Standard English are essential to success in your career and in today's vast social network. This course will help you develop the key skills that will make you a good communicator and a valued member of the workforce: reading and comprehending, building a substantial vocabulary, and speaking and writing the language that is necessary for success in the workplace—grammatically correct English. *English for Careers* will also help you develop the habit of self-directed learning through use of the technology-based supplements that align coursework with your individual needs.

THE LANGUAGE OF CAREERS

The language we use, both spoken and written, significantly affects our ability to earn a good living, advance in a career, and even enjoy good social contacts. What kind of language does a business, professional, or technical career require? "Career English" is not a special or separate language. It is the common language used for writing and speaking across all fields of endeavor: Standard English. The extent to which your use of English is "standard" versus "nonstandard" depends on your cultural and social environment and the English principles you've learned and put into practice.

In our culture, it is common to use several language styles to communicate with different people in various situations.

- ***To a child:*** Imagine talking with a group of adults at a party; now picture yourself warning a young child away from a hot stove. Think about how your communication style would differ.

- ***To friends and family:*** Perhaps you use slang or a regional or community dialect in everyday conversation with certain friends and family. You might use a different communication style with other friends or acquaintances. We all vary our communication style in different situations.

- ***English as a second language:*** If you were not born in an English-speaking country or if you grew up in a bilingual community, this might influence your use of English grammar and vocabulary.

- ***In the workplace:*** If you work in a business, professional, or technical career, you will need to speak Standard English—the style essential for career success as well as success in personal relationships with business and professional colleagues. *English for Careers* will help you communicate confidently and correctly in the workplace.

THE *ENGLISH FOR CAREERS* LEARNING SYSTEM

This book is different. You don't browse through it. You don't read it like other books. You learn your way through it! In *English for Careers,* you don't focus on grammar terms and rules. You focus on oral and written Standard English to communicate successfully and confidently in the workplace. The information you need is presented in an interesting and efficient way that makes learning easier. You will read succinct summaries about language usage and then apply them immediately. You learn the Standard English principles as used by well-informed and well-educated people.

CHAPTER ORGANIZATION

Chapter Opening Pages

Each of the 14 chapters opens with a photograph of people at work and a list of chapter objectives that tell you exactly what skills and knowledge you should acquire by the time you complete the chapter.

Read, Recap, and Replay

Each chapter has a set of learning steps called Read, Recap, and Replay. When you Read, you get information about one key aspect of the chapter's topic. These short learning units are more efficient than longer ones, and you enjoy a feeling of accomplishment as you complete each portion. Along the way, you apply what you just read by doing a Recap. At the end of each Read, you verify what you've learned by responding to the Replay questions.

Self-Evaluation

As soon as you complete a Recap or a Replay, you will be told where to check your answers in Appendix F, beginning on page 431. Write answers with a blue or black pen; then use a different color pen to show corrections. When ready to review, you'll know which ones, if any, you originally had wrong. Then if you have a question, you can reread that text portion or ask your instructor for help.

Concept Review & Skill-building Applications

Each chapter concludes with a review and applications that give you the opportunity to confirm what you know well and where you need more practice.

- *Checkpoint:* A summary of key principles that helps you assess your knowledge.
- *Special Assignment and Proofreading for Careers:* Applications that provide real-world examples of written communications and opportunities for you to practice writing and proofreading. Your instructor has the answers to these exercises.
- *Practice Quiz:* A chance to test your overall knowledge of what you have learned. Your instructor has the answers to this quiz.

The Checkpoint and Practice Quiz are minimum essentials for testing your knowledge of each chapter. Your instructor will decide whether to assign the Proofreading or Special Assignments.

Self-Study Practice and Tutorials

At the end of each chapter's applications, you will find a list of extra practice options.

- *Vocabulary and Spelling for Careers* in Appendix B helps you expand your vocabulary and improve your spelling and should be completed at the end of each chapter.
- *Replay Drills* can be used as needed for more practice on mastering key chapter principles.
- *MyWritingLab* is an online learning system that provides a diagnostic test to assess your learning needs and provide you with a study plan. Read more about this on the next page.

English for Careers Online

Additional exercises are provided on the *English for Careers* Companion Website (www.prenhall.com/Smith). You have the option of completing the Proofreading for Careers and Practice Quiz exercises online or in your textbook.

These icons are a visual cue telling you when a resource or activity is available online, only in the textbook, or both, and when to do writing assignments at the computer.

THE SYSTEM WORKS

The *English for Careers* learning system results in student success—but you must follow the steps: Read, Recap, and Replay. Skipping steps results in lower achievement. So please play the game according to the rules. Check your answers carefully, and ask about anything not clear to you.

One optional step is a pretest before studying each chapter. Your instructor has the option of assigning this or not. However, because doing the Replays is interesting and challenging, some students are tempted to pretest their English knowledge by responding to the questions without reading the explanations and studying the examples. Please resist such shortcuts. By following the recommended steps, you learn more, do better on tests, and end up saving time. Most students are enthusiastic about this way of learning.

WHAT'S IN IT FOR YOU?

A proven method that works

What's in *English for Careers* for you? Because you are interacting with the textbook so often, you immediately apply what you learn, enabling you to understand it better and remember it. Immediate feedback (with answers in the back of the book) is satisfying and encourages you to continue with enthusiasm.

Incidental learning

While learning *English for Careers,* you also learn more about today's workplace, and you increase or develop a success-oriented attitude. Many of the example and application sentences illustrating English deal with business practices, workplace cultural diversity, expected behavior in today's international marketplace, workplace etiquette, and helpful attitudes for self-development.

Respect and confidence

After successfully completing this textbook, you will enjoy confidence in the correctness and effectiveness of your speech and writing. Good communication skills, more than any other single factor, determine who gets the good job, who keeps it, and who gets the promotion. You'll find that coworkers and even supervisors will come to you for business English help. They will soon sense that you are the company expert in grammar, punctuation, spelling, and communication style.

Fun and games

Although learning isn't all fun and games, people don't learn very much unless they enjoy the experience at least some of the time. You'll find bits of humor hidden in the various exercises; smiling helps us feel better and puts our minds in a learning mode. Enjoy *English for Careers*. With a positive attitude, you'll have some fun along the way. Give it a chance; you'll find your command of English will be a lifelong asset to your career (and personal life too)!

NEED MORE PRACTICE? NEED HELP WITH SPECIFIC WRITING PROBLEMS? WANT BETTER GRADES?

MyWritingLab is an online learning system that provides diagnostic assessment and progressive exercises to help identify grammar, mechanics, and other writing problems. It will help you become a better writer. If a MyWritingLab access code was not packaged with your textbook, a code can be purchased online at www.prenhall.com <http://www.prenhall.com/> (ISBN 0-205-66897-6).

Here is how MyWritingLab can help you save time and improve results:

✓ **Individualized study plans** help you assess your strengths and weaknesses for targeted study.

✓ **Thousands of exercises** give you a chance to improve skills and your grades.

✓ **Video tutorials** assist you when your instructor isn't available.

✓ **Track your progress** and see results!

Registering for MyWritingLab

1. Go to www.mywritinglab.com.

2. Follow the onscreen instructions for students.

3. Ask your instructor if he or she has set up a course for your class. If so, select that course. If no course is set up by your instructor, select the *English for Careers* version of MyWritingLab.

4. After you register, you can log on at any time at www.mywritinglab.com.

REPLAY

Write your answers in the blanks of this sample Replay. If you don't know an answer, look for the information in the preceding Dear Student letter on page xiv. Fill in the blank for Question 1 and answer T (true) or F (false) for the rest of the questions.

_____ 1. The language style appropriate for most business, professional, and technical careers is called _____ .

_____ 2. It's wrong to use slang when writing a letter to a friend.

_____ 3. You should be sure to use the same style of language in all communications.

_____ 4. Standard English is always superior to other types of English.

_____ 5. To succeed in this course, you must memorize a long list of traditional grammar rules and terms.

_____ 6. This course includes self-directed learning opportunities.

_____ 7. The single most important ability required to get a good job or a promotion is communication ability.

_____ 8. "Incidental learning" means picking up information about other topics while focused on learning the main topic—in this case, English.

_____ 9. If you look at the answers in the back of the book (*after* doing the exercise), you are cheating.

_____ 10. The most successful students start by first answering the Replay questions and then reading the explanations and examples.

_____ 11. By completing *English for Careers* carefully, you achieve thorough mastery of traditional grammar terms and rules.

_____ 12. Look up the answers in the back of the book the day after you complete the Recaps and Replays.

_____ 13. The Checkpoint near the end of each chapter usually summarizes the chapter.

_____ 14. The last item in nearly every chapter is Proofreading for Careers.

_____ 15. After completing this course successfully, you will be confident of your ability to speak and write English in a style that leads to a successful career.

Check your answers below.

How did you do? _____

Answers to Replay

1. Standard English   **2.** F   **3.** F   **4.** F   **5.** F   **6.** T   **7.** T   **8.** T   **9.** F
10. F   **11.** F   **12.** F   **13.** T   **14.** F   **15.** T

COURSE PRETEST

Take this test just to get an idea of where you stand before you begin the course. Write the letter of the correct answer in the blank. Your instructor has the answer key.

_____ 1. The carton of books and papers (a) have been (b) has been (c) were lost.

_____ 2. Etymology is the study of (a) insects (b) synonyms and antonyms (c) grammar and word usage (d) the history of words.

_____ 3. If the first line of the inside address of a business letter is "Mr. Samuel E. Smith," the preferred salutation is (a) Ladies and Gentlemen: (b) Dear Sir: (c) Dear Sirs: (d) Dear Mr. Smith: (e) Dear Mr. Samuel E. Smith:

_____ 4. *Outsource* means to (a) import needed supplies for manufacturing (b) export high-technology products (c) use services of workers who are not employees of your organization (d) wastefully use valuable natural resources (e) help laid-off employees find new jobs.

_____ 5. Such a (a) phenomena (b) phenomenae (c) phenomenon (d) phenomeni (e) phenomenae has never before occurred.

_____ 6. George's wife is the (a) president of the company (b) President of the Company (c) President of the company (d) president of the Company.

_____ 7. When preparing slide presentations, the words are relatively unimportant. (True or False)

_____ 8. After three (a) year's (b) years' (c) years of being on this merry-go-round, George decided to get off and get a new job.

_____ 9. When you're laying out material for a Web site, place the most interesting and important information at or near the beginning. (True or False)

_____ 10. Please give the reports to Frank Hitt and (a) I (b) me (c) myself.

_____ 11. Ms. Denova is the one (a) who (b) whom we believe danced the hoochie koochie.

_____ 12. If you had (a) gone (b) went to work today, you would have seen the sunset.

_____ 13. Which would be (a) more easy (b) easiest (c) easier (d) most easiest for you to prepare, a letter or a short report?

_____ 14. We hope to receive (a) a (b) an 18 percent discount.

_____ 15. After working at the computer all day, his eyes were tired.
The preceding sentence has a (a) comma splice (b) lack of parallel construction (c) misplaced part (d) dangling verbal (e) lack of subject-verb agreement.

For items 16–20, write C in the blank if all the punctuation is correct; otherwise, correct the punctuation.

_____ 16. "Telecommuting," he said, "is good if you are disciplined."

_____ 17. Money, beauty, intelligence, and charm—she has them all, said George's friend Jesse.

_____ 18. Mr. Crane is not here however, I can help you.

_____ 19. We've mailed you a copy of the new book we told you about and hope it will reach you before the end of the month.

_____ 20. Greet your clients by name then welcome them with a smile.

After you find out how many you answered correctly, read your "fortune."

*Number Right*_____

18–20	You have a good command of English for your career. This course will serve as a brushup, and you will become an expert.
15–17	Your English skill is fair. After the practice provided in this course, you'll have excellent skill in the English required for careers.
12–14	Your English for your career needs improvement. Because your basic language skill is all right, you'll enjoy the rapid learning that will result from completing all assignments.
0–11	You came to the right place! Taking this course is a wise decision. Because you are now motivated to learn English for your career, you'll capture those principles that escaped you in the past.

ABOUT THE AUTHORS

Leila R. Smith, Los Angeles Harbor College Professor Emeritus of Office Administration, has a New York University Bachelor of Science degree in business education and a University of San Francisco Master's degree in education. In addition to Harbor College, Professor Smith taught at Bay Path College in Massachusetts, in California's Pierce and Valley Colleges, and in New York City proprietary schools. Among her many professional activities, she has been a Fulbright exchange instructor, teaching English and communication in the business department of City and East London College in London, England, for an academic year.

A federal grant enabled her to study methods of applying brain research to business English instruction, as reflected in the unique teaching/learning styles of this text. This study also culminated in the writing of the text *RSVP—Relaxation, Spelling, Vocabulary, Pronunciation.* Other publications include the texts *Communication and English for Careers* and *Basic English for Business and Technical Careers,* as well as professional newsletters and articles in professional journals.

She has served as Communication Editor for the *Business Education Forum,* the journal of the National Business Education Association. Professor Smith, a recipient of the Pimentel Award for Excellence in Education, has conducted workshops and seminars on business English and communication and on teaching and learning methods for educators, corporate groups, and government agencies and has worked in various business capacities.

Roberta Moore is a writer, editor, and author residing in New York City. She holds a Bachelor of Arts degree in English literature from Wayne State University in Detroit, Michigan. She has held editorial and executive positions with some of the nation's leading publishing houses, specializing in business education, office technology, and business English and communications. In addition to developing hundreds of educational programs, she has traveled throughout the country conducting training workshops for teachers and publishing professionals and speaking at educational conferences and on college campuses.

In 1992, Ms. Moore formed her own company, Roberta Moore Publishing & Communications, which provides professional writing and editorial services and manages the development of publications for corporations, nonprofit organizations, and public agencies. Ms. Moore also does consulting in the field of corporate communications, specializing in employee diversity training and issues of special interest to the small business community, as well as writing speeches for top executives, newsletters, and a variety of corporate literature.

Ms. Moore is coauthor of the *Pearson Business Reference and Writer's Handbook* and several textbooks: *The Attitude Advantage, College Success, Telecommunications, Telephone Communication in the Information Age,* and *Applied Communication Skills Series: Grammar* and *Writing Sentences.*

ACKNOWLEDGMENTS

The authors and editors of *English for Careers,* Tenth Edition, thank you for your assistance:

Susan Guzman-Trevino, Temple College

Sissy Copeland, Piedmont Technical College

Janet L. Myszkowski, Chattahoochee Technical College

Mandy Burrell, Holmes Community College

Pat Donahue, Monroe Community College

Cynthia S. Becerra, Humphreys College

Susan Payneer, City College of San Francisco

A finely crafted book can result only with the assistance of a talented and dedicated publishing staff. The authors of *English for Careers,* Tenth Edition wish to thank the following Prentice Hall team members for their invaluable contributions to this work: Gary Bauer, Linda Cupp, and Christina Taylor. We also extend a special thanks to Kathy Smith and Paul Fennessy of Nesbitt Graphics, Inc.

1 Mastering Language— Resources and Words

After completing Chapter 1, you will be able to do the following:

- Acquire the "dictionary habit"—using dictionaries regularly to improve vocabulary, word choices, spelling, and pronunciation.

- Locate and use the full range of information provided in dictionaries.

- Choose a dictionary that best meets your needs for everyday use.

- Use print and online thesauruses to broaden your vocabulary, expand your use of language, and improve your writing style.

- Use a reference manual to revise content and correct errors in your writing.

READ 1   YOU ARE WHAT YOU SPEAK

Words are the foundation of speaking and writing.

Your words—the **vocabulary** you use to communicate—tell a listener or reader about you. Words can make you appear to be a foggy or a clear thinker. Words can make you sound well-educated and informed or they can make you sound ignorant. They *a*ffect (or is it *e*ffect?) how people react to you or to the organization you represent.

Being able to choose the right word—the word that is precise and that has the most impact on your reader or listener—makes you a clearer and more confident communicator. This is true for both oral and written communication. You will not be able to write well unless you can speak well and have mastery of a large vocabulary. Have you ever said, "I know what I mean, but I just can't explain it"? While it is perfectly normal to have those moments when you simply can't call up the right words or can't remember a word, this is different from not having the vocabulary available to be called upon. Throughout this course you will become more *articulate* (look up the definition if you aren't familiar with this word) by expanding both your vocabulary and your awareness of how you use language.

To supplement your course work, please make a commitment to develop the following habits:

■ Read books, magazines, and newspapers on various subjects (current events, lifestyle, business/finance, special interest and trade magazines; biographies, as well as fiction and nonfiction books; and a daily newspaper).

■ Listen to articulate and well-informed speakers (radio, TV, lectures, etc.).

■ Converse with well-informed, educated people.

■ Make a habit of looking up the meaning of unfamiliar words rather than ignoring them and moving on.

Investing time in the goals of improving your language skills and developing a large and precise vocabulary will give you all kinds of advantages, including the following:

■ You will speak with confidence and authority, knowing you are making yourself clear.

■ You will be able to more easily persuade others to your point of view.

■ You will be able to say what you mean without using words or phrases, such as "you know what I mean," that make you sound inarticulate.

■ You will enjoy using a wide variety of information resources and use them fully.

■ You will become a better writer, and you will be more comfortable with the task of writing.

Lexicographers at Work

Lexicographer Noah Webster spent 20 years handwriting the first comprehensive American dictionary, *An American Dictionary of the English Language.* This dictionary had 70,000 entries. Today's dictionaries have up to 250,000 entries, and many dictionary publishers include "Webster" in their titles because of his fame.

Who decides which words get into the dictionary? The people who compile dictionaries are called **lexicographers.** It's probably not a job you would want, but you can appreciate the people who do this work. Lexicographers collect information from books, magazines, trade journals, brochures, radio and TV programs, speeches, the Internet, and all other forms of spoken and written communication. They record new words, new meanings, new usage, spellings, and pronunciations of our very complex and ever-changing English language. They review tremendous numbers of words used throughout the English-speaking world—both formally and informally, and in various activities—from *a*rmed robbery to zoology.

Dictionaries—Descriptions, Not Prescriptions

Dictionaries describe how people worldwide are using English *at the time of compiling that particular dictionary*.

Modern dictionaries don't prescribe—or tell you what to do—the way a physician writes a prescription. They tell you which pronunciations, spellings, and vocabulary are **Standard English** or **preferred usage**—that is, widely used and respected by well-educated people—and which are non-Standard, informal, slang, or vulgar. They also tell you the meanings that are modern and those that are outdated—*archaic* is the word used by many dictionaries.

Dictionaries also provide guidance on *how to use* the language. For example, contrary to the slogan you may have heard in your childhood, "*Ain't* ain't in the dictionary," *ain't* has been in some dictionaries since 1951. Knowing dictionary information about *ain't,* you wouldn't use it during job interviews; however, you might write "He ain't here" as dialogue to show that a character in a film script is uneducated.

Types of Dictionaries

A dictionary is one of the most valuable reference tools for acquiring good language skills, and it's one you have probably used often. Think of it as a friend you wish to know better as you work your way through this chapter. The information will help you in the selection of a current dictionary that best meets your needs. It will also help you appreciate the full range of information contained in a good dictionary.

Unabridged Dictionaries

An **unabridged dictionary** typically has at least 250,000 entries, or all the words the lexicographers believe belong in a dictionary. Information for each entry is extensive, as are the **front matter** (explanatory information in the front) and **back matter** (appendixes or other sections containing additional information about language and usage). Unless you have a professional or a strong personal interest in language, you probably don't need an unabridged dictionary. When you do need one, visit your local or college library. Because they are so comprehensive, unabridged dictionaries are not updated as often as abridged dictionaries, so be aware of this when you are using one.

Abridged Dictionaries

Abridged dictionaries are available in paperback, hardcover, and electronic formats. They have fewer entries and are updated frequently—some as often as annually. It is important for your career as well as home use to own up-to-date pocket-size and college dictionaries.

Hardcover **college dictionaries** are large books with at least 100,000 entries and include ample front and back matter. Keep a current one at home and at work. Paperback **pocket dictionaries** have far fewer entries than college dictionaries and less front and back matter, but are convenient to carry to classes.

When you shop for a new dictionary, look for the latest copyright date (on the copyright page) and get the newest one available. Don't buy sight unseen; your online bookstore might have a feature that lets you see inside the book, but, if not, go to a bookstore and compare dictionaries. Each one has its own "language" for explanations, formats for entries, and categories of information given about words. They also offer different material in the front and back matter. The following college and pocket dictionaries are good for workplace communication as well as for home and family use. When you select one of these, be sure it is the latest edition.

- *American Heritage Dictionary of the English Language*
- *American Heritage College Dictionary*
- *Merriam-Webster's Collegiate Dictionary*
- *Microsoft Encarta College Dictionary*
- *Random House Webster's College Dictionary*
- *Webster's New World College Dictionary*
- *Oxford American College Dictionary*

RECAP   If you already own a dictionary, use this checklist to determine whether you need a new one.

_____ A.   I have a hardcover or pocket college dictionary.

_____ B.   I do not have a hardcover or pocket college dictionary.

_____ A.   I own one of the dictionaries recommended here.

_____ B.   I do not own one of the dictionaries recommended here.

_____ A.   The copyright date on my dictionary is the newest one available for that publication.

_____ B.   There is a newer edition of my dictionary available.

If you checked any of the B answers, now is the time to buy a new dictionary. We recommend a hardcover college dictionary for use at home and a pocket dictionary if you like to carry one with you.

Electronic Dictionaries

Most of the top-selling print dictionaries come in electronic format and have online versions that you can access on the Internet. You can also buy handheld electronic dictionaries. These formats are convenient, but they do not replace the need for a college dictionary in book form.

There are some great online dictionaries that offer a wide range of information and links to many language sources. Some of these are listed below. Try them out and discover the features that you like best. Every effort has been made to provide accurate and current Internet information. However, due to possible changes of Internet addresses, some web links may not be functional.

Merriam-Webster Online
http://www.m-w.com

yourDictionary.com Online Dictionary and Thesaurus
http://www.yourdictionary.com

OneLook.com Online Dictionary
www.onelook.com

Cambridge Dictionaries Online
http://dictionary.cambridge.org

Dictionary.com Online Dictionary and Thesaurus
www.dictionary.com

REPLAY 1

Fill in the blanks based on answers obtained from your dictionary and Read 1.

Example: Name a dictionary recommended in Read 1.

Oxford American College Dictionary

1. What is the full name and copyright date of your newest dictionary?
   _____ .

2. A comprehensive dictionary containing at least 250,000 entries is known as an _____ dictionary.

3. A hardcover college dictionary with at least 100,000 entries is known as an _____ dictionary.

4. You should have an up-to-date _____ dictionary at home and at work, and a _____ dictionary to carry with you.

5. Unabridged dictionaries are not updated as often as smaller dictionaries.
   True _____ False _____ .

6. If you have an electronic dictionary, there is no reason to buy a printed one.
   True _____ False _____ .

7. The pronunciations, spellings, and vocabulary widely used and respected by well-educated people is known as _____ .

8. Meanings of words change; old meanings are referred to in dictionaries as

   _____ .

9. The place to find the publication date of a dictionary is on the _____ .

10. The people who compile dictionaries are called _____ .

Check your answers on page 431.

READ 2   GETTING TO KNOW YOUR DICTIONARY

This section is like an owner's manual for using your dictionary. Step one is to get an overview. It is vital to know what's in it, where to find the information, and how to use it, along with this text, to improve your English usage.

College dictionaries are divided into three major parts:

1. **Front matter**—everything before the first *A* word, including the inside front cover.

2. **Entries**—all the *A* to *Z* words (including word parts like prefixes and suffixes) with information about each.
3. **Back matter**—everything after the last *Z* word (including the inside back cover).

Each of these parts has unique features that you need to get to know. For an overview, read the table of contents and scan the front and back matter. Also look at the inside back and front covers to see all the categories of information contained in *your* college dictionary and where to find them. For example, in good, current dictionaries, you might find such assistance as A Guide for Writers, Avoiding Insensitive and Offensive Language, American Holidays, Science and Math Symbols, Currency (money) of various countries, Proofreader's Marks, Roman Numerals, Metric System, Foreign Language Expressions, Geographical and Biographical Information, Synonyms, Calendars used in various parts of the world, and even Commonly Misspelled Words.

Cracking Dictionary "Code"

Dictionary entries include some or all of the following: syllables, pronunciations, definitions, parts of speech, alternative spellings, etymology (history of the word), usage label (in what context the word is used), picture of the item, synonyms, run-ins (which are words derived from the entry word, such as *typographical* near the end of the *typography* entry), plurals, capitalization, year the word was first seen in print, and other helpful notes. This is what is meant by "the code."

Your dictionary will have a complete explanation of how to interpret its code.

The following section provides a review of some of the basics of layout and "code" that you will find in most dictionaries.

Guide Words

Guide words at the top of each page show the alphabetic range of that page so that words can be located quickly.

Get in the habit of using the guide words rather than skimming the page so that you can locate words quickly. For example, in *Merriam-Webster's Collegiate Dictionary*, Eleventh Edition, the guide words on page 369 are:

dodgem ■ dog's breakfast   369

This means the first entry on page 369 is *dodgem* and the last entry on that page is *dog's breakfast*. In between, you will find only words that begin with the letters *dod* through *dog*; if you are looking for the word *dough*, for example, you know it is a few pages ahead. On page 375 the guide words are:

double-ring ■ dovishness   375

You can see at a glance that this is the page on which you will find *dough*.

Syllables

Dictionaries separate the syllables of each entry with a symbol—usually a centered dot, for example:

di·vi·sion   in·ter·pret

Syllables help you with spelling, pronunciation, and word division at the end of a line.

When a hyphen separates syllables, you know that the entry is a compound word that requires a hyphen (this is a rule of spelling). (Some compound words are not hyphenated, which means you might not find them listed at all.) Look up *multiplication* to see how your dictionary shows syllables. Next, look up *full-fledged:* Notice that a hyphen divides the first and second syllables.

Pronunciation

Pronunciation follows the entry word in italics, within parentheses ( ), or within back-slashes \\. You need to fully understand this code if you have trouble pronouncing a word.

Words can have more than one correct pronunciation. Usually the most commonly used and preferred one is given first.

In most dictionaries the pronunciation key is at the bottom of every page or alternate page, or in the front matter, or back matter. Although the codes may differ from one dictionary to another, they result in the same pronunciation.

The syllables of words are spoken with either more or less force, commonly called *accent*. A word is mispronounced when the speaker puts the emphasis on the wrong syllable. **Diacritical marks** and **accent marks** show the relative amount of stress for each syllable. The three degrees of stress are weak—no accent, strong—primary accent, and medium—secondary accent. To interpret this code, see the pronunciation key in your dictionary.

RECAP Look up the syllables of the following words. Write them in the blanks with a slash (/) between the syllables. Circle the syllable that is accented in each word.

1. multiplication _____
2. mumbo jumbo _____
3. lexicographer _____
4. colloquial _____

Check your answers on page 431.

5. With help from the pronunciation key and the accent marks, say these words aloud correctly: *decadence, either, hors d'oeuvre, incognito, nausea, sadism, secretive*

Etymology

The origin or historical development of a word is its **etymology.** Etymology of words is sometimes important to business communication and is often interesting. Most important now, however, is to recognize and interpret etymology so that you avoid the common error of confusing it with a definition. In some dictionaries the etymology follows the definitions, and in others it comes before. Etymology is not provided for every word. When it is included, you usually find it within brackets [ ], double brackets [[ ]], or double backslashes / /.

Definitions

Many words are used in more than one way; that is, they have more than one definition and may also be used as more than one part of speech.

For such words, two or more numbered definitions may follow the entry word. If a definition has several shades of meaning, letters are used in addition to numbers. For words often used as more than one part of speech—for example, *fence* means one thing as a verb and another as a noun—separate definitions may be shown for each and sometimes even separate entries.

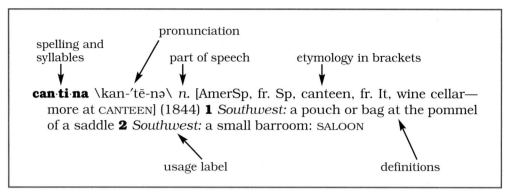

Figure 1.1
By permission. From *Merriam-Webster's Collegiate Dictionary, Eleventh Edition* © 2007 by Merriam-Webster, Incorporated.

Usage, Style, and Field Labels

Usage, style, or field labels note something special about how the word is used.

Certain words, definitions, and spellings are "labeled" according to systems that vary with the dictionary. Examples are *archaic, technical, informal, humorous, slang, taboo, used mainly by children, regional, nonstandard, American, British*. The labels are usually abbreviated in dictionaries. Most words in the dictionary are Standard English and don't require identifying labels.

The labels *archaic* or *arch.*, mean the word is currently used only in special contexts, although it was appropriate for general use in the past. Archaic differs from obsolete in that *obs.* means the word is no longer used except historically. A word labeled *rare* is, as you can guess, rarely used. Certain other examples are known as field labels, such as *chemistry, biology, medicine;* usage labels, such as *British, Scottish, Southwest;* and style labels, such as *slang, colloquial, obscene, poetic, informal, taboo, technical, American.*

Consult your dictionary's front matter for the labeling system and translations of the labeling code.

Parts of Speech

The different ways in which a word can be used to convey meaning in a sentence are indicated with an abbreviation of the part of speech, for example, n. = noun, adj. = adjective, conj. = conjunction, v or vb = verb, vt or vi = transitive verb and intransitive verb. In the next chapter, you will learn about how words are used as different parts of speech in sentences.

Word to the Wise

When looking up the meaning of a word, be sure to distinguish between the *etymology* and the *definition.* If the meaning has changed over time, some dictionaries list the earliest definitions first, right after the etymology, and continue in more or less chronological order. Other dictionaries give the modern meaning first and end with older meanings, followed by etymology. Find out the system in your own dictionary by consulting the front matter.

Synonyms, words with similar meanings, are included in the definitions of a word. Synonyms help a writer get the exact shade of meaning desired.

REPLAY 2

To answer the following questions, use your own dictionary so that you'll become accustomed to its "code"—that is, the various symbols and abbreviations used.

Example: What part of speech is *faux pas* and what does it mean?

noun: a social blunder

1. What two letters are silent in *faux pas?* _____

2. How many syllables does *quarterback* have? _____

3. Which syllable in *quarterback* has the primary accent: first, second, or third?
_____

4. Which syllable in *quarterback* has the secondary accent: first, second, or third?
_____

5. Which syllable in *quarterback* has no accent? _____

6. What part of speech is *quarterback* when it means directing or leading?
_____

7. Which syllable has the primary accent in the preferred pronunciation of *incomparable:* first, second, third, fourth, fifth? _____

8. Based on the pronunciation key in your dictionary, the first *e* in *wrecker* is pronounced the same as the *e* in what word?
_____

9. *Disinterested* and *uninterested* mean the same. (a) true _____
(b) false _____ (c) maybe _____

10. What words in the pronunciation key of your dictionary illustrate the schwa (∂) sound? _____

11. What does *gymnasium* mean in Germany?
_____

12. According to the preferred pronunciation, which syllable has the primary stress in *affluent* and *affluence?* _____

13. Divide these words into syllables, and circle the syllable that has the primary accent according to your dictionary's code: subtle _____ rationale _____ infrastructure _____

14. What is the other correct spelling of *catalog?* _____ Which does your dictionary show first? _____ What two parts of speech are most common for this word? _____

Answers are on page 431 or specific to your dictionary.

READ 3   NO "BAD SPELLERS"

If you often consult a dictionary for spelling help, you're not a bad speller. In fact, you're probably a good speller because you correct your mistakes before anyone sees them. If no one sees your mistakes, no one needs to know your secret. The reader sees the words correctly spelled, and that's all that matters.

Never succumb to the notion that you are a "bad speller." Most important is to want to spell correctly and to believe you can.

What you can believe, you can achieve. Spend five minutes a day consciously looking at some words in a newspaper, book, or magazine. That's all it takes to store a tremendous number of words in the magnificent computer between your ears.

More Than One Correct Spelling

Some words have more than one correct spelling. The dictionary entry will show them joined by *or.*

the·ater or the·atre   mea·ger or mea·gre   pi·zazz or piz·zazz

Although both spellings are correct, the *preferred spelling* is given first, and that is the one you should use; if you happened to use the second spelling it would not be considered a mistake.

However, when *also* precedes a second spelling, the second one is less acceptable; avoid it in workplace writing—unless you have a special reason to use it.

lovable *also* loveable   lasagna *also* lasagne

Some second spellings are shown as separate entries. If a second spelling is a separate entry, it is not the preferred form. A note such as *non-Standard* or *disputed sp.* may appear in the separate entry. For the definition, look up the preferred spelling. For example, the second spelling for *all right* is shown in *Webster's New World College Dictionary,* Fourth Edition, as follows:

al·right (ol rit′) adj., adv., interj. disputed sp. of ALL RIGHT

This means *alright* isn't all right and is a disputed spelling, not generally recognized as correct. The *Microsoft Encarta College Dictionary* has a "usage note" that states "*Alright* has never gained wide acceptance even though it is to be seen in the prose of many well-known writers such as Langston Hughes, Gertrude Stein, ..."

Open your dictionary now to see how this word appears in your dictionary.

Compound Words

A **compound word** means two or more words expressing one concept. These words may be one connected word, two words with a space, or two words connected with a hyphen.

chocolate chip   nationwide   hand-me-down

Common usage dictates whether compound expressions are hyphenated, and this usage changes over time.

When you are unsure of a compound word spelling, use your dictionary. If the word is not listed, then it is spelled as two words with a space. Otherwise, your dictionary will show it as either one word or hyphenated.

Note also that some words are hyphenated when they are used together as a compound modifier, but are not otherwise hyphenated. For example, in the expression *low-level position, low level* is a compound adjective modifying *position,* and needs a hyphen. On the other hand, no hyphen is needed in the expression in the following sentence: *"Please place the shelf at a low level."* In this case the two words *low* and *level* do not form a compound expression; *low* is an adjective modifying the noun *level.* You will learn more about hyphens and compound words in Chapter 11. Your reference manual will also have extensive information on forming compound words.

Prefixes and Hyphens

A hyphen might also be required between a prefix and a main word.

In some dictionaries, a hyphen follows the first *e* in *de-escalate.* In other dictionaries a second spelling with a dot between the *e*'s shows the word is correct either hyphenated or written as one word. Use the preferred form—the one listed first in your newest college dictionary.

Your Computer or Your Dictionary?

Although the electronic spell checker is important, it doesn't replace the "computer" between your ears for intelligent proofreading.

When writing at your computer, use the spell checker, even though it won't always find *miss steaks* (mistakes)—an example of what it's likely to overlook. This is why you should always use a good current dictionary in book form as well as your word processing dictionary.

Errors result when writers hastily accept the spell checker's "word" that there are no mistakes. Spell checkers do not know when you have used the *wrong* word, such as *their* for *there* or *past* for *passed.* In other words, it does not check sense; it only checks spelling. You can use this to your advantage by typing in your first idea of how to spell a word; if the spelling is incorrect and not an actual word you can save time by not having to go to a dictionary.

Word Power

In Appendix B on page 321, you will find extra practice to expand your vocabulary and improve your spelling. Accurate spelling and proofreading are important to success in many careers. Employers and coworkers often view inaccurate spellers as uneducated, careless, or incompetent. Support your spell checker usage with your own strong spelling skills.

RECAP   Write **T** for true or **F** for false beside each statement.

_____ 1. To be a good speller requires a special, inborn talent.

_____ 2. Reading newspapers and magazines is a waste of time for spelling improvement.

_____ 3. If *also* separates two spellings in the dictionary, both spellings are equally acceptable.

Check your answers on page 432.

REPLAY 3

A. Write **T** or **F** in the blank.

Example: __T__ Some compound words require a hyphen and others do not.

_____ 1. Prospective employers tend to assume a poor speller is uneducated or unintelligent.

_____ 2. Almost anyone who wants to be a good speller can be a good speller.

_____ 3. Being a good speller is unimportant because your spell checker corrects any mistakes you might make.

_____ 4. Poor spellers are always looking up words in the dictionary.

_____ 5. If a comma separates two spellings of the same word in the dictionary, it means the first spelling is non-Standard.

_____ 6. If *also* appears between two spellings of the same word, it means the first spelling is preferable to the second.

_____ 7. A computer's spell checker enables you to avoid homonym errors—for example, writing *you're* when the spelling should be *your.*

_____ 8. If *or* is between two spellings of the same word in the dictionary, it means either spelling is correct.

_____ 9. In a dictionary entry, if a dot or accent mark appears between two syllables it means you should spell it as two separate words.

10. Circle the misspelled words: pronounciation, weird, seperate, reccomend, congradulate, persue, villain, persistent, conscience, bachlor

B. Write the letter of the answer in the blank. Use your dictionary.

_____ 1. Which is spelled correctly? (a) counter-sign (b) countersign (c) counter sign

_____ 2. Which is correct? (a) epilog (b) epilogue (c) both a and b

_____ 3. Which is correct? (a) antitrust (b) anti-trust (c) anti trust

_____ 4. The adjective *buttondown* is (a) one solid word (b) hyphenated (c) two words

_____ 5. Which is correct? (a) ocurred (b) occured (c) occurred

C. Fill in the missing letters; then rewrite the word in the blank.

1. w _____ rd _____

2. ac _____ date _____

3. bach _____ or _____

4. priv _____ _____

5. persist _____ _____

6. congra _____ late _____

7. pro _____ ciation _____

8. re _____ end _____

9. emba _____ ed _____

10. p _____ sued _____

D. Use your dictionary to correct these frequently misspelled words. Then write the word correctly in the blank.

1. accomodations _____

2. indispensible _____

3. judgement _____

4. concensus _____

5. reccurence _____

6. acknowledgement _____

Check your answers on page 432.

READ 4 — MORE LANGUAGE RESOURCES

A good dictionary is an essential tool, but it isn't the only reference source you need. A *thesaurus* will help you expand your use of words and have a more precise command of language, and a *reference manual* will help with finding solutions to your writing problems.

Thesauruses—Saying It Right

Thesauruses list **synonyms** (words with similar meanings), **antonyms** (words with opposite meanings), and other related words.

Using a thesaurus will help you appreciate the variety of options you have for saying what you mean and saying it well.

Among thesauruses, the most famous name is Roget (pronounced *ro·ZHA).* It is comparable to the name Webster in dictionaries. Dr. Peter Mark Roget's first edition of *Roget's Thesaurus* was published in 1852. Roget's approach was to group words and phrases together based on their association with a single thought or concept. *The Original Roget's International Thesaurus* (latest edition) can be purchased in paperback, and there is also a *New American Roget's College Thesaurus in Dictionary Form* with *A* to *Z* entries. *Merriam-Webster's Collegiate Thesaurus* is also arranged in dictionary format.

The Thesaurus or the Dictionary?

A thesaurus with the *A* to *Z* arrangement of words is the easiest to use, but don't use your thesaurus for definitions, pronunciation, or other information that requires dictionary reference. Do use it when you need to find the "right" word, that is, the word with the most precise meaning for your purpose.

A thesaurus can help you improve your writing.

Here are some of the things you can achieve by using a thesaurus:

- Avoid repeating the same word or using clichés or tired expressions by finding words with similar or the same meaning.

- Liven up your writing with a more descriptive, interesting, emphatic, or "colorful" word.

- Make your writing clearer or less wordy by substituting a more precise word.
- Avoid harsh or inappropriate words by finding more tactful, less emotional substitutes.
- Find the "right" word when you can't recall it by looking up a similar word.

Word Power

A combination dictionary-thesaurus provides both references under one cover. Though a convenient combination, the dictionary portion might not be as complete as a college dictionary by itself. Compare the number of dictionary entries with one of the college dictionaries recommended here to determine whether the dictionary portion is sufficiently comprehensive.

Electronic Thesauruses

The convenience of an electronic thesaurus is that you can access it with a click of your mouse as you write at the computer. The widely used word processing programs Microsoft Word and WordPerfect both include an online thesaurus. Figures 1.2 and 1.3 show how to access the thesaurus using the Tools menu in Microsoft Word 2003. In Microsoft Word 2007, the thesaurus is located in the Review menu, but the pane on the right side of your screen will be the same.

You can also access thesauruses on the Internet, including Roget's and Merriam-Webster's. Figure 1.4 shows how an online thesaurus can help you quickly find a replacement for the word *great,* a word that is highly overused in our culture. Merriam-Webster online gives you five alternatives and their meanings. Next time you are online, compare Roget's thesaurus with Merriam-Webster's. Note the differences and see which one you find easiest to use.

Word to the Wise

When you look up a word in a thesaurus, you will sometimes need to use the root word to find the synonym you want. For example, if you want a synonym for *walking* or *walked,* look under the root word *walk.*

RECAP	Using a thesaurus find a synonym (a word with a similar meaning) for the following words:

1. *incomparable* _____

2. *incredible* _____

3. *distasteful* _____

Check your answers on page 432.

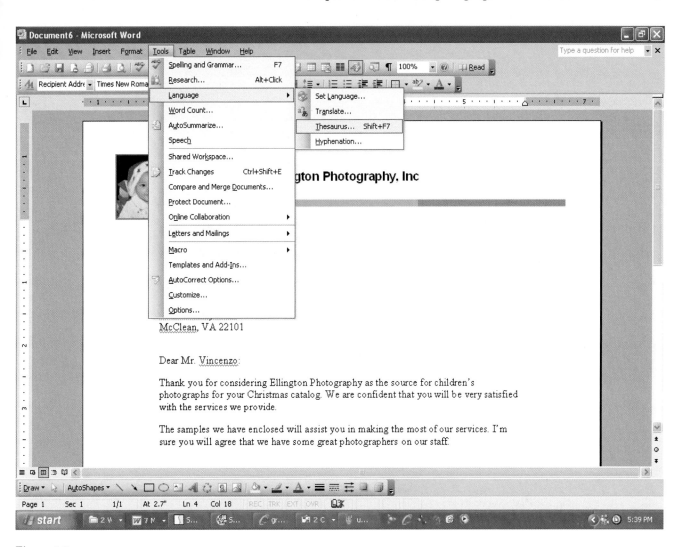

Figure 1.2
Microsoft product screen shots reprinted with permission from Microsoft Corporation.

Reference Manuals—A Resource for Writers

In case you thought good writing is simply a natural talent, by now you will begin to realize that it isn't. Like any creative task, talent comes into play—especially in creative writing. But in business writing, the right tools can carry you a long way. This course will help you recognize your personal writing weaknesses, and it will provide plenty of practice to improve them.

Using available resources to help you do the best possible job is an important habit to carry with you into any career. When it comes to writing, having a reference manual is essential. A reference manual such as the one we recommend, the *Pearson Business Reference and Writer's Handbook,* covers rules of grammar, punctuation, spelling, capitalization, and standard business usage and style for language and numbers. You will also find in-depth guidelines for writing the most common types of business communications, from letters, memos, and reports to employment application documents. In addition to including specific standards for formatting, the handbook also covers easy-to-follow steps for approaching your writing tasks and communicating the appropriate tone and content.

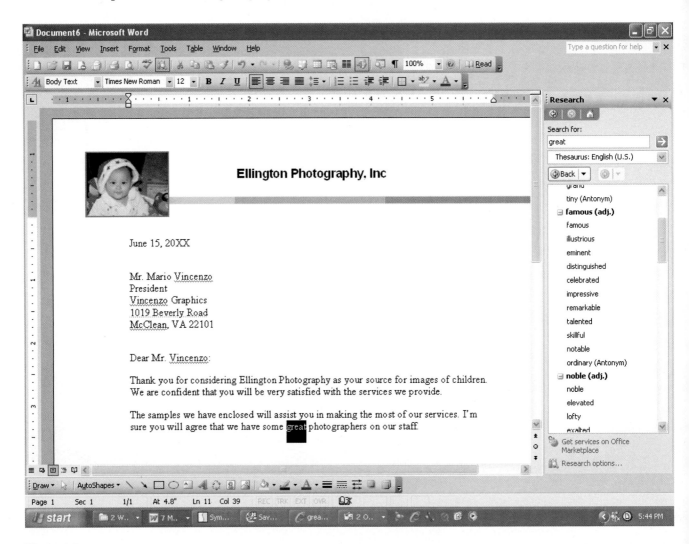

Figure 1.3
Microsoft product screen shots reprinted with permission from Microsoft Corporation.

A reference manual helps you solve writing problems as they arise so that you don't feel stuck or develop writer's block.

The **"Mini-Reference Manual"** in Appendix D in this book is an introduction to the use of a reference manual. It contains a selected number of answers to basic questions about numbers, capitalization, abbreviations, and letters. It also has guidelines for editing and proofreading. Use this mini reference for convenience, but do purchase a complete manual and take it with you to use on the job.

REPLAY 4

Using a **thesaurus,** replace the italicized words in the following sentences with a word that better expresses the writer's meaning shown in brackets.

Example: The young lady *galloped* ahead of the crowd [more precise].

raced

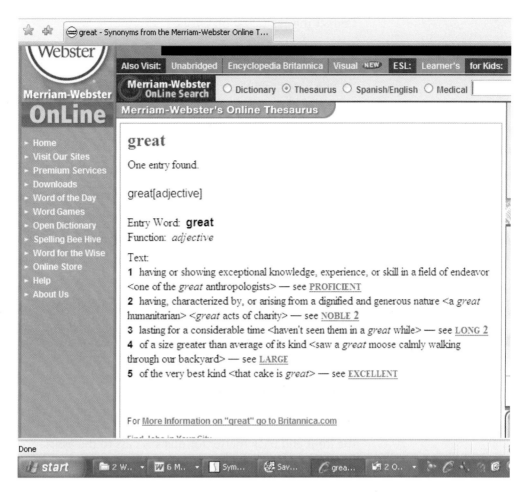

Figure 1.4
By permission. From *Merriam-Webster Online* © 2008 by Merriam-Webster, Incorporated (www.Merriam-Webster.com).

1. I hope you have a *pleasant* time in Denver. [less clichéd]

   _____

2. Please don't be *hasty* in making your decision [more emphatic].

   _____

3. You lack the *know-how* needed for this position. [less blunt]

   _____

4. I am very *angry* with the way you handled the situation. [softer]

   _____

Complete the following exercises using the **Mini Reference Manual** in Appendix D. Correct the number style where necessary:

5. Almost 5,000 people attended the Alliance for Survival rally.
6. I know about 50 ways to make about 5 million dollars.
7. The prime interest rate went to eleven % today.

Correct the capitalization errors:

8. we flew on american airlines last summer with the president of israel and the senator from maine.

9. the judge said that the supreme court decision was favorable to my company.

10. i will know chinese well enough by september to take a university course in chinese literature.

What do the following abbreviations mean?

11. SEC _____

12. CEO _____

Check your answers on pages 432–433; then take the Pop Quiz on page 294.

CONCEPT REVIEW & SKILL-BUILDING APPLICATIONS

Checkpoint

After completing this chapter, you are familiar with the full range of information to be found in a comprehensive, up-to-date college dictionary. Be sure to use the front and back matter for quick access to the assistance and facts they contain. Because a good dictionary is such a versatile reference book, keep a current one on your desk at home as well as at work. Many new words added to the latest editions are workplace-related and useful for your career.

You also know how to use a thesaurus and have some experience with finding rules in a reference manual to help you make sure your writing follows English and business standards.

Check your learning by completing the following exercise. Open your college dictionary to any page. Randomly point to an entry word, and then open your eyes. Write a check in the blank if you understand the dictionary code for interpreting the following:

_____ Spelling and variations of the spelling, if any

_____ Pronunciation

_____ Syllables

_____ Parts of speech

_____ Definitions

Write a check in the blank if you:

_____ Have read the table of contents or index of a college dictionary.

_____ Know the order in which definitions are listed in your college dictionary; i.e., oldest to current or current to oldest.

_____ Understand the labeling system in your college dictionary; for example, "labels" such as slang, vulgar, obsolete.

_____ Can locate and interpret the etymology of a word.

_____ Know what categories of special information are in your dictionary's front and back matter.

_____ Can find synonyms for *house* in your thesaurus or in an online thesaurus (abode, living quarters, etc.).

_____ Can explain the difference between homonyms, synonyms, and antonyms.

_____ Can find information in the Mini-Reference Manual at the back of this book to help you with your writing and proofreading.

_____ Own a business reference manual.

Special Assignment

A. These words are frequently mispronounced. To increase confidence in your communication ability, practice saying them correctly.

affluence—AF·loo·ens

affluent—AF·loo·ent

asked—askt (not ast or axed)

genuine—JEN·u·in

grievous—GREEV.us

irrelevant—ir·EL·e·vint

irrevocable—ir·EV·uh·cu·bel

grievous—GREEV·us

Illinois—ILL·in·oy

incomparable—in·COM·per·a·ble

Italian—i·TAL·yin

jewelry—JEW·el·ree (not JEW·ler·ree)

library—LI·brer·ee (not LI-bare-ee)

naive—ny·EEV

nuclear—NOO·clee·er

picture—PIK·cher (not pitcher)

preface—PREH·fis

preferable—PREF·er·a·ble

preferably—PREF·er·a·bly

realtor—REEL·tor

realty—REEl·tee

recognize—REK·og·nize

similar—SIM·i·ler

statistics—sta·TIS·tiks

subtle—SUT·l

superfluous—su·PERF·lu·us

B. Say each word aloud before responding to these questions. Use your dictionary to check your answers. How many syllables does each word have?

1. grievous _____

2. superfluous _____

3. mischievous _____

4. probably _____

5. naïve _____

Which letters are silent in these words?

6. Des Moines _____

7. Illinois _____

8. debris _____

9. subtle _____

10. vehicle _____

Date to submit this assignment: _____

Proofreading for Careers

Each chapter of this book has a proofreading exercise called **Proofreading for Careers.** You will improve your spelling, grammar, and usage of English by completing these exercises.

Proofreading is more than checking for spelling and typographical errors—often called "typos."

- Proofreading tests alertness and knowledge.
- Proofreading is slower than other types of reading.
- Proofreading requires more than one reading.

Don't let anything get past your desk that doesn't make sense to you or is incorrect. Proofread to eliminate:

- Typographical or spelling errors
- Omitted words
- Misused words
- Grammar, punctuation, and capitalization errors
- Number style and abbreviation errors
- Errors in standard format for business documents

Using Proofreading Marks

Proofreading marks are universally used symbols that show where errors occur in printed copy and how to correct them. Use them whenever you proofread your own work or that of someone else.

Take time now to review the **Proofreader's Marks** on the inside back cover of this book. You will find similar charts in your college dictionary, reference manuals, and other textbooks. The marks will be the same—the only thing that might differ is more or fewer symbols may be shown.

Proofread and make corrections in the following:

A. From a classified ad in a Tennessee newspaper:

Telephone receptionish needed for doctors' office. Duties are to relay massages between patients and doctors.

B. Under a supermarket advertisement in a Los Angeles newspaper:

NOT RESPONSIBLE FOR TYPORGRAPHICAL ERRORS

C. An answer from a science student's test that made biology history:

An example of animal breeding is the farmer who mated a bull that provided good meat with a bull that gave a great deal of milk.

D. Another newspaper typographical error:

Downtown has its fair share of buried treasurers.

E. Your computer's spell checker will find only two of the preceding errors. Which ones?

_____   _____

Practice Quiz

Take this Practice Quiz as though it were a real test. You'll find all the information in your college or unabridged dictionary or within Chapter 1.

1. In the blank, write the correct spelling of the two misspelled words: rediculous, personnel, occurred, ocassion, fulfilled. _____ _____

2. Use a thesaurus (electronic or print) to find more tactful ways to express the underlined word:

   You did a very <u>bad</u> job on this project. _____

   The decision you made was <u>wrong</u>. _____

3. What does OPEC stand for? _____
   _____

4. Illiterate expressions, vulgarities, and slang are not found in better dictionaries. True or False? _____

5. What does *colloquial* mean? _____

6. In what year was Geronimo (the leader of the Apaches) born? _____

7. What was the birth name of famous composer George Gershwin? _____

8. Give three synonyms for *small.* _____

9. In your dictionary, where is the etymology in relation to the definitions?
   _____.

10. If you look up a word in a college dictionary and don't find a usage label, what does this mean? _____
    _____

11. In college dictionaries, a pronunciation key may be at the _____
    _____.

12. The word *also* between two spellings of the same word means _____
    _____.

13. Show with a dot how to divide *twinkling* between syllables. _____

14. The noun *pair* has two correct plural spellings. What are they? _____

15. Correctly spell the seven misspelled words in this list: accomodate, seperate, weird, persue, villain, bachlor, congradulate, superintendant, dilemma, pronunciation, priviledge

    _____

    _____

16. The *i* in the word *juvenile* is pronounced like the alphabet sound of *i*. True or False?

    _____

17. College dictionaries have a pronunciation key _____
    _____ and _____.

18. Where in a college or unabridged dictionary do you find detailed instructions and
    explanations for intelligent use? _____

19. What is the plural of *addendum* and from what language does the word originate?
    _____

20. What is a *tittle*? _____

21. A word with the same pronunciation as another but with a different meaning is
    a/an (a) homonym (b) synonym (c) antonym. _____

22. Name three categories of information in the back matter of your college dictio-
    nary. _____

23. Name three categories of information in the front matter of your dictionary.
    _____.

24. What is the capital of Spain? _____

Self-Study Practice and Tutorials

Vocabulary and Spelling for Careers
For additional practice go to Appendix B, page 321.

Replay Drills
For additional practice go to Appendix C, page 355.

Companion Web Site: www.prenhall.com/smith
Go to the companion Web site to test your knowledge on self-grading quizzes and for
links to other helpful online resources.

MyWritingLab
Use this online learning system for an assessment of your progress on topics covered in
this chapter and progressive exercises that fit your individual needs.

2 Getting to Know the Parts of Speech

After completing Chapter 2, you will be able to do the following:

■ Name and define the eight parts of speech.

■ Use the correct forms of words as different parts of speech when writing sentences.

■ Apply your knowledge of the parts of speech to English principles in your speaking and writing.

READ 5   WHY STUDY THE PARTS OF SPEECH?

The parts of speech are the system for organizing words into the following categories: *pronouns, verbs, adjectives, adverbs, prepositions, conjunctions,* and *interjections*—depending on how the words are used in a sentence.

Whether or not you've learned the parts of speech in the past, this chapter will help you improve your command of English and be prepared for the material in upcoming chapters. Granted, studying the parts of speech is not most students' favorite thing to do in English class. It's much easier just to try to use the English language properly than to label and categorize words. Breaking sentences down and analyzing their parts is considered a painful exercise called "learning grammar." Why do you need to do this? Unless you plan to be an English teacher, it actually isn't essential to study grammar in depth. What you *do* need to be able to do is identify, so that you'll use correctly, the basic "tools of the English trade"—and these are the parts of speech.

Although you may dislike grammar, or feel you could never master it, approach it with an open mind. The *English for Careers* method is different. You'll discover an enjoyable and efficient way to acquire language skills and use them to become a more confident writer. Being able to communicate correctly and effectively is essential to success in any career.

The Parts of Speech in Sentences

Following are definitions of the eight parts of speech and their roles in sentences:

Nouns	**Naming** words, such as *Joe, doctor, table, books,* name people, animals, places, and things; abstract concepts and qualities; activities; time and measurements. Nouns tell *who, whom, what,* or *where* in sentences. They play the roles of subjects and objects.
Pronouns	**Substitution** words for nouns, such as *he, she, it, them, who, everybody,* enable us to avoid needless repetition. They also play the roles of subjects and objects.
Verbs	**Action** words, such as *eat, love, count;* **being** and **helping** words, such as *be, am, seem;* **possession** words, such as *have, has, had,* which double as helping verbs. They play the role of the predicate in sentences—telling what the noun or pronoun is doing or being.
Adjectives	**Modifying** words, such as *comfortable* shoes, *yellow* banana, *sexy* guy, *expensive* homes, *the* mouse, *an* alligator, tell something about nouns or about pronouns, such as it is *expensive,* she was *polite,* they are *yellow,* we are *happy.*
Adverbs	**Modifying** words tell something about verbs, such as run *fast* (*fast* tells about the verb *run*); about adjectives, such as *extraordinarily* graceful child (*extraordinarily* tells about the adjective *graceful*); and about other adverbs, such as ran *very* fast (adverb *very* tells about adverb *fast*).
Conjunctions	**Connecting** words, such as *or, and, but, yet, so, although, because,* join words or parts of sentences. Examples: Would

you prefer to attend Harvard *or* Yale? Start with a rough draft and then do a great deal of revising. (*Then* joins the sentence parts.)

Prepositions
Linking words, such as *under, through, with, beside, between, to;* a preposition is the first word of a prepositional phrase. A **prepositional phrase** begins with a preposition and ends with a noun or pronoun, which is called the *object* of the preposition. Example: The name "Jeep," according <u>*to* the captain</u> came <u>*from* the abbreviation</u> used <u>*in* the army</u> <u>*for* General Purpose Vehicle.</u>

Interjections
Expressive words used alone or in a short phrase to show emotion. They are usually followed by an exclamation mark. Examples: Never! Wonderful! You don't say!

REPLAY 5

You've reviewed the "tools of the trade"—the eight parts of speech. Write the name of the part of speech in the blank after its definition.

1. Expresses action or being. _____
2. Modifies—tells something about—a noun or pronoun. _____
3. Substitutes for a noun. _____
4. An exclamatory word or phrase that is used to show emotion. _____
5. Connects two or more words or parts of sentences. _____
6. Linking words such as *under, with, to.* _____
7. Modifies—tells something about—a verb, an adjective, or an adverb. _____
8. Names something, somebody, or someplace. _____

Check your answers on page 433.

READ 6   NOUNS AND PRONOUNS—NAMES AND SUBSTITUTES

Nouns

Nouns name people, animals, places, and things; ideas, concepts, and qualities; activities and events; measures of time, space, and quantities.

You also need to know that there are three categories of nouns: proper, common, and collective. These categories determine how you treat nouns in sentences—for example, whether they begin with a capital letter and whether they require a singular or plural verb. Here are the definitions of these three categories:

1. **Proper nouns** are specific names and begin with a capital letter: *White House, Professor Alicia Holmes, Toronto, Fido, Republican Party, Halloween.*
2. **Common nouns** are nonspecific names and begin with lowercase letters: *house, instructor, city, dog, organization, holiday.*

3. **Collective nouns** name a group: *team, committee, herd, jury.* You determine whether to use a singular or plural verb according to how the collective noun is used in the sentence.

Here are examples of nouns and how they are used in sentences.

Persons	professor accountant woman Kathleen members brother My **brother Bob,** who is an **accountant,** is also a **professor.** **Kathleen** and the **woman** with her are long-time **members.**
Animals	goldfish Fido eagle dog flea dinosaur **Fido** has **fleas.** **Dinosaurs** were prehistoric **animals.**
Places	island city New Zealand San Francisco Southern Hemisphere The **island** of **New Zealand** is in the **Southern Hemisphere.** **San Francisco** is known as the "**city** by the bay."
Things	piano sandwich *People Magazine* subway seat pen A **piano** and a **pen** were advertised in ***People Magazine.*** The **sandwich** was left on a **seat** in the **subway.**
Ideas, Concepts, and Qualities	integrity modesty beauty success democracy My **beauty** is exceeded only by my **modesty.** **Integrity** in business contributes to **success.** **Democracy** is practiced widely in the United States.
Activities and Events	drinking running sleeping driving eating crying The baby spent the entire day **sleeping, eating,** and **crying.** **Drinking** and **driving** are dangerous.
Measures of Time, Space, and Quantity	week decade mile million number A **number** of people—more than a **million**—voted. Last **week** we drove a **mile,** although we could have walked. In which **decade** were you born?

RECAP   Four of the preceding example sentences have nouns not printed in bold type. Find these nouns and write them in the blanks.

1. _____ 2. _____ 3. _____ 4. _____

5. Circle the nouns in the following sentence (there are eight):

   When interviewers speak with applicants, they look for energy, competence, loyalty, skill, ambition, and flexibility.

6. Look around the room and write three common nouns that name what you see:

   _____   _____   _____

7. An example of a proper noun is *Katherine*. Some common nouns that could refer to Katherine are mother-in-law, friend, sister, wife, mathematician. Write one proper noun and three common nouns that may be used for someone you know:

Proper Noun: _____

Common Nouns: _____ _____ _____

Check your answers on page 433.

Recognizing Nouns

Most nouns have two forms: singular when naming one and plural when naming more than one. Some nouns—such as honesty, ethics, helpfulness—do not have plurals.

Most nouns form the plural by adding *–s* or *–es;* some change their spelling as shown in the examples below. You will practice forming plurals of nouns in Chapter 4.

Singular	Plural
country	countries
child	children
loaf	loaves
boy	boys

Pronouns

Pronouns substitute for nouns.

We often substitute pronouns for nouns to avoid repeating the nouns.

Nouns:	**Jerry Sider** has finished **Jerry Sider's work.**
Pronouns:	Jerry Sider has finished **his** work. **He** has finished **it.**

Like nouns, pronouns tell *who, whom,* or *what.* For example, the pronouns *she, her,* and *herself* could substitute for any of the following nouns.

Sue woman stockbroker lady Ms. Gilchrist daughter student

A pronoun may replace a noun or pronoun previously mentioned or understood. For example, "**It** is hot today" really means "The **air** is hot today." We understand that *it* substitutes for *air.*

Nouns:	**Dick Tracy** won the **prize.**
Pronouns:	**He** won **it.** **Who** won **it?**
	Somebody won **that.** Did **anyone** win **this?**

Personal Pronouns

Personal pronouns have three categories—first person, second person, and third person. Each person has a singular and a plural form.

First-person Pronouns	The person or people speaking or writing:				
Singular	I	me	my	mine	myself
Plural	we	us	our	ours	ourselves

Second-person Pronouns	The person or people spoken or written to:		
Singular or Plural	you	your	yours
Singular only	yourself		
Plural only	yourselves		

Third-person Pronouns	The person(s), people, or thing(s) spoken or written about:				
Singular Masculine	he	him	his	himself	
Singular Feminine	she	her	hers	herself	
Singular Neutral	it	its	itself		
Plural Neutral	they	them	their	theirs	themselves

Word to the Wise

hisself?   theirself?   theirselves?   theyselves?   mines?   **NO! NEVER!**
Job applicants who use these incorrect expressions (they are not actual words) will not get the better jobs!

Indefinite Pronouns

Indefinite pronouns don't specify whom or what they substitute for:

Everyone is responsible for keeping **his** own locker secure. [Personal pronoun *his* substitutes for indefinite pronoun *everyone*.]

Indefinite Pronouns

who	this	everyone	everybody	everything
whoever	that	someone	somebody	something
whom	these	anyone	anybody	anything
whomever	those	no one	nobody	nothing
whose	each			

Chapter 6 covers when to use specific pronouns like **I/me** and **who/whom.** For now, just know a pronoun when you see one.

REPLAY 6

A. Circle the 24 nouns in the following sentences. If a noun is made up of two or more words, use one circle.

Example: *Don't tell ethnic (jokes) while on the (job) at (Abernathy Jones, Inc.)* (3)

1. A smile is likely to help even the most challenging situation. (2)
2. Business correspondence in the United States is often less formal than it is in Asia, South America, Europe, and Africa. (6)

3. It is important to your career to accept people of various cultures and to judge them as individuals. (4)
4. Avoid using slang when you speak with coworkers for whom English is a second language. (4)
5. The multicultural neighborhood, classroom, and workplace are typical in the United States, Canada, Great Britain, and many other parts of the world. (8)

B. Insert pronouns in the blanks to replace the words in brackets.

Example: *[My brother and my father] <u>They</u> found [a strange item] <u>it</u> in [the person I'm writing to] <u>your</u> house.*

1. [The temperature] _____ is too hot today for running in the park.
2. [This man] _____ will be the next president of the club.
3. [Which person] _____ will be the next governor?
4. [Ashley] _____ talks to [Ashley's] _____ friends on the phone for hours.
5. [These friends] _____ urged [Ann] _____ to marry [George] _____.

Check your answers on page 433.

READ 7   VERBS—WHERE THE ACTION IS

Verbs express action or a state of being. Every sentence has at least one verb. **Action** or **being verbs** are sometimes preceded by one or more **helping verbs,** thus creating a **verb phrase.**

Action Verbs

Most verbs express some kind of action; for example:

work	worry	invite	write	dance	receive	have	own	love	pay
read	call	run	think	relax	proofread	do	hop	work	play

Being Verbs

State-of-being verbs (also called "being" or linking verbs) include forms of the verb *to be*, verbs of the senses (taste, smell, touch, sound, and sight) and a few other verbs.
Being verbs "link" the subject of the sentence to a word or words that tell something about the subject. Examples of being verbs:

be	being	been	am	is	are	was	were	become	seem
remain	appear	feel	sound	taste	smell	look		

The **being verbs** are highlighted in the following sentences:

You **seem** calm and **sound** happy.
She **is** glad that you **feel** good.

The soup **looks, smells,** and **tastes** good.

The food **was** good.

Some **being verbs** are also used as **action verbs.**

Action verbs	Being verbs
Did you **taste** the pasta?	The stew **tastes** good to me!
Did you **smell** the stew?	They **smell** good, too.
She **looks** at everything before deciding.	That cat **looks** healthy.

RECAP

A. Circle the eight action verbs and underline the ten pronouns:

He wrote the application letter and proofread it. When the manager received it, she looked it over. After she read all the applications, she invited a few applicants for interviews. She has an assistant who helped her.

B. Circle the ten being verbs:

She is capable. He appears efficient. I am glad the program sounds interesting. All employees were on vacation last week. It seems as though Gene was at the beach all summer. Fresh apple pie smells good. The raincoat doesn't feel wet. Eric remains on the Dean's List.

Check your answers on page 434.

Helping Verbs

Helping verbs (also called auxiliary verbs) show time, possibility, or emphasis.
A helping verb may precede the main verb—either action verb or being verb. Together, the helping verb and main verb are called a **verb phrase.** Notice the helping verbs in bold in the following sentences; each one precedes a main verb. The helping verbs show emphasis, possibility, or time (now, before, or later). The verb phrase is underlined.

My boss **is** reading the report, but the staff **did** not finish it.

He **has** worked with them for years.

I **have been** working here for five years.

They **were** enjoying their vacation, but they **are** returning home today.

Ms. Moultry **does** sign all the letters herself.

Some *being* verbs also function as *helping* verbs:

be   been   am   is   are   was   were

A few *action* verbs also function as *helping* verbs:

do   does   did   have   has   had

The following are always *helping* verbs:

may   must   might   shall   will
could   can   should   would

RECAP   Circle each helping verb and underline each verb phrase.

She does enjoy the work and has stayed late often.

She had seen him every afternoon, but had not greeted him.

He will select the date and is planning to notify us tomorrow.

Check your answers on page 434.

Recognizing Verbs

Some words look like verbs but aren't verbs.

ing Words

Most verbs can add *ing.* Here are some examples:

see/seeing   have/having   eat/eating   be/being

When *ing* words express action or existence, they are verbs and are always preceded by a helping verb.

Verb: Recent studies show that honesty **is paying** off in business.

When an *ing* word *names* an activity, however, it is a noun. In grammar terms this is called a **gerund;** a gerund is **not** preceded by a helping verb.

Noun (Gerund):   **Paying** bills has never been my favorite activity. (gerund— *paying*; verb—*has been*)

To + Verb

When *to* precedes a verb—such as *to eat, to work, to swim*—the result is a noun naming an activity, not a verb. *To* plus a verb is called an **infinitive.** Infinitives are used as **nouns.** That sounds hard to believe; so just look at the sentence below to see how it works:

To know me is **to love** me.

To know and *to love* are *infinitives*; the verb is **is.** Notice that *to know* and *to love* name activities; thus, they are used as nouns, not verbs, and are therefore infinitives.

REPLAY 7

A. Circle the nine being verbs and underline the one action verb.

1. She is an assistant.
2. He seems qualified.
3. I am surprised that the tests are not ready.
4. All shipments were on time last week.
5. They think you are the best employee.

6. The music sounds good.

7. Edward appears enthusiastic about being on the program.

B. Circle the complete verbs—helping and main.

1. I do work on the executive floor, but I haven't met the president.
2. Judge Hoover has read the lawyer's motion.
3. The jury members are reading the transcripts.
4. He has chosen to take the new job.
5. Professor Dowd will be going to Cairo to teach.
6. In June you will have been working here for five years.
7. He might have noticed the change in tone.
8. Ms. Moultry does sign all the letters herself.

C. Fill in the blanks with verbs that make sense in the sentence.

Example: *A word to the wise ____is____ enough.—Laurence Sterne*

1. From time to time most office professionals _____ more computer training, but they may not _____ time for regular college classes.
2. Four out of five companies _____ a great deal of money training their employees.
3. We _____ for your opinion. (helping verb and main verb needed)
4. Workplace etiquette _____ important to employers.
5. Many firms _____ thousands of dollars for etiquette seminars for their employees.

D. First, underline the verbs in the following sentences. When a main verb is combined with a helping verb, underline both. (See *could help* in the example.) Second, circle the nouns and draw a triangle around the pronouns.

Example: (Paul) could help (Ms. Adams) with her (work)

	Number of Marks
1. Applicants are judged on their behavior as well as their knowledge.	6
2. Etiquette is part of all activities on the job.	5
3. No one has much data on that topic.	4
4. Do not call clients or colleagues by their first names until you are sure it is customary in your organization.	12
5. Sheila Danielle was the winner of the scholarship.	4
6. The secretaries were typing the answers in the blanks.	4
7. Someone should have completed the job by Tuesday.	4
8. Who should go to the conference in Las Vegas?	4
9. The manager's husband is known for his courtesy.	5

10. He will ask for the mail.	3
11. These have been sent to Southeastern Community College.	3
12. They know a lawyer in the building who will represent me.	7
13. Kelly Clarkson rescheduled three performances in Europe.	4
14. Larry should deliver the tickets to you.	4
15. It is in the drawer next to the computer.	4
16. Their receptionist will mail these on Monday.	5
17. The Aldrich Company received everything.	3
18. Our auditors checked everyone's books for accuracy.	5
19. The contractor built a factory in a city on the coast.	5
20. The children dressed themselves.	3

Check your answers on pages 434–435.

Word Power—Recognizing Helping Verbs

The most common helping verbs are:

am	could	may	should
is	do	will	would
are	done	might	was
be	have	must	were
been	has	ought	
can	had	shall	

READ 8 ADJECTIVES AND ADVERBS— THE MODIFIERS

Modifiers—adjectives and adverbs—are words that describe, limit, or explain.

Adjectives

Adjectives modify (describe) nouns and pronouns. They add information about *which, what kind,* or *how many.*

Following are examples and definitions of several kinds of adjectives. In the examples, the adjectives are in bold print. The noun or pronoun they describe is underlined.

Descriptive Adjectives

Descriptive adjectives are words that tell "what kind." To tell what kind of *house,* you might choose *yellow, brick, contemporary, shabby, two-story, luxurious,* and so on. By carefully selecting descriptive adjectives, your words create a picture for the reader or listener.

> **Respectful** <u>employees</u> work well with people from **diverse** <u>backgrounds</u>.
>
> **Upscale gourmet** <u>dinners</u> are served in that **elegant** <u>restaurant</u>. [*that* is a pointing adjective]
>
> The **new work** <u>environment</u> emphasizes **individual** <u>responsibility</u>.

Limiting Adjectives

Words that "limit" nouns in the sense of quantity are also adjectives. They tell "how many." Limiting adjectives are words such as these:

more	all	50 or fifty
enough	each	no
most	any	every
several	many	numerous
few	some	

> I bought **several** <u>reams</u> of paper at Cheapo Depot.
>
> In a **few** <u>months</u>, we will be moving our offices.
>
> We have **enough** <u>employees</u> to pack **50** <u>boxes</u> properly.

Articles

A, an, and *the* are articles. These adjectives tell *which one*. You can easily memorize them because there are only three.

> **An** <u>apple</u> **a** <u>day</u> keeps **the** <u>doctor</u> away.

Use of *a* or *an* depends on the **sound** of the word following *a* or *an*, not necessarily the written letter with which the word begins. If a word following an indefinite article begins with a vowel sound (the sound of *a, e, i, o,* or *u*) use <u>an</u>. Otherwise use <u>a</u>.

> a politician   an apple   a monument   an old movie   a job   an awful job

In Chapter 8 you'll have further review of when to use *a* and when to use *an*.

Pointing Adjectives

Pointing adjectives tell *which one*. Like articles, they are easy to memorize because there are only four: *this, that, these,* and *those*.

> **this** book   **these** books   **that** jacket   **those** jackets

Do you remember from Read 5 that the words *this, that, these,* and *those* are pronouns? Can they be both? Yes! *This, that, these,* and *those* are adjectives when they modify a noun; they are pronouns when used *instead* of a noun:

Adjective:	**This** <u>book</u> is the one I want to read. [*This* points at *book*.]
Pronoun:	**These** are the ones I want to read. [*These* replaces the noun *books*, which is understood.]
Adjective:	**Those** <u>labels</u> don't match what is in the box. [*Those* points at *labels*.]
Pronoun/ Adjective:	**This** belongs on **that** <u>box</u>. [*This* replaces label; *that* points at box.]

The adjectives in the following sentences are in bold print. Underline the nouns or pronouns they describe.

1. Adjectives usually precede nouns:
   He has **an** idea that she ordered **a blue** carpet, **a new** desk, and **a large** fan.
2. Adjectives often follow "being" verbs:
   You seem **smart.** Ethics is **important.** Ms. Parks appears **happy.**
3. Pointing adjectives tell which one:
   This building is almost completed and that is a good thing.

Check your answers on page 435.

Adverbs

Both adjectives and adverbs describe or explain. Adjectives describe or explain nouns or pronouns.

Adverbs describe, limit, or explain verbs, adjectives, or other adverbs.

Adverbs add information about *when, where, how,* or *how much.* Many adverbs—but not all—are formed by adding *-ly* to an adjective. Following are examples of adverb usage. In the examples, the adverbs are in bold print and the words they modify are underlined.

Adverbs modifying a verb:	**Always** <u>prepare</u> invoices **carefully.** [The adverb *always* tells "when" about the verb *prepare*. The adverb *carefully* tells "how" about the verb *prepare*.]
Adverbs modifying adjectives:	This **extremely** <u>expensive</u> book is required for an **especial**ly <u>important</u> course. [The adverb *extremely* tells "how" about the adjective *expensive*. The adverb *especially* tells "how" about the adjective *important*.]
Adverbs modifying other adverbs:	Ms. Persley works **so** <u>efficiently</u> that she **almost** <u>never</u> makes a mistake. [The adverb *so* describes the adverb *efficiently; efficiently* describes the verb *works;* the adverb *almost* describes the adverb *never; never* describes the verb *makes.*]

Insert an adverb in the blank to describe, limit, or explain the words in bold.

1. He **was hired** _____.
2. The children in that class **read** _____.
3. Do you think that I **drive** _____?
4. You **added** the figures _____.
5. They **should** _____ **use** good quality paper for resumes.

Check your answers on page 435.

Recognizing Adverbs

Many adverbs—but not all—are formed by adding *ly* to an adjective.

Adjective	Adverb
peaceful	peacefully
quiet	quietly
exceptional	exceptionally
intelligent	intelligently
attractive	attractively
final	finally
real	really

While many adverbs end in *ly*, some words often used as adverbs don't end in *ly:*

almost

more

never

so

very

even

much

not

too

well

REPLAY 8

A. Circle the nouns; underline four limiting and five pointing adjectives and one article:

Example: Please pay this bill within five days.

1. These rooms don't have any air-conditioning.
2. They have several windows, however.
3. That office is mine; this is his.
4. Some homes on this street are tri-level.
5. Ten attorneys left the firm this year.

B. The following paragraph is from a sales letter meant to bring business to a resort hotel. In the blanks, write the adjectives (descriptive, pointing, or articles) that modify the ten nouns in bold type. Numbers in parentheses tell how many adjectives to look for. For example, in item 1, write just one adjective *(an)* in the blank to modify the noun *individual*. For item 2, write the three adjectives describing the noun *hotel*. Continue until you complete all ten items.

Surveys show you are an **individual** who would be interested in visiting an exclusive resort **hotel** on the beautiful **Pacific,** where the crystal blue **waters** meet the white sand **beaches.** You will enjoy exquisite guest **villas** in Mediterranean **decor** with luxurious **jacuzzis.** The **climate** is smogless, sunny, and mild. You will want to stay in this **paradise** forever.

1. _____ individual (1)
2. _____ hotel (3)
3. _____ Pacific (2)
4. _____ waters (3)
5. _____ beaches (3)
6. _____ villas (2)
7. _____ decor (1)
8. _____ jacuzzis (1)
9. _____ climate (4)
10. _____ paradise (1)

C. Write three different sentences. In each sentence, use an article, a limiting adjective, a describing adjective, and a pointing adjective. Circle each adjective.

Example: (The) woman bought (those two red) dresses.

1. _____
2. _____
3. _____

D. In each blank, insert a one-word adverb to describe or explain the word in bold type. The adverb you select will tell when, why, where, how, or how much.

Example: Dolores Denova **speaks** _____.

1. When you **go** _____ you will need a car to drive.
2. A new computer **would cost** _____ than upgrading the old one.
3. Although Dan is on the team, he _____ **plays** in important games.
4. We didn't believe Anne when she said she **had** _____ **cut** her own hair.
5. This _____ **designed** home was featured in *Architectural Digest.*
6. Those are _____ **expensive** restaurants.
7. Nutrition is one of the _____ **important** aspects of health.
8. Good inexpensive food is _____ **hard** to find.
9. Employees who ignore etiquette while at work **are** _____ **disliked.**
10. I think Billie Horton is _____ **more suitable** for the job than Harvey Lewis.

Check your answers on pages 435–436; then take the Pop Quiz on page 296.

READ 9   CONJUNCTIONS AND PREPOSITIONS— THE CONNECTORS

The connecting words—conjunctions and prepositions—help us understand how words within a sentence relate to one another to create meaning.

Conjunctions

Conjunctions connect words, phrases, and clauses.

The relationship between the words or groups of words is shown by the choice of conjunction. The following sections describe the different types of conjunctions.

Coordinating Conjunctions

The coordinating conjunctions are used to join parts of speech in a series (nouns, pronouns, adjectives, adverbs, verbs) and parts of sentences (clauses) or let you join two sentences together to make them one sentence. This is a good idea when two thoughts are very closely connected.

The coordinating conjunctions are *and, but, or, nor, for, yet, so*.

Study the following examples so that you can identify conjunctions. The conjunctions are in bold and the words they connect are underlined.

and	Studies show that <u>honesty</u>, <u>ethics</u>, **and** <u>social responsibility</u> pay off in business. [connects a series of nouns]
but	Raymond said, "<u>It's hard to get a job</u> as a news anchor, **but** <u>the pay is good</u>." [connects two sentence parts (clauses)]
or	Workplace ethics include not violating civil <u>law</u> **or** company <u>policy</u>. [connects two nouns]
nor	He will neither <u>attend</u> the convention **nor** <u>visit</u> the showroom. [connects two verbs]
for	<u>Samantha decided not to become a movie star</u>, **for** <u>she feared the money and fame would go to her head</u>. [connects two sentences into one]
yet	<u>English is the international language of business</u>, **yet** <u>we should all know how to say "please," "thank you," and "hello" in several languages</u>. [connects two sentences into one.]
so	<u>The new manual is very complex</u>, **so** <u>be sure to read every word</u>. [connects two sentences into one.]

RECAP   Say the seven coordinating conjunctions quickly now to help you remember them.

Then write them here: _____ _____ _____ _____ _____ _____ _____

Check your answers on page 436.

Dependent Conjunctions

Dependent conjunctions (also called subordinate conjunctions), introduce a phrase—a word group that cannot stand by itself as a sentence.

The words below are often used as dependent conjunctions. The sentences following the list show the dependent conjunction in bold type; the phrase that it introduces is underlined.

after
although
as
because
before
even though
if
since
so that
than
unless
until
when
which
while

Business letters in the United States and Canada are less formal **than** <u>in most other parts of the world</u>. [*Than* is used as a dependent conjunction to introduce the phrase *in most other parts of the world.*]

The new branch office will be successful **if** <u>Petrina manages it</u>. [*If* is a dependent conjunction preceding the noun *Petrina* and the verb *manages.*]

To change emphasis, the dependent conjunction can be placed at the beginning of the sentence.

Because Petrina manages it, the branch office will be successful.

Unless it is repaired this week, we can't use the copier for the report.

Conjunctive Adverbs

Conjunctive adverbs, also called transitional expressions, join two complete sentences into one.

See the examples below and note the use of the semicolon. You will learn more about these words and this sentence construction in later chapters.

however
therefore
consequently
moreover
furthermore
also
for example
nevertheless
yet
in addition

My friend in Spain works from 8 a.m. to 6 p.m.; **however,** she has an hour and a half for lunch.

Your proposal was incomplete; **consequently,** we were unable to process it prior to the closing deadline.

We cannot afford to miss our plane; **therefore,** we're leaving at the crack of dawn.

RECAP   Observe how the conjunctions are used in the following sentences. Circle the dependent conjunctions, underline the coordinating conjunctions, and draw a rectangle around the conjunctive adverbs.

1. What kind of car would you drive if you could have any one you want?
2. The European Summit in Germany was supposed to last two to three days, but it ended up lasting a full week.
3. Some people don't accomplish their goals because they either don't set specific goals or don't keep them in mind.
4. Dinner in Turkey often begins with soup and ends with dessert and fruit.
5. In Turkey it is customary to have three sit-down meals a day; therefore, household members are together at mealtime and share events of the day.

Check your answers on page 436.

Prepositions

Prepositions link to other words in a sentence to show relationships. A **prepositional phrase** begins with a preposition and ends with a noun or pronoun, which is called the **object of the preposition.** The preposition and its object *plus any words between* them make up the **prepositional phrase.**

Please place the napkins <u>on the table</u>.

On is the preposition, *table* is the object of the preposition, and *on the table* is the prepositional phrase, which tells *where* the napkins were placed.

These words are often used as prepositions:

about	between	over
above	during	since
across	except	through
after	for*	to
against	from	toward
along	in	under
among	inside	until
around	into	up
at	like	upon
behind	near	with
below	of	within
beneath	off	
beside	on	

*For is a conjunction when it means "because;" otherwise, it's a preposition.

A prepositional phrase never has a subject or a verb. If the word group has a verb, it is not a prepositional phrase.

Study the following prepositional phrases. The prepositions are in bold type, and the objects are underlined.

under the antique <u>table</u>	**below** the newly painted <u>roof</u>
with Victoria's little <u>sister</u>	**through** the <u>air</u>
on the decrepit <u>plane</u>	**across** the <u>street</u>
from the airplane <u>window</u>	**in** the leather <u>briefcase</u>
to <u>you</u> and <u>me</u>	**after** <u>lunch</u>

You can sometimes use a preposition without stating its object, which may be understood. When the object of the preposition can be easily understood, it is all right to omit it. Here are some examples in which the object of the preposition is understood:

Please stop **by.**   Don't jump **across.**   She went **under.**   I'll go **up.**

Some prepositions are also used as dependent conjunctions—but only when a noun or pronoun and a verb are part of the word group that follows.

He hasn't been here **since** he spoke to the manager.

Since is a dependent conjunction joining the two clauses in the sentence; *he spoke to the manager* has a subject and a verb, and, therefore, cannot be a prepositional phrase.

He hasn't been here since last month.

Since last month is a prepositional phrase.

Study the following sentences. The prepositions are in bold type and the prepositional phrases are underlined.

a. Gregory filed the records **<u>under</u>** <u>the wrong name</u> **<u>in</u>** <u>the wrong drawer</u>.
b. Alexander will go **<u>with</u>** <u>you</u> **<u>in</u>** <u>the single-engine plane</u> **<u>to</u>** <u>a villa</u> **<u>beside</u>** <u>a mountain</u>.
c. They went **<u>into</u>** <u>the city</u> **<u>by</u>** <u>bus</u> and then dined **<u>at</u>** <u>a restaurant</u>.
d. The staff wanted to attend the meeting and see the fantastic view **<u>of</u>** <u>the city</u> **<u>from</u>** <u>the conference room window</u>.

Writing for Your Career

A preposition cannot usually function in a sentence on its own; it is likely to be meaningless without its object. However, you can sometimes use a preposition without stating its object, which may be understood. The standard rule used to be "Never end a sentence with a preposition." Now it is sometimes all right to do so, especially in conversation, to avoid sounding awkward. It is acceptable to say "Which person do you want me to give this to?" instead of "To which person do you want me to give this?" The latter sounds too stiff and formal. However, sometimes bad habits of speech cause us to add a preposition at the end of a sentence when none is necessary. For example, "Where did you take them to?" or "Where is your car parked at?" In both cases the prepositions are not necessary and to the educated ear sound like non-Standard English. If you have this habit, reading and listening to excellent speakers will help you correct it.

1. What are the objects of the prepositions in sentence (b)?

———   ———   ———   ———

2. How do you know "filed the records" in sentence (a) and "to attend the meeting" in sentence (d) are not prepositional phrases?

_____ is a verb and _____ is an infinitive. A prepositional phrase begins with a preposition, ends with a noun or pronoun, and never includes a verb.

Check your answers on page 436.

Recognizing Prepositions

Conjunctions connect (or join) words, groups of words, or complete sentences. **Prepositions** are also connecting words; they show the relationship between an object and another word in the sentence. To recognize a preposition, ask "whom" or "what"; if you see an answer, that word is the object. But remember that a verb cannot be part of a prepositional phrase, so don't confuse objects of verbs with objects of prepositions.

Although prepositions are usually small words, they are important for showing the exact meaning of a sentence. Notice how the preposition shows the relationship between *pen* and *desk* in the sentences that follow:

The pen is **on** the desk.	The pen is **in** the desk.
The pen is **under** the desk.	The pen is **near** the desk.
The pen is **beside** the desk.	The pen is **behind** the desk.

Writing for Your Career

If *of* can be omitted after the following—*all, half, none, any, more, most, some,* a fraction, or a percentage— do so. The preceding words are then adjectives describing the subject (instead of a prepositional phrase). It isn't important, however, to analyze the grammar. Just avoid prepositional phrases if you can express an idea more concisely without them.

Half the apples instead of **Half of the apples.**

All the software instead of **All of the software**

REPLAY 9

A. Insert a suitable coordinating conjunction, dependent conjunction, or conjunctive adverb in each blank.

1. Neither Lennie _____ Michael wants to move to New York.
2. Yaling has led many tour groups through Europe, _____ she has never taken a group to South America.
3. I was there to meet Keira _____ Steve _____ they arrived.

4. Victoria has worked for Pacific Telephone Company for many years, _____ she would prefer to work in the medical industry.

5. _____ Victoria was an administrative assistant _____ she took management classes, she understands the problems of office support workers.

6. Management consultant Peter Drucker said the better employees are, the more mistakes they make _____ the more new things they try.

7. We won't know whether this department will be profitable _____ we check the records.

8. _____ you want the rainbow, you must put up with the rain," said Dolly Parton.

9. She did not make personal phone calls at the office _____ she wanted to be known for her good work ethic.

10. "Do you prefer Chicago _____ Atlanta for our convention?" asked Roseanne.

B. Write a preposition in each blank to show a relationship between the verb and the object.

Example: Richard and Marissa walked _____ the mountain.

1. The movers carried the furniture _____ the new office building.

2. _____ this time, you should know how to find the errors in your writing.

3. She is a person who will be your friend _____ the end.

4. _____ all of our setbacks, the team has stuck together.

5. _____ the long haul, you will be rewarded for hard work.

6. The overpass moves cars _____ the highway quickly.

C. Underline the prepositional phrases and circle the prepositions.

Example: Victoria looked(at)the return address and threw the envelope(into)the trash.

1. Courtesy in the workplace means the practice of kindness and consideration toward other employees and customers. (3 phrases)

2. Advertising has a profound influence on the behavior of people and on their lifestyles. (3 phrases)

3. Do you know the difference between a dream and a goal? (1 phrase)

4. Fax the letter from your office to my home. (2 phrases)

5. Radio advertisers are experts at producing spot announcements for their customers. (2 phrases)

Check your answers on pages 436–437.

READ 10　PARTS OF SPEECH—VERSATILE TOOLS

Tools are versatile when they do more than one kind of job. So it is with words—most of them can be used as more than one part of speech. The idea is simple.

How you use a word in a sentence determines the part of speech.

Consider the word *dancing*. It looks like a verb, doesn't it? After all, it represents *action*. It sounds like a verb too—because it ends in *ing*. As a matter of fact, it *is* a verb

. . . sometimes. The *ing* form is a verb only when a helping verb precedes it. Otherwise, the *ing* word is a noun or an adjective. Compare the following examples:

Verb	He **is dancing** with Fergie. [The complete verb consists of the helping verb *is* and main verb *dancing*.]
Noun	**Dancing** is fun. [*Dancing* is a noun because it names an activity; the verb is *is*.]
Adjective	The child attends a **dancing** class. [*Dancing* is an adjective because it describes the class; *attends* is the verb.]

Some words called **verbals** can function as verbs, adjectives, or nouns. An *ing* word, such as *dancing*, can't be a verb unless a helping verb precedes it. For example, what part of speech is *brown*? It can be a:

Verb	Did you *brown* the onions?
Adjective	She has beautiful *brown* hair.
Noun	Is *brown* your favorite color?

REPLAY 10

A. The word *fish* may be a noun, an adjective, or a verb. What part of speech is *fish* in each of these sentences?

Example: *Let's go to the fish market.* _____adjective_____

1. We'll fish every day while we're on vacation. _____
2. We'll have a fish dinner every evening. _____
3. Dietitians say that fish is a healthful food. _____

B. The word *trade* may also be a noun, an adjective, or a verb. What part of speech is *trade* in each of the following sentences?

Example: *Would you like a career in international trade?* _____noun_____

1. That was not a fair trade. _____
2. I will not trade that stock. _____
3. He reads several trade papers. _____

C. *Reading* is another word that readily changes part of speech. Write a sentence using *reading* as each part listed.

1. verb _____.
2. noun _____.
3. adjective _____.

D. Write two sentences using *plant*—first as a verb and next as a noun.

1. (verb) _____.
2. (noun) _____.

E. Please respond to the following:

1. What part of speech are *city* and *country* in the sentence below?
   Do you prefer **country** life to **city** life? _____

2. Write a sentence with *city* and *country* as nouns.

   _____

   _____.

Check your answers on page 437.

Writing for Your Career

You've reviewed the "tools of the trade": seven of the eight parts of speech. The eighth is the **interjection,** an exclamatory word or phrase such as *No! Congratulations! That's great!* Perhaps you have special ones for certain occasions that fit your way of expressing your emotions or enthusiasm.

There isn't much more you need to know about interjections except this caution: Use them sparingly in workplace writing and, generally, avoid too many exclamations in your writing. The more you exclaim, the more likely your reader will become weary of the excited tone. Emphasis is effective only when it is used sparingly.

CONCEPT REVIEW & SKILL-BUILDING APPLICATIONS

Checkpoint

You should now recognize parts of speech well enough so that you can learn and apply the information provided in the chapters that follow.

Check each blank after you know the definition and understand the examples.

_____ **NOUN** Names something, somebody, or someplace.
Beauty is in the eyes of the beholder.
Typing is a basic skill needed by most employees.

_____ **PRONOUN** Substitutes for a noun. To decide whether a word is a pronoun, see if it can substitute for a noun.
Give the tape to Debra. Give that to her.
Students were selected to fill out forms. They were selected to fill them out.

_____ **VERB** Expresses action or being.
Long paragraphs look difficult and discourage concentration.
Well-written paragraphs are about one subject.

_____ **ADJECTIVE** Modifies—tells something about—a noun or pronoun. The four kinds of adjectives are pointing, descriptive, articles, limiting.
This clever accountant has a job with many responsibilities. [*This* is a pointing adjective; *clever* is a descriptive adjective; *a* is an article; *many* is a limiting adjective.]

_____ **ADVERB** Modifies—tells something about—a verb, an adjective, or an adverb. Many, but not all, adverbs end with *ly*.

Yesterday I walked really fast. [The adverbs *yesterday* and *fast* tell when and how, modifying the verb *walked*. The adverb *really* modifies the adverb *fast*.]

_____ **CONJUNCTION** Joins—or connects—two words or groups of words. Coordinating conjunctions are *and, but, or, nor, for, so,* and *yet.* Dependent conjunctions precede a word group made up of a noun or pronoun plus a verb and may either begin a sentence or join parts of a sentence. A few examples are *when, as, if, since, because,* and *although.*

Although he likes Los Angeles and Sacramento, he has to choose one or the other.

_____ **PREPOSITION** Introduces a prepositional phrase. A prepositional phrase begins with a preposition and ends with a noun or pronoun that is the object of the preposition. Describing words may come between the preposition and its object. A verb cannot be part of a prepositional phrase.

During the past month he took each woman to dinner at his parents' home near Dallas.

_____ **INTERJECTION** Expressive words or phrases usually followed by an exclamation mark.

No way! Great!

_____ **PART OF SPEECH** depends on how a word is used in a sentence. You may look up the part of speech in a dictionary; however, many words have more than one part of speech—depending on the definition. The pronunciation may even differ.

He wound the bandage around the wound.

They will service the vehicle, but the service manager doesn't give very good service. [This sentence is a special example; ordinarily avoid repeating words.]

Special Assignment

After reading the letter on page 47, answer the following questions. Use your dictionary along with what you've learned in this chapter. Remember that although a word may be used as several different parts of speech, only one of them is correct for a particular meaning.

 A. First Paragraph: For each of the following words, write the part of speech in the blanks:

 1. My _____

 2. are pleased _____

 3. on _____

 4. The _____

 5. and _____

 6. prompt _____

 7. service _____

 8. which _____

 9. appreciated _____

B. Second Paragraph: Write the verbs in blanks 1–10 and the pronouns in blanks 11–15.

1. _____
2. _____
3. _____
4. _____
5. _____
6. _____
7. _____
8. _____
9. _____
10. _____
11. _____
12. _____
13. _____
14. _____
15. _____

C. Third Paragraph: Write the prepositional phrases in the blanks.

1. _____
2. _____
3. _____
4. _____
5. _____
6. _____
7. _____

2301 Garnet Place
Sioux Falls, SD 57107
July 1, 0000

Customer Services Manager
Rollex Motors Ltd
33 Edgemont Drive
Presque City, ME 04769

Dear Customer Services Manager:

My husband and I are pleased with the new Humvee we purchased on June 25. The dealer, Goniff Imports, Inc., provided courteous and prompt service, which we appreciated.

We believe this dealer and your organization conduct business fairly and honestly. However, after we had driven the vehicle only 32 miles, we found that the wheels needed balancing. Yesterday we paid $115 (copy of bill enclosed) to have this service performed, although the problem apparently existed when we drove the vehicle out of your showroom.

When we returned the vehicle, we were billed for this adjustment because of the exclusion provisions on page 3 of the warranty. The third paragraph reads,

"Normal maintenance services . . . such as . . . wheel balancing . . ." are not covered. However, we believe a condition existing at the time of purchase is not "normal maintenance" and surely should be corrected without charge.

Although we assume a misunderstanding occurred, the dealer would not release our Humvee without payment. Will you please instruct Goniff Imports, Inc., to send us a check for $115?

Sincerely,

Leila R. Smith

enclosure
c: Goniff Imports, Inc.

Date to submit this assignment: _____

Proofreading for Careers

If you want good grades or career advancement, don't let others see your mistakes! Instead, proofread, *proofread,* **proofread.** You began your proofreading practice with Chapter 1, and it will continue throughout the course. If you need to, review the proofreader's marks on the inside back cover of this book, and then correct the errors in the following article. Your instructor will tell you whether to use proofreader's marks on the copy in your textbook or do this activity online.

Developing Good Study Habit

Adults frequently report they have'nt been taught to study and that they need practical and specific suggestions. Here is a breif list of recomendations that will put in control of your study time:

- Keep in mind that study is an activity involving more then just looking a book. study is an active process, not a passive one.

- Work with pen, paper,computer, and necesary referance materials.

- If possible, plan to do all studying in one place. We are all creatures of habit. We have places for warship, amusement, sleep, and taking a bathe; why not hae a place for study?

- Begin to study the very minute you sit down at your desk. Do not dilly dally (search for your favorite pin or sharpen pencils), for frequently that is an unconscience attempt to put off a task.

- Plan a well-balanced work-study schedule and try to adhere to it, if you must depart from your schedule at least you will have something definite and planned to which you can return.

- Take a short rest or activity break after 20 to 30 minutes of concentrated study. Short periods of relaxashion or change in activity enable you to renew your study with increased viger.

- See that fiscal factors such as heat lightnig, and ventilation are satisfactory. to do affective study and reading, you must be comfortable and ready for work.

How did you do? Excellent _____ Good _____ Need More Practice _____

(Don't be hard on yourself. This exercise contains some errors you haven't yet studied.)

Practice Quiz

A. Fill in the blanks with the name of the part of speech.

1. To name persons, animals, things, ideas, places, times, or activities, use a/an _____.

2. To show or suggest action or existence, use a/an _____.

3. To describe a verb, adjective, or adverb, use a/an _____.

4. To begin a prepositional phrase, use a/an _____.

5. To describe a noun or pronoun, use a/an _____.

6. A prepositional phrase may not include a/an _____.

7. The coordinating conjunctions are _____.

8. *Because* is an example of a _____ conjunction.

9. A word that substitutes for a noun is called a/an _____.

10. *I, me, my, mine,* and *myself* are examples of _____.

B. Insert the part of speech for each word.

While Sarah slept soundly, she dreamed about snowboarding with Jonathan at the new Utah resort. Wonderful!

11. While _____

12. Sarah _____

13. slept _____

14. soundly _____

15. she _____

16. dreamed _____

17. about _____

18. snowboarding _____

19. with _____

20. Jonathan _____

21. at _____

22. the _____

23. new _____

24. Utah _____

25. resort _____

26. Wonderful! _____

Self-Study Practice and Tutorials

Vocabulary and Spelling for Careers

For additional practice go to Appendix B, page 321.

Replay Drills

For additional practice go to Appendix C, page 359.

Companion Web Site: www.prenhall.com/smith

Go to the companion Web site to test your knowledge on self-grading quizzes and to find links to other helpful online resources.

MyWritingLab

Use this online learning system for an assessment of your progress on topics covered in this chapter and progressive exercises that fit your individual needs.

3 Writing Complete Sentences

After completing Chapter 3, you will be able to do the following:

- Identify the parts of complete sentences.
- Define independent and dependent clauses.
- Identify and correct sentence fragments, run-ons, and comma splices.
- Identify and correctly punctuate transitional words and expressions in sentences.
- Write complete sentences to achieve clarity and emphasis.

READ 11   BASIC NEEDS OF A SENTENCE

When you combine the following letters in the order shown, you can pronounce a word:

S-P-E-L-L

You can't, however, be sure whether SPELL refers to magic or to arranging letters to form a word. To increase your reader's understanding, you can use more than one word, and arrange the words in a group:

A when not word spell how to you sure are.

The preceding word group looks like a sentence. It begins with a capital letter and ends with a period. But something basic is missing from this sentence—sense. The words are not arranged properly, so you don't receive a sensible message. Now read the following:

When you are not sure how to spell a word.

These words seem to be in order. They also begin with a capital letter and end with a period, but something is still not right. Do you have a feeling of incompleteness? Do you sense something is missing? Although you understand the word group, you still don't have a sensible message. Try again:

When you are not sure how to spell a word, use the dictionary.

At last the familiar signals—capital letter and period—enclose a *complete thought* that you understand.

Just as people have basic needs, so too does a sentence. A **complete sentence** needs three characteristics:

■ **Identity**—the subject—who or what

■ **Action**—the verb—doing, having, being, helping

■ **Independence**—the ability to stand alone as a complete thought

Identity—the Subject

A sentence includes at least one word to identify who or what the sentence is about. This part of the sentence is the *subject* and is always a noun or a pronoun.

The following subjects in bold type identify **who** or **what** the sentence is about.

Who	**Mr. Escobar** is our newest call center supervisor.
	He received the promotion after a year as a telemarketer.
	Do **you** want to improve your pronunciation and vocabulary?
What	**It's** a good job.
	Learning a second language takes time and effort.
	To leave now would be a mistake.
What and Who	A **book** can help you learn English, but **you** also need to listen to English-speaking radio, TV, and films.

Understood Subjects

Sometimes a subject is a "missing person." Look at these examples:

Let me know when the report is finished. [The understood subject is *you*.]

Leave the file on my desk. [The understood subject is *you*.]

    In **commands** (also called **polite requests**)—sentences that tell somebody what to do—*you* is understood as the subject even though the word isn't used. Often commands are expressed more courteously by adding "please," but the subject is still **you.**

        Let me know when you want to meet.

        Send me the report by close of business today.

        Please show your identification to gain access to the elevators.

Action, Having, Being, or Helping—the Verb

A sentence must have at least one verb—the word that tells what the subject *does* (action), *has* (having), or *is* (being). A helping verb sometimes precedes the action, having, or being verb.

In the following sentences the verbs are in bold type. A sentence may have more than one verb, as in items 4 and 7. Sometimes a verb consists of more than one word; that is, a helping verb and a main verb, as in items 5 and 8.

1. We **saw** the new building on January 6. [action verb]
2. Ms. Hirsch from Green Investments, Inc. **is** our financial consultant. [being verb]
3. You **have** the right of way. [action (having) verb]
4. The crime **was** embezzlement, and the punishment **fits** the crime. [being and action verbs]
5. They **will** both **speak** at the annual meeting in Omaha. [helping plus action verb]
6. Most successful companies **operate** with honesty and social responsibility. [action verb]
7. Please **show** me the building and **describe** the facilities. [two action verbs]
8. **Does** he **know** Jonathan Edwards **is** the CEO? [helping plus action verb and being verb]

RECAP

A. Here are the verbs from the preceding examples. Write the subject(s) in the blanks.

1. _____ saw

2. _____ is

3. _____ have

4. _____ was
   _____ fits

5. _____ will speak

6. _____ operate

7. _____ show
   _____ describe

8. _____ does know
   _____ is

B. Read the following sentence:

Successful multicultural communication is vital to the nation's productivity.

What is the subject? _____ What is the verb? ___ What is the prepositional phrase? _____

Check your answers on page 437.

Word Power

Just because a word is a noun or a pronoun doesn't mean it is the subject. For example, the object of a preposition is always a noun or a pronoun but is *not* a subject. To identify a subject, first find the verb. If the noun or pronoun *does, is,* or *has* what the verb states, it is the subject.

Independence

Every sentence requires at least one independent clause, a word group that has a subject and verb and is a complete thought.

An independent clause that begins with a capital letter and ends with a period, question mark, or exclamation mark is a complete sentence.

A word group with a subject and a verb is called a clause.

A clause may be either dependent or independent. A clause that cannot stand alone as a complete sentence is a **dependent clause.** If a capital letter begins a dependent clause and a closing punctuation mark ends it, the result is a **fragment.**

Sentence	Prices will continue to fall.
Fragment	While prices will continue to fall.
Sentence	PCs are relatively cheap.
Fragment	Since PCs are relatively cheap.

Recognizing Dependent Clauses

You can recognize a **dependent** clause by its first word—a dependent conjunction. The two fragments above begin with the dependent conjunctions *while* and *since.* Learn to recognize the dependent conjunctions listed below. You don't need to memorize them:

after	as
before	if
since	that
until	where
which	who(m)
although	because
even though	provided
so that	unless
when	whether
while	why

REPLAY 11

A. Subjects tell who or what the sentence is about. Verbs tell what the subject does, is, or has. Write the subject(s) in the left blank and the verb(s) in the right blank. One sentence has the "understood subject" *you*. Another has two subjects and two verbs.

	Subjects	Verbs
Example: The new secretary is in the office now.	secretary	is

1. The director could have filmed the scene much faster. _____ _____
2. You must be computer literate to get a good job. _____ _____
3. The winner sees an answer for every problem. _____ _____
4. The loser sees a problem in every answer. _____ _____
5. The books were put on the shelf. _____ _____
6. What you earn depends on what you learn. _____ _____
7. The new members of the team have uniforms. _____ _____
8. Three visitors arrived yesterday. _____ _____
9. Please give me the ledger. _____ _____
10. Professor Friede found five errors. _____ _____

Word to the Wise

Notice that "of the team" in no. 7 above is a prepositional phrase. The object in this phrase is "team." An object of a preposition can't be a subject.

B. A clause is a word group with a subject and a verb. Each item below is a clause. Six clauses are independent and six are dependent.

First, in the blanks write *I* for **independent** or *D* for **dependent.**

Second, cross out the word that makes the clause dependent and then make the clause independent by adding capitalization and closing punctuation.

Third, change the independent clauses to sentences using the proofreader's mark for capitalization.

Example: ___D___ since the new assistant didn't know the meaning of *chronological.*

_____ 1. she couldn't arrange the reports in chronological order.

_____ 2. because many organizations have similar problems with employees.

_____ 3. although an information technology professional needs excellent communication skills.

_____ 4. in the workplace you may converse with many people.

_____ 5. since they have limited English skill.

_____ 6. don't laugh at someone's pronunciation or grammar error.

_____ 7. when the trucker arrived with the shipment.

_____ 8. it's better than I thought.

_____ 9. although she prefers driving to flying.

_____ 10. after you've learned a few phrases in other languages.

Check your answers on page 438.

READ 12   CORRECTING SENTENCE FRAGMENTS

A fragment is an incomplete word group beginning with a capital letter and ending with a period. Avoid fragments in most business writing.

As you just learned in Read 11, one type of fragment is a dependent clause that begins with a capital letter and ends with a period, question mark, or exclamation mark. In Replay 11 you corrected sentence fragments by crossing out the dependent conjunction, beginning the next word with a capital letter, and inserting a closing punctuation mark at the end.

1. when she dines at the college cafe.
2. where the beans taste like caviar.

Another way to correct a fragment is to add an independent clause before or after the dependent clause. Then you have a complete sentence. The dependent clause is in bold letters in the following examples; the independent clause is not bold.

a. **Since prices will continue to fall,** competition will get stronger.
b. Competition will get stronger **because prices will continue to fall.**
c. **Although Web sites are now easier to create,** well-trained people still command high salaries.
d. Well-trained people still command high salaries **although Web sites are now easier to create.**

You'll become a comma expert in Chapter 9. In the meantime, use a comma between clauses if the dependent clause precedes the independent—as in sentences (a) and (c)—but not when it follows—as in (b) and (d) above.

> **RECAP**   Convert the fragment to a sentence by adding an independent clause of your choice. Replace a period with a comma where required.

1. When she dines at the college cafe, _____

_____

2. Rewrite No. 1 so that the independent clause you used above opens the sentence and the dependent clause follows. _____

_____.

Check your answers on page 438.

Recognizing Fragments

A word group without a subject that begins with a capital letter and ends with a period is a fragment.

This type of fragment occurs when clauses or phrases are written as two separate sentences when they should be written as one:

NO	While jogging around the block. Mr. Henry sprained his ankle. [fragment followed by a complete sentence]
YES	While jogging around the block, Mr. Henry sprained his ankle.
OR	Mr. Henry, while jogging around the block, sprained his ankle.
NO	Mr. Henry's office, which is closed today. It will reopen next week. [fragment followed by a complete sentence]
YES	Mr. Henry's office, which is closed today, will reopen next week.
OR	Mr. Henry's office is closed today. It will reopen next week.

Accidentally leaving words out of sentences or omitting them intentionally are common causes of fragments. Some people mistakenly believe it is acceptable to omit a subject in certain commonly used phrases, but in business writing, full sentences are preferable.

NO	Hope to hear from you soon.
OR	Hoping to hear from you soon.

These fragments are acceptable for a postcard or informal email, but in regular business writing, use a complete sentence:

YES	We hope to hear from you soon.

Omitting the subject is correct only in a command or request with *you* as the understood subject.

YES	Reply immediately.
OR	Please reply immediately.

Writing for Your Career

Do not omit subjects to write sentences more concisely. Concise writing is important—but not if the result is poor grammar or sentence construction.

REPLAY 12

A. Write **F** in the blanks next to the fragments and **S** next to the sentences.

Examples: __F__ Whether it can be done.
__S__ We do not know.

_____ 1. If you do a good job on the Mendocino project.

_____ 2. You will get a salary increase after the first of the month.

_____ 3. Although most corporations use the services of an auditor to examine the books.

_____ 4. Some errors may never be found.

_____ 5. Don't ever think.

_____ 6. That you know it all.

_____ 7. Because sexual harassment is illegal and immoral.

_____ 8. Julia filed a complaint.

_____ 9. When Mr. Lopez became general manager.

_____ 10. He asked the staff to greet Spanish-speaking customers in Spanish.

B. Use the ten items in Part A to write five sentences. Combine each fragment (dependent clause) with one of the sentences (independent clauses).

Example: We do not know whether it can be done. (See Part A examples.)

1. _____
   _____

2. _____
   _____

3. _____

4. _____

5. _____
   _____

C. Write **F** for fragment or **S** for sentence in the blanks below.

Example: __F__ A stock certificate, which is a valuable document.

_____ 1. The man whom we met yesterday in Fullerton.

_____ 2. Our Human Resources Department on the third floor.

_____ 3. Keisha, believing that she was right.

_____ 4. Richard also felt that he was right.

_____ 5. Mr. Yee continued to argue the point.

_____ 6. Lester, having been on vacation last week.

_____ 7. The staff was on vacation last week.

_____ 8. The team that won all the games in Oklahoma City last year.

_____ 9. That team won all the games in Philadelphia last year.

_____ 10. The Bridgeport team that won all the games last year is losing today.

D. Five items in Part C are fragments. Write the item number for each fragment in the blank; then change the fragment to a sentence. Make up necessary information to complete the sentence.

_____ _____

_____ _____

_____ _____

_____ _____

_____ _____

Check your answers on pages 438–439.

Writing for Your Career

Experienced writers who clearly understand sentence structure sometimes use fragments to create certain effects, particularly in advertising material. After you're confident of your business writing expertise, you may intentionally use a fragment. Until then, keep fragments out of your writing.

READ 13   CORRECTING COMMA SPLICES AND RUN-ONS

Now that you understand how to handle sentence fragments, you need to know how to avoid two other common types of sentence errors: the comma splice and the run-on sentence. Fragments, run-ons, or comma splices may keep the reader from understanding the message in a letter or report. They may also cause the reader to wonder about the writer's education.

A comma splice occurs when you join two or more independent clauses with a comma but without a coordinating conjunction.

If the independent clauses just run together with neither conjunction nor punctuation, we call the error a **run-on**.

Run-ons occur when the writer goes on and on and doesn't insert a period or a connecting word where needed.

Correcting with a Capital and a Period

A run-on and a comma splice may have the same wording. The comma splice, however, has a comma between independent clauses; the run-on does not.

One way to correct either error is to separate independent clauses with a period and capital letter, resulting in two sentences.

Run-on	Use gestures to reinforce your message don't cross your arms.
Comma splice	Use gestures to reinforce your message, don't cross your arms.
Correct	Use gestures to reinforce your message. Don't cross your arms.

Run-on	The vigorous handshake common in American business is inappropriate in France it is seen as rude behavior.
Comma splice	The vigorous handshake common in American business is inappropriate in France, it is seen as rude behavior.
Correct	The vigorous handshake common in American business is inappropriate in France. It is seen as rude behavior.
Run-on	Business is part of our society there is no escape.
Comma splice	Business is part of our society, there is no escape.
Correct	Business is part of our society. There is no escape.
Run-on	Microsoft Corporation is worth billions of dollars it is one of the giants of American business.
Comma splice	Microsoft Corporation is worth billions of dollars, it is one of the giants of American business.
Correct	Microsoft Corporation is worth billions of dollars. It is one of the giants of American business.
Run-on	Arnold said that the recession is over salaries and prices are rising.
Comma splice	Arnold said that the recession is over, salaries and prices are rising.
Correct	Arnold said that the recession is over. Salaries and prices are rising.

Word Power

As you learned in Chapter 2, you can also use a coordinating conjunction to join two independent clauses. This is another way to correct commas splices and run-ons. You will have a chance to practice this in Read 14.

REPLAY 13

Correct run-ons and comma splices in the following sentences. Write **C** for correct, **R** for run-on, and **CS** for comma splice. Use a period and capital letter to correct the run-ons and comma splices. Remember, don't place a period after a dependent clause; if you do, you create a fragment.

Example: _CS_ Sticks and stones will break my bones, words will never harm me.

_C_ Sticks and stones will break my bones. Words will never harm me.

_____ 1. The winner always has a program the loser always has an excuse.

_____ 2. The English translation of a sign in the window of a travel agency in Spain reads, "Go Away."

_____ 3. These statistics deal only with symptoms, they do not reveal the fundamental economic problems.

_____ 4. Geriatrics, the study of dealing with problems of the aged, is a relatively new science.

_____ 5. Geriatrics is the study of dealing with problems of the aged it is a relatively new science.

_____ 6. This tax return is inaccurate ask your accountant to prepare a new one.

_____ 7. As your tax return is inaccurate, ask your accountant to prepare a new one.

_____ 8. Many students are attracted to a business career, they like the challenges and rewards it offers.

_____ 9. Because of the challenges and rewards it offers, many students are attracted to a business career.

_____ 10. Each year _Fortune_ magazine publishes a list of the top five hundred American corporations.

_____ 11. Many of today's corporations started in colonial times, they became far bigger than anyone expected.

_____ 12. Most large corporations are multinational, they do business in many foreign countries.

_____ 13. Our in-service training includes instruction in Excel and in PowerPoint.

_____ 14. After you have made your list of goals, prioritize them in order of importance.

_____ 15. Set a realistic, but ambitious, timetable for each of your goals.

Check your answers on page 439; then review Reads and Replays 11-13 before taking the Pop Quiz on page 297.

READ 14   THREE IMPORTANT CONNECTIONS

Some ideas should be connected (or joined) and others separated. When writing business documents, you must decide quickly whether to separate or connect clauses. In Read and Replay 13, you **separated** independent clauses with a period followed by a capital letter for the first word of the next sentence. In Read and Replay 14, you will **connect** them correctly. If independent clauses are closely related and not too long, connecting is often preferable to separation. The example sentence in Replay 13 illustrates this. The more common (and better) way to write this old adage is as follows:

Sticks and stones may break my bones, but words will never harm me.

Connecting Independent Clauses

Three correct ways to connect independent clauses are with a semicolon, a comma and a coordinating conjunction, or just a coordinating conjunction.

1. **Connecting with a semicolon:**
    Closely related independent clauses may be connected with a semicolon.

    Get organized; handle each piece of paper only once.

2. **Connecting with a comma and coordinating conjunction:**
   Closely related independent clauses may be connected with a comma followed by a coordinating conjunction: *and, but, or, nor, for*, and sometimes *so* or *yet*.*

   You cannot control what anyone else does, **but** you can take charge of your own life.

3. **Connecting with a coordinating conjunction only:**
   If the independent clauses total no more than ten or eleven words and you join them with *and* or *or,* a comma isn't needed.

   Get organized **and** handle each piece of paper only once.

   Take the report with you **or** leave it on my desk.

   Efficiency helps, **but** skill is also required. [Because *but* is the conjunction, add the comma.]

   Here are examples of how to use these methods to connect the independent clauses instead of separating them.

Run-on	Business is part of our society there is no escape.
Comma splice	Business is part of our society, there is no escape.
Correct	Business is part of our society; there is no escape. [Connect with a semicolon.]
Or	Business is part of our society and there is no escape. [Connect with a coordinating conjunction. A comma isn't needed since *and* is joining short clauses.]
Run-on	Microsoft Corporation is worth billions of dollars it is one of the giants of American business.
Comma splice	Microsoft Corporation is worth billions of dollars, it is one of the giants of American business.
Correct	Microsoft Corporation is worth billions of dollars; it is one of the giants of American business. [Connect with a semicolon.]
Or	Microsoft Corporation is worth billions of dollars, and it is one of the giants of American business. [Connect with a comma and a coordinating conjunction. When connecting clauses longer than a few words, use a comma.]

RECAP

Run-On	Don't fill a business letter with long sentences or with words of many syllables it doesn't impress anyone.
Comma Splice	Don't fill a business letter with long sentences or with words of many syllables, it doesn't impress anyone.

For is a coordinating conjunction when it means *because*; otherwise, it is usually a preposition. Use of *so* and *yet* as joiners are explained later.

Correct the preceding run-on and comma splice in three different ways:

1. Connect with a comma and a coordinating conjunction. _____
   _____

2. Connect with a semicolon._____
   _____

3. Separate with a period and capital letter. _____
   _____

Check your answers on page 439.

Using Transitional Words and Phrases

In grammar, transitions are words and phrases that help readers move effortlessly from one idea to the next *closely related* idea. Here are some common transitional words and expressions:

also
consequently
for example
furthermore
hence
however
in addition
in fact
moreover
nevertheless
otherwise
that is
then
therefore
thus
yet

When a transitional word or phrase connects *independent* clauses, insert a semicolon or a period—not a comma—before the transition. A comma would result in a comma splice.

The following examples show how to fix comma splices by separating independent clauses or connecting them with transitions (in bold type).

Comma splice	About 50 percent of our employees are engaged in the distribution of goods and services, **however,** about 20 percent are in production.
Run-on	About 50 percent of our employees are engaged in the distribution of goods and services however, about 20 percent are in production.

Correct	About 50 percent of our employees are engaged in the distribution of goods and services; **however,** about 20 percent are in production.
OR	About 50 percent of our employees are engaged in the distribution of goods and services. However, about 20 percent are in production.
Comma splice	In the United States eye contact is extremely important, **in fact,** Americans don't trust someone who won't look them in the eye.
Correct	In the United States eye contact is extremely important; **in fact,** Americans don't trust someone who won't look them in the eye.
OR	In the United States eye contact is extremely important. **In fact,** Americans don't trust someone who won't look them in the eye.
Comma splice	Order the new computers, **then** you can find out about training.
Correct	Order the new computers; **then** you can find out about training.
	Order the new computers, and **then** you can find out about training. [coordinating conjunction makes comma correct]
	Order the new computers. **Then** you can find out about training.

Use commas before and after a transitional word that does *not* connect independent clauses.

NO	We; therefore, will be pleased to help you. [Test for independent clauses by imagining a period after *we* and a capital *T* for *therefore;* then decide whether two sentences would result.]
YES	We, therefore, will be pleased to help you. [*Therefore* doesn't join independent clauses but merely separates a subject and a verb.]

So and Yet

So is a common coordinating conjunction used frequently in speech. It tends to make writing sound informal; therefore, be cautious about using it in formal business writing. Here is an example of how you could appropriately word and punctuate a sentence using *so* in business writing:

> We can place the room on hold for 24 hours, so we will need to have your confirmation by close of business tomorrow.

Here is an example of when its use would not be appropriate.

> Our policy is to keep items on hold for 72 hours, so we need to have your deposit no later than close of business tomorrow.

A better tone is achieved when you use a transitional word:

> Our policy is to keep items on hold for 72 hours; therefore, we need to have your deposit no later than close of business tomorrow.

Yet is also used infrequently in business writing, mainly because it tends to create too formal a tone. However, it is appropriate to use with either a comma or a semicolon to join independent clauses. If in doubt, use the comma for a short sentence and the semicolon for a longer sentence. A period **separating** the two independent clauses is also correct. If a sentence seems too long, the period or the semicolon is better than the comma, but any one of the three is correct in the following examples.

Comma	Average business letter cost is increasing, **yet** the percentage of increase is declining.
Semicolon	Average business letter cost is increasing; **yet** the percentage of increase is declining.
Period	Average business letter cost is increasing. **Yet** the percentage of increase is declining.

Word to the Wise

A comma **after** a transitional expression has nothing to do with whether a word group is a comma splice or run-on. Do use a comma **after** a transition of more than one syllable—except the short word *also*. Do not use a comma after one-syllable transitions like *yet, thus,* and *then*. (Details of the correct use of commas are in Chapter 9.)

REPLAY 14

A. Write **C** beside the two correct sentences, **R** beside the run-ons, and **CS** for comma splices. Insert semicolons to correct the run-ons and comma splices.

Example: __CS__ A stock does not have a fixed worth; it's only as valuable as people think it is.

_____ 1. Teenagers are very fashion-conscious, however, they closely follow the dictates of their friends.

_____ 2. Consumers have the last word, that is, if they buy a fashion, retailers profit and continue to stock the item.

_____ 3. Some people buy because they want to be distinctive they want to be recognized as leaders.

_____ 4. Many businesspeople wear the latest fashions because they want to make a good impression on their colleagues and clients.

_____ 5. Greet your clients by name welcome them with a friendly smile and a handshake.

_____ 6. Greet your clients by name and welcome them with a smile.

_____ 7. Greet your clients by name, then welcome them with a friendly smile and a handshake.

B. Write **C** for correct, **R** for run-on, and **CS** for comma splice. Then make corrections with a comma and one of the seven coordinating conjunctions (*and, but, or, nor, for, yet, so*); or insert an appropriate dependent conjunction.

Example: __R__ You can vote in person by attending a corporation's annual
                        or
                  meeting you can vote by using an absentee ballot.
                         ∧

_____ 1. Professor Wayne was able to repair the motor quickly, he has had no formal
         training in mechanics.

_____ 2. He didn't notice any of the errors, there was no way he could have corrected
         them.

_____ 3. The Personnel Department is on the third floor the interviewers are out to
         lunch now.

_____ 4. The new equipment is being shipped to you at once, you should receive it by
         the end of the week.

_____ 5. Possibly Joyce can attend the conference maybe Michael can go in her place.

_____ 6. Sticks and stones will break my bones, words will never harm me.

_____ 7. Goods are delivered either to the receiving area of a department store or to
         the central warehouse of a chain.

_____ 8. "Experience is an expensive school, but fools will learn in no other."—
         Benjamin Franklin

C. Answer the following questions.

1. List six commonly used transitional words and expressions:

    _____ _____ _____ _____ _____ _____

2. If a transitional expression joins **independent** clauses, use a semicolon or a period
    before the transition. True _____ False _____

3. When a transition is between a **dependent** and an **independent** clause, use a
    semicolon before the transition. True _____ False _____

4. Use commas before and after a transitional expression that does not connect inde-
    pendent clauses. True _____ False _____

D. Replace a comma with a semicolon before a transitional expression that joins
independent clauses. Write **C** beside the three correct items. Insert corrections for the
others.

_____ 1. He will not, however, take the blueprints to the laboratory until the end of
         next week.

_____ 2. He will complete the blueprints today, then he'll send them to the contractor.

_____ 3. High achievers do mental rehearsals, that is, they visualize themselves per-
         forming tasks successfully.

_____ 4. High achievers can picture themselves doing something well; for example,
         they might visualize crossing the finish line of a marathon.

_____ 5. Your mind never sleeps, consequently, visualization is effective just before
         falling asleep since your mind probably continues to work on the desired
         achievement as you sleep.

_____ 6. The instructor was right, however, in advising students to get a good night's
         sleep before the exam.

Check your answers on page 440.

MAKING MORE CONNECTIONS

A run-on or comma splice results when two (or more) independent clauses are joined without a coordinating conjunction or semicolon. One way to correct such a sentence is to make one clause dependent by beginning it with a dependent conjunction.

When a dependent clause is connected to an independent clause, the result is a complete sentence. [Review dependent conjunctions in Chapter 2, pages 38–39.]

Usually the dependent conjunction slightly changes the emphasis or meaning of the original sentence and might help express a particular idea.

A sentence needs at least one independent clause; it may be either before or after the dependent clause(s), whichever sounds better for that sentence. In the following examples you see how to correct a run-on or comma splice by making one clause dependent. The dependent conjunction is in bold type:

Run-On	He thought he would be sick something was wrong with the potato salad.
Comma Splice	He thought he would be sick, something was wrong with the potato salad.
Correct	He thought he would be sick **because** something was wrong with the potato salad.
	Because something was wrong with the potato salad, he thought he would be sick.
Run-On	The picnic was fun the ants thought so too.
Comma Splice	The picnic was fun, the ants thought so too.
Correct	The picnic was fun **although** the ants thought so too.
	Although the picnic was fun, the ants thought so too.

Deciding When to Join Ideas

When two ideas are closely related, you decide whether to join or separate them, depending on what you want to convey to your reader. Which idea do you want to emphasize or are they equal in importance? Practicing writing, reading well-written business communications, and using good judgment enable you to decide quickly.

Skillful business writers often use a dependent clause to de-emphasize an idea they don't want the reader to focus on and use an independent clause to *emphasize* another idea. With this writing technique, you emphasize the positive and make the negative less important.

Dependent Clause   Independent Clause

Although we don't give refunds on earrings, we'll be happy to exchange them for any other jewelry in the store.

Dependent Clause   Independent Clause

With this writing technique, you emphasize the positive and make the negative palatable.

Deciding *Not* to Join Ideas

Oscar Wilde, a witty British playwright of the late 1800s, wrote, "The English have really everything in common with the Americans except of course language." One of many examples of the differences between British and American English is the word for the mark that ends most sentences. In the United States, we say *period;* in Britain, it's a *full stop.*

Sometimes, the best way to correct a comma splice or run-on is to make a full stop; in other words, to change one sentence to two. How will you know when to do this? The flow of your words will tell you. Think about whether you have written a complete thought. Then analyze your intent: What part of the sentence do you want to emphasize? Will your emphasis be clear to the reader? Practice deciding between commas and periods in the following exercise.

> **R**ECAP   Insert periods and capitalize the first letter of the new sentence to correct this letter. Use the proofreader's symbols on the inside back cover to mark your corrections. If you close the sentences at the correct places, you will have no fragments, comma splices, or run-ons.

Dear Professor Head: **[Salutation]**

Thank you for the time and courtesy you extended to our representative Laura Mann at your college last month; she enjoyed her visit with you;

At Laura's request, we have sent you the new edition of *Mathematics for Business;* this was sent to you several weeks ago, and you should have it by now, we do hope you'll look it over carefully; in addition, your name has been placed on our mailing list to receive an examination copy of *Business Math: Practical Applications,* a new edition of this book by Cleaves, Hobbs, and Dudenhef is expected off the press sometime next month.

We'll send your copy just as soon as it is available, if there is any way we can be of help to you, Professor Head, please let us know, best wishes for a happy holiday season

Cordially, **[Complimentary close]**

Hal Balmer **[Handwritten signature]**

Hal Balmer **[Writer's name and title]**

Vice President

Irs **[Initials of assistant who typed the letter]**

Check your answers on page 440.

Writing for Your Career

As you read the letter in the preceding exercise and other examples of well-written business letters throughout the text, notice the friendly, easy-to-understand style. This is the style to aim for in your business writing. Take a look at these examples when you work on your writing assignments. Note that the sample letters in the text exercises show only the salutation (greeting), body (message), and closing information, not the date or address, which you will need to include in your actual business correspondence. Chapter 13 and Appendix D cover business letter formatting, and you can find extensive coverage of this topic in your reference manual.

REPLAY 15

A. Write **R** for run-on, **CS** for comma splice, or **C** for correct sentence. Underline the dependent conjunctions. Insert needed punctuation and capitalization.

Example: __C__ When you buy more shares of stock, you increase your voting power at the corporation's annual meeting.

_____ 1. He knows the definition of *workaholic* that is a person who is addicted to work.

_____ 2. He knows the definition of *workaholic,* which is a person who is addicted to work.

_____ 3. The highest achievers are passionately committed to their work they are not workaholics.

_____ 4. Although the highest achievers are passionately committed to their work, they are not workaholics.

_____ 5. The highest achievers are passionately committed to their work, although they are not workaholics.

_____ 6. High achievers take more short vacations than the average person, they often get new ideas for their work during these vacations.

_____ 7. High achievers take more short vacations than the average person they often get new ideas for their work during these vacations.

_____ 8. Workaholics work long hours because they fear losing the job or not impressing the boss favorably.

_____ 9. Because high achievers feel a strong sense of commitment to their work, they work long hours.

_____ 10. High achievers define skills needed for their career and set out to get them.

_____ 11. Observations about high achievers are from Charles Garfield's book *Peak Performers,* Mr. Garfield studied hundreds of top achievers.

_____ 12. Always leave a job on good terms, for you may need a reference some day.

_____ 13. During an interview, don't forget to ask *your* questions also remember to thank the interviewer for the appointment.

_____ 14. Listen attentively during an interview make eye contact with the interviewer.

_____ 15. Personnel directors are skilled at asking questions that cannot be answered by a simple "yes" or "no."

_____ 16. The winters are long and cold in Indianapolis, but this gives IVY Tech students more time to study.

_____ 17. Love competence in the performance of your tasks begin now.—Lao Tzu

_____ 18. A rolling stone gathers no moss, yet it does get a certain smoothness from its rolling.

_____ 19. Mix a little foolishness with your serious plans it is lovely to be silly at the right moment.—Horace (Roman poet and philosopher, but he wrote it correctly.)

_____ 20. Mix a little foolishness with your serious plans, as it is lovely to be silly at the right moment.

B. Correct these sentences by adding a dependent conjunction that makes one clause dependent. Write **C** beside the one sentence that is already correct.

Example: When A company finds its high stock price is discouraging new investors, it might initiate a stock split.

_____ 1. The future, therefore, is that time when you'll wish you had done what you're not doing now.

_____ 2. He places big orders with us, George gives him a special discount.

_____ 3. The plant was operating on a 24-hour basis, management refused to adopt a three-shift schedule.

_____ 4. Professor Brown explained that studying business communication at Wright Business School is enjoyable, the new student wouldn't believe it.

_____ 5. Then Veronica said we need the latest dictionary for Chapter 3 language changes constantly.

Check your answers on page 441; then take the Pop Quiz on page 299. Be sure you have checked all Recap and Replay answers before proceeding to Checkpoint.

CONCEPT REVIEW & SKILL-BUILDING APPLICATIONS

Checkpoint

Place a check next to each item below when you're sure you understand it.

_____ A subject is a noun or pronoun that tells who or what a sentence is about.

_____ A verb tells what the subject does, is, or has.

_____ A clause is a word group with a subject-verb combination. A clause beginning with a dependent conjunction is a dependent clause. A clause _not_ beginning with a dependent conjunction is an independent clause.

_____ An independent clause may be used as a sentence

_____ A fragment is an incomplete idea masquerading as a sentence since it begins with a capital letter and ends with a period. A fragment might be missing a subject or verb, or it could be a dependent clause.

_____ A run-on is two or more independent clauses with neither punctuation nor a coordinating conjunction between the clauses.

_____ A comma splice has a comma between the independent clauses of a run-on.

_____ Structure, not length, determines whether a group of words is a fragment, a run-on, or a comma splice. [Identify fragments, run-ons, and comma splices not by length, but by structure.]

_____ Run-ons and comma splices are unacceptable in workplace writing; fragments are usually unacceptable—unless in a very informal note.

_____ A run-on or comma splice may be corrected with a semicolon (;) between the independent clauses, or with a comma and a coordinating conjunction (*and, but, or, nor, for, yet*) between the independent clauses. The comma may be omitted if the sentence is short and the conjunction is *and* or *or*.

_____ A comma splice or run-on may be corrected by separating the independent clauses with a period followed by a capital letter.

_____ A comma splice or run-on may be corrected by making one of the clauses dependent.

Special Assignment

Speaking vs. Writing

A. In conversation, sentence fragments are frequently used. Imagine this conversation:

Instructor	What did you study in Chapter 10?
Student	The difference between sentences and fragments.

If you were to write your reply, you would insert a subject and a verb. This would change the acceptable conversational fragment above to an acceptable written sentence. Write the acceptable **written** reply in the blank. _____
_____.

Special Assignments B and C begin on page 74. Do them after you complete the Practice Quiz and check your answers.

Proofreading for Careers

More Proofreading Tips

1. Use your spelling checker, proofread from the screen, and make corrections before printing.

2. Proofread again from printed pages.

3. Proofread for sense, not just for spelling and correctness.
4. Don't rely on anyone else's accuracy or skill when a document is your responsibility. When someone has prepared a document for you, do not submit, sign, or okay the document until you proofread it yourself.
5. Remember, everyone makes errors, but successful people find and correct their own errors before anyone else finds them.

Using your dictionary, correct the following section of an article on career preparation. Look for spelling and typographical errors, poor sentence construction, and other errors that your spell checker will not find. Change punctuation **only to correct a run-on, comma splice, or fragment.** Keep the wording as is. Your instructor will tell you whether to use proofreader's marks on the copy in your textbook or do this activity online. If you correct the errors in the text, type a version of the article with all errors corrected.

Career Planning: Know the Marketplace You Plan to Enter

You should know what's going on in your field of interest, start keeping abreast of facts and trends long before you jump into the marketplace. What sourcs should you use? Most fields have professional journals or newsletters in print and online. Which provide "insider" information on what's new and important. Web sites of trade organizations and government agencys are also good sources.

Also, your local newspaper's busness section will contain articles on a board range of businesses and their activities. You never know what type of business and industries will be featured therefore reading the paper daily is a plus. You may find a company profile useful when you're ready for interviewing, another article may forecast job opportunities or salary trends. Other sections of the newspepar might be relevant to your interest as well perhaps you want to work in the sports, entertainment, food, or travel industries. Many newspapers have sections and regular columns devoted to these topics, if yours does not, check with your local library.

Start a career planing file for articles and sources of information about your field or industry now, you'll be glad you did when it comes time to apply for jobs.

How did you do? Excellent _____ Good _____ Need More Practice _____

Practice Quiz

Take the Practice Quiz as though it were a real test. After the quiz is corrected, review the chapter if needed.

A. Write **C** in the blank for correct sentences, **F** for fragments, **R** for run-ons, and **CS** for comma splices.

_____ **1.** About an hour later the CEO arrived.

_____ **2.** Anthony is the new accountant in our office he is not a CPA.

_____ **3.** Here's the truth, the difference between achieving and not achieving is goal setting.

_____ **4.** Wal-Mart's employees must recite and practice founder Sam Walton's "10-foot rule."

_____ **5.** The "10-foot rule" is explained in item 22, it is good advice for anyone working in retail sales.

_____ **6.** The carpenter is working very hard, nevertheless, we don't think she can finish by one.

_____ **7.** While the carpenter is working hard, we don't think she can finish by one.

_____ **8.** The carpenter is working hard, we don't think she can finish the job on time.

_____ **9.** Although Macy's first efforts at the dry goods business in Boston failed miserably.

_____ **10.** After trying his luck with six other doomed retailing ventures.

_____ **11.** It is the weak who are cruel, gentleness can be expected only from the strong.

_____ **12.** Leaders have different styles, they all need, however, to be skilled in handling people.

_____ **13.** Meetings must proceed according to rules furthermore, business must be conducted fairly.

_____ **14.** Because many informal meetings occur.

_____ **15.** Stay calm and don't blame or name-call.

_____ **16.** Service can come in many forms, for example, it can mean having the right merchandise at the right time.

_____ **17.** The word _business_ originally meant the state of being busy with anything.

_____ **18.** Ms. Scott flew to Spain last year then she took a Mediterranean cruise.

_____ **19.** A characteristic of high achievers is that they believe they are responsible for most of what is good or not good in their lives.—Charles Garfield

_____ **20.** Mrs. Powell, carrying the coffee in one hand and the keys in the other.

B. Correct these run-ons and comma splices by inserting a dependent conjunction in each sentence. Your corrected sentence will have an independent and a dependent clause. If the dependent clause is first, follow it with a comma.

Example: Setting goals may be scary, but it is necessary.

21. You can do all the common things of life in an uncommon way, you will command the attention of the world.

22. A customer comes within 10 feet, the employee stops what he or she is doing, speaks to the customer, and offers help—Sam Walton's 10-foot rule for Wal-Mart employees.

23. The manager was finishing the report her husband was busy baking a chocolate cake.

24. In France dinner guests send flowers they arrive at the host's home.
25. You point your forefinger to your chest in Japan, it means you want a bath.

Special Assignment (continued from page 71)

B. Select the fragments from Nos. 1–20 of the Practice Quiz. On a separate sheet of paper, or on the computer, write the number of the fragment, followed by a complete sentence to correct the fragment.

Example 14: *Many informal meetings occur. OR Because many informal meetings occur, the conference room must always be ready.*

C. Now select the run-ons and comma splices from Nos. 1–20 of the Practice Quiz. Write the item number, and then correct each one by either separating or correctly connecting the independent parts.

Example 2: *Anthony is the new accountant in our office, but he is not a CPA.*

Date to submit this assignment: _____

Self-Study Practice and Tutorials

Vocabulary and Spelling for Careers
For additional practice go to Appendix B, page 321.

Replay Drills
For additional practice go to Appendix C, page 364.

Companion Web Site: www.prenhall.com/smith
Go to the companion Web site to test your knowledge on self-grading quizzes and for links to other helpful online resources.

MyWritingLab
Use this online learning system for an assessment of your progress on topics covered in this chapter and progressive exercises that fit your individual needs.

4 Mastering Nouns— Plurals and Capitals

After completing Chapter 4, you will be able to do the following:

- Form regular and irregular plurals of nouns.
- Form plurals of compound nouns.
- Capitalize proper nouns correctly.
- Correctly spell, pronounce, and use the words presented in this chapter.

READ 16   FORMING PLURALS OF NOUNS

A noun is singular when it names one; it is plural when it names more than one. Spelling most plural nouns is easy; just add *s* to the singular form to make it plural: one *check* but three *checks*. When a singular noun ends with *s, z, x, ch,* or *sh*, add *es* to spell the plural: one *box* but three *boxes*.

Whenever you are unsure about spelling a plural, check your dictionary. In most dictionaries the plural is not given if all that's needed is to add *s* or *es*.

If you don't find the plural in the dictionary, spell it in the "regular" way; it is not an exception. When plurals are "irregular," you sometimes find two spellings in the dictionary. This means both are correct, but it's better to use the one listed first.

Exceptions to *S* and *Es*

Most English rules have exceptions. Three types of exceptions to *s* and *es* are the plurals of nouns ending in *y, o,* and *f.*

1. **Nouns ending in *y*:** Do you add *s* or change the *y* to *i* and add *es*? If a **vowel** (*a, e, i, o, u*) precedes *y*, simply add *s*.

    valley, valleys   attorney, attorneys   turkey, turkeys

    If a **consonant** (all letters other than vowels) precedes *y*, change the *y* to *i* and add *es*.

    industry, industries   company, companies   hobby, hobbies

RECAP   Spell the plurals of these nouns.

1. ally _____
2. accessory _____
3. injury _____
4. facility _____

Check your answers on page 441.

2. **Nouns ending in *o*:** Is the plural formed with *s* or *es*?

    If a vowel precedes the *o*, add just an *s*.

    studio, studios   rodeo, rodeos   radio, radios

    If a noun ends in *o* preceded by a consonant, look it up to find out whether to add *s* or *es*.

    memo, memos   domino, dominos, dominoes (both are correct)

    tomato, tomatoes   potato, potatoes

    banjo, banjos   solo, solos

RECAP Spell the plurals of these nouns. For words with two correct spellings, write both in the blank.

1. tattoo _____
2. domino _____
3. alto _____
4. potato _____ _____

Check your answers on page 441.

3. **Nouns ending in *f*:** Is the plural formed with *s* or do you change the *f* to *v* and add *es*? If a word ends with *ff*, just add *s* to make it plural. Otherwise, no useful rules determine how to spell plurals of nouns ending in *f*. When in doubt, check the dictionary because some simply add *s* and others change the *f* to *v* and add *es*.

　　rebu**ff**, rebu**ffs**　　chie**f**, chie**fs**　　belie**f**, belie**fs**
　　wi**fe**, wi**ves**　　kni**fe**, kni**ves**

RECAP Spell the plurals of these nouns. For words with two correct spellings, write both in the blank.

1. thief _____
2. handkerchief _____
3. half _____
4. safe _____

Check your answers on page 441.

Word to the Wise

In general, apostrophes (') do not make a noun plural. The occasional exceptions are in Read 56 of Chapter 11, which is all about apostrophes. Most nouns become plural by adding *s*, not by adding an apostrophe and *s*.

REPLAY 16

Spell the plurals of these nouns. For words with two correct spellings, write both in the blank. Have your dictionary handy.

1. itinerary _____
2. portfolio _____
3. ferry _____
4. money _____
5. wolf _____
6. zero _____

    7. piano _____   14. survey _____

    8. authority _____   15. plaintiff _____

    9. hero _____   16. wife _____

    10. melody _____   17. chief _____

    11. knife _____   18. cargo _____

    12. tariff _____   19. attorney _____

    13. proxy _____   20. memento _____

Check your answers on page 442.

READ 17   IRREGULAR NOUN PLURALS

Read 16 covered the regular noun plurals; now we will look at nouns that form their plurals in irregular ways. The following poem points out some of these exceptions to the rules.

> The plural of *box* we all know is *boxes,*
> Yet the plural of *ox* is *oxen,* not *oxes.**
> A goose is a *goose,* but two are called *geese,*
> But why isn't more than one *mouse* quoted *meese?*
> A *mouse* and his family are mentioned as *mice,*
> But the plural of *house* is *houses,* not *hice.*
> You can readily double a *foot* and have *feet,*
> But try as you might, you can't make *root reet.*
> If the singular's *this* and the plural, *these,*
> Should the plural of *kiss* ever be *keese?*

This poem points out why remembering how to spell words is usually more helpful than trying to apply a set of "spelling rules" to our unpredictable language. Some irregular nouns are less obvious than those in the poem, even to people who have used English all their lives.

    The following nouns are irregular because each changes its spelling in a different way to form the plural. Do not add *s* to these nouns.

Singular	man	woman	mouse	tooth	child	foot
Plural	men	women	mice	teeth	children	feet

    Below are examples of another group of irregular nouns. They are spelled the same whether they are singular or plural.

Singular or Plural   aircraft, British, corps,† deer, Dutch, fish, Japanese, salmon, series, sheep, statistics

    Check some of the preceding words in your dictionary; notice that the word is repeated following the abbreviation *pl.* This tells you that the plural spelling is the

---

*Sometimes acceptable—but not preferred.
†See your dictionary for the singular and plural pronunciation of *corps.*

same as the singular. For some nouns, however, dictionaries show two correct plurals—either without an *s* or with it—like "deer n. pl. deer, also deers." Choose the first spelling when you see the word *also*, as you learned in Chapter 1.

Some nouns ending in *s* are singular or plural depending on the meaning.

Your dictionary shows which meanings are singular and which are plural. If one of these nouns is the subject of a sentence, be sure to choose the correct verb form.*

>   politics   mathematics   economics   mechanics

>   The **politics** of issues **have** often outweighed common sense. [plural]

>   **Politics is** the focus of his life. [singular]

Writing for Your Career

Provide clues for the reader before a noun spelled the same for both singular and plural forms. For example, the words *a, one, few, several,* or *this* are possible clues.

   A deer stopped at the pond. [*Deer* is singular]

   Several deer munched on our yellow roses. [*Deer* is plural.]

Some nouns ending in *s* are always singular, while others are always plural.

Always Singular   news   aeronautics
Always Plural   scissors   proceeds†

>   The latest **news is** that the **scissors were** lost. [not *was*]

>   **Aeronautics** is the principal industry in that town, and the **proceeds** from it **have** doubled. [not *has*]

Plurals of Proper Nouns

To make a proper noun plural, just add *s* or *es*.

Do not add an apostrophe or change the spelling of a name (proper noun) to form a plural even though it may end in *y, o,* or *f*. To form the plural of *wolf*, you change the *f* to *v* and add *es* to get *wolves*. But if you mean *Mr. and Ms. Wolf*, you wouldn't say "The Wolves are coming for dinner," but rather "The Wolfs . . ."

Also, never use an apostrophe to form the plural of a proper name.

   Notice that the plural proper nouns in the following sentences do not have apostrophes:

>   Four hundred **Taylors** are listed in the telephone directory.

>   The **Lopezes** have a new Web site for their business.

---

*In Chapter 7 you'll have more opportunity to review using a singular or plural verb form to agree with a singular or plural subject.

†See your dictionary for the noun *proceeds* and distinguish it from the pronunciation and meaning of the verb *proceeds*.

REPLAY 17

A. In the blanks write plurals of the nouns. See your dictionary if in doubt about common nouns (those beginning with lowercase letters). Some of these plurals are spelled the same as their singular form.

Example: Perkins <u>Perkinses</u>

1. corps _____

2. economics _____

3. deer _____

4. George _____

5. series _____

6. Chinese _____

7. Jones _____

8. aircraft _____

9. fish _____

10. stepchild _____

11. foot _____

12. Flores _____

B. Write **S** or **P** in the blank to show whether the noun is singular or plural. If a noun may be used either way, write **S/P.** Consult your dictionary as needed.

Example: premises ____P____

1. trousers _____

2. corps _____

3. mumps _____

4. statistics _____

5. news _____

6. politics _____

C. Use the dictionary or word clues to decide whether the noun subjects (shown in bold type) require a singular or a plural verb. Then circle the correct verb for that subject.

Singular Verbs	is	was	has
Plural Verbs	are	were	have

Example: The new **pants** (was/were) shortened.

1. The **scissors** (have/has) sharp edges.
2. **Mathematics** (is/are) my favorite course.
3. These **statistics** (is/are) accurate.
4. The **proceeds** (was/were) counted yesterday.
5. All **earnings** from this show (are/is) being given to charity.
6. **Clothes** (is/are) all over the floor.
7. **Genetics** (is/are) an important field in modern science.
8. Each day's **news** (was/were) carefully edited.
9. Do you think **politics** (is/are) a subject to avoid discussing at a party?
10. Several lecture **series** (was/were) offered in anthropology.

Check your answers on page 442; then take the Pop Quiz on page 300.

READ 18   UNUSUAL PLURALS

The English language has many words that we have "adopted" from other languages. Some of these words follow the spelling rules of their original language. Sometimes an English plural spelling has been adopted as well; then we have two plurals to choose from. It's helpful to know both forms as they may have different uses. Following are examples of these unusual plurals.

Singular	Original Language Plural	Singular Ending	Plural Ending	English Plural
formula	formulae	a	ae	formulas
vertebra	vertebrae	a	ae	**or** vertebras
alumnus	alumni	us	i	alumni
stimulus	stimuli	us	i	stimuli
analysis	analyses	is	es	analyses
diagnosis	diagnoses	is	es	diagnoses
criterion	criteria	on	a	criterions
phenomenon	phenomena	on	a	phenomena
medium	media	um	a	mediums
curriculum	curricula	um	a	curriculums
datum	data	um	a	data
memorandum	memoranda	um	a	memorandums
addendum	addenda	um	a	addendums

Check your dictionary for pronunciation and usage of foreign plurals.

Careful communicators recognize nouns that require a change other than adding *s* to become plural. Yet some words look as though the plural might be irregular when it isn't. For example, just add *es* to make *sinus* plural; it's not *sini.* Develop an "instinct" for noticing words like the examples in the preceding chart, and refer to the dictionary when in doubt. If you're sure a word has two plurals that mean the same, use the one appearing first in the dictionary entry.

If you use these words often, you will begin to remember the proper forms. Here are a few that cause common errors:

- *Formulae* is used in scientific and technical communication, but otherwise use *formulas.*

- *Criteria,* not *criterions,* is preferred in American English usage.

- One *criterion <u>is</u>* but two *criteria <u>are</u>*

- *Media* is the preferred plural for newspapers, radio, etc. *Mediums* is preferred in expressions such as "mediums of exchange" to refer to various kinds of money, and "mediums" who claim to communicate with "other entities."

- *Data* and *media* are now widely used as both singular and plural forms, and are accepted as singular in some newer dictionaries.

REPLAY 18

A. With the help of your dictionary, spell the plurals of these words. If two plurals are correct, write them both in the blank.

Example: bureau <u>bureaus, bureaux</u>

1. formula _____
2. alumnus _____
3. basis _____
4. census _____
5. criterion _____
6. axis _____
7. parenthesis _____

8. crocus _____
9. appendix _____
10. concerto _____
11. index _____
12. analysis _____
13. medium _____
14. diagnosis _____

B. Write **S** or **P** to show whether these nouns are singular or plural. Use your dictionary.

Example: nucleus ___S___

1. alumna _____
2. criteria _____
3. alumnus _____

4. data _____
5. hypotheses _____
6. kibbutzim _____

C. Circle the correct form.

Example: The (media/medium) is sometimes as important as the message.

1. Television is the preferred (media/medium) for our ad campaign.
2. She broke several (vertebra/vertebrae/vertebraes) in the accident.
3. How many (criterion/criteria/criterias) did they consider?
4. Many people forget to type the closing (parentheses/parenthesis).
5. Several (alumnus/alumni/alumna) attended the opening game.

Check your answers on page 442. Then review Reads and Replays 15–18 before taking the Pop Quiz on pages 301.

READ 19   PLURALS OF COMPOUND NOUNS

A noun made up of more than one word is a **compound noun,** such as *high school*.

Compound nouns are written in three ways: as one word, as two or more words with a hyphen, or as separate words:

One word	dollhouse, checkbook
Split with Hyphen	tie-in, follow-up
Separated	doggy bag, time clock

Some compound nouns may be written in more than one way; when you are unsure, check the dictionary. If a dot or an accent mark (but no space) appears between the parts, write the expression as one word. The dot or accent mark indicates syllables, not separations or spaces.

Dictionary entry	brick•lay•er (dots between syllables) means bricklayer (one word)

If the words have a space between them or if they are not listed in your college dictionary, write them as separate words. Use a hyphen only if you see a hyphen between the parts of the dictionary entry.

Dictionary entry	Swiss cheese (space between syllables—two words)
Dictionary entry	stand-in (hyphenated word)

To form the plural of a compound noun spelled as one word, usually add *s* or *es* to the end of the word—unless the noun is irregular.

> bookcases   spoonfuls   headlines   businesswomen (irregular)

For compound nouns with a hyphen or space between the parts, the dictionary shows which part to make plural.

> sister**s**-in-law   letter**s** of credit   write-off**s**   trade-in**s**

If the dictionary shows two ways to form the plural, choose the first.

Dictionary entry	notaries public or notary publics
Use the first	notaries public

RECAP Use proofreading symbols from the inside back cover of this text to correct the compound noun errors in the following paragraph.

My brother in law asked me to design a letterhead for his stockcar company, which accepts tradeins. Because his cars have high pricetags, he wants the letter head to be classy.

Check your answers on page 443.

Word to the Wise

Compound nouns change their spelling over time and new formations of compound words come into usage.

Many new compound words eventually progress from separate words to hyphenated compounds to one-word forms as they become a part of everyday usage. When basketball, baseball, and football were invented, they were separate words: *basket ball, foot ball,* and *base ball.* As each game became more popular, it became hyphenated: *basket-ball, foot-ball, base-ball.* Eventually all became the one-word compounds they are today. Reading will help you keep up with changes in spelling of compound nouns.

REPLAY 19

Use your dictionary for help with spelling these compound nouns. Show whether the expression is one solid word, a hyphenated word, or two or three separate words. Some dictionaries give more than one spelling for certain plurals; if yours does, include both.

	SINGULAR		PLURAL
Example: notarypublic	notary public	notaries public	notary publics

1. followup   _____   _____
2. textbook   _____   _____
3. tradein   _____   _____
4. editorinchief   _____   _____
5. runnerup   _____   _____
6. spaceflight   _____   _____
7. headhunter   _____   _____
8. bushleague   _____   _____
9. chiefofstaff   _____   _____
10. volleyball   _____   _____

READ 20   A BRIEF TOUR OF THE CAPITAL

A noun beginning with a capital letter is a proper noun. Nouns that do not begin with capitals are common nouns.

A complete guide to capitalization is in the Mini Reference Manual, Appendix D. Following, however, is a review of noun capitalization principles most often needed in the workplace.

Capitalize official titles used directly before a person's name or used in "direct address" instead of the name:

Before the Name	Did you know that **President** Jimmy Carter owned a peanut farm?
	A letter of recommendation was received from **Sister** Mary Margaret.
Direct Address	We hope, **Madam President,** that you will like this gift. [Direct address means you call a person by name or title in speech or writing.]

Generally do not capitalize an official title when it is used as a general term of description:

Maynard Jackson was elected **mayor** of Atlanta, Georgia in 1973.

BUT   **Mayor** Maynard Jackson served two terms, left office, and then was re-elected to a third term.

The **colonel,** Rachel Rothstein, is a West Point graduate. [No capital is used for *colonel* because a comma separates it from the name.]

BUT   **Colonel** Rachel Rothstein graduated at the top of her West Point class.

Capitalize titles written after the name as part of the person's official identification.

Note that some companies have their own style for titles and may not capitalize them. Some reference manuals may also recommend not capitalizing titles; when you are in the workplace, always follow your company's style.

The keynote speech will be delivered by Mr. Gene Gilmore, Director of Student Affairs, University of Michigan.

Typed name at the end of a letter:

> Sincerely yours
> Rosalyn Amaro*
> Vice President
> Human Resources Department

Capitalize a family title when used as part of the name or instead of the name.

I attended **A**unt Jane's 90th birthday party at the Town Club.

Do not capitalize if the family title is not being used as part of the name.

I asked my **U**ncle Henry about the old days.

BUT   I asked my **u**ncle about the old days.

My **c**ousin Billy's **w**ife, Janice, is an accountant.

Words such as *company, college*, and *association* are usually capitalized only when used with the name of the organization.

Microchip **C**ompany is on 5th Street.

BUT   The **c**ompany is on 5th Street, near the college.

Capitalize the official name of a department or a committee.

Prepare a requisition and send it to the **P**urchasing **D**epartment.

Our company's **S**ocial **C**ommittee is planning the company picnic.

Capitalize words such as *town, city, state*, and *county* when they are part of the official name or if a governing body uses the geographic term officially; otherwise do not capitalize them.

New York **S**tate   Kansas **C**ity

Mayor Bloomberg said the **C**ity of New York is requesting bids for the new baseball stadium.

---

*Do not include "honorifics"—Mr., Ms., Dr., Professor, and the like—in signatures. Do include official titles that follow the names, such as Web Master, Administrative Assistant, Manager.

The state of Iowa is a great place to live, so we moved to Sioux City.

The newspaper said the city budget is running high deficits.

Capitalize specific geographic regions with compass point names. Do not capitalize directions or general locations.

He lives in the East, but he talks like a Westerner. [The East, North, South, West, and Midwest are considered definite geographic regions in the United States.]

Disneyland is east of Los Angeles and north of the South Pole.

Drive three blocks east on Disney Lane.

Use lowercase letters for the names of seasons.*

The office will close for a week this summer.

Always capitalize names of languages; do not capitalize names of courses unless they are languages or official course names.

He is studying Business English, bookkeeping, Accounting 101, Spanish, and Greek at Gonzaga University. Next year he will take a sociology course, Business Law 230, and French. He already speaks Hindi and Farsi.

Races named by color begin with lowercase letters, but sociological names of races and ethnic groups are capitalized. Religions are also capitalized.

white/Caucasian   black/African American   Latino   Asian American

Islam   Christianity   Judaism   Buddhism

REPLAY 20

A. Read Appendix D, Capitalization, page 414, and then correct the capitalization (use the proofreading mark) where needed in the following sentences.

1. the atomic age began on August 5, 1945, when the atomic bomb was dropped on the city of hiroshima.

2. we flew on american airlines last summer with the president of israel and the senator from maine.

3. eric a. smith, cfp, manages investment portfolios of $100,000 or more in seattle.

4. winston churchill wrote *triumph and tragedy*, an important book about world war II.

5. the judge said that the supreme court decision was favorable to my company.

6. i will know chinese well enough by september to take a university course in chinese literature.

7. the atlantic and pacific oceans are natural borders of the united states.

8. use hunt's tomato sauce for making lasagna on tuesdays in march.

9. Dr. lalitha, a hindu woman from the south of india, received her md from an American university.

10. the salutation of the letter is, "dear customer," and the complimentary close is, "sincerely yours."

*Exceptions are explained in Appendix D.

B. Write **C** in the blanks if the capitalization is correct, or make the corrections.

Example: If their $ales Manager calls, let me talk to her.

_____ 1. The General Manager of Horizon telephone likes Tostadas and Tacos.

_____ 2. We hire former Business Teachers to work in our office.

_____ 3. The secretary of the ski club is taking Art 101.

_____ 4. Macy's expects sales associates to speak spanish when needed.

_____ 5. The president of the United States has just entered the White House.

_____ 6. Did the Cardinal discuss the issue with other catholic leaders?

_____ 7. The typed signature at the end of the letter should be capitalized like this: Patty Killman, Professor of Office Technology.

_____ 8. We drove East last Summer until we reached Kansas city.

_____ 9. The City of Azusa, which is in the State of California, is named after everything from A to Z in the USA.

_____ 10. The clerk in our Credit Department needs to take the Business English course.

_____ 11. My sister has taught anthropology 101 at several Colleges.

_____ 12. Until the 1960s African American, Mexican American, Asian American, and Jewish office workers were not offered employment in this Company.

_____ 13. Some African Americans and Chinese Americans did factory work but had to eat in a separate lunchroom.

_____ 14. I believe Governor Shawn A. Taylor joined his famous sisters, Krista and Ashley, at the Inauguration Ball.

_____ 15. Krista won the academy award for her performance in *The Iron Magnolia,* and Ashley was awarded the nobel prize for her efforts on behalf of world peace.

Check your answers on page 443.

READ 21 EXPANDING YOUR VOCABULARY

An extensive, varied, and current vocabulary is needed for better jobs in business, technology, or the professions. Vocabulary expansion involves not only learning new words and adding meanings to words previously acquired, but also spelling, pronouncing, and using more words correctly. Building your vocabulary can be broken down into stages, although you will be unaware of them as they occur:

1. Recognizing a written word; that is, it looks familiar.
2. Understanding the written word in context.
3. Next, understanding the word when listening.
4. Using the word correctly in your own writing.
5. Using the word correctly in conversation, which means the word has been mastered.

You will build new vocabulary as long as you continue to seek out new and varied sources of written information in books, magazines, newspapers, and on Web sites; listen to a variety of radio programs and watch different kinds of films, live plays, and TV; and communicate with educated people.

You can speed up vocabulary growth with conscious effort. As you read the sentences that follow, give special attention to the underlined nouns for spelling, definition, capitalization, and/or pronunciation. If you look carefully at the words and say them, you'll probably spell them correctly when you do the Replay. Even some you're not sure of will look "funny" if misspelled, prompting you to refer to a dictionary. Use the dictionary to check on both singular and plural spellings, definitions, and pronunciation.

1. My allies found the cargo mentioned in both memoranda.
2. Please put the bills of lading in the portfolio, as they will be a good tie-in with the data.
3. The alumni were given copies of the itinerary as a memento.
4. The notaries public gave the banjos to the editors in chief.
5. An importer must know the criteria for determining the amount of the tariff as well as how to get the letters of credit.
6. The embargo on dynamos and dominos affects our earnings and causes several weird phenomena.
7. An addendum to the contract states that the attorneys distribute the proceeds from the sale according to these criteria.
8. The plaintiffs are technicians in our Aircraft Division but do not understand the phenomenon.
9. A survey of the co-owners shows that two speak Swahili and three, Hindi.
10. According to the media, proxies from 1,000 stockholders were received at these facilities.
11. According to the alumnae, Native Americans used the shells and clay pots stored on the premises.
12. When my proposal was rejected in all three memoranda, I accused the authorities of bias.
13. The altos sang solos for the Civilian Conservation Corps.
14. The author of the textbook about college curriculums received the Nobel Prize.
15. Her credentials show she worked for the Vietnamese in Saigon and studied aeronautics, mathematics, and monkeys' vertebrae.

REPLAY 21

Test your spelling and vocabulary with the following nouns. The first letter of each word is given.

Example: My sister's husband: ___brother-in-law___

1. Nongender-specific words for *businessmen*: **b**_____ **b**_____
2. One who starts a legal action: **p**_____
3. A compound noun meaning programs for use in a computer: **s**_____

4. The place where you work or live: **p**_____
5. Plural of publishing executive: **e**_____
6. Freight carried by a ship: **c**_____
7. The singular and plural are spelled the same but pronounced differently:
   c_____
8. Carrying case for holding papers or a list of investments: **p**_____
9. Written authorization to act for another: **p**_____
10. A plural noun that means profits from a commercial or other venture; when the same word is a verb, the accent is on the second syllable: **p**_____
11. A travel plan: transportation, times, dates, hotels: **i**_____
12. An object that is a reminder of the past, such as a souvenir: **m**_____
13. Persons authorized to guarantee signatures on legal documents:
    n_____
14. The plural of chassis: **c**_____
15. Something we want more of at income tax time (compound noun):
    w_____

Check your answers on page 443; then take the Pop Quiz on page 301.

CONCEPT REVIEW & SKILL-BUILDING APPLICATIONS

Checkpoint

A regular noun becomes plural by adding *s*—or by adding *es* to nouns ending in *s, x, z, sh,* and *ch.* However, irregular nouns (the exceptions) don't follow this principle. In this chapter you've reviewed irregular plural spellings and pronunciations, and forming plurals of compound nouns. You have also learned rules of capitalization for proper nouns and had some practice at increasing your vocabulary.

Special Assignment

Words, Words, Words

A. The words represented by the following definitions rhyme with *bird*. Fill in the blanks. The first letter of each word is shown.

Example: Slang for a person regarded as socially inept and dull ____nerd____

1. Listened ____h____
2. Next after second ____t____
3. You should put one in each blank ____w____

4. A group of large animals _____h_____
5. Unreasonable and ridiculous _____a_____
6. The thick part of sour milk _____c_____
7. Went astray or made a mistake _____e_____
8. Postponed _____d_____
9. Came together to discuss _____c_____
10. Agreed; we're of the same opinion _____c_____

B. Use the proofreader's mark (=) to show which words should be capitalized. See Appendix D, "Mini Reference Manual," if you want help with capitalization.

Example: <u>s</u>usan is an occupational therapist in <u>n</u>ew <u>y</u>ork <u>s</u>tate.

1. joseph flew via united airlines to uganda on veteran's day.
2. world war II preceded the era known as the fabulous fifties.
3. our english professor met reverend perez in this city last fall.
4. Did senator charles west from pennsylvania give a speech in northern maine?
5. to get to monroe college, go north on jerome avenue until you reach fordham road.
6. we ate a bag of yum yums and drank coca cola while we watched the film *father's day.*
7. my uncle was the first to do accounts payable auditing for department stores.
8. if you speak german and take business 101, you might qualify for that job.
9. although she has a bs and an ma degree, she does not have a doctorate.
10. The salutation is "dear credit manager"; the complimentary close is "sincerely."

Date to submit this assignment: _____

Proofreading for Careers

Any time you write a business letter, absolutely error-free copy is required. Proofreading is challenging because it requires concentration on so much at the same time: errors in spelling, word choice, meaning, noun usage, numbers, capitalization, and consistency (did you treat like things alike?).

If you proofread on your screen, start by running your spell checker, and make needed corrections. Next, either on the screen or in a printout, slowly read each line of type for sense, correctness, and clearness. Looking at each sentence individually focuses your attention.

The following letter to Ms. Gonzalez has noun errors—capitalization, spelling, and typographical. Use your dictionary and spell checker as needed. In addition, be sure you end each sentence with a period, and begin the next sentence with a capital letter. Your instructor will tell you whether to mark the copy in your book or make the corrections online. (See the inside back cover of this book for proofing marks and Appendix D for proofreading guidelines.)

Dear Ms. Zonzalez:

We can help your Sales Staff by providing you firm with a new dimention of client service—an inferior design tie in with the sale of office space and studioes. clients looking for new office facilitys often ask about desks, filling cabinets, chairs, and carpeting. They are interested in prices and availability of these items, this is were we come in to help close the sale for you. At no charge to you, we can furnish a complete floor plan to fit any offices you offer this will be an important sales aid to you that will pay off in faster and increased sales.

Alert Reality Firms like yours are always looking for new and creative consepts in selling. We would be happy to met with you or one of your key sales representatives to provide more information and discuss how we might work to gether. Please give us a call the next time you have a client with an office furnishing need, we will prove that this service will work for you.

Yours Truely,

Manny Kahlil

President

21st Century Office Interiors LLC

How did you do?   Excellent _____ Good _____ Need More Practice _____

Practice Quiz

Write the letter of the best answer in the blank. It's all right to use your dictionary.

_____ 1. The birds fly (a) south (b) South in

_____ 2. the (a) winter (b) Winter.

_____ 3. Stockholders mail in their (a) proxys (b) proxi (c) proxyes (d) proxies.

_____ 4. Aeronautics (a) were (b) was my favorite subject.

_____ 5. They are our (a) alleys (b) allys (c) allies (d) alloys in the controversy.

_____ 6. Her (a) sister-in-laws (b) sisters-in-laws (c) sisters-in-law manage the office.

_____ 7. To import from Thailand, we need two (a) letters-of-credit (b) letters of credit (c) letter of credits (d) letters of credits (e) letter's of credit.

_____ 8. Our office in the (a) midwest (b) Midwest (c) Mid west will be

_____ 9. closed on (a) labor day (b) Labor day (c) Labor Day.

_____ 10. The Ohio (a) senator (b) Senator voted for a grant to Casper College.

_____ 11. Both (a) secretarys (b) secretaries (c) secretarys' (d) secretary's seemed confident as they interviewed for the data control position.

_____ 12. The inventory indicates we have three (a) celloes (b) cello (c) cellos (d) cello's (e) cellos' in our Music Department.

_____ 13. Although James McCarthy is the president, three other (a) McCarthy's (b) McCarthies (c) McCarthys' (d) McCarthys are on the Board.

_____ 14. The (a) Jones's (b) Jones (c) Joneses (d) Jones' invited us to dinner.

_____ 15. Our (a) Advertising department (b) advertising Department (c) advertising department (d) Advertising Department is

_____ 16. headed by the (a) vice President (b) Vice president (c) Vice President (d) vice president.

_____ 17. The nouns (a) cargo and embargo (b) vertebra and chassis (c) addenda and appendix (d) tariff and bill of lading have almost the same meaning.

_____ 18. The (a) diagnosis (b) diagnosises (c) diagnoses (d) diagnosis's are accurate.

_____ 19. These (a) criteria (b) criterion (c) criterias (d) criteriae were developed for us.

_____ 20. Which word is incorrect in the following? An alumnae and an alumnus broke their vertebrae when they placed the bric-a-brac on top of the chassis. (a) alumnae (b) alumnus (c) vertebrae (d) bric-a-brac (e) chassis

_____ 21. Which word is incorrect in the following? We sent two memorandas about the new formulas for dealing with the two nuclear crises publicized by the media. (a) memorandas (b) formulas (c) nuclear (d) crises (e) media

_____ 22. The new curricula (a) seems (b) seem more challenging than the old.

Self-Study Practice and Tutorials

Vocabulary and Spelling for Careers

For additional practice go to Appendix B, page 321.

Replay Drills

For additional practice go to Appendix C, page 369.

Companion Web Site: www.prenhall.com/smith

Go to the companion Web site to test your knowledge on self-grading quizzes and for links to other helpful online resources.

MyWritingLab

Use this online learning system for an assessment of your progress on topics covered in this chapter and progressive exercises that fit your individual needs.

5 Mastering Nouns— Possessives

After completing Chapter 5, you will be able to do the following:

- Show the possessive relationship between nouns.
- Correctly form possessives of singular and plural nouns.
- Correctly form possessives of compound nouns.
- Use the possessive form to write clear and concise sentences.

READ 22   POSSESSIVES VERSUS PLURALS

In Chapter 4 you added *s* to nouns to make them plural. Because the *s* also makes nouns **possessive,** be careful to avoid confusing plurals with possessives.

To form the possessive of nouns, use an apostrophe (') and an *s*. Do not use an apostrophe in plural nouns that are not possessive.

Showing Possession

Possessive nouns show the relationship between one noun and another noun. The first noun shows *who* or *what possesses;* the second shows *who* or *what is possessed.* The relationship is made clear by the use of an *s* and an apostrophe in the first noun.

Use a Possessive or Prepositional Phrase

A possessive noun can replace a prepositional phrase.

Prepositional phrases (word groups beginning with a preposition) may convey the same meaning, but possessive nouns are more concise. Compare the expression of possessive relationships in the following examples:

POSSESSIVE NOUN	PREPOSITIONAL PHRASE
Latisha's brother	brother **of Latisha**
the **auditor's** friend	friend **of the auditor**
teachers' salaries	salaries **of the teachers**
women's hats	hats **for women**
girls' pearls	pearls owned **by girls**
boy's toys	toys belonging **to a boy**

When a possessive sounds natural, use it instead of a prepositional phrase. If the result seems awkward or changes the meaning, use a prepositional phrase. For example, **the interior of the house** sounds better than **the house's interior.** In "The Star Spangled Banner," however, **the dawn's early light** is better than **the early light of the dawn.**

The following examples show how replacing prepositional phrases with possessive nouns can make your writing clearer and more concise. Notice it is always the **first** of the two nouns—the possessor (or owner)—that gets the apostrophe.

> The records prepared **by the accountants** were taken to the **office of the secretary.**

> **The accountants' records** were taken to **the secretary's office.**

In revising this sentence, the writer assumes the reader will know the records were "prepared by" the accountant. If that were not the case, the first prepositional phrase should stand.

> Is the **population of Nevada** smaller than the **population of Arizona**?

> Is **Nevada's population** smaller than **Arizona's**?

In the second example, "population" is understood but not stated after "Arizona's," thus avoiding needless repetition.

> **Clothes for children** are on this floor, and **clothes for infants** are on the fourth floor.

> **Children's clothes** are on this floor, and **infants' clothes** are on the fourth floor.

> **A delay of two hours** would be disastrous.
>
> **Two hours' delay** would be disastrous.

To find out whether to use an apostrophe and *s* (*'s*), reverse the order of the nouns and put "of" between them: **Carol's** brother—brother **of Carol.** If reversing the nouns and inserting "of" delivers the intended meaning, then the first noun needs an apostrophe: **Carol's** brother.

Word Power

Which butler would be fired for extreme rudeness? No.1 or No. 2? _____

1. The butler stood at the doorway and called the guests names.
2. The butler stood at the doorway and called the guests' names.

RECAP   Circle the possessor and the possessed. In the blank write the "understood" word for item 2.

1. "Five minutes' planning might save an hour's work on New Year's Day," said Alicia's mother to Ben's father.
2. The purchase of Alaska was called "Seward's Folly," but history proved the foolishness was his critics' rather than Secretary of State William Seward's.

_____

Check your answers on page 444.

Forming Possessives of Regular Nouns

To form possessives of regular nouns add an apostrophe before the *s* if the noun is singular and after the *s* if the noun is plural.

Singular Possessive	**Springfield's** population is larger than I thought.
	Tennessee's weather is a lot warmer than expected.
	The **chairperson's** report is very brief.
	A **week's** vacation goes by too fast.
Plural Possessive	The **representatives'** speeches can be no more than five minutes.
	Soldiers' uniforms from past wars are on exhibit.
	Please deliver the **secretaries'** new desks by Friday.
	The citizens will not tolerate another **two years'** delay.

When a plural noun ends in *s*, use the apostrophe only when you need to show possession.

Here are some sentences with plural nouns ending in *s*, but no possessive connection is needed. Apostrophes would be incorrect:

The **brothers** are **partners** in software consulting **businesses.**

The **Browns** each play a few **instruments** in several **orchestras.**

The **Joneses** wear straw **hats** on **holidays.**

Your **records** indicate the **Lees** made several **errors.**

The **Nguyens** own **factories** in both small **towns.**

Word to the Wise

Study the difference in meaning between the following two sentences. What part of speech is *work* in each sentence? 1. _____ 2. _____

1. We would like you to see our students' work.
2. We would like you to see our students work.

Check your answers on page 444.

REPLAY 22

Some nouns in the following sentences are possessive, but the apostrophes are left out. Insert the apostrophe where it belongs and underline the noun that names what is possessed. Write **C** for correct if a sentence doesn't require an apostrophe.

Example: The artist's <u>books</u> were left in Mr. Fox's <u>office</u>.

_____ 1. The Byrneses have sent four altos to try out for the operas.

_____ 2. Our editors stories please his readers greatly.

_____ 3. His brothers-in-law manage the offices.

_____ 4. His brother-in-laws manager has been transferred to Guam.

_____ 5. The Schwartzes own property in the swamp lands of Brazil.

_____ 6. The attorneys offices are in new buildings.

_____ 7. South Dakotas resources are listed in the back pages of two almanacs.

_____ 8. Mens and womens clothes are on sale in all our stores today.

_____ 9. Have you shipped Ms. Lopezs orders yet?

_____10. One of the film industrys most talented directors, Steven Spielberg, lectures at UCLA.

_____11. The crews strength was spent in useless maneuvers. (one crew)

_____12. Californias gold mines were less profitable than its orange groves.

_____13. These vineyards supply more than 75 percent of this nations wine and raisins.

_____14. Mattel and Lego are among the worlds largest toy manufacturers.

_____15. The former Claremont Mens College is now simply Claremont College.

_____16. Oral communications on the job include making introductions, giving directions, and greeting visitors.

_____17. Toms new book was used twice before the errors were found.

_____18. Several hours work took more than three days to do.

_____19. Important to James Cash Penneys success was how he treated employees.

_____20. Barbies worldwide fame is probably Mattels greatest success.

Check your answers on page 444.

READ 23   APOSTROPHE BEFORE OR AFTER?

When forming possessives, the general rule is that the apostrophe is placed before the _s_ when the noun is singular, and after the _s_ when the noun is plural.

Several hundred years ago possession was expressed by using the pronoun "his" after the first noun. Instead of saying _the clerk's desk,_ they said _the clerk his desk._ If you say this old-fashioned possessive form fast, you hardly hear the first two letters of "his." Therefore, people of that day, when spelling was much more individualized than it is today, began spelling the expression _the clerk s desk._ Since the apostrophe had previously been used to show omission of one or more letters, writers began to use this mark to show that the first two letters had been left off "his." That's how we ended up with the modern form, _the clerk's desk._

If more than one clerk shared the desk, the original wording would have been _the clerks their desks._ This, in turn, was shortened to _the clerks' desks_—with the apostrophe after the _s_ to show that "their" was left out after the plural word _clerks._

This method still works for determining whether to place the apostrophe before or after the _s:_ Once you've decided the noun is possessive, see whether it's singular or plural. If it's singular, put the apostrophe where _his_ would have been in the 1700s. If it's plural, insert the apostrophe where _their_ would have fit. Various singular and plural possessive relationships are shown below:

Ownership	the **banker's** salary, **students'** books
Relationship	the **Joneses'** twins, **Joey's** wife, **Mr. Harris's** daughter
Type or kind	**women's** hats, **girls'** pearls, **boy's** toys
Place of origin	**Springfield's** population, **Niagara Falls'** weather
Authorship	**representatives'** speeches, **chair's** report
Time	**two years'** delay, **a day's** vacation

Making Nouns Possessive

Although the _his_ and _their_ trick still works, here are three modern rules to help you form possessives correctly.

Singular Nouns

Add _'s_ to make a singular noun possessive.

The toothbrushes are on the **dentist's** desk. (one dentist)

We do not believe the **witness's** testimony. (one witness)

Please send the **technician's** reports to the lab. (one technician)

The **city's** need for extra funds has not been met. (one city)

Mr. Hawkes's office is at Kent. (one Mr. Hawkes)

Exception: If adding 's to the singular noun makes the word hard to say, then add only the apostrophe.

This exception applies only when you have a singular **_proper_** **noun** with two or more syllables and ending with an *s* sound.

Mr. Seagrams' executive assistant relocated from Washington, DC.

Joyce Simons' office is on the main floor.

The **Schwartzes'** art gallery opening is on Sunday at 3 p.m.

Compound Singular Nouns

All words, whether individual words or compound nouns, form possessives at the end, not somewhere in the middle.

If a compound singular noun (made up of two or more words) is possessive, add *'s* to the end.

The reporters were amused by the **editor-in-chief's** remarks.

My **brother-in-law's** appetite amazes me.

RECAP   Insert six apostrophes in items 1 and 2.

1. Mr. Smiths and Ms. Perkins assistants will tour New York Citys tallest buildings during a weeks vacation. (Her name is Pat Perkins.)
2. My son-in-laws business is as successful as my sons. (one son)

Check your answers on page 444.

Plural Nouns Ending in s

Add only an apostrophe to make a plural noun that ends in *s* possessive.

The **dentists'** desks are on wheels. (more than one dentist)

The **witnesses'** statements are false. (more than one witness)

Send the **technicians'** report to the lab. (more than one technician)

Three **days'** work is needed to complete the job. (more than one day)

The **Hawkeses'** office is in Rock Springs. (more than one person named Hawkes)

Word Power

The exception rule shown under the "Singular Nouns" heading is for singular possessives only—*not* for plurals. *Men's, women's, children's, man's, woman's,* and *child's* (all possessive nouns) are always written with an apostrophe before the *s*. No exceptions!

Plural Nouns that Don't End in s

If a plural possessive noun does not end in *s*, add *'s* to make it possessive.

> **Men's** suits are very tailored this year.
>
> The trustee controls the **children's** assets.
>
> The **alumni's** contributions to the **Women's** Fund were small.

Compound Plural Possessives

If a plural compound noun is possessive, first spell the plural. Then add the *'s* to the end of the compound noun.

> What are the reasons for so many local business **start-ups'** declining profits?
>
> Two of the **four-year-olds'** test scores were above average in preschool.

Some compound words become plural by adding *s* to the first word—like *sons-in-law*. This plural word does not end in *s* but in *w*.

> Newspaper reporters listened attentively to five **editors-in-chief's** speeches. [The *s* after editor makes the compound expression plural. The *'s* after *chief* makes it possessive.]
>
> My **brothers-in-law's** appetites amaze me. [plural possessive]

Word to the Wise

Before placing an apostrophe, decide whether the **possessive** noun is singular or plural. Then make certain this noun is correctly and completely spelled before making it possessive.

Plural possessive noun	The ladies' purses
Singular possessive noun	The lady's purses [one lady with more than one purse]

It doesn't matter whether the second noun—what is possessed—is singular or plural. Just consider the first—the possessor—and decide whether it's singular or plural.

RECAP Insert *s*, *es*, and apostrophes where needed. Correct item 1 so that you can tell the writer has more than one brother; then make Martinez plural. Item 2 needs three apostrophes. In item 3 two of his sons' wives are business partners.

1. The meeting was held at my brother office, and both the Martinez attended.
2. The old saying, "Women work is never done," is harmful to women and men roles in modern society.
3. His daughter-in-law business is bankrupt.

Check your answers on page 444.

Special Cases

Sometimes an organization's name sounds as though it should have an apostrophe, but some do and some don't. Always check organization names and write them exactly as the organization does.

Vons (a supermarket chain) has no apostrophe.

Macy's (the department store chain) has an apostrophe.

If a possessive sounds clumsy, reword the sentence to avoid the need for a possessive form.

My **brothers-in-law's** huge appetites amaze me. [correct but clumsy]

Rephrase	I am amazed that my **brothers-in-law** have such huge appetites.
or	I am amazed that my **husband's brothers** have such huge appetites.

REPLAY 23

A. Write the singular possessive, the plural, and the plural possessive.

Singular	Singular Possessive	Plural	Plural Possessive
Example: *lawyer*	*lawyer's*	*lawyers*	*lawyers'*
1. representative			
2. week			
3. witness			
4. James			
5. country			
6. Filipino			
7. man			
8. Asian			
9. wife			
10. father-in-law			
11. congresswoman			
12. family			
13. Webster			
14. hour			
15. Wolf			
16. wolf			
17. organization			
18. boss			
19. woman			
20. child			

B. Insert an *'s* or just an *s* where needed, or write **C** for correct. Show clearly whether an apostrophe is before or after the *s*. Make any necessary spelling changes to nouns. Do not change verb forms. Read for sense before correcting.

Example: Mr. Williams' book is the manager‸choice.
                                            ^'s

_____ 1. The Columbuses never dreamed Chris would become so famous.

_____ 2. Two year interest is due on the note.

_____ 3. Health is a person most valuable possession.

_____ 4. Men fashion change almost as quickly as women.

_____ 5. Be prepared to come at a minute notice.

_____ 6. Mr. Childress signature was needed two day ago.

_____ 7. The store was having a sale on lady coat.

_____ 8. The Goldstein of West Palm Beach will join us in two day.

_____ 9. Brunswick population has increased during the past five year.

_____10. Mr. Jenkins desk is to your right.

_____11. Several coach reports included details about their player health.

_____12. We studied Keats poetry in our literature class.

_____13. Montreal and Quebec are in Mr. Hendrix territory.

_____14. Three Marx brother film were shown on TV.

_____15. The butler stood at the doorway and called all the guests name.

Check your answers on page 444; then take the Pop Quiz on page 302.

CONCEPT REVIEW & SKILL-BUILDING APPLICATIONS

Checkpoint

Place a check beside each principle you're sure of. If you are not sure, review the Reads 22 and 23 explanations.

_____ Use apostrophes in singular and plural possessive nouns.

Maria's office and the managers' offices are always open.

_____ If a plural noun is not possessive, don't use an apostrophe.

The brokers work from 6 a.m. to 3 p.m.—the New York Stock Exchange hours.

_____ A possessive noun ends with apostrophe ('s) and precedes another noun or "an understood" noun.

Charlene's aunt is eccentric.
Of all the aunts here, Charlene's is the most eccentric. [*aunt* is understood after *Charlene's*]

_____ To test for possessives, reverse the order of the two nouns and insert **of** between them.

aunt **of** *Charlene* is *Charlene's aunt*

_____ Make a singular proper noun possessive by adding '*s*.

Shinji's job pays well.

_____ If adding '*s* to a singular proper noun with two or more syllables makes the word hard to pronounce, add an apostrophe only.

Mr. Watkins' home is near mine. [instead of *Watkins's* home]
BUT Morris's home is far away. [*Morris's* doesn't sound awkward.]

_____ A plural noun that ends in *s* becomes possessive by adding an apostrophe only.

Ladies' shoe styles sometimes result in injuries to their feet.

_____ A plural noun that does *not* end in *s* becomes possessive by adding *'s*.

Please don't buy children's toys that encourage violence.

 ## Special Assignment

A. Write sentences in which you shorten these phrases by using a possessive noun or a contraction.

Example: son of Mr. Ames _____ Mr. Ames's son is the auditor. _____

Possible answers:

1. books of George _____
2. wife of Mr. Adams _____
3. vacation of a week _____
4. home of the Adamses/office of Mr. Adams _____

   _____
5. store of my sisters _____
6. name of the server _____

   _____
7. problems of the members _____
8. commissions of the salespeople _____

   _____
9. work of two years _____

   _____
10. studio of my mother-in-law _____
11. words of Moses _____
12. streets of Dallas _____
13. report of the auditor _____
14. notice of ten minutes _____
15. expense accounts of the supervisors _____

    _____

B. Correct the following sentence and fill in the blank:

Student's who put apostrophe's into plain plural's will receive shock's when they get grade's on the examination's in a few day's. Remove _____ apostrophes from this sentence.

_____

Date to submit this assignment: _____

Proofreading for Careers

Add eight apostrophes to this short essay, and correct all other errors.

Whistler's Mother

In the worlds most famous museum, the louvre in Paris, hangs a painting by Americas celebrated artist, James McNeill Whistler. This paintings formal title is *An Arrangement in Gray and Black,* but it is better known by the simple name *Whistlers Mother.*

Studies have been made to explain this portraits almost universal appeal, but what criterias can an art Critic use to judge a painting? Critics are not like scientists. They cannot set up controlled experiment's in which a number of stimulus are shot into subjects and data collected on the subjects reactions. No, an art critic relys on inner emotions and sensitivity when analyzing a painting. Analyses of a painting is very personal.

When you visit Paris and look at *Whistlers Mother,* what will you see? Will you, like most of us, be left wondering about the source of this portraits greatness?

How did you do? Excellent _____ Good _____ Need More Practice _____

Practice Quiz

Insert apostrophes where needed, delete unneeded apostrophes, and fix incorrect plurals. Write **C** for correct to the left of sentences needing no change.

Example: The architects͝ report includes the data regarding the workers͝ cafeteria. [one architect]

_____ **1.** The deans view is that your attitude needs drastic changes. [one dean]

_____ **2.** Hiring 1,000 employees for the merger will add to the company's 22,000-member workforce.

_____ **3.** Many Americans take their mothers out to restaurants on Mothers Day.

_____ **4.** Yesterdays techniques cannot succeed in todays marketplace.

_____ **5.** Green Interiors Inc. has two weeks to accept or reject our companys offer.

_____ **6.** My sister-in-laws bookkeeper completed three years of college. [Two of my brothers' wives are partners and share a bookkeeper.]

_____ **7.** Yamada and Jones is one of the citys finest law firms.

_____ **8.** Emily Jones reputation as a criminal lawyer is excellent.

_____ **9.** The MIS personnel have the CEOs attention in this company.

_____ **10.** Send the proposal to the PTA's president.

_____ **11.** Within the last 50 years, many pieces of invention history have been discarded in landfills across the world.

_____ **12.** These losses are painful for historians because many items would have been important artifacts.

_____ **13.** Some of the items were as revolutionary as Gutenbergs printing press and James Watts steam engine. [These inventors' names are spelled Gutenberg and Watt.]

_____ **14.** During the World War II era, British Colossus computers helped crack the Nazi war codes.

_____ **15.** Xeroxs Palo Alto Research Center developed the Alto, the first computer to use a mouse.

_____ **16.** Womens roles have changed enormously since comedies like _Charlie's Aunt_ were written.

_____ **17.** Businesss consistently rank communication skills' as a top requirement for they're employee's.

_____ **18.** Shakespeare's play _A Midsummer Night's Dream_ is about fairies, magic, king's, and queen's.

Self-Study Practice and Tutorials

Vocabulary and Spelling for Careers

For additional practice go to Appendix B, page 321.

Replay Drills

For additional practice go to Appendix C, page 372.

Companion Web Site: www.prenhall.com/smith

Go to the companion Web site to test your knowledge on self-grading quizzes and for links to other helpful online resources.

MyWritingLab

Use this online learning system for an assessment of your progress on topics covered in this chapter and progressive exercises that fit your individual needs.

6 Mastering Pronouns

After completing Chapter 6, you will be able to do the following:

- Use the correct forms of pronouns to substitute for nouns and other pronouns.
- Identify pronouns used as subjects and objects.
- Correctly form possessives of pronouns.
- Avoid confusing possessive pronouns with contractions.
- Define and use correct forms of indefinite pronouns.
- Use pronouns to make your writing free of gender bias and vague references.

READ 24   PRONOUNS AS SUBSTITUTES

A pronoun is a word that substitutes for a noun. A pronoun refers to someone or something previously named by a noun.

When writing and speaking, you substitute pronouns for nouns all the time to avoid repetition and awkward sentences. For example, after using the noun *pencil,* you would later use the pronoun *it;* the reader or listener understands *it* means *pencil.* To substitute for the plural noun *pencils,* the pronoun *them* or *they* might be used.

The reason for studying about different forms of pronouns is to make sure you use them correctly in your writing. Some habits of speech may not be the Standard English usage; this review will help you clear up any habits of pronoun usage that don't conform to the expectations for workplace writing.

Types of Pronouns

Pronouns are divided into types so you can gain a better understanding of their usage. We will begin with three common types of pronouns and work our way to others later in this chapter: **personal pronouns,** used to refer to specific people and things; for example, *I, you, me, he, she, they, it;* **reflexive pronouns,** used to reflect either emphasis or action back to the noun or pronoun to which they refer; and **indefinite pronouns,** used to refer to groups of people and things; for example *everyone, no one, someone, something.*

Understanding these types of pronouns will help you use the correct form when you reference a noun with a pronoun. This is called **pronoun reference.**

Personal Pronouns

Personal pronouns (*I, you, me, they,* and so on) have different forms that are known in grammar as **pronoun case.**

Subjective case	When a pronoun is used as the **subject** of a sentence; it tells *who* or *what* a sentence is about. Subjective case is also called **nominative case** in grammar.
	She gave a good presentation at the meeting.
	You and I will make a good team.
Objective case	When a pronoun is used in a sentence as an **object** of a verb or a preposition.
	The company owes **me** money for my expenses. [*Me* is the object of the verb *owes.*]
	Please get the money for **me** as soon as possible. [*You* is the understood subject of this sentence; *me* is the object of the preposition *for.*]
Possessive case	When a pronoun **shows possession** (ownership).
	That book is **mine** and this one is **yours**.
	Kevin asked that you return **his** book by tomorrow.

Most personal pronouns change their form (spelling) as they change case and person.

The following chart lists the forms of personal pronouns in the subjective, objective, and possessive cases.

Pronoun Reference Chart

PERSONAL PRONOUNS	SINGULAR			PLURAL		
Person	Subjective*	Objective	Possessive	Subjective	Objective	Possessive
First person	I	me	my, mine	we	us	our, ours
Second person	you	you	your, yours	you	you	your, yours
Third person	he, she, it	him, her, it	his, hers, its	they	them	their, theirs
	who	whom	whose	who, whoever	whom, whomever	whose

Reflexive Pronouns

Pronouns that end in *self/selves* are called **reflexive pronouns.** You use these pronouns all the time in speaking and writing. The thing to remember is that *they cannot be used as the subject of a sentence.* They are used to reflect either emphasis or action *back* to the noun or pronoun to which they refer, for example:

> I asked **myself** whether or not I was making the right decision.

> If you want a job well done, do it **yourself.**

> They treated **themselves** to a big lunch.

> I bought **myself** a birthday present.

These are the reflexive pronouns:

First person	myself, ourselves
Second person	yourself, yourselves
Third person	himself, herself, itself, oneself, themselves[†]

Indefinite Pronouns

Indefinite pronouns refer to nonspecific people or things, so they do not have a first, second, and third person form. Indefinite pronouns also do not change form when used as subjects or objects. Those that have a possessive form show it by adding *'s.*

> **Someone's** jacket was left in the conference room.

Word to the Wise

Do not confuse the possessive form of indefinite pronouns with a **contraction.** In the sentence *Everybody's going to the company picnic,* everybody's is a contraction meaning *everybody is.*

These are the indefinite pronouns:

- everyone, anyone, no one, someone
- anybody, everybody, nobody, somebody
- anything, everything, nothing, something
- some, several, both, few, any, one, all (when not followed by a noun)

---

*Also known as the nominative case.

[†]Never use the "nonwords" *themself, theirself,* or *theirselves* (note: *Merriam-Webster calls this form* "dialect.").

REPLAY 24

A. Using the chart on page 107 as needed, circle the correct pronoun in each of the following sentences and write in the blank whether it is in the subjective or objective case.

1. Marie, Larry, and _(me, I, myself)_ lost all our quarters at the casino. _____ case

2. Please give the instructions to the president and _(he, him, himself)_ . _____ case

3. Bob and _(me, I, myself)_ went to the concert. _____ case

4. When you hear the test results for _(she, her, herself)_ and Kirby, you'll be very surprised. _____ case

5. _(Who/Whom)_ is the best person to talk to about the position? _____ case.

B. Write a subject pronoun in the subject blank of each sentence and an object pronoun in the object blank. If in doubt, see the chart at the beginning of this chapter.

Subject	**Object of Verb**	**Subject**	**Object of Preposition**
1. _____ believe _____		5. _____ am staying with _____	
2. _____ admires _____		6. _____ are starting with _____	
3. _____ respects _____		7. _____ is leaving with _____	
4. _____ knows _____?		8. _____ are going with _____?	

C. Use a reflexive pronoun or an indefinite pronoun that makes sense in each of the following sentences:

1. My group had _____ to represent us at the meeting because _____ was busy.

2. The receptionist needs _____ to replace him while he goes to lunch.

3. The manager _____ gave me permission to use a company car.

4. If there is _____ that can be done to help meet the deadline _____ should volunteer to do it.

5. I threw a big party for _____ to celebrate my promotion.

6. _____ needs to be done about the terrible service in the cafeteria.

Check your answers on page 445.

READ 25   CHOOSING THE RIGHT PRONOUNS

How do you choose the right pronoun to act as a noun substitute?

Refer to the pronoun reference chart on page 107 while reading the guidelines below:

Subjective case pronouns	Use subject pronouns as the subject of a sentence to tell *who* or *what* with an *action (doing)* verb or a *being* verb.

> **Joan** and **he** are **majoring** in business administration. [*Joan* and *he* are the subjects; *he* is a subject pronoun; the action verb *majoring* tells what they are *doing*.]
>
> **He** and **she are** graduate students. [*He* and *she* are subject pronouns; *are* is a being verb.]
>
> **They were** the first to make the suggestion. [*They* is the subject pronoun; *were* is the being verb.]

Objective case pronouns	Use object pronouns as the objects of action verbs or prepositions, such as *between, among, under, below, over, with, of, to, in, into.*

> Pease call **Janet** or **me** with the information. [*Janet* and *me* are the object of the verb *call*.]

Also use object pronouns as the objects of prepositions.

> Among the five **of us,** two have attended training and three have not. [*Us* is the object of the preposition *of*.]

Subject Pronouns

The subject of an action verb is the "doer" of the verb's action and must be in the subjective case.

> **You** and **I** plan to attend graduate school and study for our MBAs. [*You* and *I* are subjects of the action verb *plan*.]

Most pronoun subject errors occur when two or more pronouns are used together, such as *he and I,* or when a noun is used with a pronoun, such as *Jonathan and I/me/myself.*

You will usually make the right choice if you imagine one of the pronouns or the noun omitted; then decide whether the sentence "sounds right."

The following examples show how to use this "trick."

NO	Jonathan and **me** went to the concert. OR Jonathan and **myself** went to the concert. [Leave *Jonathan* home, and you know that "Me or myself went to the concert" sounds terrible.]
YES	You would change the sentence to: Jonathan and **I** went to the concert.

> **NO** **Him** and **me** attended the concert. [Both pronouns are wrong; you wouldn't say "Him attended the concert," or "Me attended the concert." Therefore, change objective pronouns—*him/me*—to subjective pronouns *he/I*.]
>
> **YES** **He** and **I** attended the concert.

No Conjunction? Imagine Omitting the Noun

Sometimes the noun and pronoun have no conjunction *(and/or)* between them. This happens when you combine a noun and a pronoun that have the same meaning to show emphasis or to make your meaning clear. Which is right?

> we clerks **or** us clerks   we boys **or** us boys

The four combinations above are Standard English. You can tell which to use when you see the rest of the sentence. You'll make the right choice if you imagine omitting the **noun;** then decide whether the sentence sounds right:

> **NO** **Us students** need a longer lunch break.

Omit the noun *students:*

> **NO** "**Us** need a longer lunch break" sounds wrong.
>
> **YES** "**We** need a longer lunch break" sounds right.
>
> **YES** **We students** need a longer lunch break.

Word to the Wise

Habits of speech carry over to writing and can cause mistakes in pronoun usage. Many people make the mistake of using *me* in this kind of sentence:

NO   **Shirley** and **me** are having lunch together next week.

If you are one of them, remembering the rule *being verb = subject pronoun* will help you avoid making this error. Say it often, until *I* begins to sound right.

YES   **Shirley** and **I** are having lunch together next week.

Object Pronouns

> The object of an action verb or of a preposition tells *what* or *whom* is *doing* or *being;* if the object is a pronoun, then it must be in the *objective case,* not the subjective case.

Objects of Verbs

To find out if a verb has an object, say the subject and verb, and then ask *whom?* or *what?* If you get an answer, the answer is the object. The following sentences show objects of verbs in bold type:

> I like **peaches.** [I like *what?* peaches]
>
> Nick expects **Beverly** and **her** to attend. [*Whom* does Nick expect? Beverly and her]

If you don't get an answer to *whom* or *what,* the clause has no object.

> I dance well. [*well* answers *how,* not *whom* or *what*]
>
> We kissed **Marty** and **her** goodbye. [The objects of the verb *kissed* are *Marty* and *her.*]

Objects of Prepositions

Prepositions, usually direction or position words, begin prepositional phrases. A prepositional phrase ends with an object, which is a noun or an object pronoun. If you say the preposition followed by *whom* or *what,* the answer is the object. In the following sentences, the prepositions are underlined, and the objects of the prepositions are in bold type.

> Gregory is <u>in</u> the **group** <u>with</u> **him.**
>
> Victoria wrote <u>to</u> **me** <u>about</u> the **position.**
>
> She gave the pizza <u>to</u> **Joan** and **me.**
>
> My sister bought the theater tickets <u>for</u> **Jordan** and **us.**
>
> Let's divide the pie <u>between</u> **you** and **me.**
>
> Give it <u>to</u> my **sister** and **him.**
>
> Just <u>between</u> **you** and **me,** the meeting was dull.

Just Between You and Me

What is the correct way to say it? Should it be "Just between you and I"? Definitely not! Well, how about "Just between us"? You know it can't be "Just between we"! With two pronouns—*you* and *me* or *you* and *I*—it's harder to tell which is right. Because *between* is a preposition, an object pronoun is needed. "Just Between **You** and **Me**" (not **I**) is right—*me* is an object of the preposition *between.*

> **As with subject pronouns, you can imagine omitting the object pronouns one at a time to make sure you are using the correct one.**

NO	Professor Boone will discuss the problem with **he** and **I.** [Omit *he* or *I* and you know "Professor Boone will discuss the problem with **he**" {or with **I**} is wrong. Change subjective pronouns *he/I* to objective pronouns *him/me*—objects of the preposition *with.*]
YES	Professor Boone will discuss the problem with **him** and **me.**
NO	Give the report to Pat Garner and **I** tomorrow. [Omit *Pat,* and then you know "Give the report to **I** tomorrow" can't be right.]
YES	Give the report to Pat Garner and **me** tomorrow.

No Conjunction

Also as with subject pronouns, when no conjunction separates object pronouns from a noun, use the omission test.

NO	Would you consider giving **we salespersons** longer lunch breaks? [Omit the noun *salespersons,* and you immediately know that "Would you consider giving **we** longer lunch breaks" can't be right.]
YES	Please give **us salespersons** longer lunch breaks.
NO	Please give **we students** a voice in setting campus rules. [Omit the noun *students,* object of action verb *give,* and you know that "Please give **we** a voice in setting campus rules" can't be right.]
YES	Please give **us students** a voice in setting campus rules.
NO	Send a car for **Ms. Dahlberg** and **I** immediately. [Omit *Ms. Dahlberg,* object of preposition *for,* and you immediately know that "Send a car for **I** immediately" can't be right.]
YES	Send a car for **Ms. Dahlberg** and **me** immediately.

REPLAY 25

Circle the correct pronouns.

1. If (she and me/her and I/she and I/her and me) study, we'll do better work.
2. Please tell Walter and (I/me) the best way to get to your office.
3. (They/Them) as well as Carla are involved in the Texas City project.
4. (We/Us) paralegals need more training in the procedures.
5. Ms. Garcia and (I /me) should work together frequently.
6. Joining the union would be good for (we/us) pasta chefs.
7. Deborah of Denmark, South Carolina, phoned Suzy and (I/me).
8. Mr. Townsend authorized Stephen and (she/her) to go to Fort Lauderdale.
9. Do (we/us) students have a vote on whether to have a final exam?
10. Ms. Denova and (he/him) could travel to the sales meeting together.
11. Should Luanne show Mr. Byrnes and (I/me) the new outlines?
12. Christopher asked both you and (we/us) to visit her.
13. This committee needs Terry as well as (they/them).
14. Everyone except Ms. Rosenblatt and (he/him) works in Omaha.*
15. (Him and me/He and I) have an advantage in this situation.
16. The money should be divided between Mr. Park and (I/me).
17. Jamal Hendricks and (him/he) will share the Pulitzer Prize.
18. (We/Us) Americans transfer the fork to the right hand after cutting food.
19. We sent Ms. Papas and (her/she) to London.
20. All the responsibility was given to the auditor and (they/them).
21. The director told Ms. Ray and (I/me) about downtown Lancaster.
22. Were you and (he/him) preparing a PowerPoint presentation that day?
23. Ms. Little invited you but not (he/him).
24. Professor Newsom wants Lee and (I/me) to work on the project.
25. You and (them/they) should devise a new production schedule.
26. Let's keep the surprise ending to the program just between you and (I/me).

Check your answers on pages 446.

READ 26   SUBJECT/OBJECT CONFUSION

Some subject and object pronouns are oddly confusing. *Me* and *I* are examples. Is it "John and **me** can work late this evening" or "John and **I** can work late"? Based on the "omit one" test, you now know that *John and I* is the correct way to say it. (Remove *John* and you know the right pronoun is *I*.) This section covers some other ways to test whether you are using the correct pronoun case.

---

*The subject is everyone; except is a preposition.

Understood Words

Pronoun usage gets confusing when understood words are left out to avoid wordiness. These understood words are verbs or subject-verb combinations that complete comparisons but are unnecessary because the sentence is clear without them.

If you're not sure whether to use subject or object pronouns when understood words are missing, just complete the expression or imagine it completed.

The words *than* or *as* are clues that a sentence may have "understood words" that are omitted.

> Did Mr. Ngueyen sell more tickets than (**she/her**)? [Than *she sold* or than *she did* is understood—not *her sold* or *her did*.]

Here are some more examples; the omitted words are in parentheses. Say the underlined phrase to know which pronoun is correct.

NO   No one wants to please you more than the manager and <u>**me** (want to please you]</u>.

YES   No one wants to please you more than the manager and <u>**I** (want to please you).</u>

Do you like him better than (**I** or **me**)? [If you add the understood words *like him* or *do* after the questionable pronoun, you easily choose *I*, not *me*.]

NO   Do you like him better than **me** (do)?

YES   Do you like him better than **I** (do)?

Go by the Meaning

In some sentences either a subject pronoun or an object pronoun is correct. The choice depends on what you want the sentence to mean. Let's take another look at the preceding example:

YES   Do you like him more than **I** [like him]?

If you add the understood words *you like* **before** the pronoun in question, the meaning changes—and you need a different pronoun.

NO   Do you like him more than [you like] **I**?

YES   Do you like him more than [you like] **me**?

To be certain you choose the right pronoun, complete in your imagination any sentence that omits understood words in a comparison. If more than one meaning is possible, use the words that deliver the meaning you intend.

RECAP   Circle the correct answers for items 1 and 2.

---

1. Mr. Swanson sold more tickets than (her/she).
2. Marilyn is just as tall as (him/he).

   Items 3 and 4 are both correct but have different meanings. Circle the number of the statement that sounds like a marriage in trouble. In the blanks, write the understood word(s) in parentheses.

3. My husband likes golf better than I. _____

4. My husband likes golf better than _____ me.

Check your answers on page 446.

Reflexive Pronouns—Self, Selves

The *self* and *selves* pronouns that follow are compound personal pronouns but are also called **reflexive pronouns** or *reflective pronouns* because they may be used to reflect back on a noun or another pronoun with the same meaning. They're also used to add emphasis or clarity.

Use a reflexive pronoun only when another pronoun will not make sense in that position in the sentence.

Misspellings of these words often occur; they are shown in parentheses below. Check your written work and your spoken vocabulary to remove these unacceptable "non-words."

Reflexive Pronouns

Singular	Plural
myself	
itself	
oneself	
yourself	yourselves
himself (never use *hisself*)	ourselves (never use *ourself*)
herself	themselves (never use *theirself, theirselves,* or *themself*)

Using Reflexive Pronouns Correctly

Use reflexive pronouns in two situations only:

1. To emphasize the noun (or pronoun) to which the pronoun refers:

    I did that job **myself.**

    You yourself know better than that.

    We ourselves are to blame.

    Vicki **herself** always does the hardest work.

2. To direct the action back to the subject of the sentence:

    They took care of **themselves.** (reflects *They*)

    He frequently talks to **himself.** (reflects *He*)

    He corrected **himself** immediately. (reflects *He*)

    She does the easy work by **herself.** (reflects *She*)

    She placed **herself** at great risk. (reflects *She*)

The most common error writers and speakers make with reflexive pronouns is to use them in place of objective pronouns:

NO	The store gave a discount **to** Ms. Beckham and **myself.**
YES	The store gave a discount **to** Ms. Beckham and **me.**

NO   The documents must be signed **by** your boss or **yourself.**

YES   The documents must be signed **by you** or your boss.

REPLAY 26

A. Fill in the parentheses with the understood completion word or words.

1. He loves the job more than she (_____).
2. He loves his job more than (_____) her.
3. I know the vice president better than he (_____).
4. I know the vice president better than (_____) him.
5. Ms. Guthrie can operate the device as well as he (_____).

B. Draw a line through the incorrect words, and write the correct pronoun in the blank. Write **C** in the blank if the sentence is already correct.

_____ 1. The president himself will attend the meeting.

_____ 2. The twins learned how to dress theirselves at an early age.

_____ 3. She can do the work faster than him.

_____ 4. Neither his sister nor himself is willing to take care of the situation.

_____ 5. Always give copies of memorandums to Joyce Moore and myself.

_____ 6. Victoria usually leaves earlier than Ramon and I.

_____ 7. The others usually leave as soon as Ms. Hixon and me.

_____ 8. Wallace runs just as fast as he.

_____ 9. Rhoda and Isabelle often ask themself that question.

_____ 10. Only Ms. Englehart and yourself know how to fix the equipment.

_____ 11. Deborah and myself listened to them with great interest.

_____ 12. I may find myself looking for a new manager.

_____ 13. We ourselves are excluded from the contract.

_____ 14. They felt like themselves again after the crisis had passed.

_____ 15. She injured herself while they were in Oshkosh.

_____ 16. The Indiana team members voted theirself a pay increase.

_____ 17. Good table manners require that you spoon soup away from yourself.

_____ 18. He gave hisself a raise.

_____ 19. I gave me a perm and a manicure.

_____ 20. Gomez himself should have known better than to buy 100 shares of GYPCO in a bear market; don't blame yourself.

Check your answers on page 446.

READ 27   POSSESSIVE PRONOUNS

It is easy to remember the pronouns used to show possession because you use them all the time. The most important thing to remember about possessive pronouns* is this:

Do not use an apostrophe with any of the personal possessive pronouns.

They already show possession in the way they are spelled.

Use apostrophes only with possessive nouns and contractions.

Personal Possessive Pronouns

That is **my** idea.	That idea is **mine**.†
This is **his** idea.	This idea is **his**.
That is **her** business.	That book is **hers**.
These are **our** jeeps.	Those jeeps are **ours**.
This is **your** dollar.	That money is **yours**.
These are **their** jeans.	Those jeans are **theirs**.
The lizard lost **its** tail.	**Whose** tail is that?

Confusing Possessive Pronouns and Contractions

Errors often occur because some *possessive pronouns* and *contractions* sound alike but are spelled differently. Be aware of the differences below and make sure you have used the right word in your writing, depending on the meaning you want.

Possessive Pronouns	**Contractions Requiring Apostrophes**
your—Your job pays well.	**you're** (you are)—You're a rich man.
its—Its wing was injured.	**it's** (it is)—It's a short distance away.
whose—Whose responsibility is it?	**who's** (who is)—I know who's here.
their—Their problem is serious.	**they're** (they are)—They're in debt.

To make indefinite pronouns possessive, add 's (see Read 24 for a list of indefinite pronouns).

That could be **anybody's** calliope.	This isn't **anyone's** trumpet.
It must be **somebody's** saxophone.	**Someone's** guitar is on the piano.
That is **everybody's** banjo.	**Everyone's** song sheets are here.
One should mind **one's** own business.	

Indefinite pronouns may also be part of a contraction.

Everyone's going to the office party. [everyone is]

Everything's fine. [everything is]

Somebody's in the conference room. [somebody is]

---

*Possessive nouns are covered in Chapter 5 and contractions are covered in Chapter 11.

†Never add *s* to *mine* unless you mean the underground sources of valuable materials.

REPLAY 27

Draw a line through the pronoun and contraction errors and write the correct word in the blank. Write **C** beside the only correct sentence.

_____ 1. Everybodys going to the Dodger game today.

_____ 2. Nobodys here to mind the store.

_____ 3. Reserve the apostrophe for it's proper use, and omit it when its not needed.

_____ 4. Its color has faded.

_____ 5. The new printer is our's, not yours'.

_____ 6. Your's is on the room with the green door.

_____ 7. The one on the right is her's.

_____ 8. The CDs are mines; the DVDs are their's.

_____ 9. Your to use your own books today.

_____ 10. If your running behind schedule, let you're sister help.

_____ 11. Everybodys notebook is closed.

_____ 12. No ones' work was checked.

_____ 13. Whether or not we'll get that account is anyones' guess.

_____ 14. Whose going to do the graphics?

_____ 15. Who's work do you prefer?

Check your answers on page 446.

READ 28   *WHO* AND *WHOM*

If you're a fan of whodunits (mystery stories, books, and films), then you'll like this section. The best known English-language whodunit is "The Mystery of Who and Whom" (although it qualifies as a mystery, it's not exactly a thriller).

Those who truly care about their English try hard to use who/whom correctly, yet they often err by using *whom* where *who* belongs. Some people correct themselves like this: "Who ah whom ah who ah is the treasurer of this company?" Then we have who/whom cowards who mumble the mystery word and hope the listener won't notice. Many well-educated people, however, do use *who* and *whom* correctly. Now here's the good news: Some language experts recommend eliminating *whom* from **speech** to avoid awkward pauses and mumbles.

BUT—for **writing** in the workplace, we recommend taking some care and making sure you are using *who* and *whom* correctly. It takes just a few seconds if you know the "clue." In **speech,** just use *who* unless you're certain about your choice of *whom.*

Clue: Imagine *He* or *Him*

Here is the secret to correct usage:

Imagine replacing *who* or *whom* with *he* or *him* (disregard whether the person is male or female). If *he* fits, use *who* or *whoever*; if *him* sounds right, use *whom* or *whomever.* Both *him* and *whom* end with *m,* making it a good memory device.

Mr. Agresta is the man (**who**/whom) gave me the package. [*He* gave me the package—not *him* gave me the package; therefore, choose *who.*]

Jim Young, (**who**/whom) we understand visited you yesterday, is a database expert. [Jim Young is a database expert; we understand *he* visited your office yesterday—not *him* visited; therefore, choose *who.*]

Dr. Perry, (who/**whom**) Prudential hopes to hire, has the highest qualifications. [Dr. Perry has the highest qualifications; Prudential hopes to hire *him*—not hire *he;* therefore choose *whom.*]

Assign the report to (whoever/**whomever**) you wish. [Assign the report to *him;* therefore, choose *whomever.*]

If either *he* or *him* fits in the same place, choose *who* or *whoever,* not *whom* or *whomever:*

You should go with (**whoever**/whomever) is ready first. [*Him* fits after *with* (objective case), but *he* fits before *is* (subjective case). Therefore use *who.*] Why? Always allow a subject to have priority over an object.

RECAP   Circle the correct pronoun.

1. She is the expert (who/whom) we told you about.
2. He is the one (who/whom) will receive the Teacher of the Year Award.
3. Joseph can invite (whoever/whomever) he pleases.
4. Give* the extra supplies to (whoever/whomever) you think needs them.
5. Send the money to (whoever/whomever) will use it wisely.
6. Jacqueline is the woman (who/whom) I chose for the job.
7. I want to hire (whoever/whomever) will do the job efficiently.
8. (Who/Whom) should she choose for the job?
9. To (who/whom) did Alex reveal the master plan?
10. Margaret, (who/whom) Jesse planned to call, was away on business for the week.

Check your answers on page 446.

Clue: Imagine a Statement

If the sentence is a question, imagine it as a statement before making the *who/whom* choice.

(Who/Whom) are you going with?

Change to a statement:

You are going with **whom.** [*Him,* not *he,* sounds right after *with.*]

Another way to look at it is *You* is the subject of the verb *are going;* therefore, the object pronoun *whom* is needed as the object of the preposition *with.*

---

*You is the understood subject of *give;* you is the subject of *think;* whoever is the subject of *needs.*

RECAP Circle the correct answer.

1. (Whom/Who) do you think won the contest?
2. The question of (who/whom) should go will be discussed.
3. Bring anyone (who/whom) would like to come.
4. Mr. Valdez, (who/whom) we expected, can't attend.

Check your answers on page 447.

REPLAY 28

Choose *who/whoever* or *whom/whomever;* apply Read 28 clues. (Practice, not guessing, makes perfect.)

Example: We referred a programmer to you ____whom____ we believe you will like.

1. You should go with _____ is leaving first.
2. I will give the money to _____ will take it.
3. People _____ never make a mistake never make anything else.
4. Mohammed is the one _____ should do the work.
5. _____ does Professor Serrano prefer for the job?
6. _____ would you like to join me?
7. _____ do you believe will win the election?
8. _____ should we ask to investigate?
9. _____ is willing to work hard will be given the responsibility.
10. Each candidate will support _____ the convention chooses.
11. We think he is the professor _____ you will want at Carl Sandburg College.
12. Give the scholarship to the one _____ needs it most.
13. She is the woman _____ I took to be your sister.
14. You are the court reporter _____ I requested for the deposition.
15. Professor Costner is the instructor _____ I believe could help you.
16. Give it to _____ you wish.
17. Ms. Ferguson is the one _____ helped me most in Seattle.
18. We selected Ms. Serrano, _____ we know is a Renton professor.
19. Ms. Faries-Tondi, _____ we met yesterday, is giving a speech.
20. The prize will be awarded to _____ writes the best essay.
21. The board will approve _____ we select for vice president.
22. Ms. Stranix, _____ I told you about last week, will speak on business education at Yuba College.
23. The question of _____ should do the artwork will be discussed.
24. Give the package to _____ can identify it.
25. He _____ has courage and faith will never perish in misery.—Anne Frank

Check your answers on page 447.

Read 29   # INDEFINITE PRONOUNS IN-DEPTH

Use indefinite pronouns to refer to nonspecific persons or things.

Indefinite pronouns can be tricky, so we are going to spend some extra time looking at their usage and some of the things about them that trouble writers. First, here's a review of the indefinite pronouns listed earlier in this chapter.

Indefinite Pronouns

each	any	some	none	both	most
everyone	anybody	somebody	nobody	few	several
everybody	anyone	someone	no one	all	many
everything	anything	something	nothing	others	more

One Word or Two?

Except for *no one,* the compound indefinite pronouns (those combining two words into one) are written as one word. In some sentences, however, these expressions are not pronouns; the first part is an adjective and the second, a noun. In that case, write them as two words. Fortunately, you don't need to analyze the grammar to know whether to use one word or two. Just apply these two word tricks:

Any one and *every one* are two words when *of* follows.

> **Any one of** you might go to Topeka.   **Every one of** you might go to Omaha.
>
> **Anyone** may go to Houston.   **Everyone** might go to Brunswick.

Sometimes a special meaning makes it right to use two words instead of one—use your own judgment of what fits your meaning.

> The professor told the medical students they could examine **any body** in the morgue.
>
> The man I met at Muscle Beach has **some body.**

Here's another example of where you can decide how you want to say it. If you were writing a commercial about milk (this was once a commercial slogan of the dairy industry), which one would you choose?

> **Every body** needs milk.
>
> **Everybody** needs milk.

Every body stresses the body's need for milk, and *everybody* stresses that all people need milk.

Recap   Make the corrections needed for written English. Use the proofreading mark for insert space [#] and use the close space symbol [◖] where no space is needed.

1. Noone from this office responded.
2. Everyone of the books was sold yesterday.

3. Everyone has their own access code.
4. In American business situations, keeping some one waiting is considered rude.
5. The designer is willing to use anyone of the three colors.

Check your answers on page 447.

Indefinite Singular Pronouns

The following words are often **singular indefinite pronouns.** However, when the words in the first column precede a noun, they become adjectives. Good news: It isn't necessary to identify the part of speech—just remember they are all singular.

When using these words as the subject of a sentence, be sure to use the singular verb form.

each	everyone	everybody
every	someone	nobody
either	anyone	somebody
neither	no one	anybody
	one	

Everyone is going to the party.[Although *everyone* might include five hundred people, it is singular because it refers to each one acting individually.]

Neither of us **is** interested in a subscription.

Each color **is** beautiful, but you can only pick one. [In this case *each* is an adjective describing the subject *color*.]

Everybody in the class **dances** well.

Use singular pronouns such as *his, her,* or *its*—not the plural *their*—to substitute for words in the preceding list. In informal speech this rule is frequently ignored, but it is still important in workplace writing.

USE	**Every** student in men's physical education needs **his** own locker. [*Every* means *every one.*]
AVOID	**Every** student in men's physical education needs **their** own locker.
USE	**Each** building has **its** own heating unit.
AVOID	**Each** building has **their** own heating unit.
USE	**No one** is consulting a lawyer about it. [No one is consulting **his** or **her** lawyer about it.]
AVOID	**No one** is consulting **their** lawyer about it.

Indefinite Plural Pronouns

The following words are often adjectives but are also used as indefinite plural pronouns: *all, any, both, few, more, most, none, some.* When using these words as the subject of a sentence, be sure to use the plural verb form.

Both are beautiful.

Few tourists **go** there.

Some were better than others.

More seem interested this year.

Most have attended.

Many are here today.

Writing for Your Career

Avoid using *they* in a vague sense and *you* when you mean people in general or those in authority. Use specific nouns instead, or rephrase to omit the need for a noun or pronoun.

NO   *They* give *you* grants or loans if *you* can prove *your* income is at or below the poverty level. [Use nouns instead of *they* and *you* so that you communicate clearly.]

YES   The Financial Aid Office arranges grants or loans for students who can prove their income is at or below the poverty level.

NO   *You're* prohibited from driving in this state if *you've* been drinking.

YES   State law prohibits driving after drinking alcoholic beverages.

Pronoun Gender and Number

Gender refers to male, female, and neutral words.

When both sexes are represented, avoid the shortcut of using only male gender—*his, he,* or *him.*

Instead, use the expression *him or her,* reword the sentence to use the plural forms *they* or *their,* or find some other way to say it.

Number refers to singular or plural; nouns and pronouns should agree in number.

Use singular pronouns to represent singular nouns or pronouns.

NO   **Each** employee did **his** work quietly. [No women on the job?]

NO   **Each person** did **their** work quietly. [A plural pronoun *their* should not be used to represent singular words: *each person*.]

YES   **Each person** worked quietly.

    Everyone worked quietly.

    The students worked quietly.

NO   **Each employee** has **their** job to do.

YES   **Employees** have **their** jobs to do.

    An employee has **his or her** job to do.

    Each employee has **a** job to do.

REPLAY 29

A. Rewrite the following sentences to correct gender and number agreement.

1. Everyone in this department should be sure their nouns and pronouns agree in number in their written communications. [When correcting this sentence, note that "Everyone" is a singular pronoun, but *their* is plural.] _____

_____

_____

2. Every mechanic finished their work quickly. _____

_____

3. Every boy and girl in the class needs (his or her/their) own book. _____

_____

4. Each applicant should write their name in the blank. _____

_____

B. Draw a line through the incorrect form in the following sentences.

Example: (No body/~~Nobody~~) was found where the fatal accident occurred.

1. (Any body/Anybody) at this meeting may speak on the subject.
2. (Every one/Everyone) of you can do well in this class.
3. (No one/Noone/) but Patti knows the combination to the safe.
4. Please distribute the flyers to (any one/anyone) who wants them.
5. (Every body/Everybody) should learn touch typing.
6. Ms. Kato asked that (some one/someone) from this office visit her store.
7. (Any one/Anyone) of you is qualified to prepare the report.
8. Although we believe the pilot was killed, (no body/nobody) was found.
9. Senators must use (his or her/their) own funds for this project.
10. The corporation publishes (its/their) annual report in the first quarter.
11. Each building has (its/their) own security guard.
12. A few mechanics completed (his or her/their) work by 4 p.m.

C. In the blank below "Best," write the letter of the best form for written workplace communication. In the next blank, write the letter of the only incorrect form.

BEST   INCORRECT

___   ___   1. a. A person can usually improve if he really tries.

b. A person can usually improve if they really try.

c. People can usually improve if they really try.

d. A person can usually improve if he or she really tries.

___   ___   2. a. When customers express their dissatisfaction, listen courteously.

b. When a customer expresses his dissatisfaction, listen courteously.

     c. When a customer expresses his or her dissatisfaction, listen courteously.

     d. When a customer expresses their dissatisfaction, listen courteously.

___ ___   3. a. Every one of the contractors submitted his or her bid today.

     b. Every one of the contractors submitted bids today.

     c. Each contractor submitted his bid today.

     d. Every contractor submitted their bid today.

___ ___   4. a. Did anyone here lose his notebook?

     b. Did anyone here lose a notebook?

     c. Did anyone here lose their notebook?

___ ___   5. a. Everyone should write his name on the form.

     b. Everyone should write their name on the form.

     c. Everyone should write his or her name on the form.

     d. You should each write your name on the form.

Check your answers on page 447.

READ 30   AGREEMENTS AND COMPLEMENTS

Pronouns Referring to Collective Nouns

One final area where confusion about pronouns occurs is agreement when a pronoun is used to refer to a collective noun.

Collective nouns name groups of people, animals, or things. When a pronoun refers to a collective noun, it must agree in number.

Gaggle (geese), herd (cattle), flock (sheep), pride (lions), fleet (ships), and faculty (teachers) are all examples of collective nouns.

audience	committee	crowd	group	navy	staff
class	congregation	family	jury	squad	team

Here is the rule for using pronouns that agree with collective nouns:

Use a singular pronoun—*it, its, itself*—to substitute for a collective noun if the members of the group act as one; that is, as a single unit. If the pronoun can be eliminated, do so.

An example of a collective noun is *jury;* when a jury announces a verdict, it acts as a single unit.

    NO   The **jury** announced **their** verdict. [The plural pronoun *their* is incorrect when members of the collection act as one.]

YES	The **jury** announced **its** verdict. [The singular pronoun *its* refers to *jury* acting as a unit.]
OR	The **jury** announced the verdict. [Change the sentence to omit the pronoun]

Use a plural pronoun—*they, them, their/s, themselves*—to substitute for a collective noun if the members of the group act separately or disagree.

NO	The **jury** put on **its** coats as it prepared to leave. [*Jury* acts as single unit arriving at a verdict but as separate individuals when putting on coats.]
OK	The **jury** put on **their** coats as they prepared to leave. [This is technically correct but awkward.]
BETTER	The **members of the jury** put on **their** coats as they prepared to leave.
YES	The **committee** believed **it** had been right to take strong action.
NO	The **committee** disagreed about whether **it** should take strong action. [The committee as a whole did not disagree.]
YES	The **committee members** disagreed about whether **they** should take strong action. [Individuals acted separately in disagreement with each other.]

Use a singular pronoun to substitute for names of organizations—for example, companies, unions, stores, schools, governments, and government agencies.

Though the college named below has many students and employees, use a singular pronoun because it is **one** organization.

NO	Davenport College opens **their** offices at 8 a.m.
YES	Davenport College opens **its** offices at 8 a.m.
BETTER	Davenport College offices open at 8 a.m. [The same idea is expressed smoothly and with fewer words.]

Use a plural pronoun to substitute for a plural noun—juries, companies, colleges, classes, teams.

YES	The **companies** announced **their** merger simultaneously in New York and in Chicago.

By recognizing collective nouns, you can avoid choosing incorrect pronouns to substitute for them. Your understanding of collective nouns will help with "subject-verb agreement" in Chapter 7.

Writing for Your Career

Rephrasing to omit the pronoun when referring to collective nouns usually improves the wording.

NO	The Internal Revenue Service revised **their** 1099 form. [IRS is a collective noun requiring a singular pronoun (its), if a pronoun is used.]
YES	The Internal Revenue Service revised **its** 1099 form.
BETTER	The Internal Revenue Service revised the 1099 form.

1. Nordstrom's will open (their/its) doors early for the sale.
2. The Navy recalled (its/their) ships from dry dock.
3. Committees often make (its/their) decisions too slowly.

Check your answers on page 448.

Subject Pronouns After *Being* Verbs

You have learned that a pronoun following a *being* verb must be a subject pronoun. This rule is important in *written* English. In 21st-century spoken American English, however, either an object or a subject pronoun is acceptable after a *being* verb. Adjectives are also often used after *being* verbs—but not adverbs. A subject pronoun or an adjective after a *being verb* is called a complement. (Notice *e*, not *i*, before *ment*.)

Being Verbs	*am, is, was, were, been, be*
Subject Pronouns	*I, we, you, he, she, they, it, who;* these are correct as *complements.*
YES	It **is he,** not Jerry, who sold it.
	It **was I,** not she, who sent it.
Object Pronouns	*me, us, you, them, it, whom;* these are incorrect as *complements.*
NO	It **is him,** not Jerry, who sold it. OR It **is them,** not Jerry, who sold it.
YES	The only experts in the group **were** she and **I.** [not *her* and *me*]
	The winners might have **been** Raul and **he.** [not *him*]

A. List collective nouns in the six blanks below. See how many you can think of without referring to the preceding pages.

1. _____
2. _____
3. _____
4. _____
5. _____
6. _____

B. Circle the correct answer within the parentheses.

1. When the members of the group named by a collective noun—such as *team*—act separately or disagree, the pronoun is (singular/plural).
2. When the group named by a collective noun acts as one, a pronoun substituting for it is (singular/plural).
3. When writing, use (an object/a subject) pronoun after a being verb.
4. Aerojet Corp. has (its/their) offices in Escanaba, Michigan.
5. The Sales Office is on the third floor; (they are/it is) open until five.
6. Segal Institute always pays (its/their) bills promptly.
7. Metro College revised (its/their) application form.
8. It was not (me/I/myself) who made the suggestion.
9. Her family is planning (its/their) vacation for August this year.
10. The Board of Directors will hold (its/it's/their) next meeting at Mount Hood.
11. The city should regulate (its/it's/their) hiring policies more carefully.
12. The committee will review the new data at (its/it's/their) next meeting.
13. Why can't (they/the janitorial service) keep this place clean?
14. We all know (you shouldn't throw trash/trash shouldn't be thrown) from a car window.
15. Our best district managers in Dallas are Ron and (she/her).
16. The two who will join the department are Jill Edelson and (he/him).
17. The guests of honor were Janice Bragia and (me/I/myself).
18. I think it was (they/them) who requested the report.
19. It is (me/I) who should go to Auburn Hills.
20. He wants (we clerks/us clerks) to bear responsibility for the project.

Check your answers on page 448. Then review the entire chapter before taking the Pop Quiz on page 303.

CONCEPT REVIEW & SKILL-BUILDING APPLICATIONS

Checkpoint

Along with rapidly changing technologies and lifestyles, language styles also change. As with all change, some people use their energy defending the old, and others lead the parade. For your career, being in the middle is advisable when it comes to language. Your objective is for others to concentrate on your message and not be distracted by something unusual you say or write.

Whether preparing a report for the president of your company, a letter to an important customer, or an informal email message, you should not have to ponder over whether to use *I* or *me, who* or *whom,* and so on. You should *know* how to decide. When speaking with colleagues or clients, you should not have to be self-conscious about your grammar. You should be *confident* your grammar is correct.

Place a check in the blank when you understand the principle.

_____ Use a subject pronoun as subject of a verb and an object pronoun as object of a verb or of a preposition.

_____ *Who* is acceptable in speech for subjects and objects. However, when writing, use *who* as a subject and *whom* as an object.

_____ Use a reflexive (self/selves) pronoun only when another pronoun will not make sense in that position in the sentence. Never use *hisself, theirselves, themself,* or *theirself!*

_____ The pronouns *hers, ours, yours,* and *theirs* never have apostrophes. However, indefinite possessive pronouns (such as someone or everybody) do have apostrophes before the *s* when used in possessive forms. Distinguish between possessive pronouns and contractions that sound alike but are written differently, such as *its/it's* and *your/you're.*

_____ Pronouns should agree in number (singular or plural) and in gender (masculine or feminine) with the noun or other pronoun for which they substitute. Reword sentences to avoid pronouns suggesting gender bias.

_____ Except for *no one,* compound indefinite pronouns are written as one word (*someone*)—unless "of" follows or the meaning indicates two words are required.

_____ Singular pronouns substituting for singular collective nouns are singular if the members of the group act as a single unit. If the members act separately or disagree, use a plural pronoun. Names of organizations are always considered singular.

_____ In workplace writing, use subject pronouns after "being" verbs.

_____ Avoid the pronouns *you* and *they* when you refer to people in general or an authority; use specific nouns instead.

  ## Special Assignment

This assignment will give you the opportunity to practice your speaking and writing. First you will conduct an interview and take notes; then you will write about your findings.

To begin, choose a career field or a company that interests you and identify someone who is willing to be interviewed for approximately 30 minutes. Your goal is to get enough information to form an opinion about whether or not the career field or job would be right for you. You might start by doing some "networking" to find your interviewee—ask people you know or call or visit a company or organization and explain your purpose. Before the interview, prepare questions that will help you get a more in-depth understanding of what it is like to work in the field and the kinds of opportunities that exist for someone with your education and experience. You might want to do some research on the Internet, read some magazine articles, or talk with someone for advice in advance.

Questions you might ask include: What does the work consist of? What is a typical daily routine? What types of entry-level jobs are available? What about salary and advancement possibilities? What are the advantages and disadvantages of this kind of work? What kind of training is needed to qualify? Ask only questions that interest you; that is, what do *you* want to know about this kind of work?

Be aware during your interview that your report is not a biography of your subject. People enjoy talking about themselves and telling their "life story," but it will be your job to steer the conversation to get the information you need. Take good notes and immediately after the interview summarize the information and prepare a 175- to 200-word report.

Start with a topic sentence that tells the reader in an interesting way about the subject of the report. However, don't begin your report with "I am going to write about . . ."

Sample Topic Sentences

1. "Accounting is an excellent career for women," states my friend, Abbi Hobson, who has held several high-level positions with top accounting firms.
2. I learned a great deal about the work of a systems analyst in a government agency by interviewing Harold Marvin, head of Information Technology for the City of Davenport's Department of Transportation.
3. Like other careers, a teaching career has advantages as well as disadvantages.

Follow through with what you promise in the topic sentence. The rest of the report for Topic Sentence 1 should tell why accounting is a good career, especially for women. For Topic Sentence 2, the writer will tell about the work of a systems analyst. The report beginning with Topic Sentence 3 will explain advantages and disadvantages of a teaching career.

Stay on track right to the end. Effective closings conclude or summarize what went before and do not introduce new ideas. Here are sample closing sentences:

1. Business management sounds like an exciting career filled with challenges and rewards.
2. A human resources department manager requires a vast knowledge of many subjects as well as excellent people skills.
3. Now that I've learned about the training a neurosurgeon needs, I realize I do not have the tremendous drive, ambition, and ability required to prepare for this career.

Date to submit this assignment: _____

Proofreading for Careers

Please correct sentence construction, spelling, capitalization, noun and pronoun usage, and typographical errors in the following e-mail message. Do not change wording except to correct errors of the type brought to your attention in preceding chapters.

Dear Mr. McIntyre:

I am responding to you're advertisement for a customer service associate at the new spa you are opening at Greenville mall. I am familiar with your Company's services and have expereince working the fitness industry that would fit well with the qualification's your requesting.

My last positon was with the health club at the downtown hyatt hotel, were we provided a variety of services to hotel guests, including personnel fitness training and spa treatments. An associate and I was responsible for managing the center. Him and me oversaw operation of the facility for six hours daily. This job helped myself develop outstanding communictions, problem solving, and other customer service skills that was mentioned in your ad.

Details of my background are listed in the attached resume. I would like to request and appointment for a personal interview to discuss how you and me can apply my knowledge of quality spa services to ensure the success of your newest business adventure.

Sincerely,

Jared Underwood

Jared Underwood

How did you do?   Excellent _____   Good _____   Need More Practice _____

Practice Quiz

Circle the correct pronoun—or word group for written English.

1. (Every one/Everyone) must make (his or her/their) own decision.
2. They make you stand in the registration line for hours. The applicants must stand in line for hours.

3. (No one/Noone) regrets this incident more than (I/me/myself).

4. Is Mike Terry better qualified than (her/she)?

5. They completed more of the programming than (I/me).

6. Yoshi has a better background in Hebrew than (they/them).

7. The Rock Springs plant is owned by Martinez and (me/I/myself).

8. Neither Ms. Yamomoto nor (I/me/myself) will visit the Maryland plant.

9. (Some one/Someone) left (his or her/their) keys at the reception desk.

10. Mine is faster than (your's/yours'/yours) and (her's/hers).

11. (Everybody's/Everybodys/Every body's) getting a raise.

12. (Who's/Whose/Whos) laptop computer is missing?

13. (Who/Whom) did you say will handle the new account?

14. The host seated (hisself/himself) between Artie and (me/I/myself).

15. Lee became acquainted with the planner (who/whom) was in charge of the convention.

16. (Him/He) and (me/ I /myself) will report it to (whoever/whomever) is in charge.

17. If (anyone/any one) of the men would like a ticket, (he/they) may have one.

18. If (it's/its/its') too late, give the information to (whoever/whomever) needs it.

19. We sent letters to all (who/whom) we thought might visit our showroom.

20. Each officer was issued (his/their/a) new uniform yesterday.

21. The guests of honor were Nancy Burnett and (I/me/myself).

22. Her family members are taking (it/it's/their) vacations at different times this year.

23. The Internal Revenue Service revised (its/it's/their) forms again this year.

24. The Maintenance Department is on the third floor; (it's/they are) open every day.

25. (It's/Its) (I/me) who should take the risk.

Self-Study Practice and Tutorials

Vocabulary and Spelling for Careers
For additional practice go to Appendix B, page 321.

Replay Drills
For additional practice go to Appendix C, page 374.

Companion Web Site: www.prenhall.com/smith
Go to the companion Web site to test your knowledge on self-grading quizzes and for links to other helpful online resources.

MyWritingLab
Use this online learning system for an assessment of your progress on topics covered in this chapter and progressive exercises that fit your individual needs.

7 Mastering Verbs

After completing Chapter 7, you will be able to do the following:

- Identify verb forms in sentences.
- Form verb tenses correctly when writing sentences.
- Explain the difference between regular and irregular verbs.
- Recognize irregular verbs and use the dictionary to find their correct forms.
- Use subjects and verbs that agree in number and person.
- Correct your speech and writing to avoid common verb errors and bad habits.

READ 31   VERBS: WHERE THE ACTION IS

In this chapter you will learn how to correctly use verbs in sentences. We will start with an overview.

Some Basics about Verbs

1. **Every sentence has at least one verb.** The verb tells what the subject **does (action verbs)** or what the subject **is (being verbs)**.

   Some verbs consist of one word:

   > The bank manager **interviewed** two loan applicants. [action verb]

   > Our systems analyst **purchased** a new firewall program. [action verb]

   > The sales director **was** in the office. [being verb]

   Other verbs consist of two or more words: one or more helping verbs and a main verb.

   > The human resources director **has been interviewing** those applicants all day. [*Has* and *been* are helping verbs; *interviewing,* an action verb, is the main verb.]

   > The software engineer **should have been** here today. [*Should* and *have* are helping verbs; *been,* a being verb, is the main verb.]

2. **Infinitives are the basic forms of verbs preceded by *to*.** Examples are *to cook, to dance, to have, to be, to love, to work, to send.* Do not confuse an infinitive with the action or being verb in a sentence. An infinitive is not used as a verb; the verb is elsewhere in the sentence. In the following sentences, the infinitive is in bold.

   > The manager wants **to hire** a new assistant. [The subject is *manager*; the verb is *wants*.]

   > The applicant seems **to want** the job. [The subject is *applicant*; the verb is *seems*.]

3. **Choosing a verb form depends on tense (time), number, and person.**

Tense	When does the action or being take place—past, present, or future?
Number	Does the verb have a singular or plural subject?
Person	Is the subject of the verb in first person, second person, or third person?

Word to the Wise

Make Standard English a habit in your speech and writing. Although learning about correct verb use requires concentration and practice, the principles presented here enable you to avoid verb errors often occurring in the language of intelligent adults.

BUT

If you grew up in:

- a community where non-Standard English is usually used
- a non-English-speaking country
- a community where English is a second language for many residents

THEN

Applying these rules could mean the difference between success and failure in a career. Most of the non-Standard English verb forms brought to your attention in this chapter are noticeable in business or professional environments. For that reason it is important that you acquire this information about verbs and develop the habit of using Standard English.

Verb Tenses

Action or *being* occurs in three principal time periods: *before*, *now*, or *later*; in grammar these are referred to as **past**, **present**, and **future**, and the term **tense** is used for *time*. Some action or being includes more than one period of time; that is, something may start in the past and continue into the present. Other action might start in the present and continue into the future. English can express a complex range of time. Here are some ways we express time:

> I **am working** on the project. [It is being done at the present time.]
>
> I **have been working** on this project for days. [It started in the past and is continuing in the present.]
>
> I **worked** on the project earlier today. [It was done in the past.]
>
> I **will work** on this for days if necessary. [It will be done in the future.]
>
> I **will be working** on this until at least 7 p.m. tonight. [It is being done in the present and will continue in the future.]

Regular Verb Forms

Verbs are classified as regular or irregular, based on how the basic word changes to form the tenses that show the time of the action or state of being.

A verb is regular if it changes form by adding *s*, *ed*, or *ing* to the basic form.

walk	walk<u>s</u>	walk<u>ed</u>	walk<u>ing</u>
call	call<u>s</u>	call<u>ed</u>	call<u>ing</u>

Look up the verb *walk* in your dictionary. (Be sure to look at the verb *walk*, not the noun.) In some dictionaries, *walks, walked, walking* are next to the entry word. This means all forms of regular verbs are included in that dictionary. Other dictionaries, however, don't show the forms of regular verbs, because it is assumed you will know how to add *s, ed,* or *ing.*

Forming Tenses of Regular Verbs

Present Tense + *s*	For action or being happening in the present, use the basic verb form ending with *s* if the subject is a singular noun or pronoun—except *you* or *I*.
	In Spain a **visitor** to a home often **receives** a gift from the host. [singular noun]
	It appears to be a mistake. [singular pronoun]
Present without *s*	If the action or being is happening now, use the basic verb form without *s* if the subject is a plural noun or pronoun—or *you* or *I*.
	Evelyn and **Jermaine take** cream in their coffee. [plural subject—two nouns]
	They seem qualified for the job. [plural pronoun subject]
	I walk home from work every day. [subject is *I*]
	Please **mail** the checks. [subject is understood to be *you*]
In Progress (Present Participle)	For "in progress" action or being, always use a helping verb before a main verb ending with *ing.*

If you **are inviting** any coworkers to your wedding, invite them all.

They **are talking** about Elliot and Robert.

They **will be working** on the new design every day from now on.

Past Tense If the action or being was in the past or if *has, have,* or *had* precedes the verb, add *ed* or *d* to the basic verb form:

The baby **crawled** to the table.

The baby **has crawled** to the table every day this week.

Future If the action or being will be in the future, use *will, shall, would,* or *should* before the basic verb form.

Zell **should stay** home today if he isn't well.

I **would talk** to him today if I could.

Shall I walk with you today?

He **will call** the office tomorrow.

Irregular Verb Forms

Irregular verbs do not follow a set pattern when changing tense. Dictionaries include the various forms for irregular verbs.

Some verbs change spelling for past, present, and future; some change spelling only for one tense. The verb *begin* is an example of a common irregular verb:

Present Tense **begin**—with singular subject

Please **begin** the presentation. [The subject is understood— *You.*]

begins—add *s* with singular subject

Ms. Gina Hecht **begins** a new assignment today. [singular noun subject—verb ends with *s*]

In Progress (Present Participle) **beginning**—double the final letter before adding *ing*; needs a helping verb

I **am beginning** to understand the new regulations.

Past Tense **began**—change the *i* to *a* instead of adding *ed;* no helping verb

The band **began** to play the national anthem.

Past Participle **begun**—change the *i* to *u* instead of using the basic form with a helping verb; this form also needs a helping verb

By the time we arrived the meeting **had begun.**

Sentences with Two or More Verbs

When a sentence has two or more verbs, generally express them in the same tense.

She **thinks** I **am** a millionaire. [both verbs are present tense]

Mr. Meek **wrote** me a note in which he **said** I **passed** the accounting final. [three verbs in past tense]

For a general truth or something still going on, use the present tense, even if a verb elsewhere in the sentence is past tense.

YES	Mr. Chung **told** us that Tokyo **is** larger than New York City.
NO	Mr. Chung **told** us that Tokyo **was** larger than New York City. [Even though he told us in the past, Tokyo **is** still larger.]
YES	Joan **demonstrated** in Binghamton that our printer **performs** better than any other.
NO	Joan **demonstrated** in Binghamton that our printer **performed** better than any other. [Since our printer still performs better **now**—*performed* (past tense) is wrong.]
YES	What **are** the titles of the books you **borrowed** from the library?
NO	What **were** the titles of the books you **borrowed** from the library? [Although you borrowed the books in the past, the titles are still the same.]

Word Power

If English is your second language, be especially alert to adding *ed* to regular verbs if:

■ The past tense is required: *call, called*

■ *Have, has,* or *had* precedes the verb: *have, has,* or *had called*

REPLAY 31

A. In the blank write the correct form of the verb in parentheses based on the **tense** indicated in parentheses at the end of the sentence. Add a helping verb if necessary.

Example: They (talk) _____talked_____ every day on the telephone last week. (past)

1. He (work) _____ very accurately. (present)

2. The president (need) _____ your decision now. (present)

3. Ms. DeVries (move) _____ to Lakeport. (past)

4. They (sail) _____ to Catalina this week. (*ing* form)

5. The floor is slippery because the custodian (wax) _____ it. (past)

6. Good manners in the workplace (be) _____ essential to success. (present)

7. The world (look) _____ brighter from behind a smile. (present)

8. Dr. Perry (climb) _____ up the ladder to reach the carton. (past)

9. Left of the plate, you (find) _____ an entrée fork and a salad fork. (future)

10. They (want) _____ something they cannot have. (present)

11. She (want) _____ something she cannot have. (present)

12. He (want) _____ something he could not have. (past)

13. She (want) _____ something she cannot have. (future)

14. An employee's appearance (influence) _____ the way he or she is treated. (present)

15. He believes Ms. Oh (select) _____ a business career. (past)

16. Michael (consider) _____ that problem tomorrow. (future)

17. Dennis (consider) _____ that problem now. (*ing* form)

18. I (stay) _____ at that hotel every July. (present)

19. We (watch) _____ television all day. (past)

20. Marketing people (discuss) _____ international sales. (past)

B. Each of the following sentences has a verb error. Cross out the incorrect verb and write the correct form in the blank.

Example: ____has____ We knew that Orlando ~~had~~ a parade every Wednesday year round.

_____ 1. The officer said that obeying traffic laws was necessary for accident prevention.

_____ 2. Seth asked if New York was the biggest city in the USA.

_____ 3. I brought with me the data that you said you needed.

_____ 4. Who were the authors of the books on yesterday's best-seller list? (Hint: Authors haven't changed since yesterday.)

_____ 5. Gary said the old HP 150 color printer was now in Lois's office.

_____ 6. The people meeting in the conference room were former employees of General Motors. (Hint: They haven't died.)

_____ 7. He taught us that rivers flowed into oceans. (They still do.)

_____ 8. We learned that no scientist knew with certainty how the universe originated.

_____ 9. The Chicago Police have not discovered where the $5 million dollars was.

_____ 10. The CEO praised the office staff for having been so efficient. (Hint: The office personnel are still efficient.)

Check your answers on page 448.

Check your answers on page 448.

Word Power

Remember that the word *tense* is used in grammar to mean *time*—to indicate *when*. Look up the word *tense* in your dictionary to see how it is defined as a term of grammar and its other definitions.

READ 32   RECOGNIZING IRREGULAR VERBS

Recognize verbs that might be irregular; look them up in the dictionary to be sure of form or spelling.

Present and Past

The chart on page 138 lists common irregular verbs. The words in Column 1A are the basic forms. Use them alone with *you, I,* or a plural subject. Also use them after the helping verbs *will, shall, would, should, do, did, does, might, may, can,* and *could*—no matter what the subject is.

Common Irregular Verbs

Column 1		Column 2	Column 3
Present	**Present**	**Simple Past** (no helping verb)	**Past Participle** (use helping verb)
A	B		
begin	begins	began	begun
break	breaks	broke	broken
choose	chooses	chose	chosen
do	does	did	done
drink	drinks	drank	drunk
freeze	freezes	froze	frozen
give	gives	gave	given
go	goes	went	gone
hang (suspend)	hangs	hung	hung*
ring	rings	rang	rung
rise	rises	rose	risen
run	runs	ran	run
see	sees	saw	seen
speak	speaks	spoke	spoken
stand	stands	stood	stood
swing	swings	swung	swung
take	takes	took	taken
understand	understands	understood	understood
wear	wears	wore	worn

No Helping Verbs—No s

You drink smoothies too fast. [subject is *you*]

I choose the beach for today's trip. [subject is *I*]

They break easily. [plural pronoun subject]

These **surfers wear** identical clothing. [plural noun subject]

With Helping Verbs

He **would drink** smoothies all day if he could.

He **did choose** me for the competition.

I **should take** the best one.

Ms. Flood **does run** the business.

For present tense, use the verb forms ending with *s*—Column 1B in the chart—with any singular subject except *I* or *you*.

Everybody goes to lunch at the same time. [singular pronoun subject]

Professor Seilo understands the problem. [singular noun subject]

Simple Past

Use Column 2 verbs—the simple past—for past tense with any subject. Do not use a helping verb. (For some verbs, Columns 2 and 3 forms are the same.)

She **ran** away.   The glass **broke.**   The bells **rang.**

Hang meaning a method of putting to death is regular: hang, hangs, hanged.

Past Participle

Use Column 3 forms—past participles—with a helping verb, such as *have, has, had, been, was, were*, and with any subject.

SINGULAR

She has run away.

The **glass had broken.**

PLURAL

They have run away.

The **glasses had broken.**

Word to the Wise

Although the irregular verbs in the preceding table are among the most commonly misused verbs, they aren't the only ones. To avoid incorrect use of irregular verbs, careful writers refer to the dictionary when in doubt.

REPLAY 32

Cross out the incorrect irregular verb and write the correct form in the blank.

Example: _____hung_____ I ~~hanged~~ up all my clothes.

_____ 1. I thought it was broke, but it had just wore out.

_____ 2. He begun to work when the bell rung.

_____ 3. He choose the best one for himself.

_____ 4. He had chose the best one for himself yesterday.

_____ 5. She do all the complaining, and he just stand around.

_____ 6. He had drunk all the tea before the sun had rose.

_____ 7. The children have ate all the fresh strawberries.

_____ 8. We seen that Smith done a good job on the pricing.

_____ 9. They had flew to Taiwan last year.

_____ 10. They went to the convention before she quitted her job.

_____ 11. The child had ran away after he had broke the window.

_____ 12. She had wore the new suit yesterday.

_____ 13. He had gave me a ticket to the luncheon.

_____ 14. I seen him before he had spoke.

_____ 15. I had took it with me before you went away.

_____ 16. They always wears suits to the office.

_____ 17. She seen that file before.

_____ 18. "If a man don't know what port he's steering for, no wind is favorable," said the Roman philosopher Seneca.

_____ 19. David swinged his tennis racket and then flung it down on the ground.

_____ 20. Last week they give him three days to do the job.

Check your answers on page 449.

Check your answers on page 449.

READ 33   DICTIONARY DATA FOR IRREGULARS

The Irregular Verbs chart in Read 32 lists just a few of more than 100 irregular verbs. If English was your principal language during your growing up years, you've probably mastered most irregulars. However, a few of these verbs still cause even native English-speaking adults to hesitate or to use them incorrectly. Since it is not practical to memorize all the irregular verbs, it helps to know how to interpret a verb's "principal parts" in the dictionary.

Principal Parts of a Verb

- **Basic form**—break, see, walk
- **Present participle form**—breaking, seeing, walking
- **Simple past form**—broke, saw, walked
- **Past participle form**—broken, seen, walked

Basic Form Present—the Dictionary Entry

The basic form in the present tense (infinitive without "to") is the dictionary entry for that verb. See Column 1A, Read 32. Column 1B shows the basic form ending in *s*.

Present Participle

The present participle is easy to recognize because it always ends with *ing*. Be aware, however, of other spelling variations.

- Usually the *ing* is simply added to the unchanged basic form: *see, seeing*
- Sometimes, however, a final *e* is omitted before adding *ing*—*love, loving*
- Sometimes a final letter is doubled before adding *ing*—*win, winning*

Simple Past and Past Participle

Regular Verbs (Please place your dictionary beside you now.)

For regular verbs, the simple past and the past participle are the same: just add *ed*—as in earn*ed.* Use the *ed* form of any regular verb either with or without a helping verb. Both *I earned* and *I have earned* are correct, depending on the idea you wish to express.

Irregular Verbs

- **Simple past**—all Column 2 verb forms in the chart that begins Read 32 are simple past. This means use them **without** a helping verb. In the dictionary, the simple past either follows the entry word or follows the *ing* form. Look up *begin* now to see where *began* (the simple past) appears in your dictionary.

- **Past participle**—follows the simple past and could be listed in Column 3 of Read 32. A helping verb **is required**. Notice how *begun* follows *began* in the dictionary.
- **Simple past/past participle**—if only one *past* form appears, that form is *both* simple past *and* past participle. In that case use that form either **with** or **without** a helping verb. Now look up *bring*. You find only one past form: *brought*.
- **Or/also:** If *or* is between two words in the dictionary, either word is correct—although often the meaning or customary usage differs. The word *also* in a dictionary entry means the second word is less acceptable or less often used. Look up *broadcast*. You'll find that the simple past is either *broadcast* or *broadcasted*. Since no other form follows, the same two words are correct for the past participle.
- Now look up *show*. The first form after the entry (or after the *ing* word) is *showed*, meaning it is the simple past—the form to use with no helping verb. Following *showed* is *shown* or *showed*; this means use either one **with** a helping verb. With that particular word, you can't go wrong with *showed*; however, *shown* without a helping verb is wrong.
- Finally, look up *occur*. Notice the double *r* before adding *ed* or *ing*. When you're not certain whether to double the last letter before adding *ed* or *ing* or whether to drop a final *e* before adding *ing*, **look it up.**

Word Power

Memo to the Conscientious but Restless Student

Did you take the necessary few minutes to look up each word suggested in the preceding dictionary-use hints? Did you also refer to the Irregular Verbs chart in Read 32? If you did, you can now use a dictionary competently to get verb information. It's not necessary to memorize hundreds of forms once you become adept at quickly look them up!

REPLAY 33

A. Fill in the blanks with the "principal parts" of these irregular verbs. Consult your dictionary if you're unsure of the correct form.

BASIC VERB	PRESENT PARTICIPLE (*ing* ending)	SIMPLE PAST (no helping verb)	PAST PARTICIPLE (requires helping verb)
Example: beat	beating	beat	beaten or beat
1. be*	_____	_____	_____
2. bite	_____	_____	_____
3. blow	_____	_____	_____
4. come	_____	_____	_____

*Other "parts": *am, are, is*

5. cost   _____   _____   _____

6. fall   _____   _____   _____

7. forget   _____   _____   _____

8. freeze   _____   _____   _____

9. hide   _____   _____   _____

10. lead   _____   _____   _____

11. pay   _____   _____   _____

12. shake   _____   _____   _____

13. sink   _____   _____   _____

14. sing   _____   _____   _____

15. throw   _____   _____   _____

B. Each sentence below has one or more incorrectly used irregular verbs. Make the corrections. When in doubt, consult your dictionary for spelling.

1. Ms. Bogue has beat all records and is wining.
2. Sean payed the bill because the job was done right.
3. Ed has broke two rules and has hid the evidence.
4. Ms. Farrell hanged the picture but had forgot about it.
5. Mr. James could have stood another day if he had wrote to me.

Check your answers on page 449.

READ 34 — IDENTIFYING SUBJECTS AND VERBS

As you learned in Chapter 3, every sentence has at least one **independent clause**; that is, a group of words that includes a subject and verb, and communicates a complete thought.

> **The verb is the *action* or *being* word; the subject is the *noun* or *pronoun* that tells who or what is doing or being.**

A sentence always begins with a capital letter and ends with closing punctuation such as a period or question mark.

> The manual is short.   Have you read it yet?

To find a subject, first find the verb. Then ask "who" or "what" before the verb. The answer is the subject.

> The engineers **study** mathematics. [The verb is *study*. Who studies? The subject is *engineers*.]

If a sentence has more than one independent clause, each clause has its own subject-verb combination.

> Some **students study** and **others daydream**. [Who studies? Students. Who daydreams? Others. The subjects are *students* and *others*; the verbs are *study* and *daydream*.]

Although the subject is usually in front of the verb, sometimes the order is reversed. The order is almost always reversed in questions.

> After 9 a.m. **will be** the best time to call me. [The verb is *will be*; the subject is *time*; *after 9 a.m.* is a prepositional phrase.]

> **Are** six laptops enough? [The verb is *are*; the subject is *laptops*.]

Questions are usually worded in either of two ways:

1. A helping verb precedes the subject, and a main verb follows the subject:

   > **Do** the girls study? [*Do* is the helping verb; *study* is the main verb; *girls* is the subject. You can test this by turning the question into a statement: *The girls do study.*]

2. If a helping verb isn't needed, the verb simply precedes the subject:

   > **Are** the girls smart? [*Are* is the verb; *girls* is the subject; *smart* is an adjective.]

A subject is always a noun or a pronoun; however, it may look like a verb when it names an activity.

> **Studying** is my favorite activity. [*Studying* looks like a verb, but in this sentence it is a noun (naming an activity) and is the subject of the sentence.]

> **To run** would be foolish. [*To run* looks like a verb, but it is a noun (naming an activity); the verb is *would be*.]

The understood *you* may be the subject of a sentence that gives a command or makes a polite request.

> Put a new cartridge in the printer. [The subject *you* is understood; the verb is *put*.]

> Please **call** before Friday. [The subject *you* is understood; the verb is *call*.]

RECAP   Circle the subjects and underline the verbs in these sentences.

1. When you finish the soup, leave the spoon in the plate.

2. Everyone except your brothers was discharged.

3. Lewis and Martin told jokes and sang.

4. Should we tell him the truth?

Check your answers on page 449.

A related word group within a sentence that does not have both a subject and verb may be a phrase or a clause.

> This morning, the receptionist will open the office. [The verb is *will open*. Who will open? The subject is *receptionist*. *This morning* is a phrase.]

Introductory or describing words (phrases) may precede the subject.

> In Schenectady, students study history. [The subject is *students*; the verb is *study*.]

> Ambitious and diligent students study every day. [The subject is *students*; the verb is *study*; *ambitious* and *diligent* are adjectives.]

Sometimes a prepositional phrase separates the subject from the verb. *The subject is never within a prepositional phrase.*

The seminar in Washington, DC begins promptly at nine in the morning. [The verb is *begins.* Who or what *begins*? The subject is *seminar.* The prepositional phrase *in Washington, DC* is not part of the subject.]

Word Power

A **prepositional phrase** begins with a preposition and ends with a noun or pronoun called an **object**. A prepositional phrase never includes a subject-verb combination. Some common prepositions are *in, to, with, by, of,* and *for.* Examples of two- or three-word prepositions are *alongside of, along with, in addition to, as well as.* You can review prepositions and prepositional phrases in Read and Replay 9.

Sometimes one clause "interrupts" another clause; that is, a clause may separate the subject and verb of another clause.

> Alice, who has many skills and talents, is an RN. [The **independent clause** is *Alice is an RN;* the **dependent interrupting clause** is *who has many skills and talents.*]

A compound subject has two or more nouns or pronouns.

> Laziness and irresponsibility impede success. [The compound subject is *laziness and irresponsibility.*]

A compound verb has two or more verbs.

> Robin works and goes to school at night. [The compound verb is *works and goes.*]

REPLAY 34

Underline each verb and circle the subject. If a verb has a helping verb, underline the two or three words making up the "verb phrase." Remember that a sentence may have more than one subject-verb combination or may have a compound subject or verb.

Example: A (company) may issue preferred stock only after (common stock) has been issued.

1. Do you enjoy the sunset?
2. The financial analysts are doing their jobs well.
3. Will she get a salary increase?
4. The clothing you select for the workplace should be appropriate.
5. Ask yourself if your appearance sends a message that will benefit your career.
6. For a professional look, women should limit jewelry to a watch, necklace, earrings, and no more than two rings.
7. According to American-style table manners the diner puts the knife back on the plate, not the table, after he or she cuts a piece of food.
8. However, the knife remains in the diner's right hand in most parts of Europe.

9. Career advancement is more likely for employees who get along well with coworkers, supervisors, and clients or customers.

10. Hard, steady work turns daydreaming into reality.

11. Playing Monopoly is fun.

12. During the past year our sales have risen dramatically.

13. In 1905 former president of the United States Grover Cleveland said, "Sensible and responsible women do not want to vote."

14. Everyone in the shop is working on the blueprints.

15. Xerox made its name as a manufacturer and seller of photocopying equipment.

16. My assistant, who is very efficient, will gladly help you.

17. Would you like my assistant's help next week?

18. Considerable turnover of personnel is prevalent in the fast-food business.

19. Both poverty and riches are a state of mind as well as of pocketbook.

20. Good grammar and correct spelling are important in workplace email.

Check your answers on page 450.

READ 35   MAKING THE SUBJECT AND VERB AGREE

A subject and its verb must agree—if the subject is singular, then use a singular verb; if the subject is plural, use the plural verb form.

Most agreement errors occur when a verb form is used that ends with s when it shouldn't or that does not end with s when it should.

Although most *nouns become plural* by adding s, *verbs become singular* when you add s. It is important not to confuse these two spelling principles.

Singular Subject

Singular subjects, except *you* or *I*, typically add an s to the verb form for the *present tense* and use helping verbs that end in s, such as *is, has,* and *was.*

Singular pronoun subjects:	**He runs** five miles every day.	**It was running** away.
Singular noun subjects:	The **honor means** so much to me.	Your **help has been** vital.

You, I, and plural subjects require a verb that does *not* end with s.

Subjects *you, I*:	**You are** the winner. **I work** across the street.
Plural pronoun subject:	**We ship** widgets everywhere on earth.
Plural noun subject:	**Text messages are** ubiquitous.*

*If you're unfamiliar with *ubiquitous,* look it up.

Compound Subject
Joined by or/nor

If the words in a compound subject are joined by *or* or *nor*, make the verb agree with the noun or pronoun following the *or* or *nor*.

> Martha Jagel or **Petrina Noor has** the key. [singular noun—singular verb ends with *s*]
>
> Christine or the **clerks** usually **sort** the mail. [plural noun—plural verb doesn't end with *s*]
>
> Either Ms. Grover or **I am** holding the winning ticket. [singular pronouns—singular irregular verb]
>
> Neither Mr. Fairley nor the **teachers** left Blairsville. [plural noun—plural irregular verb]

Word Power

Pair *neither* with *nor,* not *or.*

NO   Neither Charles **or** Dolores leaves at 5 p.m.

YES   Neither Charles **nor** Dolores leaves at 5 p.m.

Joined by and

A compound subject joined with *and* is plural and, therefore, requires the verb form without *s.*

> A **report** and a **letter provide** the information.
>
> **Victoria** and **he are** guarding the secrets.

Indefinite Pronouns

For indefinite plural pronoun subjects—*both, many, several, few*—use the verb form without the *s.*

> **Several have** been chosen.
>
> **Few take** advantage of the opportunity.

If *each, every, many, a, an, one, either, neither, another,* or a pronoun ending with *one, body,* or *thing* precedes a subject, the subject is singular and requires the *s* verb.

> **Each man and woman needs** an application form.
>
> **Many an applicant is** denied an interview because of a spelling error.
>
> **Everyone dines** after 9 p.m. in Spain.

Separating Words

When choosing a verb form, ignore words, phrases, or clauses separating a subject from its verb.

> **NO**   The **box** of tools **are** on the table.
>
> **YES**   The **box** of tools **is** on the table.

WHY?   The subject is the singular noun **box.** Therefore, use the singular verb form *is.* Ignore the prepositional phrase *of tools* when choosing the verb.

NO   The **supervisors,** as well as the CEO, **is** here today.

YES   The **supervisors,** as well as the CEO, **are** here today.

WHY?   Ignore the prepositional phrase *as well as the CEO* when deciding on the verb.

RECAP   Circle the correct verb in each of the following sentences.

1. The **reason** for his difficulties seem/seems clear.
2. **Nobody** like/likes this background music.
3. The book and the DVD fit/fits in the same package.
4. **Something** has/have arrived from the printer.
5. The **reasons** his job was difficult seem/seems clear.

Check your answer on page 450.

Introductory Words

In a sentence introduced by *here*, *there*, or *where*, the subject usually *follows* the verb.

NO   There **was** several **boxes** of tools on the table.

YES   There **were** several **boxes** of tools on the table. [Since the subject is the plural noun *boxes*, use the plural verb form *were*.]

NO   Here **comes** my **sisters.**

YES   Here **come** my **sisters** [The plural subject *sisters* requires the plural verb *come*.]

NO   Where**'s** your **sisters?** [The *'s* is a contraction of *where is*; the **singular** verb *is* does not agree with the **plural** subject *sisters*.]

YES   Where **are** your **sisters?** [The verb *are* precedes the subject *sisters*.]

The Pronouns *Who, Which,* and T*hat*

If *who*, *which*, or *that* is a subject, the verb must agree in number (singular or plural) with the word for which the pronoun is substituting.

NO   This is the **man who talk** with you on the phone every day.

YES   This is the **man who talks** with you on the phone every day. [The pronoun *who* is substituting for the singular noun *man*. Therefore, the verb *talks* ends with *s* to agree with *man*.]

NO   These are the **men who talks** with you on the phone every day.

YES   These are the **men who talk** with you on the phone every day.

The Word *Number*

The word *number* is a singular subject if *the* precedes it. If *a* precedes *number*, it is a plural subject.

NO	**The number** of restaurants in this neighborhood **are** growing.
YES	**The number** of restaurants in this neighborhood **is** growing.

NO	**A number** of books **has** been written on that subject.
YES	**A number** of books **have** been written on that subject.

Subjects That Go Either Way

Subjects referring to "parts"—the words *all, none, any, more, most, some,* and a fraction or a percentage—may be singular OR plural depending on whether they refer to a plural or singular word.

Singular	**All** of **it is** lost. [Use singular verb *is* because *it* is singular.]
Plural	**All** of **them are** happy. [Use plural verb *are* because *them* is plural.]

Here's a helpful trick to determine whether "part" subjects are singular or plural: If the item referred to can be counted, it's plural; otherwise, it's singular.

Singular	At least **10 percent** of the **applesauce has** been eaten. [Applesauce can't be counted.]
Plural	**Half** the **apples are** in the refrigerator. [Apples can be counted.]

Writing for Your Career

Contractions of subject/verb create one word. These are so common in speech that you needn't think twice about agreement. What about contractions in workplace writing? Are they acceptable?

NO: Avoid contractions, in legal and other formal documents, such as important business letters. Also, do not use *would* or *should* contractions (such as *I'd* for *I would* or *I should*) in workplace writing, although these contractions are fine in speech.

> **We'd** be pleased if **you'd** join us. [OK for conversation or informal email.]

> **We would** be pleased if you would join us. [Preferred in more formal workplace writing.]

YES: Use contractions in informal workplace writing; they sound concise and friendly. For that reason, this includes some business letters.

> **I'm** going to send you the information right away.

> **We're** always here to help you.

> **He's** an auditor.

> **You'll** always be welcome here.

> **We've** shipped the widgets.

> **It's** a good buy.

> **Here's** the document you requested.

REPLAY 35

Decide whether the subjects and verbs agree in the following sentences. Draw a line through incorrect verbs and write the correct form in the blank. If the verb agrees with the subject, write **C** for *correct* in the blank.

_____ 1. Every one of the passengers were waiting in line quietly.

_____ 2. Neither of your responses seem satisfactory.

_____ 3. The report and the letter was on my desk.

_____ 4. Either the report or the letter was on my desk.

_____ 5. Neither the report nor the letter were on my desk.

_____ 6. Both Richard's story and Alicia's reasons seem valid.

_____ 7. Neither Richard's story nor Alicia's reasons seems true.

_____ 8. Every battery, radio, and antenna are missing.

_____ 9. Everything that was in the garages are gone.

_____ 10. Many a quotation have been memorized and then forgotten.

_____ 11. About half the papers is gone from the file.

_____ 12. All employees except the manager rides the elevator.

_____ 13. Any one of us is willing to help with the report.

_____ 14. A number of members are able to contribute to the fund.

_____ 15. When in Sweden, don't touch your drink until the host says "skoal."

_____ 16. Only one of the books have been translated into French.

_____ 17. Half the peach pies has been eaten.

_____ 18. The number of books translated into French are small.

_____ 19. She don't want to go to the workshop.

_____ 20. There was several people waiting for the tickets.

_____ 21. The latest figures on yesterday's sale is available.

_____ 22. Each report and letter are on my desk.

_____ 23. A report on the accounts have been completed.

_____ 24. Close friends often greets each other with a hug.

_____ 25. Each of the countries have distinct cultural characteristics.

_____ 26. Neither he nor his assistant pack the items carefully.

_____ 27. Here's the software you ordered.

_____ 28. "We like to meet you when you visit Chicago," he wrote.

_____ 29. Michelle and her aide, who drive in from Kenansville, leaves early.

_____ 30. He usually do his work carefully.

_____ 31. The new copier don't work well.

———————— 32. My cousin, as well as a number of my aunts and uncles, work here.

———————— 33. Neither the attorney nor the paralegal are able to be here.

———————— 34. There goes the new models down the runway.

———————— 35. Another batch of envelopes have arrived incorrectly addressed.

Check your answers on pages 450–451.

READ 36   IF I WERE ...

We've all indulged in fantasies about what we would do if we were someone else or if conditions were enormously different from our present reality. The English language provides a special verb form for the unreal—that is, to express ideas contrary to reality.

Use this special form—*were*—principally when the subject follows *if* or *wish*.

We ordinarily use *was*, *is*, or other verb forms ending with *s* when the subject is a singular noun or a singular pronoun.

Use *were* regardless of what the subject is if the statement is contrary to reality.

Continue to use *was* or *is* if the statement is true or **might** be true (except, of course, with *you* or *I*).

ORDINARY OR MIGHT BE TRUE	CONTRARY TO REALITY
I was not at home Monday.	If *I were* you, I would stay at home on Mondays. [I can't be you.]
Everyone is going to the meeting.	If *everyone were* to go to the meeting, who would mind the store? [Everyone *won't* go.]
He was staring at the princess, but he is not a prince.	Peter wishes that he *were* a prince. [His parents are not king and queen.]
I was a millionaire last year.	If I *were* a millionaire, I would buy a 22-carat diamond for you at Tiffany's. [Guess what? I am not a millionaire.]

REPLAY 36

Draw a line through incorrect verbs and write the correct form in the blank. If the sentence is already correct, write **C** in the blank.

———————— 1. If you was ready to take the final, you would not need a tutor.

———————— 2. If I were not sure of how to get there, I wouldn't give you directions.

———————— 3. If he was a better writer, we would offer him the job.

———————— 4. Because she was ill so often last year, she couldn't complete her work.

_____ 5. I wish I was your secretary instead of your husband.

_____ 6. He was a millionaire who spent his money to help the poor.

_____ 7. I wish I was a millionaire.

_____ 8. When I were your assistant, your office weren't in this building.

_____ 9. Cinderella wishes that she was a princess.

_____ 10. We wish the apple tree was healthy, but it never will be.

Check your answers on page 451.

Word Power

Arithmetic Problem:

　2 plus 2 _is_ 4, but 2 and 2 _are_ 4, and 2 times 2 _is_ 4.

　I don't know why; that's just the way it is . . . are?

READ 37　AGREEMENT WITH COLLECTIVE NOUNS

Collective nouns are words like _club, herd, staff, management, family, class, faculty, company, committee, crowd, jury,_ and names of organizations. A collective noun is like a single package containing several items. When you refer to the entire "package," the collective noun is thought of as a single unit. If the package is broken up into its parts, you consider the items separately—resulting in ordinary plural nouns.

If a collective noun acting as a single unit is a subject, use a singular verb—the one ending with _s_—for the present tense or for a helping verb.

> **NO**　The **faculty are** meeting in Room 406.
>
> **YES**　The **faculty is** meeting in Room 406. [_Faculty_ is a collective noun acting as a unit and, therefore, singular.]
>
> 　　　The **members** of the faculty _are_ meeting in Room 406. [A plural verb is correct with the plural subject _members; of the faculty_ is a prepositional phrase and cannot include a subject.]
>
> 　　　The **teachers are** meeting in Room 406. [_Teachers_ is a plural subject.]
>
> **NO**　**Macy's have** many employees. [Organizations are always singular.]
>
> **YES**　**Macy's has** many employees.

If the members of a collective noun act as separate individuals or disagree, use a plural verb.

> **NO**　The **faculty disagrees** about the new grading policy.
>
> **YES**　The **faculty disagree** about the new grading policy. [If members disagree, they are not acting as a unit.]

Sometimes the grammatically correct way just doesn't sound right. In that case, change the wording of the sentence so that it is both grammatically correct *and* sounds right.

NO	The **jury goes** home every weekend. [Twelve people go off in different directions to different homes. They don't act as one.]
CORRECT	The **jury go** home every weekend. [Collective noun is plural, thus requiring the plural verb *go*. Singular would be *goes*. However, the sentence just sounds wrong.]
YES	The **jurors go** home every weekend. [Subject is now *jurors*, a plural noun requiring the plural verb form—*go*.]
OR	The **jury members go** home every weekend.

Writing for Your Career

Collective noun principles are more important in business and professional writing than in speech. If in doubt about whether a collective noun is singular or plural, just rephrase the sentence.

Note: If you are a native speaker of British English, you'll find that collective noun principles of British English differ from those of American English.

REPLAY 37

Draw a line through incorrect verbs and write the correct form in the blank; don't change the rest of the sentence. Write **C** for correct in two blanks. Review Read and Replay 35 now so that you'll find two pronoun errors below.

—————— 1. The members of my family takes separate vacations each year.

—————— 2. At noon today my family piles into the truck, leaves the old homestead, and heads for Anchorage, Alaska.

—————— 3. Wong & Lopez, Inc., have their offices at 10 Park Avenue.

—————— 4. Hiteki Corp. also need new headquarters.

—————— 5. Several groups was invited to the meeting.

—————— 6. For years J. C. Penney stores was called The Golden Rule Stores.

—————— 7. The Senate favor new tax laws.

—————— 8. The company was warned by the fire chief to clear the aisles.

—————— 9. The Social Services Department are submitting their applications.

—————— 10. This class work quietly.

Check your answers on page 451; then take the Pop Quiz on page 304.

CONCEPT REVIEW & SKILL-BUILDING APPLICATIONS

Checkpoint

In the 1600s mathematician and grammarian John Willis was disturbed to discover that *shall* and *will* had about the same meaning. He worked out a plan to give them different meanings, and defenseless students have suffered ever since.

If you studied grammar in the past, you may wonder how you made it through a verb chapter without *will/shall–would/should*. Well, the simple truth is that our ever-changing language makes this instruction unnecessary. Some people who use British English still distinguish between these pairs of words. Other equally careful writers and speakers in business, politics, and the media now ignore these rules dating back to Mr. Willis. Only currently required verb principles are included in this chapter.

Repeat the correct forms aloud until they sound natural. For example, perhaps you noted a principle you've been careless about following before. Practice saying (to yourself) "If I *were* you" several times a day. Then, try saying (to yourself) "If I *was* you" and you'll find it no longer sounds correct.

The three most serious common verb errors follow. If you make errors like these, hurry to acquire the habit of using Standard English verbs.

1. Using the present verb form when the past is needed

   Yesterday Ms. Wong talk to the business class about being flexible on the job. [should be *talked*]

2. Not adding *s* to a verb when it is needed—or adding *s* when it should not be there

   Ms. Hoover always explain the business English principles carefully. [For present tense, use *explains*; for past, use *explained*.]

   Professors Johnson and Ward teaches in Washington. [The verb should be *teach* or *taught*, depending on the meaning intended.]

3. Using the simple past with a helping verb or the past participle without a helping verb

   He had wore that same shirt yesterday. [The verb should be *worn* OR He wore that same shirt yesterday.]

   I know he done a good job because I seen it. [Use *did* and *saw*, or use helping verbs before *done* and *seen*.]

Special Assignment

A. Compose sentences with any **singular subjects** except *you* or *I*. Use the present tense form of the verbs.

Example: beat   **She beats** her husband regularly at tennis.

1. go _____

2. drive _____

3. see _____

B. Compose sentences using the *ing* form of these verbs; use them as **verbs, not adjectives or nouns.**

Examples: dance   **YES**   My husband is dancing. [*Dancing* is a verb.]

   NO   My hobby is dancing. [*Dancing* is a noun.]

   NO   My husband attends dancing school. [*Dancing* is an adjective.]

1. run _____

2. rise _____

3. raise _____

C. Compose sentences using these verbs to show past tense **without a helping verb**.

Example: talk   He **talked** on the phone for an hour.

1. win _____

2. sing _____

3. quit _____

D. Compose sentences using these verbs to show past tense **with a helping verb.**

Example: drink   The guests **had drunk** the last glass of punch before the party ended.

1. hide _____

2. pay _____

3. be _____

E. Compose sentences showing the present tense of these verbs with a plural subject. **Be sure to use the words as verbs.**

Example: give   **They give** shoe polish with all shoe purchases.

1. cost _____

2. ship _____

3. produce _____

Date to submit this assignment: _____

F. Solve an Action-Word Puzzle.

Across

   1. Simple past and past participle of *catch*

Down

   1. Past participle of *choose*

   2. Form of *have* for use with *he, she,* or *it*

5. Past participle of *sing*
6. Simple past and past participle of *lose*
7. Adjective meaning *uncooked*
10. Past participle of *run*
11. Antonym of *down*
13. Past participle of *see*
14. Simple past and past participle of *put*
16. Simple past of *ring*
18. Simple past and past participle of *need*
21. Singular masculine subject pronoun
22. Past participle of *be*
25. Form of *beat* with singular masculine pronoun subject (present tense)
27. Past tense of *seal*
28. Two guys named Ed
30. Coordinating conjunction; somewhat informal for business writing
31. Simple past tense of *feel*
34. They do it to your groceries at the register
35. Past participle of *swim*
36. Simple past tense of *do*

3. Present tense of *went*
4. Simple past tense of *tear*
8. Simple past tense of *an*
9. Present participle of *tune*
10. Present tense of *run*
12. Past participle of *put*
15. "To _____ or not to _____," wrote Shakespeare
17. To grow older
19. Past participle of *do*
20. Present form of *do* with a singular noun subject
21. Doing Recaps and Replays are good ones
23. Verb meaning to show agreement silently
24. Present tense of *be* with *she* as the subject
26. Present tense of *be* with *you* as the subject
29. Past participle of *dig*
30. Simple past of *see*
32. Past tense of *lead*
33. Present tense of *be* with *I* as the subject

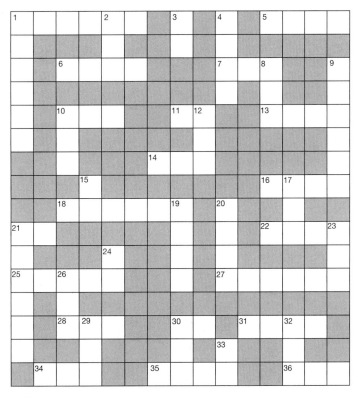

Date to submit this assignment: _____

Proofreading for Careers

A. Please save the English language by undoing these atrocities to verbs:

1. It don't seem right. _____
2. If you had wrote, he would of answered. _____
3. He done the work. _____
4. We seen her yesterday. _____
5. He ain't goin'. _____

B. Correct spelling, capitalization, pronoun, sentence completeness, and subject-verb errors in this article. Do not make changes other than correcting specific errors just mentioned. Glide your pen or pointing finger below each line as you proofread and correct the letter. Never let written material leave your desk without careful proof-reading.

A Financial Healthcare Plan

Maintaining financial solvency doesn't just happen; it takes careful planning. Here is some tip's to help you stay financially healthy:

■ Practice delayed gratification—put off buying today what you can do without until you has more money.

■ When you need to make a majer purchase, save for them instead of using credit.

■ when you have to by, be a bargain hunter and comparison shopper.

■ If you shop to fill the time or as a relaxing leisure activity. Get involved in a hobby, do volunteer work, or make up a list of free activities (like taking a walk, exercising, playing games, fixing things, cooking) that you can do instead.

■ Don't make money a source of worry and irritation. focus on what you have, not what you don't have. A positive attitude toward money free your mind to handle it constructively and create opportunities for financial improvement.

■ Learn about investments, assume that this information will be a necessity in your financial future.

■ Have financial goals. Don't assume that you will automatically get better job's and higher salaries or that you will "grow into" the habit of saving. Financial goals helps you identify and stay focused on what you needs to do to achieve it.

How did you do? Excellent _____   Good _____   Need More Practice _____

Practice Quiz

Circle the correct answer. Refer to your dictionary when in doubt.

1. Ms. Nixon explained that many more people (live/lived) in Torrance now.
2. The people of this country (believe/believes) it can be done.
3. If I (was/were) not certain how to get there, I wouldn't give you directions.
4. Mr. Sedirko has (chose/chosen) three people to take deposition notes.
5. The film industry (employ/employs) many extras for walk-on parts.
6. At present 3,800 extras (is/are/be) on the payroll of this film.
7. If I (were/was) you, I would take advantage of this opportunity.
8. Robert Ball, as well as all his aides, (deserve/deserves) a raise.
9. Neither the engineer nor the designer (is/are) here.
10. The costs of salaries and travel expenses (have/has) been determined.
11. Ms. Timm told me that I (did/done) the right thing in Monterey.
12. I wish that the new plans for San Antonio College (was/were) ready.
13. You have (broke/broken) one of the rules.
14. Neither the banker nor the lawyer (is/are/be) in Alabama.
15. Each girl and boy (is/are/be) doing well.
16. One-third of the pies (have/has) been sold.
17. Accuracy in figures (mark/marks) the expert accountant.
18. She is the only one of the attorneys who (do/does) the research.
19. They (sunk/sank) the ship.
20. The Bureau of Mines (is/are) now preparing to transfer its offices.
21. Rosenberg & McNeil, Inc., (insist/insists) on prompt shipments.
22. The Hartford City Council (were/was) disappointed in the results.
23. The committee (have/has) been unable to agree on the agenda.
24. The senior class (arrive/arrives) an hour before the graduation ceremony.

Self-Study Practice and Tutorials

Vocabulary and Spelling for Careers
For additional practice go to Appendix B, page 321.

Replay Drills
For additional practice go to Appendix C, page 379.

Companion Web Site: www.prenhall.com/smith
Go to the companion Web site to test your knowledge on self-grading quizzes and for links to other helpful online resources.

MyWritingLab
Use this online learning system for an assessment of your progress on topics covered in this chapter and progressive exercises that fit your individual needs.

8 Mastering Adjectives and Adverbs

After completing Chapter 8, you will be able to do the following:

- Explain the difference between adjectives and adverbs, and use them correctly.
- List pointing adjectives and articles, and use them correctly.
- Use correct forms of adjectives and adverbs to express comparisons.

READ 38 MORE ABOUT THE MODIFIERS

Adjectives and adverbs are "modifiers"; that is, they tell about, describe, tell how many, or add special meaning to other words.

Adjectives and adverbs are more fun than pronouns and verbs. They add precision, character, liveliness, and color to our language. Imagine how dull our language would be without adjectives and adverbs like *generous, happily, stingy, cheerfully, prudish, confidently, weaker, meaner, strictest, domineering, shabby, purple,* and *most comfortable*. Now imagine how vague our language would be without adjectives like *several, those, fifth, often, sometimes,* or even the little word *the*.

Communication is difficult at best; we often misunderstand one another. Skillful communicators draw from a wealth of adjectives and adverbs, using those that most effectively communicate the shade of meaning desired. In Chapter 8, you will review Standard English principles for adjectives and adverbs.

Adjectives tell something about—or *modify*—nouns and pronouns. The four kinds of adjectives are **pointing, describing** and **limiting adjectives,** and **articles.** Limiting adjectives, which describe "how many" (*three* children, *few* people) are explained in Read 8. Since they are usually used correctly, they are not covered again in this section.

Adverbs tell something about—or *modify*—verbs, adjectives, and other adverbs. Many adverbs are formed by adding *ly* to adjectives; for example, *peaceful* is an adjective and *peacefully* is an adverb. Other adverbs, however, are totally different from adjectives—words such as *well, often,* or *sometimes*.

Writing for Your Career

The adverb *very*—a word that is used to show intensity—is probably the most overused adverb in our language. If an intensifying word is used too much, it loses its power. William Allen White, famous journalist and writer from the early 1900s, was editor of the *Emporia Gazette*, a well-written Kansas newspaper. To discourage the staff from overuse of *very*, he sent them this memorandum: "If you feel you must write 'very,' write 'damn.'"

Since the copy desk had instructions to delete reporters' profanity, the writing style of the newspaper was improved: "It was a very fine victory" was written "It was a damn fine victory," and was printed, "It was a fine victory."

The Pointing Adjectives

When *this, that, these,* or *those* precede a noun, they are called **pointing adjectives**; otherwise they are pronouns. Here are the only pointers—or tips—you need for *pointing* adjectives:

> **This** soup is mine. [*This* is a pointing adjective; *soup* is a noun.]

> **This** is mine. [*This* is a pronoun.]

Use *this* and *that* as adjectives pointing to singular nouns.

> **This kind** of spice is too hot for **that type** of soup.

Use *these* and *those* as adjectives pointing to plural nouns.

NO	**Those kind** of spices are hot.
YES	**Those kinds** of spices are hot.

NO	Will **these type** of homes sell in those neighborhoods?
YES	Will **these types** of homes sell in those neighborhoods?

Incorrect	Those kind of roofs are fireproof.
OK but Awkward	Those kinds of roofs are fireproof.
Improved	That kind of roof is fireproof. OR Those roofs are fireproof.

When you use the phrase **this kind of**, avoid an unnecessary *a* or *an* after *kind of* (or *type of/sort of*).

NO	This kind of a house . . .
YES	This kind of house . . .

Never use ***them*** as a pointing adjective; it is a pronoun only.

NO	I plan to give them boys a million dollars.
YES	I plan to give those (or these) boys a million dollars. OR
	I plan to give them a million dollars. [*Them* is correct as a pronoun.]

NEVER use the following expressions: *this here, that there,* and *them there.*

You probably don't write those expressions. If, however, you might **say** them, ask a friend or an instructor to help you break the habit.

NO	This here is my office.
YES	This is my office.

NO	That there phone is out of order.
YES	That phone is out of order.

NO	Them there books should be stored in the basement.
YES	Those books should be stored in the basement.

Writing for Your Career

If a singular pointing adjective makes sense, avoid the plural construction. Instead of *these kinds* or *those kinds, types,* or *sorts,* use *this* or *that kind, type,* or *sort*—or omit *kind, type,* or *sort.* For example, *This kind of book . . .* OR *This book . . .* INSTEAD OF *These kinds of books.*

REPLAY 38

Correct the following sentences.

Example: These kind~s~ of dogs can be vicious.

1. Professor Stagnaro ordered those kind of PC bookcase.

2. Them books should be returned to the library.

3. If you are not careful, these type of errors will occur frequently.

4. Those sort of books are extremely interesting.

5. I don't like those type of people.

6. He wants to buy this here book.

7. Please give that there calculator to Michelle Miller of Milwaukee.

8. Ask them there people to do the work themselves.

9. That there is the way the cookie crumbles.

10. That kind of an advertisement doesn't attract our customers.

Check your answers on page 451.

READ 39 — THE ARTICLES—THREE LITTLE WORDS

Another kind of adjective is the *article*. **The**, **a**, and **an** are the only three articles.

The is a "definite" article because it makes the noun following it *definite*—that is, *specific*. A and an are "indefinite" articles.

Notice the difference in meaning between "the book" and "a book" or between "the apple" and "an apple."

Fine Points of Article Usage

Using articles is something we take for granted—they occur constantly in English, and it might seem odd that there is any need to study their usage. However, for those who speak English as their second language, when to use articles and when to omit them is not always clear. Look at these two sentences:

We are going to school today.　**BUT**　We are going to *the* office today.

Why don't we use *the* before *school* in the first sentence? Why do we use *the* before *office* in the second sentence? These choices "sound right" to a native of an English-speaking country, but no simple rule governs them. Differences even occur between British English and American English:

BRITISH　She is in hospital.
　BUT
AMERICAN　She is in *the* hospital.

If you're learning English now, the solution is to read English a great deal; listen to the radio, watch TV and films; and ask coworkers, teachers, and friends to correct you. Your brain will gradually develop a sense of what "sounds right."

One use of articles, however, can be a problem even for native-born speakers of English—the two little words *a* and *an*. Some people use *a* almost exclusively and rarely use *an* when it's needed. However, non-Standard English use of *a* and *an* is noticeable in workplace communication.

The rules that determine the use of *a* or *an* are quite simple. Not everyone needs to study them because many people automatically use these words correctly. The following Recap is a pretest to determine whether you need to study all, some, or none of the rules that follow.

RECAP	Write *a* or *an* in the blank before each word. Choose what comes to you immediately. Don't stop to think about it.

Example: __a__ $10 bill

1. _____ addition
2. _____ carrot
3. _____ egg
4. _____ apple
5. _____ giant
6. _____ honor
7. _____ heater
8. _____ $11 gift
9. _____ hand
10. _____ one-day sale
11. _____ manager
12. _____ onion
13. _____ owl
14. _____ uncle
15. _____ Englishman
16. _____ heir
17. _____ island
18. _____ European
19. _____ IBM office
20. _____ CIA report
21. _____ UN member
22. _____ 2 percent tax
23. _____ X-ray
24. _____ unknown admirer

Check your answers on page 451.

If your answers for the preceding Recap are correct, just go directly to the next Replay. If some of your answers are incorrect, study "Managing *a* and *an*," and refer to the information as a reference when you're writing.

Managing a *and* an

Use of *a* or *an* depends on the **sound** of the word following *a* or *an*, not necessarily the written letter with which the word begins.

> **If a word following *a* or *an* begins with a vowel sound (the sound of *a, e, i, o,* or *u*) use *an*. Otherwise use *a*.**

an apple   an egg roll   an illness   an owner   an uncle   an honor

a 10 percent raise [*t* sound]   a hot rod   a bookkeeper   a puzzle   a uniform

Some words begin with a vowel but have a consonant (all letters other than *a, e, i, o, u*) sound; they require *a*, not *an*.

For example, the *u* in *union* sounds like the consonant *y* in *you*: **a u**nion, **a u**niform, **a eu**logy, and so on. Also the *o* in *one* sounds just like the consonant *w* in *winner*: **a** one-cent stamp.

***H* beginning a word is sometimes silent. For such words, use *an*.**

The first sound of *honor* is *o*, a vowel sound: **an** honor, **an** honest person, **an** herb (pronounced "urb") garden. (In British English the *h* in herb is pronounced, so **a** *herb* would be correct.)

When using a letter of the alphabet alone or as part of an abbreviation, the letter is preceded by *a* or *an*, depending on the *sound*.

USE *AN*   an A, an E, an F, an H, an I, an L, an M, an N, an O, an R, an S, an X
USE *A*   a B, a C, a D, a G, a J, a K, a P, a Q, a T, a U, a V, a W, a Y, a Z

He needs **an FBI** report for **a CIA** officer.

Write **a T** or **an F** in each blank.

Abbreviations pronounced as words instead of individual letters are called *acronyms*, such as NASA*, pronounced *nas'uh*.

He was **a NASA** employee and **an NAACP** member.

Word to the Wise

Use **a** before a consonant **sound. Consonants are all letters except** *a, e, i, o, u.*
Use **an** before a vowel **sound. Vowels are** *a, e, i, o, u.*
Remember, it is the **sound** that matters, not the actual letter.

REPLAY 39

Write *a* or *an* in each blank.

Example: ___A___ pessimist sees the difficulty in ___an___ opportunity. ___An___ optimist sees the opportunity in ___a___ difficulty.

1. Jan Hinkle was given _____ one-day unpaid leave of absence and _____ eight-day paid vacation.

2. _____ union member took _____ overnight flight to attend _____ important meeting.

3. It is _____ unusual combination to be _____ CFP and _____ MD.

4. They left for _____ meeting in Pasadena about _____ hour ago.

5. _____ thesaurus is _____ invaluable tool for writers.

---

*If you're unsure of what any of the abbreviations and the acronym (NASA) mean, look them up in your dictionary now.

6. _____ X ray was needed to determine whether there was _____ injury.

7. _____ UNICEF* representative and _____ NATO* representative were seated next to each other at _____ UN* meeting.

8. _____ yes or _____ no in Japanese doesn't always mean what _____ American thinks it means—because of aspects of Japanese culture differing from American culture.

9. Each time he received _____ B on _____ report card, he was given _____ $11 gift.

10. He walked down _____ hall to get _____ history book for _____ honest man.

11. _____ heir expected to inherit _____ one-million-dollar home.

12. His sister, _____ heiress, was not _____ honorable woman.

13. _____ uncle of mine planted _____ herb garden. (say _herb_ as _erb_)

14. After receiving _____ AA degree, he earned _____ BA in sociology.

15. _____ European executive was _____ CEO in _____ American firm.

Check your answers on page 452.

READ 40 DOUBLE NEGATIVES—A BIG NO-NO

Adjectives and adverbs such as _no, any_, and _none_ are of great use in the English language, but they also are the cause of one of the most serious and embarrassing errors in the English language: the double negative.

When two negative words express one negative idea, the result is a double negative.

While two negative words to express a single negative idea does not really affect your listener's or reader's ability to understand, it does affect the reaction you get. If a child says, "I don't want no broccoli," you know the child doesn't want any broccoli. If your employer asks you what time it is and you reply, "I don't got no watch," she will certainly understand what you mean. BUT, she will be reluctant to involve you in written or oral communications with the public. In fact, using double negatives usually prevents applicants from being hired for better jobs.

It isn't important to identify which negative words are adverbs and which are adjectives. Just remember that two negatives shouldn't be combined to express one negative idea.

Here are examples of negative words that should not be combined:

no	none	doesn't	aren't	never	shouldn't
not	nowhere	won't	wouldn't	scarcely	neither
nobody	can't	couldn't	don't	haven't	hardly

Here is an example of what can happen when double negatives get in the way of communication: A student showed his teacher a punctuation quiz before turning it in.

---

*Pronounce acronyms UNICEF and NATO as words—_unisef_ and _naytoe_. Pronounce the abbreviation UN as two separate letters.

"I didn't put no comma there," he said, pointing to one of the sentences. Trying to save him from the horrors of a life of double negatives, the teacher said, "I didn't put *any* comma there, Joe." He replied, "Oh, good, you did<u>n't</u> put <u>none</u> there <u>neither</u>," thus increasing his original double negative to a triple.

If you suspect you use double (or even triple) negatives, kick the habit by asking an instructor or a friend to tell you privately when you say or write them.

REPLAY 40

Correct these sentences so that they conform to Standard English. Cross out the incorrect double negatives and write the correct words in the blank. Write **C** next to the two sentences that are already correct.

_____ 1. I scarcely never do that.

_____ 2. I never said nothing about it to nobody.

_____ 3. Don't put none over there as it might spill.

_____ 4. He won't eat no more pizza if he goes to Afghanistan.

_____ 5. If you have a negative attitude, you won't succeed.

_____ 6. He doesn't know nothing about chemistry.

_____ 7. Taylor won't go nowhere with me on Saturday.

_____ 8. You don't pass no serving dishes during a meal in China.

_____ 9. In China you reach for food with your chopsticks.

_____ 10. She hasn't gone nowhere yet.

_____ 11. You couldn't hardly expect Mr. Blank to join that organization.

_____ 12. You can't win no friends that way.

Check your answers on page 452; then take the Pop Quiz on page 306.

READ 41   THREE DEGREES OF COMPARISON

Degrees of comparison are an important aspect of the correct use of adjectives. Children say sentences such as "Mine is the goodest of all." Very soon, however, they learn to say "best." It just happens naturally from imitating their elders. Using the correct comparative form for most adjectives comes naturally as we speak Standard English the way we hear it spoken. However, certain adjective and adverb comparative forms still cause even Standard English speakers some problems.

Making Comparisons

Descriptive adjectives change form to show comparison. In grammar these forms are called **degrees—positive, comparative,** and **superlative.**

> The positive form of descriptive adjectives does not change; the comparative and superlative degrees are used for comparisons by adding *er/est, more/most,* or *less/least.*

He is **strong.** [positive]

He is the **stronger** of the two. [comparative]

He is the **strongest** of them all. [superlative]

Positive Degree—for One

Positive degree adjectives describe, or modify, a noun or pronoun *without making a comparison.*

old   young   happy   valuable   modern   affluent

The queen's jewels are **old.** [*old* modifies the noun *jewels*]

They are **valuable.** [*valuable* modifies the pronoun *they*]

Comparative Degree—for Two

Comparative degree adjectives compare two nouns or pronouns.

To make an adjective comparative, either add *er* to the end of the word or use *more* or *less* before the adjective.

older
younger
happier
more valuable
less modern
more affluent

Jean is the **younger** of the two sisters, but Marian's life is **happier.** [Two sisters are compared.]

That building is **older** than the one on Vine Street, but the plumbing is **more modern**. [Two buildings and the plumbing in the two buildings are compared.]

Superlative Degree—for Three or More

Superlative degree adjectives compare three or more nouns or pronouns.

To make an adjective superlative, add *est* to the end of the word, or use *most* or *least* before the adjective.

oldest
youngest
happiest
smartest
most valuable
least modern
most affluent
most careful

Melvin is the **youngest** of the three sons, and he is also the **most affluent**.

It was the **happiest** day of my life when you gave me your **most valuable** diamond. [You had three or more diamonds.]

RECAP   Underline the correct answer.

1. Who is (wisest/wiser), the judge, the minister, or the professor?
2. Who is (wisest/wiser), the judge or the minister?

Check your answers on page 452.

How Many Syllables?

To distinguish between words that add *er/est* and those that require *more/most* or *less/least*, focus on how many syllables are in the word.

One-Syllable Words

Add *er* or *est:* big, bigger, biggest   smart, smarter, smartest

Two-Syllable Words—Ending with Y

If the word ends with *y*, such as *easy*, change the *y* to *i* and add *er* or *est—easier, easiest*.

Two- or More-Syllable Words—Not Ending with Y

For words with two or more syllables that don't end with *y*, such as *careful* or *beautiful*, use *more/most* or *less/least*; for example, more or most careful, less or least beautiful, more/most or less/least important.

Avoid Double Comparatives and Superlatives

NEVER use *more, most, less,* or *least* before a modifier that ends with *er* or *est.*

NO	The problem was **more easy** to solve than I expected. [bad comparative]
YES	That problem was **easier** to solve than I expected.
NO	He is the **most laziest** child I've ever seen. [bad double superlative]
YES	He is the **laziest** child I've ever seen.
NO	I am **more carefuler** than anyone else. [bad double comparative]
YES	I am **more careful** than anyone else.
NO	Mine is **more better** than hers. [bad comparative]
YES	Mine is **better** than hers.

Word to the Wise

Avoid the comparative *more* or the superlative *most* before words like *unique* or *perfect*. These are examples of **absolute adjectives**—there are no degrees of comparison. *Unique* means *one of a kind*; therefore, it isn't logical to say something is *more* unique or *the most* unique. In the same way, *perfect* means no imperfections; therefore *more* or *the most* perfect do not make sense.

Irregular Adjectives

Some adjectives have comparative and superlative forms that differ from those just reviewed. In the dictionary, the entry word for an adjective is usually in the positive degree. Next to it you will find the irregular forms for that adjective. For example, look up the adjective *bad* right now. Next to it, instead of *badder* and *baddest,* you find *worse*, which is the comparative form, and then the superlative, *worst*, in that order.* Some other irregular adjectives are *far, ill, good,* and *many*.

REPLAY 41

A. Look up these irregular adjectives in the dictionary and fill in the blanks. You'll find the comparative and superlative forms next to the positive, which is the entry word.

Example: many ___more___ ___most___

	Comparative	Superlative
1. far	_____ or _____	_____ or _____
2. bad	_____	_____
3. little	_____ or _____	_____ or _____
4. much	_____	_____
5. good	_____	_____

B. Cross out the incorrect adjective and write the correction in the blank where necessary. In some cases you need only delete a word. Write **C** beside the only correct sentence.

Example: ___more___ This lot is the ~~most~~ valuable of the two we saw today.

_____ 1. The most safest neighborhoods are more expensive.

_____ 2. Of the two reports, his is the worst.

_____ 3. He is the younger of the two brothers.

_____ 4. He is the older of the three brothers.

---

*In newer college dictionaries, *badder* and *baddest* are somewhere in the *bad* entry with the usage label *slang* along with the definition.

_____ 5. When the figures of the two accountants were compared, the controller found Mr. Higgins' work to be best.

_____ 6. This new alloy is more heavy than any other metal.

_____ 7. This file contains recenter information than that one.

_____ 8. If you use our detergent and brand X, which one will give you the brightest wash?

_____ 9. He's more friendlier than the other sales manager.

_____ 10. When you examine the two diagrams, you discover that the one on the right is biggest.

Check your answers on page 452.

Writing for Your Career

Instead of writing *less* or *least* before an adverb or adjective, you can sometimes choose an antonym (a word that means the opposite of the adverb or adjective). For example, you could replace *less easily, less easy,* or *least easy* with *harder* or *hardest* or *more/most difficult.* Choosing an antonym can liven up your writing and make it more precise.

READ 42   AN ADJECTIVE OR AN ADVERB?

Words change from adjective to adverb, depending on what they modify.

We add *ly* to many adjectives to form adverbs. For example, adding *ly* to the adjective *occasional* results in the adverb *occasionally.* The information that follows enables you to avoid some common adverb and adjective errors.

Recognizing Adjectives and Adverbs

Most (but not all) words ending in *ly* are adverbs.

| **Adverbs** | happily | busily | attractively | cheaply | carefully |
| **Adjectives** | happy | busy | attractive | cheap | careful |

Some adverbs do not end with *ly*; for example, *always, never, often, seldom, very.* Some adjectives do end in *ly*; don't mistake them for adverbs. If the *ly* word describes a noun or pronoun—*curly* hair, *friendly* man—you know it's an adjective.

Sometimes the same word is either an adjective or an adverb.

He is a **fast** worker. [*Fast* is an adjective describing the noun *worker.*]

He works **fast**. [*Fast* is an adverb describing the verb *works.*]

Use adverbs (not adjectives) to modify verbs, adjectives, or other adverbs.

NO   He arrived on time and **worked quiet**. [The adjective *quiet* is incorrect because an adjective cannot describe a verb—*worked.*]

YES   He arrived on time and **worked quietly**. [The adverb *quietly* tells **how** he *worked.*]

RECAP   Circle the correct choice.

1. This engine runs (smooth/smoothly) and has great gas mileage.
2. The interior design looks (beautiful, beautifully), but will be hard to pull off.
3. I feel (awful/awfully) sorry about leaving, but it's time to move on.
4. His decision was made (quick/quickly), but we still lost the contract.

Check your answers on page 453.

Adjective to Adverb Comparisons

To make *ly* adverbs comparative (for two) or superlative (for three or more), use *more/less* or *most/least* before them.

ADJECTIVE	ADVERB	COMPARATIVE ADVERB	SUPERLATIVE ADVERB
efficient	efficiently	more/less efficiently	most/least efficiently
beautiful	beautifully	more/less beautifully	most/least beautifully
polite	politely	more/less politely	most/least politely

NO   Of all the custodians, the new man works the **most efficient**. [*Most efficient* is an adjective and is not to be used to describe a verb: *works*.]

YES   Of all the custodians, the new man works the **most efficiently**. [*Most efficiently* is an adverb correctly modifying a verb: *works*.]

NO   We obtain parking permits **easier** than do the other stores. [*Easier* is an adjective incorrectly modifying a verb: *obtain*.]

YES   We obtain parking permits **more easily** than do the other stores. [The adverb *more easily* correctly modifies the verb *obtain*.]

RECAP   Circle the correct choice in item 1, and write the answers in items 2 and 3.

1. He writes (clearer/more clearly) than his assistant.
2. What is the verb in item 1? _____
3. What part of speech is the circled answer to item 1?_____

Check your answers on page 453.

Word Power

Spelling tip: The *ily* ending always has one *l*—as in the adverbs *easily, busily, happily*. The *ally* ending always has two *l*'s—as in the adverbs *accidentally, occasionally, officially*.

Other Differences Between Adjectives and Adverbs

A modifier placed *after a being verb* must be an adjective modifying the subject.

The most common being verbs are forms of *be* such as *is, am, are, was, were, been.*

> She **is** intelligent. [The adjective *intelligent* modifies *she*, the subject of the being verb *is*.]

In addition to forms of *be*, verbs of the senses are often (but not always) being verbs. Typical verbs of the senses are *appear, become, seem, look, taste, sound, smell, feel.* To determine whether a verb of the senses is a being or an action verb, decide whether it refers to action or state of being in that sentence.

> She **looks** carefully for the eraser. [*Looks* is an action verb referring to the action of using her eyes to look.]

> She **looks** intelligent. [*Looks* is a being verb because she is not doing the action of looking; *looks* refers to her appearance.]

> I **tasted** the potatoes. [*Tasted* is an action verb because tasting is action.]

> The potatoes **tasted** delicious. [*Tasted* is a being verb referring to the sense of taste; potatoes are not doing the action of tasting.]

NO	I feel **badly** today. [Use of the adverb *badly* here changes *feel* to an action verb. The sentence then means "I do a bad job of feeling" as an action; for example, I can't feel the difference between hot and cold because my hand is numb.]
YES	I feel **bad** today. [*Bad* describes how the subject (which is *I*) feels.]
YES	Susan Chin seems **friendly** and her hair is **curly**. [Adjectives *friendly* and *curly* follow being verbs *seems* and *is*.]

Remember that some *ly* words—such as *curly* and *friendly*—aren't adverbs. In this case, they are adjectives describing the nouns *Susan* and *hair*.

Word to the Wise

Sometimes adverbs are acceptable without the *ly* in specialized language such as advertisements and road signs.
   "Buy direct."   "Go slow!"   "Think Different"
This practice is unacceptable for most other types of business communication.

REPLAY 42

Draw a line through the adjective and adverb errors in these sentences, and write the correction in the blank or a **C** beside the three correct sentences.

Example: ___quickly___ She works quick.

_____ 1. The fumes from the refinery smell badly today.

_____ 2. Businesspeople should write clear and correct.

_____   3. His sister feels sadly about her loss.

_____   4. Be sure to do the problems careful.

_____   5. The doctor wrote legible.

_____   6. The pie is excellent today.

_____   7. The manager should think deep about that subject.

_____   8. I hope you will treat him fair.

_____   9. This one works as efficient as the new one.

_____   10. Ms. Teller dances the most graceful of all the dancers.

_____   11. Our assistant feels badly about the mistake.

_____   12. The vegetables taste more delicious than ever.

_____   13. That which we call a rose,
By any other name would smell as sweetly—William Shakespeare

_____   14. They work more quiet today than usual.

_____   15. Some days they work quieter than other days.

_____   16. The Lexus runs smoother than the other cars.

_____   17. You did satsifactory on all the tests.

_____   18. She appears more calmly than her sister.

_____   19. Of the two Las Vegas hotels, the Luxor has the higher rating.

_____   20. The music on this boat sounds more louder today.

_____   21. He feels worser today than he did yesterday.

_____   22. The engine in the truck runs quieter than the one in the car.

_____   23. She appears the most capablest of all the candidates.

_____   24. Compared with Mr. Beligusi, Mr. Rosenberg presented his case more concise.

_____   25. Bernard is the oldest of my two children.

Check your answers on page 453.

READ 43   MORE COMPARISONS

Shakespeare compared a woman to a summer's day in these romantic lines:

Shall I compare thee to a summer's day?
Thou art more lovely and more temperate:
Rough winds do shake the darling buds of May.
And summer's lease hath all too short a date.
But thy eternal summer shall not fade.

Though less romantic, we move along to more adjective and adverb comparisons.

Good/Well and Bad/Badly

The irregular adjectives **good** and **bad**, and the irregular adverbs **well** and **badly** frequently create confusion when used to make comparisons:

	POSITIVE	COMPARATIVE (2)	SUPERLATIVE (3 OR MORE)
Adjective	good	better	best
	bad	worse	worst
Adverb	well	better	best
	badly	worse	worst

To choose between *good* and *well*, decide whether you need an adjective or an adverb. If an adjective is required, choose *good*. If an adverb is required, choose *well*.

> Professor Stagnaro wrote a **good** report. [The adjective *good* describes the noun *report*.]

YES	The report looks **good**. [The adjective *good* describes the noun *report*; *looks* is a being verb.]
	It looks **good**. [*Good* describes the pronoun subject *it*; *looks* is a being verb.]
NO	He plays the drums **good**. [*Good*, an adjective, incorrectly describes *plays*, which is an action verb; do not use an adjective to describe an action verb.]
YES	He plays the drums **well**. [The adverb *well* correctly describes the action verb *plays*.]
YES	The drums sound **good**. [*Sound* is a being verb; *good* is an adjective correctly describing the noun subject *drums*.]
NO	She knows English **good**. [Do not use an adjective to describe a verb; therefore, *good* is incorrect.]
YES	She knows English **well**. [The adverb *well* tells **how** she **knows**.]

When referring to health or state of being, either *good* or *well* is correct with the being verb *feel*.

YES	He feels **good**.
OR	He feels **well**.

When being verbs other than *feel* refer to health, use *well*, which becomes an adjective on the subject of health.

YES	They are all **well**. He is not **well**. She seems **well**. [*Good* would refer to their behavior.]

If health is not the subject, use an adjective after a being verb.

YES	The sauce smells **good**. [This is not about health. *Smells*, a being verb, requires an adjective—in this case, *good*—to modify the subject *sauce*.]

Use an adverb—never an adjective—to modify an action verb.

Use an adverb to modify the action verb *write*.

> They write **badly**. They write **poorly**. They write **neatly**.

RECAP   Circle the correct choice.

1. Greta writes (good/well/either good or well).

2. Do you get along (good/well/either good or well) with people?

3. I hope he feels (good/well/either good or well) today.

4. He spoke (good/well/either good or well) of Ms. Sorenson.

5. Professor Sanneh feels (bad/badly) about losing her motorcycle.

Check your answers on page 453.

Comparative and superlative forms are easy for *good* or *well*: The comparative is *better*, and the superlative is *best*. Both of the following sentences are correct.

YES   Our products are **better** than theirs. [The comparative **adjective** *better* modifies the noun *products*.]

YES   Our products are designed **better** than theirs. [The comparative **adverb** *better** modifies the verb *are designed*.]

Are You Really Sure?

Real and sure are adjectives; do not use them to describe other adjectives.

Adjectives can describe nouns or pronouns only. Only adverbs can describe adjectives.

  Instead of incorrectly using *real* as an adverb, use a true adverb such as *really*, *very*, *extremely*, *exceptionally*, or *truly*:

NO   I'm **real** sorry about being late.

YES   I'm **truly** sorry about being late.

NO   He's **real** good at that.

YES   He's **exceptionally** good at that.

Use *real* as an adjective meaning "genuine."

  That is a **real** diamond, not a CZ.

Here's a quick test for the adjectives *real* and *sure*:

  If you can substitute **very**, you need an adverb.

NO   She is **real smart**. [The adjective *real* cannot correctly modify the adjective *smart*; switch to an adverb like *really* or *extremely*.]

YES   She is **extremely** smart.

NO   That report is **sure good**. [The adjective *sure* cannot correctly describe the adjective *good*; replace it with an adverb such as *especially*, *certainly*, *exceptionally*.]

YES   That report is **definitely** good.

---

*Better is both an adjective and an adverb—the comparative form of *good* and *well*; see dictionary.

RECAP   Change the incorrectly used adjectives to adverbs.

1. I'm sure happy you decided to buy a new water cooler.
2. We're real disappointed about losing the Panasonic account.

Check your answers on page 453.

Writing for Your Career

Excessive use of descriptive words interferes with the effectiveness of your writing. When you see a sentence in context, decide whether to include or eliminate the *really, surely, extremely, especially, very,* or other "intensifying" word. Particularly avoid overuse of *very*. A sentence such as "The presentation is good" sometimes carries more "punch" than "The presentation is really (or very or extraordinarily) good."

REPLAY 43

These sentences provide practice for Read 43 as well as for the preceding Reads in this chapter. If the sentence is correct, write **C**. Otherwise circle the adjective or adverb error, and write the correct form in the blank. In one sentence you will have to delete a word.

Example: ___C___ The sauce smells good.

_____ 1. They are real unhappy about the declining profit. (or delete real)

_____ 2. We sure wish you would participate in the conference.
                     (or delete *sure*)

_____ 3. Tony Carter writes more logical than anyone else here.

_____ 4. Of the two trumpets, the new one sounds best.

_____ 5. Ms. Teller speaks more better than Mr. Keller.

_____ 6. These laptops are wider used than the others.

_____ 7. His cooking is more better than his brother's.

_____ 8. I did real good in the grammar part.

_____ 9. Of all our stores this one is managed the poorest.

_____ 10. The chemicals don't smell as bad today as they did yesterday.

_____ 11. This office is furnished different from the others.

_____ 12. He is feeling badly today.

_____ 13. She thinks she did good on a interview.

_____ 14. These kind of books are not suitable for a officer.

_____ 15. The view today is more beautiful than ever before.

Check your answers on page 453; then take the Pop Quiz on page 307.

Word Power

Words that end in *way* and *where*, such as *anyway* or *nowhere*, are often used as adverbs. NEVER add *s* to these words—either in writing or in speech.

NO anyways, somewheres, everywheres; adding *s* to these words makes one appear uneducated

YES anyway, anywhere, everywhere, somewhere, nowhere

CONCEPT REVIEW & SKILL-BUILDING APPLICATIONS

Checkpoint

Place a check in the blank after you review the information and understand it.

Adjectives

_____   Adjectives modify, or tell something about, nouns and pronouns.

_____   Pointing adjectives are *this, that, these, those.*

Singular   this kind, that type
  Plural   these or those kinds or types

_____   The articles *a, an, the* are also adjectives. Use *a* before a word or letter beginning with a **consonant sound** and *an* before a word beginning with a **vowel sound**.

_____   Limiting adjectives limit in the sense of quantity: 42 hats, several coats, few children, some applesauce. Limiting adjectives, explained in Read 8, are usually used correctly and therefore not studied in this section.

_____   Describing adjectives describe a noun or pronoun:

blue eyes   black hair   good manners   he is responsible

Adverbs

_____   Adverbs modify, or tell something about, verbs, adjectives, or other adverbs:

eat carefully [*Eat* is a verb modified by the adverb *carefully.*]

very good [*Good* is an adjective modified by the adverb *very.*]

so softly [*Softly* is an adverb modified by the adverb *so.*]

_____   Many adverbs, but not all, are adjectives to which *ly* has been added: *accidentally, happily, cheerfully;* not all adverbs end with *ly*—for example, *well, often, always.*

Three Degrees of Adjectives and Adverbs

_____ The positive degree modifies without making a comparison.

The plane is comfortable. [The adjective *comfortable* modifies the noun *plane*.]

The plane is extremely comfortable. [The adverb *extremely* modifies the adjective *comfortable*.]

_____ The comparative degree ends in *er* or is preceded by *more* or *less.* Use the comparative degree to compare two only.

This building is safer than that one.

He writes more neatly than his brother. [The adverb *more neatly* modifies the verb *writes.* The adjective *neater* would be incorrect since an adjective cannot modify a verb—*writes*.]

_____ The superlative degree ends in *est* or is preceded by *most* or *least.* Use the superlative degree to compare three or more.

This investment is the most secure of all those I've made.

Of the three senators, the junior senator worked hardest.

Adjective and Adverb Tips

_____ Negative words are either adjectives or adverbs, but it isn't important to identify them as such. Just be sure to use only one negative word to express one negative idea.

NO   He doesn't want nothing to do with them. (two negative words: *doesn't, nothing*)

YES   He doesn't want anything to do with them.

_____ A describing word following a being verb is an adjective; it modifies the *subject* of the being verb.

Professor Kostner feels bad about your low grade. [The adjective *bad* modifies the subject, *Professor Kostner*.]

_____ To modify an action verb, use an adverb.

She plays the saxophone loudly. [The adverb *loudly* modifies the action verb *plays*; *loud*, an adjective, cannot be used to describe a verb.]

_____ Using an adjective or an adverb where the other is needed is a common error in writing: An adjective modifies a noun or pronoun, and an adverb modifies a verb, an adverb, or an adjective.

NO   He is higher qualified than the other applicants. [The adjective *higher* incorrectly modifies *qualified*, which is also an adjective.]

YES   He is more highly qualified than the other applicants. [The adverb *more highly* correctly modifies the adjective *qualified*.]

_____ Use *good* as an adjective and *well* as an adverb. The comparative for good or well is *better*. The superlative for good or well is *best*.

The steak smells good. [*Good*, an adjective, describes the subject *steak*; *smells* is a being verb.]

He writes *well* (not good). Use an adverb (*well*) to modify a verb (*writes*).

Either *good* or *well* is correct after a being verb that refers to health or state of being.

I feel *good*. OR I feel *well*. BUT He feels *bad* (not *badly*) about that.

_____ *Sure* and *real* are adjectives; don't use them to modify other adjectives. Instead, use adverbs *surely, really,* or some other adverb—or omit them altogether, which is often the best choice.

NO   I'm sure happy that you invited me. I'm real happy that you invited me.

YES   I'm surely happy . . . OR I'm extremely happy . . . OR I'm happy . . .

_____ Never add *s* to *anyway, somewhere,* etc.

 # Special Assignment

Write a short description (about 15 to 20 typed lines) comparing two coworkers or two other people you know who differ from each other in some way. Choose a specific difference to write about—such as appearance, personality, interests, skills, or talent. Introduce both people and your subject in the opening sentence. Use concise and correct language.

Opening Sentences

Start immediately with a **topic sentence** to get the reader's interest. A topic sentence gives the main idea (the topic) of the paragraph.

These are ineffective openings:

I am going to write about ... [We know you're going to write; just get started.]

This is a comparison of two people I know who differ from each other. [Who cares? Tell me who they are and what they do so that I'll want to know more about them. Be specific.]

These are effective openings:

Amy Lopez and Josh Stern are successful department managers at Magnasoft, Inc.; however, their leadership styles differ considerably.

Although Professor X and Professor Y are both excellent instructors, their teaching styles are quite different.

Latisha is a perfect example of how a supervisor should dress for the office, while Carmen is just the opposite.

Body

Continue with sentences supporting your opening statement—or topic sentence. Describe the people with interesting, accurate, and precise words. Anything that doesn't support the topic sentence does not belong in the piece. If you have more than one paragraph, each one should have a new topic sentence. Make sure your ideas flow smoothly from one sentence to the next and from one paragraph to the next.

Conclusion

Conclude with a summarizing sentence. Avoid introducing new information in the closing.

Date to submit this assignment: _____

Proofreading for Careers

Find and correct spelling, capitalization, grammar errors, and typographical errors. The punctuation is already correct. Correct the printed copy using proofreading symbols or go online to correct the document electronically.

What Employers Want

When employer's fill positions, they are looking for more than competence in the basic skills or even real specific technical skills. They also place a higher value on personal qualities such as integrity, self-discipline, ethics, honesty, promptness, and reliability. Be sure that you conduct yourself according in your college courses and work situations so that these quality's will be noticed by professors and supervisor whom can provide you with job references. Extra responsibilities that you take on, such as tutoring, working with the more elderly, or organizing a food drive are character-building and show employers what is more better about you, your work habits, and your value system.

Here are some expectations common mentioned by employers:

1. Take responsible for yourself, your work performnce, and your career success.

2. Present yourself positive and on time every day.

3. Get along good with others and know how to perform as a member of in a team.

4. Communicate well and ask intelligently questions.

5. Have a stronger work ethic: follow up, follow through, and get things done.

6. Be a problem solver and decision makers; don't wait to be lead by others.

7. Accept feedback and criticism positive in the interest of continuously improvement.

8. Know businesses etiquette and exhibit behavior appropriately to the workplace.

Evaluate your work.
Excellent _____ Good ___ Fair ___ Other ___

Practice Quiz

Take the Practice Quiz as though it were a real test. In the blank, write the letter that identifies the correct answer. Use the dictionary when in doubt.

Example: __b__ (a) A (b) An eager history professor assigned 200 pages.

_____ **1.** She is the (a) less (b) least efficient of the two clerks.

_____ 2. (a) A (b) An union official would probably

_____ 3. refuse (a) a (b) an low hourly wage.

_____ 4. These (a) type (b) types of properties are advertised

_____ 5. in (a) this here (b) that there (c) either this or that newspaper.

_____ 6. She doesn't want to lose (a) a (b) an $11 commission.

_____ 7. If he doesn't understand the work, he will get (a) a (b) an F on the test.

_____ 8. (a) A (b) An European businessperson would probably

_____ 9. consider this award to be (a) a (b) an honor.

_____ 10. Since both brands are good, order the (a) less (b) least expensive one.

_____ 11. Which is (a) easier (b) easyer (c) easiest (d) easyest for you to do, a graph or a chart?

_____ 12. I (a) can't (b) can hardly believe what I saw.

_____ 13. Although Mr. Shue and Ms. Farr are both skilled at typing, Mr. Shue is (a) more faster (b) most faster (c) faster (d) fastest.

_____ 14. The class was asked to sit (a) quiet (b) quietly and read.

_____ 15. I hope you (a) won't do no more (b) won't do any more (c) will not do no more (d) will not do any more (e) either b or d work on that project.

_____ 16. This is the (a) newer (b) newest (c) most new of the six computers in our office.

_____ 17. Mr. Young spoke at Southwestern College (a) brief (b) briefly and to the point.

_____ 18. The sewage treatment plants don't smell as (a) bad (b) badly today.

_____ 19. When we evaluated our three facilities, we found this one is run (a) most poorly (b) most poorest (c) more poorly.

_____ 20. He seems (a) worse (b) more badly (c) badder this week.

_____ 21. Of the four letter styles, full block seems (a) better (b) best (c) more better for our correspondence.

_____ 22. The file is missing, but we know it must be (a) somewheres (b) somewhere (c) either a or b (d) neither a nor b in this office.

_____ 23. My sister is in the hospital but feels (a) good (b) well (c) either good or well today.

_____ 24. The software-design team worked (a) really well (b) really good (c) either good or well (d) real well (e) real good together.

_____ 25. We would (a) sure (b) really (c) certainly (d) b or c like to meet him.

Self-Study Practice and Tutorials

Vocabulary and Spelling for Careers
For additional practice go to Appendix B, page 321.

Replay Drills

For additional practice go to Appendix C, page 384.

Companion Web Site: www.prenhall.com/smith

Go to the companion Web site to test your knowledge on self-grading quizzes and for links to other helpful online resources.

MyWritingLab

Use this online learning system for an assessment of your progress on topics covered in this chapter and progressive exercises that fit your individual needs.

9 Using Commas Correctly

After completing Chapter 9, you will be able to do the following:

■ Use commas correctly to separate a series of items or adjectives in sentences.

■ Use commas correctly to join parts of sentences.

■ Properly place commas in sentences that contain names of locations and people, dates, abbreviations, quotations, and numbers.

READ 44 — SOME COMMA BASICS

When you speak, pauses in your flow of words help your listener's understanding. When you don't pause at the expected places, your words seem to be out of order, and your listener might stop you and ask for clarification. When you write, punctuation marks replace the pauses, and they are crucial to your reader's understanding. The comma is the mark that gives writers the most trouble. If commas have caused you problems in the past, now is the time to conquer them forever. Once you learn to apply the established principles, you will no longer rely on guesswork for comma use. These logical rules help make your writing precise and clear.

When you do the exercises in this chapter, insert a comma only when the rule applies. If you don't think of the rule first, you'll continue to make whatever errors you made in the past. So practice applying the rules in each Recap, Replay, and Skill-Building Application.

Items in a Series

Johann Voss, an 18th-century poet who may have been a bit of a reprobate,* wrote:

> *Who does not love wine, women, and song*
> *Remains a fool his whole life long.*

"Wine, women, and song" is an example of a series.

Use commas to separate items in a series of three or more words, phrases, or clauses.

Notice the commas between the items in the series below—as well as before the words *and* or *or* that precede the last **word**, **phrase**, or **clause**. Business communications experts use that final comma because it helps to ensure clarity of business information; academic and literary writers, bloggers, and journalists often omit it.

Word series	Do you prefer **Catalina, Hawaii**, or **Bermuda** for your honeymoon?
	Please order **soft drinks, sparkling water, coffee**, and **tea** for the afternoon break.
Phrase series	Joe believes in government **of the people, for the people**, and **by the people**.
Clause series	**Amish men wear black felt hats all the time, Sikh men always wear turbans**, and **Orthodox Jewish men usually wear skullcaps**. [three independent clauses]
	We believe **that your idea was good, that you planned carefully**, and **that you had a good product**. [one independent clause, *We believe*, followed by three dependent clauses]

If a conjunction precedes each item in the series, omit the commas.

No Commas	Engineers **and** physicists **and** chemists are working on the project.

*If you are not familiar with the word *reprobate*, look it up now, before you forget.

While the preceding example is correct, good writing requires that you omit extra words; therefore, edit this sentence to omit the first *and*. Use the series comma instead.

Revised   Engineers, physicists, and chemists are working on the project.

Another point to notice about these examples is that three to four items is about the maximum number that is comfortable for readers to absorb in a series. If your list is longer, find a way to break your ideas into two or more sentences, or consider using a numbered or bulleted list. This will greatly aid your reader's understanding and memory.

RECAP   Add the missing commas in these sentences.

---

1. Taiwan Hong Kong Singapore and Korea have achieved high levels of industrialization.
2. First we studied the annual report then we verified its accuracy and finally we bought the stock.
3. Major differences among cultures include language religion politics and the role of women.
4. Think about what kind of world you want to live in what you are good at and what you need to work at to build that world.
5. When you attend a business lunch dress appropriately use good table manners avoid ordering something difficult to eat and order nonalcoholic beverages.
6. The job of a top manager is to set broad objectives for the company formulate strategies to meet them and decide among alternate possibilities.

Check your answers on page 454.

Two or More Adjectives Together

Apply the "series rule" to *three* or more *items*. For adjectives, however, use a comma between just *two* or more that describe the same noun.

Test by Omitting and

Imagine *and* between consecutive adjectives. If it makes sense, then it is correct to use a comma to replace *and*, which is understood but omitted.

The seeds were dormant during the **long, severe** winter. [*And* makes sense between adjectives *long* and *severe*; therefore, use a comma instead of *and*.]

The seeds were dormant during the **long and severe** winter. [*And* is already between *long* and *severe*; therefore, no comma is needed.]

If *and* doesn't make sense between the adjectives, do not insert a comma between them. Also try the reversal test. If the adjectives don't make sense reversed, don't use a comma between them.

The seeds woke up in the **early spring** thaw. [The word *early* modifies *spring*, not *thaw*. *And* does not make sense between *early* and *spring*; therefore do not use a comma.]

Test by Reversing the Adjectives

Another clue that helps you decide whether to use a comma between consecutive adjectives is to reverse their order. If they make sense either way, you need a comma.

> She is a **loyal, intelligent** employee.

> She is an **intelligent, loyal** employee.

Since the sentence makes sense either way, use a comma between the adjectives.

> **Many elderly** people died during the long, severe winter.

Reversing the adjectives—*elderly many people*—doesn't make sense, indicating that a comma is not needed between the adjectives.

RECAP

Try the two tests—**imagining the word** *and* **between the two adjectives** and **reversing the order**—with the adjectives in bold type below. Insert a comma in the two sentences that need it, and write **C** beside the two correct sentences.

_____ 1. He is a **bright enthusiastic** student.

_____ 2. The **loud electronic** music is irritating the customers.

_____ 3. Our **new advertising** booklet was completed last week.

_____ 4. The **annual financial** report was prepared by a **highly paid famous** accountant.

Check your answers on page 454.

REPLAY 44

Apply the comma rules you've just learned. If you are tempted to use a comma for another reason, DON'T! Write **C** beside the sentence that needs no comma.

Example: That company needs strong‸aggressive sales representatives.

_____ 1. A dazed demure debutante dated a disheveled double-dealing dancer in December.

_____ 2. They are about to begin a unique exciting adventure.

_____ 3. He asked why you came what you wanted and what you expect to do.

_____ 4. Our showroom is in a small elegant building in a new part of Milwaukee.

_____ 5. Eric Smith is an ethical and expert financial planner specializing in socially responsible investing.

_____ 6. Carla will call on accounts in Fort Worth Dallas and Austin.

_____ 7. Sean Combs' marketing expertise in a profitable highly competitive industry was what the record label needed at that time.

_____ 8. The CEO was offered a million-dollar bonus a million-dollar salary and stock options.

_____ 9. Use *nd rd st* or *th* with the day of the month only when that day precedes the month or stands by itself for example the *4th of May* or the *4th*—but *May 4.*

_____ 10. That country has a settled well-educated population.

Check your answers on page 454.

READ 45   JOINING PARTS OF SENTENCES

In Chapter 3 you made decisions about how to join parts of sentences. This section will review **independent clauses** and how to join them with a comma.

Joining Independent Clauses

An independent clause has a subject and a verb. Use a comma before a coordinating conjunction that joins independent clauses.

Coordinating conjunctions are *and, but, or, nor, for, so,* and sometimes *yet.* Although *so* is a coordinating conjunction and appropriate in conversation, be careful about using it in business writing where it can sound a little too casual.

> Joe faxed printouts of the email messages, but he forgot to send the invoices. [Two independent clauses are joined by a comma and the coordinating conjunction *but.*]

> Joe faxed printouts of the email messages but forgot to send the invoices. [One independent clause; the subject is *Joe*; there are two verbs—*faxed* and *forgot*—and a prepositional phrase, *to send the invoices.* No comma needed.]

Recognizing Independent Clauses

Remember that an independent clause must have a subject and a verb *and* it must be able to stand alone as a complete thought.

Either/or, neither/nor, and *not only/but also* clauses don't *sound* independent. They *are* independent, however, if each word group has a subject and verb.

> **Either** he lives in Savannah, **or** he lives in a South Carolina suburb. [Two independent clauses are joined by the coordinating conjunction *or* and a comma. *He lives* is the subject and verb in both clauses.]

> **Either** he lives in Savannah **or** in some other Georgia city. [This sentence has only one independent clause with a subject and verb (*he lives*). *Or* connects a prepositional phrase; no comma is needed.]

Here are some more examples:

> **Not only** is she the best candidate for the job, **but she also** knows the territory. [two independent clauses; comma needed]

> She is **not only** the best candidate **but also** knows the territory. [one independent clause; no comma needed]

Neither one of us can go to the luncheon, **nor** do we want to. [two indepen-dent clauses; comma is needed.]

Neither the marketing plan **nor** the launch party made an impact on product recognition. [one independent clause; no comma needed]

RECAP	Insert commas where needed. Write **C** beside the sentence that is already correct.

_____ 1. Everyone in the office is extremely pleased with Pam's work and we especially appreciate her proofreading ability.

_____ 2. I am pleased with Rosalyn's work and I really appreciate her positive attitude.

_____ 3. Not only does Professor Caroll like sports but she also enjoys music and art.

_____ 4. Professor Carroll not only likes sports but also music and art.

Check your answers on page 454.

Exception to the Comma Rule

In a short sentence (no more than about ten words) omit the comma when _and_ or _or_ join an independent clause.

If _but, nor, for, so,_ or _yet_ joins the independent clauses, however, do use a comma before it regardless of sentence length.

He won **and** I lost.   Either he built it **or** she did.

He won, **but** I lost.   He really won, **yet** I can't believe it.

Contrasting Expressions

Use a comma (or two commas) to set off a sharply contrasting or opposite expression. Such expressions are generally introduced by _not, never, seldom, but,_ or _yet._

He often thinks about leaving his job, but never his parents' home.

She loves chocolate, yet breaks out when she eats it.

Take a bus home from the office party, not the subway.

Omitting a Verb

A comma replaces an omitted verb that is easily understood from the wording of the rest of the sentence.

A used one costs $1,245; a new one, $2,300.

Shirley is now in Ohio in a new career and George, in Alaska.

Word to the Wise

In an English grammar book written in 1582, the comma is described as "a small crooked point, which in writing _followeth_ some small branch of the sentence, & in reading _warneth_ us to rest there, & to _help_ our _breth_ a little."

REPLAY 45

Either insert or remove commas based on the rules you just learned. If you are tempted to insert a comma for another reason, resist! Write **C** beside the sentences that do not require commas.

Example: The company is opening a new office in Boston‸and the telemarketing operation will be moved there in the fall.

_____ 1. International students bring to classrooms not only a variety of cultures but also a wide range of learning experiences.

_____ 2. Not only will students be better prepared for today's international workplace but also they will be better citizens by learning about other countries and cultures.

_____ 3. Ms. Mack is a member of the prestigious Theta Alpha Delta honorary business education sorority and she will join us at the state convention.

_____ 4. He works out at the gym every morning but he never goes in the afternoon.

_____ 5. Deborah wants to move to New York but will she like it there?

_____ 6. In September we hired an administrative assistant; in October a data entry clerk; and in November a website manager.

_____ 7. Bill spoke harshly to Amelia today for she still hasn't completed the research.

_____ 8. Neither one can do the job nor is it fair to ask someone else to do it.

_____ 9. He arrived at 10 p.m., not a.m.

_____ 10. Either make a down payment or pay the total now.

_____ 11. Mr. Penney treated employees as he would want to be treated and they were appreciative.

_____ 12. Everett qualified for promotion to upper management; Luc for transfer to Antarctica.

_____ 13. Until the 1800s ice cream was only for the rich but that changed after the ice cream freezer was invented.

_____ 14. Around this time insulated ice houses also became available and even more people were able to enjoy ice cream.

_____ 15. Be sure to send for his brother, and not his sister.

Check your answers on page 455.

READ 46   COMMAS AND INTRODUCTORY WORDS

Often you need to begin a sentence with introductory words that explain something about the main part of the sentence. This **introductory expression** is always **dependent**; that is, it is not a complete thought.

Many, but not all, introductory expressions are followed by a comma to separate them from the main idea—or independent clause—of the sentence.

Use a comma after one-word or other very short introductory expressions:

Yes, we'll be glad to introduce William to Esther.

No, I don't believe we will be able to schedule a full-day workshop.

Use a comma after an introductory "direct address" of the person you're writing to.

Mr. Gregory, are you available for lunch on Friday, June 29, at noon?

A comma is not required after short "place" and "time" introductory phrases—unless the comma is needed for clearness or emphasis.

Within a year we will know the results of making this investment. ["time" introductory phrase]

In 2008 our main offices moved from downtown to the suburbs. ["time" introductory phrase]

On the higher floors the windows do not open. ["place" introductory phrase]

In the following sentences, a comma *is* needed to enclose an intervening phrase that is not essential to the meaning of the sentence.

In 2008, **after a huge fire in the building**, our main offices moved from downtown to the suburbs.

On the higher floors, **due to building regulations**, the windows do not open.

Use a comma after an introductory expression that includes a verb, even when it is short.

I'm not sure, but I believe tomorrow is the deadline for registration.

If you can, please complete the first draft by Monday.

Use a comma after an introductory expression of fewer than five words and no verb form when it is needed for clearness or if it is a transitional expression.

Once inside, the man requested food. [clarity]

In addition, a few of our suppliers make special deals. [transitional expression]

Use a comma after an introductory expression of five or more words—whether it has a verb form or not.

Because of the severe weather forecast, we are closing the office for the rest of the day.

Under the sponsorship of the university medical school, a conference on early childhood nutrition will be held on July 2.

RECAP   Insert commas after introductory expressions, apply the series rule in one sentence, and write **C** for two sentences that are already correct.

_____ 1. Since the board meets only once a month we need to have them approve the new contract the blueprints for the new wing and plans for the fall gala.

_____ 2. Before leaving for the airport, please sign the expense vouchers.

_____ 3. If you take the train you will arrive at 8:45 a.m.

_____ 4. Being in a hurry to end the meeting he skipped the first two items on the agenda.

_____ 5. He didn't make it on time because he drove too fast and rear-ended a police car.

_____ 6. Had he read the directions he would have taken the proper exit for sure.

_____ 7. Hank please let us know if you need our help.

Check your answers on page 455.

REPLAY 46

Insert commas based on the rules given so far. If tempted to use a comma for another reason—DON'T! Write **C** for five correct sentences.

Example: Although their supervisor didn't know it,Eddie and Helen worked late to finish the project.

_____ 1. When we walked through the doors of the exclusive Flintridge Inn we knew this was a special celebration.

_____ 2. As he approached her he saw that she looked nervous.

_____ 3. In this attractive modern dining room you always find a courteous staff at your service.

_____ 4. As we all know real merit is hard to conceal.

_____ 5. Examples of English words taken from American Indian languages are _igloo kayak moccasin skunk_ and _persimmon_.

_____ 6. You'll receive the engraved mugs for the holiday party if you order now.

_____ 7. By discreetly motioning to the speaker indicate when five minutes of her time remains.

_____ 8. In 1969 the world's first Internet message was transmitted at UCLA.

_____ 9. Being an alert salesperson he noticed the prospect's gesture of annoyance.

_____ 10. No he hasn't called on us either this month or last month.

_____ 11. Please email the dinner chairperson explaining why we can't attend.

_____ 12. If it is to be it is up to me.

_____ 13. No one in the world has more courage than the person who stops after eating one peanut.

_____ 14. The public relations firm thinks West Covina would be a good location for the new store but the client believes it should be in Cucamonga.

_____ 15. In Chicago people sunbathe on a beach on Lake Michigan.

Check your answers on page 455; then take the Pop Quiz on page 308.

READ 47   SETTING OFF WORDS AND PHRASES

To decide whether commas are required to separate parts of sentences, you sometimes need to consider whether a word group is necessary to the meaning of the sentence or not. In grammar, these word groups are called nonessential and essential expressions.

Nonessential Expressions

A **nonessential expression** may help the reader understand the rest of the sentence or may simply give additional information. The "nonessential" word or words do not, however, change the main idea of the sentence.

Enclose in commas a nonessential word or word group that interrupts or is added onto the main idea.

Nonessential Words and Phrases

Nonessential words and phrases include transitional words and other word groups. Each nonessential expression that follows is in bold print and enclosed in commas. If you were to remove the nonessential words, the rest of the sentence would retain its original meaning.

Anything, **little or big**, becomes an adventure, **however**, when shared with someone special.

Professor Ingram-Cotton is, **of course**, an expert in this field.

Dr. Ellis Jones, **an expert in this field**, will lead the discussion.

A training DVD, **"Banking for Tweens and Teens,"** is one of our bestsellers.

Adrian Dorado, **a Colorado Community College professor**, is an exceptionally fine instructor.

Nonessential Clauses

Remember that a clause is a word group that has a subject and a verb; it may be dependent or independent. A nonessential clause is one that can be removed from a sentence without the sentence losing its meaning.

Ms. Elaine Esperanza, **who is a nutritionist**, will chair the panel on obesity.

This business plan, **which we have studied carefully**, is unsatisfactory and needs to be rewritten.

We'll meet you at 5 p.m., **although we cannot stay long**.

RECAP Insert commas around nonessential expressions unless they end the sentence, in which case insert just one comma.

1. The Upper Peninsula where I spent childhood summers holds a special place in my heart.
2. The course is divided into two parts "Job Content" and "Work Ethics," each two hours long.
3. The job you want therefore may not be available when you want it.
4. Our electronic filing system which was devised by the Records Management Department eliminates considerable paper waste.
5. The guide gave us a fascinating tour of the old courthouse even though he was worried about sticking to his schedule.

Check your answers on page 455.

Essential Expressions

An **essential expression** is a word or group of words that is necessary to convey the main idea of a sentence.

Do not enclose essential expressions in commas.

To decide whether a word or word group is essential or nonessential, imagine the words omitted; then see how the meaning of the rest of the sentence changes. Try this with the following sentences.

A person **who is a nutritionist** should lead the discussion. [Compare this with the sentence about Ms. Elaine Esperanza in the previous section on nonessential clauses.]

Someone **like you** should lead the discussion.

Bring your resume with you **when you apply for a job**.

A national organization **that has a research bureau** stands behind our product.

A city **that can qualify as a disaster area** is eligible to receive federal aid.

The ones **who complain the loudest** are generally those who contribute the least.

My sister-in-law **Pat** lives in Detroit, Michigan. [As I have two sisters-in-law, her name is essential.]

Word to the Wise

Here are two correctly punctuated sentences with totally different meanings due to the use or absence of commas. Circle the one in which Ron is believed to be generous. Then check your answer on page 455.

Brad thought Ron was very generous.

Brad, thought Ron, was very generous.

RECAP   Use the proofreading symbol for "delete/omit" to remove commas enclosing essential word groups, or write **C** for correct.

_____ 1. Our best video, *Dealing with Customers*, shows a simple method for dealing effectively with angry customers.

_____ 2. An Arizona fireman was honored, because he exhibited extreme bravery.

_____ 3. A woman student, must not enter men's rooms, without a chaperone, approved by the principal, or her representative.—Oxford Intercollegiate Rules for Women, 1924.

Check your answers on page 455.

Prepositional Phrases

Most prepositional phrases are "essential" and shouldn't be enclosed in commas. In addition, do not use a comma to separate a subject from its verb.

NO We saw your sales representative, **at the conference**, on May 2.

YES We saw your sales representative **at the conference** on May 2.

NO The Board of Directors, **is considering Internet sales**, to increase income.

YES The Board of Directors **is considering Internet sales** to increase income.

Commas with *Which* and *That*

The words *which* and *that* are useful for introducing essential and nonessential expressions.

> Use *which* to begin nonessential expressions and *that* to begin essential expressions.

Good   Homes **that are beautifully decorated** sell faster. [essential phrase]

However, if you can shorten a modifying clause or phrase, you improve the writing style through conciseness.

Better   Beautifully decorated homes sell faster.

Good   The new office, **which has been rented by Mr. I. M. Rich**, is on the third floor.

Better   Mr. I. M. Rich rented the new third-floor office.

REPLAY 47

Insert commas to enclose **nonessential expressions** that appear to be added for extra information. No other corrections are required. Write **C** if the sentence is correct without commas.

Example: George͵who was supposed to give the party͵was locked out of his home. [The clause "who was supposed to give the party" is additional information. It could have been made into a separate sentence following *home* beginning with *He* instead of *who.*]

_____ 1. A close* corporation limits the number of stockholders often members of the same family and conducts business less formally than publicly held corporations.

_____ 2. Sales representatives who increase sales by 50 percent will win a Caribbean cruise for two.

_____ 3. Avoid introducing subjects not on the agenda when you attend a business meeting.

_____ 4. People rarely succeed at anything unless they have fun doing it.

_____ 5. We faxed your January 6 memo to the IRS auditor but have not yet had a reply.

_____ 6. Managers need to know how to realign workers quickly to meet performance goals and staff availability.

_____ 7. Professor Kleinrock of UCLA developed the prototype for the Internet the system of computer-to-computer communications that has resulted in today's cyber culture.

_____ 8. The one who complains the loudest however is often the one who contributes the least.

*Also called *closed*. Close or closed corporations are regulated by the Securities and Exchange Commission (SEC), a government agency.

_____ 9. The operating costs as you probably know are too high for us to show much of a profit.

_____ 10. A preschool administrator Gloria Rojas telephoned me.

_____ 11. My office, Room No. 103 is in the new building.

_____ 12. The Financial Aid Office which is on the third floor is open daily.

_____ 13. Martin Simon the auditor found a $100,000 error.

_____ 14. The system that was devised by Technocraft Inc. is easy to learn.

_____ 15. The coach gave the book titled _The Inner Game of Tennis_ to all of the team members.

_____ 16. Coaches who don't inspire their players should be replaced.

_____ 17. Openness fosters growth and establishes an important feeling of worth which motivates everyone to do the best possible job.

_____ 18. Harold Simon is the attorney who will try the civil case next month.

_____ 19. You can buy the new instruction booklet which gives complete information for only $23.95.

_____ 20. Sandi uses English effectively and correctly and also speaks French fluently.

_____ 21. A great idea it has been said comes into the world as gently as a dove.

_____ 22. The workshop I'm attending "Career Networking in Cyberspace " begins at 2:30 this afternoon.

_____ 23. The exchange student who just arrived from Beijing will help the Lopez family to improve their Chinese.

_____ 24. My Internet service which was working fine yesterday suddenly went down again this afternoon.

_____ 25. The No. 64 bus, which is usually on time, was delayed for over an hour.

Check your answers on page 456.

READ 48   FOUR EASY COMMAS

States

Enclose in commas the name of a state, province, or country that follows the name of a smaller unit, such as a city.

> Did you visit Paris, France, or Paris, Kentucky?

> I lived in Springfield, Massachusetts, and taught business classes at Bay Path College in Longmeadow.

Dates

When a date has the month/day/year, separate the year from the day with a comma. In the middle of a sentence enclose the year in commas.

Expressing dates in order of month/day/year is the **American date style**. Do not use commas with the **international or military date** style (day/month/year).

| **American** | The groundbreaking ceremony was held on May 5, 2004, in Prescott, Arizona, at Yavapai College. |
| **International and military** | I saw him in Amsterdam, Holland, at the international conference on 31 July 2009. |

In a date that has only the month and year, do not use a comma.

The next meeting will take place in April 2010 in Frederick, Maryland.

If the year isn't included in a date, use no commas.

The March 6 conference was held at Abbie Business Institute

Never use a comma between the state and a ZIP code:

His address is 5310 Spectrum Drive, Frederick, MD 21703.

Enclose in commas elements of a date or time that explain a preceding date.

At 9 a.m., Wednesday, January 3, the sale on women's shoes begins.

Abbreviations

Use commas to enclose the abbreviation of a college or professional degree that follows a name. Do not use periods in these abbreviations.

Millie S. Perry, PhD, and Brad Rosenberg, MD, will be the speakers at the Eclectic Convention in Visalia, Montana.

Do not separate a name from a birth order designation, such as Jr., Sr., II, III, unless the person writes it that way.

Charles Davis Jr.

Charles Davis III

If a company name is followed by a designation that indicates the type of entity it is, such as Inc. or Ltd., do not set off this designation with a comma, unless the company writes it that way.

W. H. Jones Engineering Inc.

Power Resources LLC

Names

When using the name of a person in "direct address," enclose the name in commas.

Because of your expertise, Joanne, we're inviting you to lead the discussion.

The following will explain, Dr. Spellman, just how important this research is.

Writing for Your Career

Skilled communicators tend to use "direct address," because it is courteous and because most people like to hear or read their name. This builds rapport with your reader.

Thank you, Ms. Leslie, for showing me around Grossmont last Tuesday.

Overuse of the technique, however, appears insincere.

REPLAY 48

Insert commas where required. Write **C** next to the two sentences that don't need a comma. Resist any temptation to add commas.

Example: Marietta͵Georgia͵is the home of Chattahoochee Technical College.

_____ 1. On March 2 2010 we shipped you five HP LaserJet printers.
_____ 2. In April 2004 Professor Van Vooren became the vice president of the college.
_____ 3. Steven Smith PhD will head the Industrial Arts Department.
_____ 4. One of Billy Crystal's first "gigs" was in a Long Beach New York nightclub.
_____ 5. The deposition was taken on Friday January 4 8:30 a.m. in my office.
_____ 6. Irish Linens Ltd. opened a new shop and Ms. O'Callahan is the general manager.
_____ 7. Little Rock Arkansas, was the scene of tragedy and strife in the 1960s.
_____ 8. Goldfinger's Variety Stores Inc. closed the Albuquerque New Mexico store in 2007.
_____ 9. We will be in Edinburgh Scotland, on 3 May and London on 6 May 2010.
_____ 10. I hope to interview two members of the British Parliament on 7 May 2009.

Check your answers on page 456.

READ 49   A COMMA MEDLEY

A medley, which means a mixture, usually refers to a musical arrangement made up of a series of songs or short musical pieces. What follows, however, is a medley of more comma-use principles.

Quotation Marks

Use commas to separate a **direct quotation** (the exact words of a person) from the rest of the sentence.

> George said, "Isn't that Stella Glitter signing autographs in the lobby?"

Place a comma or period *before* the closing quotation mark, never after—no exceptions.

Quote at end of sentence	Years later, my former boss admitted, "I should have done more to convince you to stay with the company."
Quote at beginning of sentence	"Money is *not* the root of all evil," he said.
Quote that is interrupted	"Money," Alicia replied, "*is* the root of all evil."
Quote in middle of sentence	Jesse whispered, "Don't reveal our plans," but I didn't hear him.

Do not add a comma when a quotation ends with a question mark or an exclamation mark.

"Did you ever tell a lie?" asked Ms. Ripley.

"No, I never did and never would!" exclaimed Mr. Ripley.

A comma is unnecessary before a word or words in a quotation that is "woven" into the rest of the sentence.

We all sang "Happy Birthday" when Georgette entered the office.

Jesse answered the big question with a simple "no."

Numbers

Commas are required in numbers of more than four digits when they refer to quantity.

10,000   1,000,000

In four-digit numbers, the comma is optional, but recommended.

$2,000 or $2000

When four-digit numbers are listed along with numbers in the ten thousands and higher, use the comma in all of them for consistency.

Sales figures for the past three years were 5,000 in the first year, 7,900 in the second year, and 10,200 in the third year.

All countries do not use commas to separate digits in numbers; some use the period:

$1,321,000 (USA and some other countries)

$1.321.000 (some parts of the world)

Do not use commas in numbers that "identify," such as addresses, serial numbers, page numbers, and so on.

page 1247

19721 Victory Boulevard

No. 23890

Addresses

When address parts are in sentence form, separate the parts with commas; however, never use a comma between the state and the ZIP.

Please return the software to Computer Learning Center, 3600 Market Street, Philadelphia, PA 19104, before June 8.

The art director lives at 35 Wynford Heights, Don Mills, Ontario M3C 1k9, Canada.

REPLAY 49

A. The best way to remember the rules for punctuating quotes is to compose sentences that apply them.

1. Compose a sentence that includes a quotation at the end. ＿＿＿＿＿＿＿

＿＿＿＿＿＿＿＿＿＿＿＿＿＿＿＿＿＿＿＿＿＿＿＿＿＿＿＿＿

2. Compose a sentence with a quotation at the beginning. ＿＿＿＿＿＿＿

＿＿＿＿＿＿＿＿＿＿＿＿＿＿＿＿＿＿＿＿＿＿＿＿＿＿＿＿＿

3. Compose a sentence with a quotation in the middle. _____

_____

_____

4. Compose a sentence with an interrupted quotation. _____

_____

5. Write a sentence beginning with a quotation that is a question or an exclamation.

_____

6. Compose a sentence with a "woven" quote that does not require a comma.

_____

B. Commas in the following sentences are correct. Fill in the blanks with the comma rules that were applied.

1. Please, Mr. Gilmore, ship the merchandise to our distributor: Pueblo Art Inc., 900 West Orman Avenue, Pueblo, Colorado 81004 _____

_____

_____

2. Our home office is at 4800 Freshman Drive, but we have offices all over the world.

_____

3. On Friday, May 27, 2010, a voucher was issued allowing us to purchase 1,250 tennis rackets. _____

_____

_____

4. Fred, if you refer to men as *Mr.* in the workplace, then use the equivalent title *Ms.* for women. _____

_____

5. For career success, an employee must be dependable, cooperative, self-disciplined, courteous to coworkers and clients, effective in speech and writing, and appropriately dressed. _____

_____

Check your answers on pages 456–457. Then take the Pop Quiz on page 310.

CONCEPT REVIEW & SKILL-BUILDING APPLICATIONS

Checkpoint

Using commas correctly is important in every sentence you write. Correctly used commas are written signals that can be as effective as a speaker's pauses and voice inflections. Misplaced or omitted commas can make a sentence difficult or impossible to understand or can totally change its meaning.

Place a check in the blank next to each comma principle you've thoroughly mastered. Review any you're not sure of.

_____ Use commas between items in a series as well as before the conjunction preceding the last item. If conjunctions are used before each item, do not add commas.

_____ Use a comma between consecutive adjectives if *and* is omitted but understood.

_____ Use a comma before *and, but, nor, for, so,* and *yet* when one of those conjunctions joins independent clauses.

_____ Use a comma after an introductory expression—

> _____ that has a verb.

> _____ that has five or more words.

> _____ when necessary for clearness.

> _____ that is one word: *yes, no, well,* or *oh.*

> _____ that addresses a person by name or title.

_____ Enclose in commas words that interrupt the main idea.

_____ Don't separate a subject from its verb with a comma.

_____ Most prepositional phrases should not be enclosed with commas.

_____ Use a comma to replace omitted verbs that are understood.

_____ Use a comma before a sharply contrasting or opposing expressions. These often begin with a word such as *but, seldom, never,* or *not.*

_____ When choosing between *which* and *that* to begin a clause, use *which* with commas for "nonessential" words and *that* with no commas for "essential words."

_____ Use commas to enclose a state, province, or country following a city.

_____ Use a comma before and after dates that explain preceding days.

_____ Use a comma before and after an abbreviation of a degree following a name.

_____ Use commas to enclose direct quotations that don't end the sentence.

_____ Do not use a comma before a quotation that blends in with the rest of the sentence.

_____ Use commas to separate thousands, millions, and billions when the number refers to a quantity. (Periods are used instead in some countries.)

_____ Use commas between parts of an addresses when written within a sentence.

 ## Special Assignment

Insert or delete commas where needed in the following essay. Think of the comma principle before inserting a mark.

Robert M. Green who sold drinks at a concession stand usually prepared a popular drink containing syrup cream and carbonated water. One day, he inadvertently invented ice cream sodas when he used up his supply of cream, and substituted vanilla ice cream in the drink. The first ice cream soda was sold in Philadelphia in 1874.

Some years later in Evanston, Illinois, ice cream sodas were banned on Sundays because ministers complained that too many young people were drinking sodas instead of going to church. Soda fountain owners came up with the idea of circumventing* the law by calling them "ice cream Sundays" which were ice cream sodas without the soda. The next development was that "Sunday" the spelling of the ice cream dish was changed to "sundae" because using the Sabbath to name a food was declared irreverent.

In New York City, during the early 1900s the "egg cream" was invented—a drink made of carbonated water (seltzer) chocolate syrup and a small amount of milk. This drink which became very popular sold in two sizes—originally at 3 cents for the small glass and 5 cents for the large size. Of course the prices increased during later years of the 20th century.

Date to submit this assignment: _____

Proofreading for Careers

Insert or delete commas, and correct any other errors in the following article. Correct the printed copy using proofreading symbols or go online to correct the document electronically.

Read the Fine Print

Make sure, that you understand the terms of any contract or financial agreement you enter into with a bank, creditor or any other lending institution. Take the time to read the agreement carefully and make sure you understand everything in it. Remember, asking after you sign is to late! Seek the advice of an expert, if you are unsure about what any of the terms mean.

Before borrowing from a public, financial institution however it is a good idea to consider financial aid, provided by the US government. Federal loans, which generally offers borrowers' lower interest rates have more flexible, repayment options. *Federal Aid First* is a brochure in English and Spanish that explains why student's should apply for loans from the federal government first, before seeking assistance from a private lenders. The brochure explain the differences between federal and private loan. In addition, it list the various kind of federal loans, and the amounts of funds available. Free copy's of this brochure can be ordered from ED Pubs, P.O. Box 1398, Jessup, MD, 20794-1398.

---

*circumventing—a handy word to have in your vocabulary.

Keep in mind, that educational loans are treated just like any other creditor arrangement, which means that failure to pay, or late payments will be noted on your credit record. Terms for paying back loans for education might be tied to your enrollment status not to your ultimate graduation date. In some cases, your grade point average might also be a factor. Having a clear understanding of the loan terms a commitment to your educational goal and a focus on gainful employment are key elements for future financial solvency. In recent years, the average amount owed by students has reached approximately $20,000. Your future earning potential, which depends on having a college degree, is worth the sacrifice off paying off a loan.

Practice Quiz

If the commas in the following sentences are correct, write **C** in the blank. Otherwise, make the corrections. Capitalize the first word of new sentences you create.

_____ **1.** On Monday March 6 I expect to meet Mr. Lombard president of Lake County Industries Inc.

_____ **2.** When you attend a meeting or business lunch do you silence the ringing on your cell phone?

_____ **3.** In a business communication class you can learn oral written and nonverbal strategies for success in a career.

_____ **4.** At business meetings wear your name tag high on the right side of your chest for maximum visibility.

_____ **5.** An advertising agency acts as an intermediary between a company that wants to advertise and the various media that sell space and time.

_____ **6.** When traveling to non-English-speaking countries for business know how to say hello good-bye please and thank you in the country's language.

_____ **7.** Of course you should also know the country's money and recognize its flag.

_____ **8.** Do not however speak entire sentences in another language if you have not mastered that language.

_____ **9.** When you speak full sentences people will respond by assuming you are fluent in the language and you will be lost.

_____ **10.** Charles Davis Jr. and Charles Davis III worked for Avco Inc. before they joined Metromedia Corp.

_____ **11.** A factory closing means the community loses jobs tax revenues and consumer buying power.

_____ **12.** Charles Darwin said, "A man who dares to waste one hour of his life has not discovered the value of life."

_____ **13.** If a dependent clause precedes an independent clause put a comma after the dependent clause.

_____ **14.** Yes, it's true that Josh Wasserman is the most popular professor on campus.

_____ **15.** "In Dayton Ohio we have two factories about to close" the manager said glumly.

_____ **16.** Dr. Waterman who was a national authority on Ninja turtles developed a video game.

_____ **17.** Working quickly he carefully organized the questions and the facts.

_____ **18.** Although the new office furniture arrived telephone service was not immediately available.

_____ **19.** My supervisor asked whether I would be willing to work over the weekend again.

_____ **20.** Thomas Carlyle referred to music as "the speech of angels."

Self-Study Practice and Tutorials

Vocabulary and Spelling for Careers

For additional practice go to Appendix B, page 321.

Replay Drills

For additional practice go to Appendix C, page 389.

Companion Web Site: www.prenhall.com/smith

Go to the companion Web site to test your knowledge on self-grading quizzes and for links to other helpful online resources.

MyWritingLab

Use this online learning system for an assessment of your progress on topics covered in this chapter and progressive exercises that fit your individual needs.

10 Punctuating Sentences Properly

After completing Chapter 10, you will be able to do the following:

- Use commas, semicolons, and colons correctly to separate parts of sentences.
- Use sentence ending punctuation (the period, question mark, and exclamation point) correctly.
- Use dashes and parentheses to emphasize and de-emphasize parts of sentences.
- Use brackets to set off words and groups of words in sentences.

READ 50   THE SEMICOLON (;)

Punctuation helps you communicate with precision and without risk of criticism—or worse—dire consequences caused by misunderstanding. If you want to "get ahead" in your career, leaving your meaning unclear is something you will try hard to avoid. After studying Chapter 9, where you mastered the fine points of comma use in the middle of sentences, you will take up the halfway mark—the semicolon.

One of the best-known examples of double meaning caused by the absence of punctuation is the prophets' written reply to Roman soldiers. The soldiers asked whether they would return from the war. Since death was often the punishment for an inaccurate prediction, the Roman soothsayers took great care with their words: *ibis redibis non morieris in bello* (you will go and return not die in war). However, as punctuation had not yet been invented, the reader could interpret the prediction either way—that is, with either a pause *before* or a pause *after* "not." Say the sentence both ways, and you will see how the absence of a semicolon enabled the soothsayers to keep their heads no matter how the war turned out.

Writing for Your Career

Although email is used for informal as well as formal communications at work, accurate punctuation is required in both. Inaccurate email punctuation leads to misunderstandings and conveys an impression of carelessness. Punctuate as carefully and skillfully in a business email as you would in preparing a business communication on paper.

Punctuation affects meaning, clarity, ease of reading, and reader's emotions and mood, as well as how important or unimportant an idea seems to the reader. Punctuation expertise adds professional polish to your business writing.

Semicolons Join Independent Clauses

The **semicolon** (;) is a halfway mark because it is midway in "pausing value" between a comma and a period. That's why it consists of one of each.

Without Coordinating Conjunctions

Use a semicolon between *closely related independent* clauses that are not joined by a coordinating conjunction—*and, but, or, nor, for, so,* and *yet*.*

> Success is getting what you want; happiness is wanting what you get.

> Please take this to the messenger center; it closes at 4:30.

Use a semicolon before a transitional expression joining independent clauses.

> When you travel in other countries, your name might sound foreign**; therefore,** have a supply of your business cards ready to exchange with people you meet.

---

*When *yet* joins independent clauses, it may be preceded by a comma, a semicolon, or a period. See page 63 for more transitions.

Use a comma *after* a transitional expression of two or more syllables. (See Read 14, Three Important Corrections, in Chapter 3.) Omit the comma after short transitions—*then, thus, hence, still, yet,* and *also.*

> The early 2000s were unforgiving years; thus marginal employees didn't survive.

The preceding sentences would also be correct if written as two separate sentences.

To *separate* two independent clauses, use a *period* after the first clause and a capital letter to begin a new sentence.

You decide whether joining or separating will read more smoothly.

With Coordinating Conjunctions

Place a semicolon before a coordinating conjunction that joins independent clauses—*if* the sentence already has two or more commas.

> Professor Dennison, who works in Huntington, will present the slideshow; but we expect others to participate also.

> Through the ages languages have gathered new words; but popular use, as Betty explained, often becomes proper use.

RECAP　　Insert semicolons and commas where needed. Be sure the clauses are independent before inserting a semicolon. Write **C** before two sentences that are already correct.

_____ 1. Job security hardly exists any more now there is only skill security.

_____ 2. When unemployment is high your skills will enable you to compete.

_____ 3. Stocks can be a surefire way to double your money they are however always a risk.

_____ 4. Our company was one of the first to eliminate ID cards and replace them with an iris-reader in high security areas.

_____ 5. My employer Mr. Anton was upset by the criticism and he refused to discuss the issue of why salary increases were unlikely.

_____ 6. Banks he explained pay depositors interest on their savings accounts but borrowers must pay interest to the banks.

_____ 7. The store promised its employees a raise that is each person would receive a five percent increase.

_____ 8. Look at the left side of the top row of letter keys on your keyboard if you don't know what a "qwerty" keyboard is.

_____ 9. The motion was passed by the City Council the vote was 6 to 3.

_____ 10. When speaking with clients whose English is limited keep in mind that their nods and smiles do not necessarily mean they understand and agree with you.

Check your answers on page 457.

Additional Semicolon Uses

Before Certain Transitions

Use a semicolon after an independent clause that precedes *for example, for instance, namely,* or *that is*—if one of these transitions introduces a list or an explanation that ends the sentence.

> When invited to dinner in Egypt, bring a gift; for example, flowers or chocolates.

> Be prepared to discuss appropriate topics; for instance, topics like Egypt's ancient civilization, Egyptian achievements, or the high quality of Egyptian cotton.

Between Series Items

If there are commas *within* the items of the series, use semicolons *between* the items.

NO   AMTRAK stops at Schenectady, New York, West Burlington, Iowa, and Pasadena, California. [It seems as though AMTRAK makes five or six stops.]

YES   AMTRAK stops at Schenectady, New York; West Burlington, Iowa; and Pasadena, California. [The reader easily sees just three stops will be made.]

Rᴇᴘʟᴀʏ 50

A. Insert semicolons and commas where needed. Write **C** for correct sentences.

_____ 1. SHAPE is an acronym that is it's pronounced as one word the meaning is *Supreme Headquarters Allied Powers Europe.*

_____ 2. Lance Armstrong winner of the Tour de France seven consecutive times did not let his battle with cancer interfere with his career.

_____ 3. Our records show from June through December that we filled six orders for you every one of them was delivered promptly.

_____ 4. Our records show that we filled six orders for you every one of them was delivered promptly.

_____ 5. The new officers are Louise Fuller president Sandra Hall vice president and Gina Hecht treasurer.

_____ 6. Gene has one overpowering ambition namely to learn to fly an airplane.

_____ 7. Mark Knowlton has many assets that people don't know about for example he has a law degree.

_____ 8. A president of a big corporation usually earns a higher salary than the president of the United States.

_____ 9. A large business is highly complex and may be difficult to understand it is divided into many departments in which people perform specialized functions.

_____ 10. Like several other applicants his computer skills are good however they selected him because of his excellent writing and oral communications abilities.

_____ 11. This year Fast Track Inc. declared a dividend that is a sum of money paid to stockholders out of the company's earnings.

_____ 12. While doing research in Irish history I learned about the Kilarney elections on 19 March 1941.

_____ 13. Typewriters were first patented in 1714 but didn't become practical to use until the 1860s.

_____ 14. I am a great believer in luck and find that when I work harder I have more of it.

_____ 15. I believe therefore that you are right about that issue.

B. If you don't believe this event took place, insert one semicolon and one comma:

> _Charles the First walked and talked half an hour after his head was cut off._

Check your answers on page 457.

READ 51 THE COLON (:)

The colon is a stronger pause than a semicolon. A few simple rules will help you remember when to use the colon.

Colons Introduce and Emphasize

Like the semicolon, the colon is used after an independent clause in the middle of a sentence. It signals to the reader: pay attention to what is coming. It may or may not be followed by another independent clause.

With Words, Clauses, and Phrases

Use a colon after an independent clause if a clause, a phrase, or even a single word explains or supplements the original clause.

> Just one word describes him: lovable. [_Do not_ capitalize words or phrases introduced by a colon.]

> In an 1899 issue of the _Literary Digest,_ a prediction was made about the horseless carriage: "Automobiles will never come into as common use as bicycles."

Use a colon after a complete sentence that introduces a quotation.

> He added this statement to the contract: "The total fee of $10,000 will be paid in four installments of $2,500 each."

BUT

> Since the contract states, "The total fee of $10,000 will be paid in four install-ments of $2,500 each," and we didn't do so, please make out a check for $5,000 to cover two installments. [A dependent clause introduces the quote.]

With Items in a Series or List

Use a colon after an independent clause (a complete sentence) when it introduces items in a series.

> His goals were clear: health, wealth, and love.
>
> These traits are required of his employees: initiative, loyalty, and honesty.

BUT

> His clear goals were health, wealth, and love.
>
> The personality traits required of his employees are initiative, loyalty, honesty, and dependability.

Notice how the use of the colon places more emphasis on the items listed.

If items are listed vertically, use the colon whether or not the introduction is a sentence.

The qualities he's looking for:	The qualities he's looking for are these:
▪ initiative	▪ initiative
▪ loyalty	▪ loyalty
▪ honesty	▪ honesty
▪ dependability	▪ dependability

Do not use a colon before a list if another sentence follows the introductory sentence.

> Please send the following people to my office. I need to see them immediately.
>
> > Shuzu Itakara
> > Frank Chang
> > Sherrill Frank

Additional Colon Uses

In Written Communications

Standard punctuation style for business letters and emails that take the place of printed letters requires a colon after the salutation and a comma after the complimen-tary close.

Salutation	Dear Mr. Archer:
Complimentary close	Sincerely yours,

With Numbers

Use a colon between hour and minutes to express time and for ratios in technical writing.

> The packages were delivered at 12:30 p.m.
>
> The ratio is 3:1. [When read aloud, this technical notation is "3 to 1."]

REPLAY 51

Replace commas or semicolons with colons and change lowercase letters to capitals where needed. Write **C** beside correctly punctuated sentences.

_____ 1. Please ship the following, two dozen Style No. 308 and three dozen Style No. 402.

_____ 2. Ship these items to Birmingham, United Kingdom; Mysore, India; and Provence, France.

_____ 3. He has just one goal in life; revenge.

_____ 4. "In three words I can sum up everything I've learned about life it goes on."—Robert Frost

_____ 5. We plan to visit these cities Winston Salem, Atlanta, Newark, and Pittsburgh.

_____ 6. Two important things can be done to prevent shoplifting, place mirrors in strategic locations and post special warning signs.

_____ 7. Los Angeles Harbor College is interesting nearby are fishing boats, oil refineries, and a home port for huge cruise ships.

_____ 8. Here is something worth thinking about; a small idea that produces something is worth more than a big idea that produces nothing.

_____ 9. Judges have a double duty protect the innocent and punish the guilty.

_____ 10. Evan Davis wrote the following: "Appearance counts greatly when an employee is to be chosen from among a number of applicants."

Check your answers on page 458. Then take the Pop Quiz on page 311.

READ 52   ENDING PUNCTUATION (. ! ?)

Using the correct punctuation to end sentences might seem obvious because you've been doing it in everything you've written for many years. Nevertheless, a review here will remind you about the rules that can provide that extra touch of confidence in the correctness of your writing.

The Period

Use a period after a statement, a command, or a courteous request or indirect question that is a statement but sounds like a question.

We sent you the bill last week. [statement]

Pay your bill this week. [command]

Please pay your bill this week. [courteous request]

Would you please pay your bill. [courteous request that sounds like a question]

A courteous request means *action* is desired, *not* a reply, even when it is stated as a question.*

I asked whether you would pay your bill. [indirect question]

Use only one period after an abbreviation that ends a sentence.

Please plan to attend the meeting from 10 to 11 a.m.

Periods are frequently used to separate the digits in telephone numbers—in place of parentheses and hyphens—although it is still correct to write phone numbers traditionally.

Traditional	(800) 234-5678 or 900-234-5678
Modern	800.234.5678

Word Power

Which one gets the job? No. 1 _____ or No. 2 _____

1. He'll wear nothing that might discourage them from hiring him.
2. He'll wear nothing. That might discourage them from hiring him.

Check your answer on page 458.

The Question Mark

Use a question mark after a direct question. A direct question calls for a reply.

Will you pay the bill this week or next?

Capitalize and use a question mark after a shortened form of a question, which in grammar is known as an **elliptical question**. Capitalize each question.

Do you intend to return my deposit? If so, when?

What transportation do you want to take to the airport? The shuttle? A limo? Let me know.

Use a question mark after a sentence that might be considered presumptuous if punctuated as a courteous request.

Would you please handle my mail while I'm away? [question in a memo to your supervisor]

BUT

Would you please handle my mail while I'm away. [courteous request in a memo to your subordinate]

The Exclamation Point

Use an exclamation point at the end of a sentence to express strong feeling.

Also use an exclamation point at the end of **an interjection** (see Chapter 2).

Please send your check today!

I can't believe it!

*When asking a customer to pay a bill, the seller wants money, not *yes* or *no.*

What great pizza!

How delicious!

An exclamation point following a statement, command, or courteous request enables the reader to sense strong emotion or urgency. If the words are spoken instead of written, voice and facial expression transmit the strong feeling to the listener. Read these three correctly punctuated sentences aloud:

Would you please order the pizza.

Will you order the pizza?

Will you order the pizza!

Writing for Your Career

An exclamation point is often used in advertising copy and sales letters. Don't use it often in other workplace writing. With overuse, the exclamation point loses effectiveness—like the parent who yells at the children frequently and finds they no longer respond. Also avoid using an exclamation point to knock the reader over the head with how wonderful, cute, or funny something is.

REPLAY 52

Add periods, question marks, and exclamation points; correct comma splices with periods and capital letters. (If you need to review commas splices, see Chapter 3.)

1. I wonder whether he uses voice recognition software
2. The pizza is good, but where's the pepperoni
3. Would you please send these items overnight mail to us
4. A winner says he fell, a loser says somebody pushed him
5. Management makes important policies and decisions; we just carry them out
6. Do you know what a subprime mortgage is
7. Would Thursday be more convenient for you
8. Take advantage of this deal today
9. Would you please fax this report before you go to lunch
10. That's wonderful

Check your answers on page 458.

Word Power

Which sentence has the exclamation mark in the right place? No. 1 _____ or No. 2 _____

1. Woman! Without her, man would be uncivilized.
2. Woman without her man would be uncivilized!

Check your answers on page 458.

READ 53   DASHES, PARENTHESES, AND BRACKETS

A business writer with good precision understands even the less frequently used marks of punctuation—the dash, parentheses, and brackets. This section will clear up the use of these marks, so you will be comfortable that you're using them correctly.

Setting Off Parts of Sentences

Use either the dash or parentheses to set off parts of sentences that are not essential to the main idea in cases where using commas would disrupt the flow and possibly make the sentence harder to understand.

Dashes emphasize nonessential expressions (as defined in Read 47) ordinarily enclosed with commas. Parentheses de-emphasize such expressions.

NO	Mr. Simon, director of the Denver, Scottsdale, and Sacramento offices, said abuses have been common in ads for many weight-loss products.
YES	Mr. Simon (director of the Denver, Scottsdale, and Sacramento offices) said abuses have been common in ads for many weight-loss products. [De-emphasis of a nonessential expression.]
NO	My plan saved the company thousands, actually, it was closer to tens of thousands, of dollars last year.
YES	My plan saved the company thousands of dollars last year—actually, it was closer to tens of thousands. [Emphasis of an important but nonessential expression.]

Notice how each mark of punctuation changes where the emphasis is placed in this sentence:

Ordinary	The president of this company, a man who once earned $50 a week as a janitor, is one of the richest men in the world.
Emphasis	The president of this company—a man who once earned $50 a week as a janitor—is one of the richest men in the world.
De-emphasis	The president of this company (a man who once earned $50 a week as a janitor) is one of the richest men in the world.

Of the preceding sentences, a good writer would probably choose dashes to emphasize an interesting—but nonessential—point. However, the commas and parentheses are also correct. In the next example you can emphasize the main idea of the sentence by choosing parentheses to de-emphasize the nonessential information.

De-emphasis	Our supervisor (a new employee) is a holography expert.

However, if you wish to emphasize that the supervisor is new on the job, choose dashes for the nonessential expression. Commas would also be correct.

Emphasis	Our supervisor—a new employee—is a holography expert.

Use a dash after a word or word group that is closely related to an independent clause.

YES	Dependability, good attitude, and efficiency—those are qualities required in our employees.
OR	These are the qualities required in our employees: dependability, good attitude, and efficiency.
OR	The qualities required in our employees are dependability, good attitude, and efficiency.

Writing for Your Career

The size of dashes is indicated as follows:

■ The *em dash* (—): Make this dash on your keyboard by typing two hyphens and then hitting the space bar.

■ The *en dash* (–): Make this dash on your keyboard by typing one hyphen and then hitting the space bar or by holding down the control key and hitting the "minus" key on your number keypad.

Type dashes with no space before or after, unless your in-house style calls for spacing around dashes.

Use the en dash to show ranges when writing numbers. A hyphen (covered in the next chapter) is also acceptable for this usage.

em dash	A diamond is the hardest stone—to get. (two hyphens)
en dash	Use for a range, such as *from 100–200*. (one hyphen)

Other Uses For Parentheses

Use parentheses to enclose information that is added to a sentence for reference or clarification:

References and dates	The profits (see chart, page 7) were the highest in the history of the company (1999–present).
Numbers or letters of listed items	Please send the following as soon as possible: (a) three copies of the project specifications; (b) a schedule outlining dates for completion of each part; (c) your availability dates between now and June 1.
Abbreviations	Eligibility for membership in the American Association of Retired Persons (AARP) begins at age 50.

Using Brackets

Brackets are a stronger way to separate words from the surrounding sentence. They are mainly used to insert your own words into quotations and to insert words inside a parenthetical expression.

In Quotations

To show that you have inserted words to add clarity or information within a quotation, enclose the words in brackets:

The report stated that, "First-quarter sales [January–March] are 0.05 percent below last year in the same time period."

Sometimes you need to quote words that contain an error. To indicate that the error is from the original source, insert *sic* (which means "it is thus in the original") in brackets. The word *sic* should be italicized.

The agreement states that "both party [*sic*] must agree and sign off on any amendments." [The agreement has a mistake: the word *party* should have been *parties*.]

Expressions within Parentheses

If you need to insert a point of clarification within a parenthetical expression, use brackets instead of a second set of parentheses.

To understand the history of the company, I suggest you read the book written by its founder, Jeremy Andrews, *Braking New Ground in the Auto Industry*. (I believe it was published [by a vanity press] in the early 90s, but check Amazon.com.)

Writing for Your Career

When a complete sentence is set off in parentheses or brackets, place the end-of-sentence punctuation inside; when the set-off words are part of a sentence, place the ending punctuation outside. The preceding examples demonstrate this rule.

Rᴇᴘʟᴀʏ 53

Insert dashes, parentheses, or brackets. The commas are already correct. If a sentence may be correctly punctuated in more than one way, use your judgment. Write **C** beside the correct sentence.

_____ 1. The new board members Dr. Duzeck and Ms. Swenson will meet with the press this afternoon.

_____ 2. Charmaine the scholarship recipient praised her parents for their love and devotion.

_____ 3. The officers of this corporation the president, the vice president, the treasurer, and the secretary are all graduates of the same university.

_____ 4. The decimal equivalents see Figure 4, page 80 will help you with the percentages.

_____ 5. Harbor Office Supply Company I'll check the address has ordered three photocopiers.

_____ 6. *Roget's Thesaurus* a treasury of synonyms, antonyms, parallel words, and related words was first published in 1852 by Peter Mark Roget look up pronunciation of Roget.

_____ 7. The 7-11 chain which featured spoon straws for Slurpees, plastic straws for sodas, and reusable straws for car cups added straws that change color as a drink changes temperature.

_____ 8. Money, beauty, intelligence, and charm Stella Glitter has them all.

_____ 9. The "soap" star has money, beauty, intelligence, and charm.

_____ 10. She has all the attributes of a star beauty, intelligence, and charm but has not made a film in five years.

_____ 11. We must see him at once not tomorrow.

_____ 12. His check for $152 not $156 was returned by the bank.

_____ 13. Roosevelt Island was described as "New York City's ideal place to live a crime-free, auto-free, dog-free new _sic_ island in the East River."

_____ 14. The report indicates that "the majority of new jobs created in America today 2010 are in small companies" fewer than one hundred employees.

_____ 15. The three branches of the United States government the executive, the legislative, and the judicial derive their authority from the Constitution.

Check your answers on page 458; then take the Pop Quiz on page 312.

CONCEPT REVIEW & SKILL-BUILDING APPLICATIONS

Checkpoint

Punctuation is the most important single device leading to easy reading. With punctuation, writers imitate spoken language on paper. Write checks in the blanks below for the punctuation principles you are confident about, and review the appropriate Reads for those you're not sure of.

_____ Use a semicolon (a) to join independent clauses that are not joined by a coordinating conjunction; (b) before a coordinating conjunction that joins independent clauses that already have two or more commas; (c) before certain transitions—can you name them?

_____ Use a semicolon between a series of items when the items have commas within.

_____ Use a colon after an independent clause when (a) words that explain the clause follow it, (b) a series or list follows it, or (c) a quotation follows it.

_____ Use a colon after the salutation of a business letter, between the hour and minutes, and in ratios (or proportions).

_____ Use a period, question mark, or exclamation mark at the end of a sentence.

_____ Use a period after a courteous request, even if it is worded like a question, and at the end of an indirect question.

_____ Use an exclamation mark at the end of an interjection.

_____ Use a question mark at the end of an elliptical (shortened) question and begin it with a capital letter.

_____ Use dashes to set off an important but nonessential expression.

_____ Use an em dash to set off parts of sentences and an en dash to join numbers. Spaces are not required unless a matter of company style.

_____ Use parentheses to enclose a word or words to be de-emphasized or important but supplementary information.

_____ Use brackets to insert your own words into quotations and to insert words inside a parenthetical expression.

Special Assignment

Select ten punctuation principles from Chapters 9 and 10. (See the Checkpoint in each chapter; note that some checkpoints contain more than one principle.) Type the principles concisely, but completely. Then compose a sentence to apply each rule. By applying more than one principle within the same sentence, you may write fewer sentences.

EXAMPLE   **Principle 1:** Use a semicolon before a transitional expression that joins two independent clauses.

Principle 2: Use a comma after a transitional expression except for the very short ones.

Sentence for 1 and 2: An executive needs to make decisions quickly; in fact, decisions are often necessary before all the data is available.

Date to submit this assignment: _____

Proofreading for Careers

Proofread and correct this letter, which has various errors including the need for punctuation. Correct the printed copy using proofreading symbols or go online to correct the document electronically.

Dear Ms. Shay,

We appreciate your inquiry about socialy responsable investing unfortunately we are not licensed in your State, however if you plan to be in Washington State in the future we'll be happy to be of service. Otherwise you might want to contact the Social Investment Forum, SIF, an organization of advisers and financial planers, in your locale. Here is their address, Social Investment Forum, PO Box 57216, Washington, DC, 20037.

You can also call SIF at 202.872.5319If or call our office at 206-448-7737 and we can refer you to a Social Investment ForumSIF member in your area.

We are however licensed in many other places across the country and would be pleased to hear from your friends and family in the following states, Washington Origon New York California Colorado Kansas Massachusetts and Florida. We specialize in socialy, environmentally, and financialy responsible investments speficialy tailored to fit each investors needs!

Thank you for your interest.

Sincerely

Eric A. Smith CFP

Certified Financial Planner

After checking your corrected letter with a key or with your instructor, answer these questions: What kinds of errors, if any, did you make in completing this proofreading practice— spelling, punctuation, carelessness? How do you evaluate your English and proofreading skills?

Excellent _____ Good _____ Fair _____
Needs Improvement _____ Other _____

Practice Quiz

A. This quiz is based on Chapters 9 and 10. If a sentence is correctly punctuated, write **C** in the blank; otherwise, correct it. Take the Practice Quiz as though it were a real test. Don't look back through the book until you've finished the test.

_____ **1.** Obviously upset by the criticism he refused to make necessary changes

_____ **2.** Have you read the article entitled "Increase Your Vocabulary"?

_____ **3.** Jennifer Crystal Imports Inc. is conveniently located that is just two blocks south of the Long Beach exit of the Long Island Expressway

_____ **4.** Although I am a great believer in work, I find that the harder I work, the more I have to do.

_____ **5.** In the Hartford office for example this plan saved the company; thousands of dollars every year for the past five years.

_____ **6.** His itinerary includes sales calls in Springfield Massachusetts Urbana Illinois and Galveston Texas

_____ **7.** He had allowed the usual discount: 8 percent off for cash payment.

_____ **8.** Keep a space for study on a table or desk also set aside a time for study each day

_____ **9.** PLEASE NOTE EACH MEMBER IS RESPONSIBLE FOR KEEPING THE LOCKEROOM TIDY.

_____ **10.** Professor Billingsley said, "The American economic system is the most powerful factor in attracting immigrants to our shores."

B. Insert parentheses, dashes, or brackets where needed, and write **C** beside the one correct sentence.

_____ **11.** In the American system only one person the president can be commander in chief of the armed forces. (emphasis)

_____ **12.** The prices of greeting cards and desk sets see page 46 of the catalog are reduced.

_____ **13.** Forget the advertiser's promise that "you'll drop from a size 14 to an 8 with three minutes a day on the ab *sic* machine" it will take a lot more than that.

_____ **14.** We were cold freezing is more accurate when we walked on the glacier. (emphasis)

_____ **15.** Wade, a gentleman with esoteric interests, collects 1962 Seattle World's Fair memorabilia.

Self-Study Practice and Tutorials

Vocabulary and Spelling for Careers

For additional practice go to Appendix B, page 321.

Replay Drills

For additional practice go to Appendix C, page 395.

Companion Web Site: www.prenhall.com/smith

Go to the companion Web site to test your knowledge on self-grading quizzes and for links to other helpful online resources.

MyWritingLab

Use this online learning system for an assessment of your progress on topics covered in this chapter and progressive exercises that fit your individual needs.

11 Mastering the Fine Points of Punctuation

After completing Chapter 11, you will be able to do the following:

- Use quotation marks correctly to quote the words of others.
- Know when to use quotation marks, italics, or underlining with words and expressions.
- Apply the various uses of the hyphen, including forming compounds and dividing words.
- Use the apostrophe to show possession and to form contractions.

READ 54   QUOTATION MARKS AND ITALICS

This section will review some of the points you've already learned about using commas and quotation marks (Read 49), and also introduce new information about using quotations marks, italics, and underlining.

Quotation Marks with Quotations

Enclose **direct quotations**—the exact spoken or written words of others—in quotation marks. Do not, however, use quotation marks when paraphrasing. **Paraphrasing** means expressing someone's stated or written ideas in your own words.[*]

Quotation	The hiring manager said, "The applicant should understand Microsoft Windows applications."
Paraphrase	The hiring manager said the applicant should understand Microsoft Windows applications.
Quotation	"A business," Elwood Chapman writes, "is an organization that brings capital and labor together in the hope of making a profit for its owners."
Paraphrase	The principal aim of a business, according to Elwood Chapman, is to bring together capital and labor to make a profit for its owners.
Quotation	In 1905 President Grover Cleveland said, "Sensible women do not want to vote."
Paraphrase	In 1905 President Grover Cleveland said that sensible women do not want to vote.

Writing for Your Career

To include the name of the original source of a quotation, a good technique is to start with the quoted words and then find a suitable place to insert the source of the statement, as the Elwood Chapman quotation demonstrates above.

Quotation Marks and Punctuation

Place commas or sentence-ending punctuation inside of closing quotation marks.

> "Some publishers are born great, some have greatness thrust upon them, and others merely survive television," said John H. Johnson, founder of *Ebony* magazine.

> Mr. Johnson received the Magazine Publishers Association award for "Publisher of the Year."

If a colon or a semicolon is needed with a closing quotation mark, place the quotation mark *before* the colon or the semicolon—no exceptions.

---

[*]Be sure to include the name or a specific reference to the original speaker or writer whether you quote or paraphrase.

The following scientists were quoted in the article entitled "Rediscovering the Mind": Carl Sagan, Georgi Lozanov, and Jean Houston.

The accountant explained, "The check was accidentally postdated"; however, we have still not received a correctly dated check from the company.

If a question mark or exclamation mark is required with a closing quotation mark, "before-or-after" placement depends on the sentence. See explanations in brackets after each example.

Jesse said, "Do you really care?" [The question mark is inside the quotation mark because it applies only to the quotation.]

Did he really say, "Will you give me a raise?" [The question mark is inside the quotation mark because both parts of the sentence are questions.]

Did you know the memo said merit increases "have been cut"? [The question mark is outside the quotation mark because it applies to the whole sentence.]

Quotation Marks, Italics, and Underlining

Quotation marks, italics, and underlining are all used to indicate special usage of words, expressions, and titles. The guidelines for using each one follow. While these three styles can be applied interchangeably to some extent, always use one style within each piece of writing. Consistency makes writing clear for the reader.

Words and Expressions

It is correct to use either quotation marks or italics to show that a word or phrase is unusual—for example, a foreign word—or might seem out of place to the reader. In general use italics for foreign words and expressions and quotation marks to denote unusual or intentionally "incorrect" usage, such as slang or very informal language.

E pluribus unum is a motto found on the Great Seal of the United States.

Insert the word *sic* into a quote inside brackets to indicate that a mistake appears in the original source.

Yesterday, the boss told Gerald to "hit the road"—in other words, he was fired.

No matter what happens, I "ain't gonna" quit this job!

Too many "don'ts" in your life can lead to frustration. [Do **not** add another apostrophe between the *t* and the *s* to make the contraction plural.]

Words Referred to as Words

No doubt you have noticed the use of italics frequently in this book, particularly in the brackets that explain examples.

Use italics or quotation marks to indicate words used as words in typed copy. In handwritten copy use underlining.

Most writers use italics because it's faster to do on the keyboard. As mentioned above, use a consistent style in each piece of writing.

The word *you* is the subject in the first sentence above; the verb is *have noticed.*

Do you know how to distinguish between *effect* and *affect*?

The memo looks fine, but please change the word "deadline" to "target date" in the last paragraph.

Titles

Quotation marks and italics are both used to indicate titles, but they denote different forms of published works.

Use quotation marks for titles of *subdivisions* of published works, such as articles in magazines or chapters of books.

> You can find the article, "Twenty-First Century Career Advancement Strategies," on my Web site.

Also use quotation marks for names of short works, such as poems, songs, lectures, and so on.

> The song "New York, New York" is played every year at the Belmont Stakes, which takes place in Long Island, New York.

Use italics for full-length published books, magazines, newspapers, films, and plays. If italics are not available (usually when handwriting), underline instead.

> David Allen wrote the best-selling book *Getting Things Done.*

> According to the *New York Times* review, the film version of *Sex and the City* was a disappointment; but, still, it was a blockbuster at the box office.

REPLAY 54

This Replay requires a variety of punctuation marks, including underlines (to show italics are needed). It covers marks discussed in this Read and in previous chapters.

1. He shouted Your house is on fire

2. Your house is on fire! he shouted.

3. Alonzo whispered Are you sure you have the right data

4. Are you positive the numbers are correct he whispered again.

5. Do you know whether Jessica said Reserve a rental car

6. If you use words like ain't and theirselves in some places you will be considered uneducated.

7. My classmate pointed out that many professionals use sloppy language all the time.

8. What does the phrase negotiable instrument mean

9. He faxed us as follows We depart from O'Hare on American Flight 23 at 8 a.m. and arrive at Kennedy at 1030 p.m.

10. Was it Mr. Higgins the character in My Fair Lady who said Results are what count

11. We need more tacos for the company party Jim yelled.

12. This shipment the manager said will arrive in time for your January sale

13. Are you all right asked Ann. Yes groaned her dad, as he lifted Merriam-Webster's Unabridged Dictionary

14. Bach's Suite No. 2 in B Minor is first on the program at the concert.

15. University of South Carolina Professor Benjamin Franklin is tired of people asking him, Why aren't you out flying your kite

Check your answers on page 459. Then take the Pop Quiz on page 313.

READ 55   THE HYPHEN (-)

Half a dash equals one **hyphen** (-), but the hyphen and the dash are two completely different punctuation marks. A hyphen is smaller than an *en dash,* which is smaller than an *em dash* (see Read 53). Correct hyphen use is shown below and builds on what you learned about compound nouns in Chapter 4.

Words Spelled with a Hyphen

Hyphens are needed in some compound words. A **compound word** results when two or more words function together to form a single unit. The hyphen helps readers understand that the words have a single meaning and function. Once the compound word becomes widely used, the hyphen, which was used to avoid confusion, is often dropped and the two words are written as one.

Because spellings change over time, the only complete guide is an up-to-date dictionary. Words spelled with hyphens show hyphens in the entry word. When a dot or an accent mark appears between the syllables, write the word closed up.

Words that need hyphenation include numbers that are spelled out and words with prefixes attached.

Numbers

The numbers from 21 to 99 are spelled with a hyphen when they are not written in figures.

twenty-one   fifty-six   forty-two   ninety-nine

The numbers *one hundred, five million,* and the like are not hyphenated.

Prefixes

Some words with prefixes are hyphenated and others are not. When in doubt, consult your dictionary.

Generally, short prefixes, such as *non, over, under, semi,* and *sub* do not require a hyphen.

nonfat   overpayment   underexposed   semisweet   subhuman

Use a hyphen after the prefix *self* when it is joined to a complete word and after *ex* when it means former.

self-control   self-respect   ex-president   ex-husband

The only exception is *selfsame.*

If a prefix ending with *e*—such as *re, de,* or *pre*—begins a word that might confuse the reader, use a hyphen.

re-cover	to cover again
recover	to get better from illness or to get something back that had been lost

Most *re, pre,* and *de* words do not require hyphens; however, some are optional if the main part of the word begins with *e.*

reheat, deplane, predict   reelect or re-elect   preexist or pre-exist

Use a hyphen after a prefix preceding a capitalized word.

mid-July   un-American

RECAP   Decide whether or not to hyphenate these words and then check your dictionary to see how they should appear.

1. brother in law _____
2. vice president _____
3. semi sweet _____
4. up to date _____
5. off limits _____
6. de escalate _____
7. ex boyfriend _____
8. re discover _____

Check your answers on page 460 or in your dictionary.

Compound Adjectives

In addition to words that always require spelling with hyphens, hyphens are used for a purpose that cannot always be verified in the dictionary: to join the elements of a **compound adjective.**

> **An adjective requiring two or more words is called *compound* and has a hyphen if it precedes the noun being modified. If it is a *permanent compound*, it will be shown in the dictionary.**

> These statistics are **up-to-date.**

OR

> These are **up-to-date** statistics. [A permanent compound adjective as shown in dictionary spelling.]

> You gave a **first-class** report about life in a **four-family** house [Compound adjectives precede the nouns *report* and *house.*]

BUT

When the compound adjective follows the noun it modifies, the part of speech often changes; it is no longer a compound adjective.

> You gave a report that was **first class** about life in a house with **four families.** [Compound adjectives follow the nouns *report* and *house,* and they are not permanent compounds.]

> **Remember to hyphenate when the modifier comes *before* the noun or if the expression *is spelled with a hyphen in the dictionary.***

Word to the Wise

To recognize a compound adjective, omit one of the words. Does the phrase still make sense? Does the remaining word keep its meaning? In the first sample sentence about the report and the house, the meaning is changed completely if you refer to a **first report** or a **four house.** Since **first class** and **four family** cannot be separated, they are compound adjectives. Join them with a hyphen if they precede the noun being described.

If the first word of the compound expression is an *ly* adverb, the hyphen is not required. If, however, the *ly* word is an adjective, do use the hyphen.

The **fashionably dressed** executive carried an **Italian leather** bag. [No hyphens are required because *fashionably* is an adverb modifying the adjective *dressed*; *Italian* and *leather* are both adjectives but not compound because *leather* can be used without *Italian*—see preceding Word to the Wise.]

My employer is a **friendly-looking** man. [Friendly is an adjective; therefore, use the hyphen to create the compound adjective modifying *man*.]

Do not hyphenate common compound expressions that represent a single idea.

A **high school** student found a **Social Security** check in a **mobile home** park.

> **RECAP** Insert hyphens where needed. Consult your dictionary when in doubt about whether an expression is a permanent compound. Write **C** beside the two sentences that don't need hyphens.

_____ 1. Buy your back to school laptop computer now and get free Windows based software.

_____ 2. If you're a charge account customer, you can buy clothes now for going back to school.

_____ 3. He has a part time job planning never to be forgotten parties.

_____ 4. This seven foot tall basketball player understands the problem solving process.

_____ 5. The state of the art coffeemaker has a built in self cleaning system.

_____ 6. To get the lowest interest rate you need to be prequalified for a home repair loan.

Check your answers on page 460.

Compound Adjectives with Interrupting Words

Sometimes an adjective consists of more than one modifier with an interrupting word (or words) in between. In this case place a hyphen and space after the first adjective to show that both modifiers are part of the same compound.

The financial adviser said, "Both **long-** and **short-term** gains must be considered."

I ordered **silver-** and **gold-embossed** nameplates for the junior and senior executives, respectively.

Word Division

Another important use of the hyphen is dividing words at the end of a line. Here is the most important principle:

If you need to divide a word at the end of a line, divide only between syllables.

If a word is divided at a place other than between syllables (fl-ower), the effect of the entire document is destroyed as the reader wonders, "*Where* did that writer go to school?" Or "*Did* that writer go to school?"

In general, avoid hyphenated words by turning off your word processor's automatic hyphenation. If you use automated hyphenation, you will need to undo the following automatic word divisions: (a) proper nouns, (b) hyphens on more than two consecutive lines, or (c) hyphens on the last line of a page.

Word processing dictionaries hyphenate at the end of almost any syllable, which is fine for newspapers and certain other written materials. For professional-looking documents, however, hyphenate words in the following ways:

- Between syllables. When consulting the dictionary, refer to syllables in the entry word, not in the pronunciation. Dots, spaces, or accent marks—depending on the dictionary—show syllables.

  fol.low.ing [may be divided between the *l*'s or after the *w*]

  stopped [may not be divided because it is a one-syllable word]

- When at least two letters—preferably three—can be typed on the line before the hyphen.

  YES   rec-ognition (3 letters)
  YES   re-veal (2 letters)
   NO   a-gainst (1 letter)

- when at least three letters can be typed on the next line.

  YES   compil-ing
   NO   compa-ny

If syllables don't permit the minimum number of letters before or after the hyphen, do not divide the word.

Never divide:

- the last word on a page
- a word containing an apostrophe
- a number expressed in figures
- an abbreviation
- on more than two consecutive lines
- a word with fewer than five letters
- a word of only one syllable
- a proper noun
- between the number and *a.m.*, *p.m.*, *noon*, *midnight*, or *percent*
- unless at least three letters can be carried to the next line

Consult your reference manual for additional guidelines on word division.

Writing for Your Career

Avoid distracting the reader by using word division that might amuse or momentarily confuse:

Please send me your cat-

alog. Just over the horizon-

tal line, you'll see a number.

He had a blind date with a dog-

matic woman.

cat? horizon? dog?

Avoid word division and you won't have to worry about confusing your reader.

REPLAY 55

A. With the goal of writing that is concise and direct (a more appealing style for your reader), revise these correct sentences with compound adjectives. **Do not change the meaning.** Keep your dictionary handy.

Example Lionel Barrymore was an actor who won an Academy Award.

Lionel Barrymore was an Academy Award-winning actor.

1. I work in a building that has 100 stories. _____

2. Do you need a ladder that is 10 feet or one that is 20 feet to do the repairs?

_____

3. My father is a man who works hard. _____

4. The case against the company that is based in Dallas was handled in Seattle.

_____

B. Some words in the sentences below need a hyphen. Write the correctly spelled word in the blank, or write **C** if no correction is needed. Use the dictionary.

5. The artist feels that recreation of the entire scene is possible. _____

6. What is your favorite form of recreation? _____

7. Our overall objectives are similar, but our methods differ. _____

8. You should report underpayments as well as overpayments. _____

9. My father in law acts like a commander in chief. _____

10. Professor Foster made an offhand comment about a selfmade millionaire.

_____

11. Do you think our country will ever produce enough oil to be self sufficient?

_____

12. The newly developed procedure is unavailable for general use. _____

13. Her goal is to complete grad school by the time she is twenty five._____

14. This financier is a Johnny come lately whose effect on the market is overstated.

_____

15. A person who acts as though intellect and reason are unimportant to solving world problems is called an anti intellectual. _____

C. Use a vertical line (|) to show the preferred place to divide the following words at the end of a line. Three words should not be divided at all.

Example   cata|log   head|ed

function   believe   horizontal   wouldn't   thousands   punctuation

aligned   impossible   interrupt   syllables   stopped   guesswork

Check your answers on page 460.

| **READ 56** | # THE APOSTROPHE (')—POSSESSIVE NOUNS |

Our fine points of punctuation could not be complete without a reminder on using the apostrophe. We'll begin with a quick review of possessive nouns, as studied in Chapter 5. Here is the rule you learned in Read 22:

Possessive nouns show the relationship between one noun and another noun.

A possessive noun shows such relationships as ownership, authorship, place of origin, type of use to which something is put, and time periods.

A possessive noun always ends with 's or s'.

The first noun shows *who* or *what possesses;* the second shows *who* or *what is possessed.* The relationship is made clear by the use of an *s* and an apostrophe in the first noun.

Singular and Plural Possessives

To make a singular noun possessive, add *'s.*

the boss's office	Franklin's *From Slavery to Freedom*
Ms. Jones's secretary	a semester's work

To form the possessive of a singular proper noun with two or more syllables that ends in an *s* sound, you could omit the added *s* to avoid a hard-to-pronounce word.

Socrates' disciples   Ms. Perkins' report   Dr. Adams' prescription

To form the possessive of a plural noun, first look at the last letter of the noun. If the last letter is *s*, add only an apostrophe; if the last letter is not *s*, add *'s.*

Last letter of plural is *s*	Adamses	The Adamses' factory is closed.
	weeks	Three weeks' work was wasted.
	ladies	He designs ladies' clothes.
Last letter of plural is not *s*	alumnae	Who collected the alumnae's contributions?
	men	The men's fortunes were lost at these gaming tables.
	children	Our children's room is neat and clean.

Possessives versus Plurals

Make sure that a plural is actually a possessive before you add an apostrophe.

Do not add an apostrophe to a nonpossessive plural.

The Joneses own factories all over the world. [*Joneses* is the plural subject of the sentence; *own* is the verb; no possessive relationship is shown.]

BUT

The Joneses' factories are all over the world. [*Factories* is the plural subject of the sentence; *Joneses'* tells whose factories and is therefore possessive.]

Joint or Separate Ownership

When two (or more) nouns are used together to show something is possessed jointly, add the apostrophe to the second noun.

Rozini and Marino's factories [jointly owned]

To show separate ownership, add the apostrophe to both (all) owners.

Rozini's and Marino's factories [individually owned]

REPLAY 56

Insert apostrophes to show possession where needed and correct any *s* errors based on Chapter 5 and Read 56 principles.

1. This sales representatives approach is to get her assistants opinion of the new hardware and software. [The sales representative has one assistant.]
2. The comments are taken from Patricia Hills pamphlets. [Her name is Hill.]
3. Our womens and girls jackets are on sale for prices that fit your pocketbook.
4. Here is a statement from Donna and Garys book: "It takes more than getting their moneys worth to satisfy buyers—a fact that must be implanted in every retailers mind."
5. Ms. Watkins memos are about scheduling dates for next years programs. [Her name is Watkins.]
6. Germanys Thyssen Co. was sold to Americas Giddings & Lewis.
7. Space Shuttle Discovery astronauts attended last weekends National Science Teachers Association convention.
8. My wifes aunt is my favorite in-law; she lives on New Yorks Upper East Side.
9. The Lopez have an Internet provider called Cyberwire.
10. Dr. Lopezs husband is Baruch Meeks; they are co-editors of an online news service.

Check your answers on page 460.

READ 57 THE APOSTROPHE (')—CONTRACTIONS AND OTHER USES

The apostrophe has several other functions in addition to showing possession. Some of them, such as contractions, are easy because you use them all the time. Others, such as making abbreviations possessive, are a bit more difficult. This section reviews various uses of the apostrophe.

Contractions

Successful written communications for the workplace have a natural and conversational style. One technique to achieve naturalness is using contractions. **Contractions** are shortened forms of words formed by removing one or more letters, and replacing them with an apostrophe: *can't, won't, couldn't, it's.* Some contractions, however, are fine for conversation, but should not be used in business writing: One example is *would* as in *I'd, we'd,* or *they'd.* Consider your reader and the situation when deciding how conversational the style of a workplace communication should be. In legal or other formal documents, avoid contractions.

Here are some words frequently contracted in business writing. Look at them carefully, and remember that the apostrophe belongs where the missing letter or letters would have been.

is not = isn't	was not = wasn't	were not = weren't
are not = aren't	would not = wouldn't	should not = shouldn't
have not = haven't	will not = won't	cannot = can't
could not = couldn't	do not = don't	does not = doesn't
has not = hasn't	I have = I've	you have = you've
we have = we've	I shall or will = I'll	we shall or will = we'll
you will = you'll	he is = he's	I am = I'm
we are = we're	you are = you're	that is = that's
they are = they're	it is = it's	what is = what's
who is = who's	she is = she's	

Possessives or Contractions

Sometimes writers confuse possessives and contractions. A few pronouns that contain the words *one* and *body* often end with *'s* and may be used as either possessives or contractions, depending on the meaning desired.

anyone's	someone's	no one's	everyone's
anybody's	somebody's	nobody's	everybody's

The apostrophe represents the missing *i* in the word *is*:

> *Everyone's* going to that party.

> *No one's* at home.

> *Someone's* on duty at all times.

Now the apostrophe makes the same words possessive:

> *Everybody's* coats are in the closet.

> *No one's* home is available for the party.

> *Someone's* hours are from two to four.

The preceding contractions are correct and appropriate in conversation and in informal business writing.

Plural Abbreviations

An apostrophe is unnecessary to form the plural of all-capital letter abbreviations. Note also these abbreviations are written without periods. This is the style for most abbreviations today; consult your reference manual to be sure. See Appendix D for abbreviations often used in the workplace.

> All CEOs on our mailing list should receive a copy.

> There are two YWCAs in Toledo.

Add *'s* to make lowercase abbreviations plural if they might be misread without an apostrophe.

NO	Please be sure to "dot your is and cross your ts."
YES	Please be sure to "dot your i's and cross your t's."
NO	The department has sold out of the Mickey Mouse pjs.
YES	They department has sold out of the Mickey Mouse pj's.
NO	Too many *etc.s* usually mean the writer isn't sure of the facts.
YES	Too many *etc.'s* usually mean the writer isn't sure of the facts.

Plural abbreviations are suitable for such documents as specifications or invoices and in tables. These abbreviations do not require an apostrophe or a period at the end.

> 5 yds   6 gals   7 lbs

Generally, in correspondence or reports, spell out "quantity words," unless the document contains heavy usage of such data.

> Thank you for shipping five gallons of Chocolate Syrup in seven cartons.

> We'll use it to make 250 quarts of chocolate egg cream drinks for the party.

Plural Numbers and Words

Do not add an apostrophe to form the plural of numbers or words.

> The temperature in New Brunswick is in the 70s.

> She graduated from college some time in the late 1990s.

> The young child wrote threes backwards.

> Please omit all *therefores.*

Possessive Abbreviations

Use an apostrophe in possessive abbreviations, just as with any other noun.

> The AMA's position is clear. [singular possessive]

> Our RNs' uniforms are yellow. [plural possessive] Make *RN* plural by adding *s*; then make it possessive by adding an apostrophe.

Miscellaneous Apostrophe Uses

As a symbol, the apostrophe has several meanings. The number *4'* means either 4 feet or 4 minutes depending on the context.

Although *'06* means 2006, avoid this style in business writing, except when referring to a year of graduation such as "the class of '06" or when referring to decades.

> The Class of '95 will hold its next reunion at the Ritz Carlton.

> In the 20th century more cultural changes occurred during the '60s than in any other decade.

Ordinarily use the full number for the century.

> In 2010 our company will celebrate 25 years in business.

Use an apostrophe to represent a single quotation mark when you are placing a quotation or title within a quotation.

> The candidate said, "It was Abraham Lincoln who spoke of 'government of the people, by the people, and for the people'; and that is also my credo."

REPLAY 57

Insert apostrophes or missing numbers where an apostrophe is incorrect. Write **C** beside the correct sentences. Draw a delete mark through incorrectly used apostrophes.

Example He's not aware that Winston Churchill was in his 80s in $\overset{19}{\wedge}$54.

_____ 1. I couldnt meet you at five oclock.

_____ 2. Dot your is and cross your ts is a way of saying, "youd better make it perfect."

_____ 3. MBAs are given preference when we recruit mid- or top-level management.

_____ 4. They experienced many ups and downs before achieving their astounding success.

_____ 5. We believe the last CFOs convention was held in 07.

_____ 6. Dont use too many _ands_ and _buts_ in your writing.

_____ 7. Several MDs and RNs routinely have lunch here.

_____ 8. In tables or charts, its all right to use abbreviations like yd's, ft, or lb's.

_____ 9. During the 19th-century era known as "The Gay 90s," worker's suffered while the wealthy held lavish parties.

_____10. Three CPAs have offices in this building.

_____11. The word committed has two ts.

_____12. "Wont you please help me with this work?" Timothy begged.

_____13. Only five As were recorded on the students record.

_____14. In the early 2000s, email was not used as much as it is today.

_____15. Couldnt you make your 1s look less like 7s?

Check your answers on page 461; then take the Pop Quiz on page 315.

CONCEPT REVIEW & SKILL-BUILDING APPLICATIONS

Checkpoint

You are now an official punctuation maven! Check off the principles you have mastered. If you feel unsure about any of them, review the Read explanations.

_____ Enclose direct quotations in quotation marks. Do not use quotation marks when paraphrasing.

_____ Place commas or sentence-ending punctuation inside of closing quotation marks. Place a colon or a semicolon outside the quotation mark.

_____ If a question mark or exclamation mark is required with a closing quotation mark, "before-or-after" placement depends on the sentence.

_____ Use quotation marks or italics (or underline in handwriting) to show that usage of a word or phrase is unusual or to indicate words used as words.

_____ Use quotation marks for titles of *subdivisions* of published works and short works.

_____ Hyphenate the words for numbers twenty-one through ninety-nine.

_____ Some words with prefixes are hyphenated and others are not. When in doubt, look it up in your dictionary.

_____ A compound adjective requires a hyphen if it precedes the noun being modified. If it is a permanent compound, it will be shown in the dictionary.

_____ Do not hyphenate common compound expressions that represent a single idea.

_____ If you need to divide a word at the end of a line, divide only between syllables.

_____ To make a singular noun possessive add *'s*; to make a plural noun that ends in *s* possessive add an apostrophe after the *s*.

_____ Do not use an apostrophe for a nonpossessive plural.

_____ When two (or more) nouns are used together to show something is possessed jointly, add the apostrophe to the second noun. To show separate ownership, add the apostrophe to both (all) owners.

_____ Apostrophes are also used to form contractions, which are acceptable in everyday business writing.

 ## Special Assignment

Add or delete punctuation in the following paragraph:

When the New York YWCA offered typing instruction for women in the late 1800s the managers were called well meaning but mis-guided ladies The female mind and constitution were considered too frail to survive a six month typing course. Upon completion of the course, the womens' desire for good jobs still faced strong opposition. The business world was a mans world. Men spoke male language smoked strong male cigars and ignored the niceties.

Date to submit this assignment: _____

Proofreading for Careers

Proofread and correct this article, which has errors related to this chapter as well as others. Correct the printed copy using proofreading symbols or go online to correct the document electronically.

Words That Respect Your Readers

Consider your the reading ability and background of your audience's before you write. If you are writing for a class taught by a college professor, you can write at a higher level than if you're message will be read by adults for whom english is a second language. It is equally important to avoid talking over the head's of your readers' or talking down to them. Readers' can tell when your trying to hard too impress or when you are lecturing to them.. Avoid jargon words specific to a particular activity or line of work unless you are certain your readers will know what you are talking about. At a minimum, always define your terms.

Use three and four syllable words sparingly when you write. Why say utilize or incorporate when use will do. Long and unfamiliar words are hurdles that your readers must leap over to get to your meaning. Remember, the propose you want to serve, and keep it simple.

Certain words and phrases can convey a smug attitude. Obviously, as anyone can see, and in my estimation are example's of words that will turn off your readers, especially if your point is not as clear as you believe it to be. College's instructors will quickly detect a superior attitude if it appear in your writing. After all, your instructor's are looking to see if you can provide a straight-forward intelligent discussion of ideas in your writing assignments, not a show of your mental-superiority.

Practice Quiz

If a sentence is correctly punctuated, write **C** on the left; otherwise correct it. Look for all of the types of punctuation errors you have studied in this chapter and others.

_____ 1. "The sale of men's and boys' coats will be held next week," said the manager.

_____ 2. Your going to hire that mechanic, arent you

_____ 3. Although Charlie's aunt was eccentric, her antics have entertained countless theatergoer's since the late 1980s.

_____ 4. During the 1990's I bought technology related stocks that made me rich.

_____ 5. Regarding unneeded commas Professor Lorraine Ray of Ohio University assigned "The Stubborn Little Mark," a funny article published in last week's San Francisco Chronicle

_____ 6. Elizabeth who is a good listener never once interrupted while I read what must have seemed to be a never ending story.

_____ 7. Show us someone who habitually "oversleep's, and well show you cause for alarm.

_____ 8. The play Les Misérables is touring throughout the United States.

_____ 9. Mens roles have changed and its not unusual for successful hardworking men to also be the primary caretakers of their children.

_____10. This booklet contains hard to find facts about Aldus Manutius a 15th century Italian.

_____11. His boss shouted, Youre fired!

_____12. What time will your plane arrive Dale asked.

_____13. Did you mean eligible or illegible

_____14. "The man who lies down on the job," the lecturer said,"deserves to get run over."

_____15. Dont use aint in formal business communications

Self-Study Practice and Tutorials

Vocabulary and Spelling for Careers
For additional practice go to Appendix B, page 321.

Replay Drills
For additional practice go to Appendix C, page 398.

Companion Web Site: www.prenhall.com/smith
Go to the companion Web site to test your knowledge on self-grading quizzes and for links to other helpful online resources.

MyWritingLab
Use this online learning system for an assessment of your progress on topics covered in this chapter and progressive exercises that fit your individual needs.

12 Polishing Your Writing

After completing Chapter 12, you will be able to do the following:

- Write complete sentences and avoid fragments and comma splices.
- Write clearly and concisely and improve the style of your writing.
- Know how to construct sentences to achieve parallel parts and avoid misplaced modifiers.
- Apply the use of active and passive voice to achieve appropriate emphasis in your writing.

READ 58 · THE BUILDING BLOCKS: STRONG SENTENCES

Written workplace communications must be clear, correct, logical, concise, and courteous. This sounds like a lot to achieve, but it isn't so hard when you approach it one sentence at a time. Writing is not a one-step process. It begins with a **draft**—the first version you write with the idea in mind that you will *always* review, revise, and proofread.

In previous chapters you learned how to write grammatically correct and complete sentences with appropriate punctuation. This chapter focuses on how to achieve clear and concise writing that will make it easy for readers to understand your message. You will learn how to correct some common sentence faults that prevent writers from achieving their objectives. Here are some of the problems you will avoid with polished writing:

- Readers are amused by an error that "sounds funny" and are distracted from the message's important content.

- Readers must write or phone for clarification, thus wasting their time and yours.

- Readers misunderstand a message, and the result is a failed or an incorrect transaction.

- Readers feel frustrated trying to figure out a poorly written message when other tasks are competing for their attention, causing them to feel negatively toward you.

- Readers get the impression that the company you work for is not efficient, knowledgeable, or competent.

Writing Complete Sentences

The basic principles for writing clear and correct sentences were covered in Chapter 3. You learned how to identify the basic sentence parts and how to write complete sentences. You also learned how to recognize and correct fragments, run-ons, and comma splices. We begin here with a short review of these key elements of good sentence writing before moving on to some important and more advanced principles.

Avoiding Fragments

A sentence is a word group with a subject, a verb, and independence. If a group of words does not contain these elements, it is a fragment.

A sentence requires at least one independent clause and may have one or more dependent clauses and/or phrases.

Sentence **Business writers use gender-neutral language** for job titles to avoid offending their readers. [The independent clause in boldface is followed by two prepositional phrases.]

A fragment does not have an independent clause and is misused when posing as a sentence.

Fragment When we use words that identify people by their work. [This word group has subjects and verbs but lacks independence; it consists of two dependent clauses and a prepositional phrase.]

Sentence We often use words that identify people by their work. [By deleting the dependent conjunction *when*, you create a sentence.]

RECAP   Write **S** in the blank for the sentences and **F** for the fragments.

_____ 1. When identifying people by what they do, avoid sexist language; for example, say *police officer* instead of *policeman*.

_____ 2. Hope to hear from you soon and that you're having a great vacation in Hawaii.

_____ 3. When you accept the idea of limitation.

_____ 4. Do you accept the idea of your ability being limited?

_____ 5. By accepting the idea of limitation, you restrict yourself unnecessarily.

Check your answers on page 461.

Run-ons and Comma Splices

**Run-ons and comma splices consist of two or more independent clauses incor-
rectly joined.**

Run-on	Chad suggested this item we approved it. [Nothing joins the independent clauses but space.]
Comma splice	Chad suggested this item, we approved it. [Only a comma joins the independent clauses.]

Here are four ways to avoid run-ons and comma splices:

**Write two or more independent clauses as separate sentences instead of join-
ing them.**

Correct	Chad suggested this item. We approved it.

**Insert a semicolon, or a semicolon followed by a transitional expression, to
join independent clauses.**

Correct	Chad suggested this item; we approved it.
	Chad suggested this item; **therefore**, we approved it.

**Insert a comma plus *and, but, or, nor, for, so,* or *yet* to join independent clauses.
Very short sentences (up to about ten words) don't require a comma if the
conjunction is *and* or *or*.**

Correct	Chad suggested this item, but the auditor rejected it in his October 21 email.
	Chad suggested this item and we approved it. [no comma]

**Change one of the independent clauses to a dependent clause or a phrase;
then the word group is not a run-on or comma splice.**

Correct	Since Chad suggested this item, we approved it. [dependent clause followed by independent clause]
	Because of Mr. Valdez's suggestion, we're making the change. [phrase followed by independent clause]
	OR

We're making the change because of Mr. Valdez's suggestion.
[independent clause followed by phrase]

_____ 1. The word *marketing* needs explanation you may have first heard it used about grocery shopping.

_____ 2. In business, marketing is everything connected with distributing a product or service, therefore, it includes transporting and advertising.

_____ 3. The professional term *marketing* means everything connected with distributing a product or service therefore, it includes transporting and advertising.

_____ 4. *Marketing* is everything connected with distributing a product or service. Therefore, it includes transporting and advertising.

_____ 5. Since the professional term *marketing* means everything connected with distributing a product or service, it includes transporting and advertising.

_____ 6. Many college students major in marketing it is a field of study encompassing varied activities.

_____ 7. Many college students major in marketing, it is a field of study encompassing varied activities.

_____ 8. Many college students major in marketing, a field of study encompassing varied activities.

Check your answers on page 461.

Putting it All Together

- A **complete sentence** has a subject, a verb, and independence. A word group lacking these sentence requirements is a **fragment**.

- Both a **run-on** and a **comma splice** consist of independent clauses joined *without* a coordinating conjunction *or* a semicolon.

- A comma joins the independent clauses of the comma splice—but not the run-on. Other correct commas, however, may be elsewhere in the sentence.

Coordinating conjunctions	*and, but, or, nor, for, so,* and *yet*
Transitional expressions	*also, however, therefore, in fact, furthermore, in addition, nevertheless, otherwise, consequently, that is*

- To avoid a run-on or comma splice, do one of the following:

  a. Separate independent clauses with a period followed by a capital letter.

  b. Join independent clauses with a comma and coordinating conjunction.

  c. Join independent clauses with a semicolon, either with or without a transitional expression following the semicolon.

  d. Make one of the independent clauses dependent.

Writing for Your Career

To de-emphasize an idea in a sentence with two or more clauses, choose option **d**; that is, create a dependent clause or a phrase for the idea you want to seem less important. To give equal emphasis to both clauses, choose **a**, **b**, or **c** depending on length and ease of readability.

For further help in avoiding fragments, run-ons, or comma splices, review Read 45 Joining Parts of Sentences and Read 50 The Semicolon.

REPLAY 58

A. Use commas, periods, and capital letters to correct this business letter (names changed) from an insurance company to its public relations firm. Notice the conversational tone and easy-to-understand language after you punctuate correctly.

April 13, 20xx

Mr. Bruce Finlay President
The Piers Agency
7 North Maryland Street
Philadelphia, PA 19106

Dear Mr. Finlay

As you requested I looked over your suggestions to let you know our preferences Since your list indicates an understanding of our newsletter I'm sure your selection of topics is valid.

I'm holding the article Five Steps to a Healthy Heart for an issue close to Valentine's Day use the other articles however as you see fit Just provide a good mix of subjects

Will you please also look through the enclosed manual about our logo then you can see the various sizes available call either Heather Scanlon or Harold Teesdale our graphic artists to request negatives of the sizes you need.

Sincerely

Janet B. Sugg

Janet B. Sugg
Creative Director

enclosure

cc: Heather Scanlon
    Harold Teesdale

B. Correct the punctuation in the following sentences. Write **C** beside the sentences that are already correct.

_____ 1. I no longer maintain an office downtown, therefore, please call me at home.

_____ 2. Regarding the map, I do have people who are supposedly working on it, however, so far nothing has happened.

_____ 3. I would be happy to have your friend try his luck with the map, ask him to call me when he's in Colombia next month.

_____ 4. We are working on this project, but nothing has been completed yet.

_____ 5. The movement of money is the fuel that keeps the machinery of our economic system working, economists call this phenomenon "money flow"

_____ 6. The US economic structure is very complicated, and few people under-stand all aspects of it.

_____ 7. Most people agree; however, that the system *produces*.

_____ 8. When you go out for a business lunch, avoid ordering food that is messy to eat for example whole lobster, pasta or thick sandwiches.

_____ 9. If you order too much to eat or foods that are clumsy to eat, you're likely to have trouble answering questions and keeping up your end of the conversation.

_____ 10. At a business meal, you need to put business first, if you're still hungry you can always eat again later.

C. Write **F** for fragment, **CS** for comma splice, or **C** for correct. Correct the comma splices by inserting a coordinating conjunction; correct the fragment by crossing out one word.

_____ 1. Answer your work phone within one to three rings, say a greeting such as "hello," "good morning," or "good afternoon."

_____ 2. Also identify yourself by your organization's (and/or your department's) name and your full name, not just your first or last name.

_____ 3. Using just your first name is too informal and unprofessional sounding, just your last name sounds too abrupt.

_____ 4. Corporations must meet their responsibilities to their employees, stockhold-ers, and society and still show a profit.

_____ 5. The prices of our kitchen utensils, as you know, have not increased.

Check your answers on page 461. (Your instructor will provide the solution to Part A.) Then take the Pop Quiz on page 316.

Writing for Your Career

Write more concise sentences by omitting an unnecessary, but understood, *that*—if you're sure the resulting sentence is clear and easy to understand.

Good	We are glad that the system works.
Better	We are glad the system works.

READ 59   POLISHED WRITING

When young children write a letter or a composition, they are taught to compose short, simple sentences like those in their beginning reading textbooks. This writing style is important in learning basic written expression, but polished writing requires varying the length of sentences. Too many short simple sentences and sentences that are too long—usually, more than 25 words—are both to be avoided. With experience, writing should be a balance of long and short sentences to achieve rhythm and a smooth flow of ideas.

Revising Short, Simple Sentences

Consider joining short, simple sentences of equal importance with a coordinating conjunction. The result might be a single smoothly written sentence.

The examples that follow are exaggerations to make a point—a quick way for you to grasp the idea.

Original   Jane likes her work. Dick likes to play.

Revised   Jane likes her work, but Dick likes to play.

Consider combining two short simple sentences by making one of the clauses dependent.

Original   Jane likes to work. Dick likes to play.

Revised   Although Jane likes to work, Dick likes to play.

Consider using a phrase, an adjective, or an adverb instead of only short clauses.

Original   Jane is wearing a new dress. She looks pretty. She approached Dick. Jane is shy.

Revised   Jane, looking pretty in her new dress, shyly approached Dick.

Consider using a transitional expression to join short sentences.

A transition is like a bridge enabling the reader to cross over from one thought to the next.

Original   Dick and Jane like to read. Dick and Jane like to dance.

Revised   Dick and Jane are very much alike; for example, they both enjoy reading as well as dancing.

Not only short, simple sentences need to flow more smoothly. Two sentences together with exactly the same construction don't read very well, whether they are long or short. The following revisions show several techniques for polishing writing by avoiding repetitive structure. You might think of other ways.

Original   You write in code. That is how you convey the information secretly.

Revised   By writing in code, you convey the information secretly.

Original   The dean's office is next to the reception room. It is on the first floor.

Revised   The dean's office is next to the reception room on the first floor.

Original	Measuring industrial output is comparatively easy. Measuring an education system's output is difficult.
Revised	While measuring industrial output is comparatively easy, measuring an education system's output is difficult.
Original	Some manufacturers engage in wholesale trade. They are not regarded as wholesalers. Their primary function is that of manufacturing.
Revised	Some manufacturers engage in wholesale trade. They are not, however, regarded as wholesalers because their primary function is manufacturing.

RECAP

1. He finished dinner. He returned to work. _____

2. You might go on a trip to China for your work. Do not give your hosts expensive gifts. They might be embarrassed. They might not accept them. _____

3. Someone in China might invite you to dinner. You will get rice. Hold the rice bowl next to your mouth. They will give you other food too. Eat from every plate on the table. _____

Check your answers against possible solutions on page 462.

Revising Long, Complex Sentences

The preceding examples suggest ways to *join* ideas for more effective writing. Too much joining, however, can result in sentences that are too long and complicated for easy comprehension. Such writing, especially when combined with needlessly technical or long words, is called *gobbledygook*.

> **Gobbledygook is speech or writing with needlessly long words, superfluous words, or complicated sentence structure. Gobbledygook is pompous and hard to understand.**

Research shows that big words and long sentences do not impress readers favorably. A simple language style that expresses ideas clearly, correctly, and concisely is more likely to get results in the workplace. Unfortunately, too much writing is gobbledygook. The technical, scientific, governmental, and legal professions are especially guilty of this type of writing. (Academic and business scholars have also been known to indulge in it.) These professions desperately need individuals who not only understand their field, but can also explain it clearly in writing; maybe you can become one of them.

Gobbledygook	Distributors of merchandise for profit in the Middle Ages kept numerical records of the merchandise they sold on "tally sticks," on which they produced a notch on a stick which was then broken in half, with the merchant retaining half and the other half being presented to the customer in order to have a record of the data for the merchant and the individual who made the purchase.

You can replace this gobbledygook with concise, straightforward writing. Separate the one long sentence into three clear sentences and use fewer and simpler words.

Revised	Merchants in the Middle Ages recorded sales on "tally sticks." The data was notched on a stick, which was then split in half. The merchant kept half and gave the matching half to the customer.

The last idea in the original paragraph can be understood by the reader from the context; therefore it isn't necessary to include it.

Original	Please be advised that your inquiry concerning the availability of our recently advertised offer is being processed at this time and the products you requested will be sent to you via our express fulfillment service, which guarantees shipment within 5 business days.
Revised	Thank you for your order. It will be shipped within 5 business days.

People in today's workplace are busy and appreciate writing like the above that "cuts to the chase."

Pronoun Reference

We need to pause for a note of caution about writing longer sentences. It is especially important to provide the reader with clear, immediate reference to the pronouns you use. When nouns become separated from the pronoun that refers back to them, take special care that the references are clear.

Each pronoun should mean to the reader precisely what you want it to mean. If necessary, rephrase a sentence or replace a vague pronoun with an appropriate noun.

Poor	Ms. May is a **good writer**, **which** she acquired from a Watterson College communication expert. [Did she acquire good writing from the expert?]
Good	Ms. May is a **good writer**, a **skill** she acquired from a Watterson College communication expert.
Poor	If **washing machines** have been tearing your fine linens and laces, let us do **it** for you by hand. [Do we want to tear your linens and laces?]
Good	If **washing machines** have been tearing your fine linens and laces, let us do **your laundry** for you by hand.
Poor	**They** keep the streets clean in Auburn Hills. [Avoid vague use of *they*.]
Good	The streets are clean in Auburn Hills. OR The sanitation department keeps Auburn Hills' streets clean.

REPLAY 59

Rewrite the following sentences to improve the sentence construction. Add and delete words where necessary for clarity and conciseness, but take care to maintain the sense of the original sentence.

1. The beautiful movie star smashed a bottle of champagne over the stern as she slid gracefully into the sea. _____

2. We got up at 6 o'clock. We had a quick breakfast. _____

3. A college pennant is in the student's room. There is also a picture by Monet. Both of these hang on the wall. _____

4. A house sits far back among the trees, and it is in need of painting. _____

5. Dennis and Mike walked to the telephone company office, from there they walked to the gas company, then they went to the electric company. They were paying their bills, it took them all afternoon. _____

6. An animal paced restlessly back and forth in the cage, it appeared to be a hyena. _____

7. We realize that people who travel by airplane make a choice of an airline based on the quality of its service to the people who fly on that airline's planes, and we are extremely regretful that we have not been able to meet your expectations. _____

8. We received your May statement. We are enclosing a check in payment. The check is for $635.23. _____

9. I missed the final exam because I had been out late the night before, nevertheless, they wouldn't give me an "Incomplete" or "Withdrew" grade, they failed me. _____

10. For those of you who have small children and didn't know it, we have a nursery downstairs. _____

11. We don't recommend that Mr. Nguyen go to Mr. Anderson's office uninvited because he is so busy. _____

12. Despite our repeated reminders regarding nonpayment of your account, which is long overdue. _____

Check your answers against possible solutions on page 462.

READ 60   WELL-PLACED AND PARALLEL PARTS

The late James McSheehy, a member of the San Francisco Board of Supervisors, addressed a group of women about his work on a finance committee. "Ladies," he said, "I have here some figures I want you to take home in your heads, which I know are concrete." Of course, Mr. McSheehy really meant that the *figures* were concrete. To avoid this kind of error in your writing, look for **misplaced words** when revising and proofreading. If the words in a sentence are not in correct order, the reader or listener may be confused or amused. Either way, concentration on your message is lost.

Misplaced Words

Avoid the sentence fault of *misplaced words*. Make sure the words in each sentence are in the best place for getting the message across.

Misplaced	I have some figures that I want you to take home in your heads, which I know are concrete. [*which I know are concrete* are the misplaced words]
Correct	I have some figures, which I know are concrete, that I want you to take home in your heads.
Misplaced	Irene hung a picture on the wall painted by Rembrandt. [Rembrandt painted the wall?]
Correct	The picture Irene hung on the wall was painted by Rembrandt.
OR	Irene hung a Rembrandt in the president's office. [Unnecessary words are omitted, and additional information is included in one concise sentence.]
Misplaced	He only had $5 when he arrived in Kenansville. [No one else, only *he*?]
Correct	He had only $5 when he arrived in Kenansville.
Misplaced	On the bulletin board of a factory building—WANTED: Worker to sew buttons on 4th floor.
Correct	WANTED ON 4TH FLOOR: Worker to sew buttons.

RECAP   Find the misplaced words in each sentence and move them to where they belong. Write the correct sentence in the blank.

1. We sat there listening to his singing in awed silence. _____
   _____

2. Ms. Griggs worked for CNN during her vacation in the Headline News Department.
   _____
   _____

3. Genevieve Astor died in the home in which she had been born at the age of 96.

   _____

   _____

4. The fire was brought under control before much damage was done by the fire department. _____

   _____

Check your answers against possible solutions on page 462.

Parallel Parts

Parallel construction enables readers to understand immediately how two or more parts of a sentence are related.

> **Express parallel ideas—that is, similar sentence elements—in the same grammatical form.**

In the following examples, words that are _not parallel_ are in boldface in the first sentence, and words that make the parts parallel are in boldface in the revision.

Not parallel	The cat chased the mouse **around** the barn, **out** the door, and **then they** ran into the yard.
Parallel	The cat chased the mouse **around** the barn, **out** the door, and **into** the yard.
Not parallel	He was **tall**, **dark**, and **had a handsome face**. [Make all three describing expressions parallel by using three adjectives and omitting the unneeded words.]
Parallel	He was **tall**, **dark**, and **handsome**.
Not parallel	His ambitions were **to join** a fraternity and **becoming** a football player. [Use _to with a verb_ (the infinitive) before each ambition. **OR** use the _ing_ form for each ambition.]
Parallel	His ambitions were **to join** a fraternity and **to become** a football player.
OR	His ambitions were **joining** a fraternity and **becoming** a football player.

RECAP   Rewrite the following sentences so that the parallel ideas are parallel in construction; that is, they have the same grammatical form.

1. With the new software we hope to improve response time, reducing input errors, and see that systems problems are identified more readily. _____

   _____

2. Typing accurately can be more important than to type fast. _____

   _____

3. Linda is a full-time securities analyst, and her husband is working part time as an insurance agent. _____

4. We would appreciate learning your views on how to introduce change, controlling quality, and the motivation of employees. _____

_____

5. Ophthalmologists and optometrists may examine eyes, and prescriptions for glasses may be issued by them also. _____

_____

Check your answers against possible solutions on page 463.

Word to the Wise

Little Girl   I know a man with a broken leg named Jones.
The Nanny   Oh really? What's his other leg named?

What is the name of the little girl's sentence fault? _____

REPLAY 60

A. Write **P** for lack of parallel parts, **M** for misplaced words, and **C** for correct.

_____ 1. Oranges are a valuable source of vitamins, which are not mentioned in your report.

_____ 2. The English teacher was sitting by the fireplace with his dog reading Shakespeare.

_____ 3. He is interested in science, math, and he likes to read good books.

_____ 4. Mr. Gorjus was frantically searching for the telephone number in his office that was missing.

_____ 5. The woman suggested that we fill out the form and to leave it with her.

_____ 6. Ad for a famous cosmetic: Lady Ester Dream Cream is recognized by leading dermatologists as highly effective in improving skin's texture, smoothness, and for counteracting aging.

_____ 7. I believe that playing a good game of chess is a better accomplishment than to play a good game of bridge.

_____ 8. Writing business documents requires excellent grammar, and they should be punctuated very well also.

_____ 9. Her hobbies are painting, to go to concerts, and reading blogs on the Internet.

_____ 10. A wholesaler's function is to buy in large quantities and sell in small quantities.

_____ 11. The father sat down in an easy chair to tell his children about his childhood after dinner.

_____ 12. According to a "Human Development Index" that includes incomes, education, and life expectancy, Norway ranks second in the world.

_____ 13. A major Norwegian industry is production and transporting oil and gas from offshore petroleum deposits.

_____ 14. Norway is heavily dependent on world trade conditions with a population under five million.

_____ 15. We would like to hear your ideas on motivating employees and how to introduce change.

_____ 16. Some employees react quickly, get things done promptly, and beat deadlines.

_____ 17. That program has too much sex, violence, and the language is bad.

_____ 18. Friendship means forgetting what one gives and remembering what one receives.

_____ 19. She believed him as well as having faith in him.

_____ 20. At the age of seven, my father gave me a kitten.

B. Type the number of each item in Part A that you marked **P** or **M**, and polish the sentence.

Check your answers for Part A on page 463.

Your instructor will provide solutions to Part B.

READ 61 GETTING TO THE POINT

Do you know someone who makes a "beeline" for the snack table upon arriving at a party? This food fancier moves in a straight, unwavering path just as a bee flies directly to its chosen flower. Similarly, a well-written sentence makes a beeline to get to its point. Good writers know that their readers are busy and do not have time to sort through ideas, make assumptions, or ask follow-up questions. In the workplace, people usually react most favorably to a **direct writing style**.

In addition to your friend who makes a beeline for the refreshments, you may have other friends who eventually get there but take their time about it. They don't want to appear to be pushy or rude. In the same way, skillful business writers sometimes use a more **indirect writing style**, when a situation requires being tactful or de-emphasizing parts of a message.

Voice of Verbs

To write a sentence in the direct or indirect style, you need to know about the **voice of verbs**. The way you construct a sentence can change verb _voice_—which may be _active_ or _passive_.

Active Voice

A direct writing style uses _active voice_, which means the subject _does_ the verb's action.

Carl ignored the boss. [The subject _Carl_ did the action—_ignored._]

The United States won 110 medals at the 2008 Summer Olympics. [The subject _United States_ did the action—_won._]

Passive Voice

An indirect writing style uses *passive voice*, which means the subject *receives* the verb's action.

> The boss was ignored by Carl. [The subject *the boss* received the action—*was ignored*]
>
> One hundred and ten medals were won by the United States at the 2008 Summer Olympics. [The subject *medals* received the action—*were won.*]

Since the required ingredients of a sentence are subject, verb, and independence, you can write complete sentences in the passive voice without mentioning who did the action.

Passive   The boss was ignored. [This sentence has a subject and a verb and is independent; it is passive because the subject *received* the action]

One hundred and ten medals were won at the 2008 Summer Olympics. [This sentence is in passive voice because the subject is the receiver even though the doer of the action, *the United States,* is not named.]

Choosing Active Versus Passive Voice

Use active, rather than passive, voice for most workplace writing. It is often more concise.

Fewer words are usually required for the active voice; it is more efficient, and it takes the reader from Point A to Point B in a straight line. In the following sentences, there is no reason to use the passive voice:

Active   Jesse accurately prepared a spreadsheet of the accounts receivable.
Passive   The accounts receivable spreadsheet was prepared accurately by Jesse.

The accounts receivable spreadsheet was prepared accurately.

Active   George presented the report to the stockholders.
Passive   The report was presented to the stockholders by George.

The report was presented to the stockholders.

Use passive voice for tact or emphasis.

Tact

You may want the reader to know about an error but prefer to omit the culprit's name or soften the impact of the news.

Passive   An error was made on the report.

The payment of your invoice has been inadvertently delayed.

Emphasis

Use the passive voice if you don't know who is doing the action, or if you want to emphasize the receiver of the action rather than the doer. The passive enables you to begin the sentence with the receiver; you can omit the doer or end with the doer. For example, the report is more important than the auditor in the following sentence:

Passive	A report was presented to the stockholders by the auditor.
	OR
	A report was presented to the stockholders.
Active	The auditor presented a report to the stockholders.

Distinguishing Active from Passive Voice

A quick test can help you detect the voice of a verb. If "by someone" makes sense after the verb, the voice is passive. If "by someone" is already there, then you *know* it's passive.

Passive	The book was purchased last week. [**Test:** The book was purchased (by someone) last week. "By someone" makes sense after the verb.]
Active	Dorothy Larson bought the book today. [**Test:** Dorothy Larson bought (by someone) the book today. "By someone" after the verb doesn't make sense.]

REPLAY 61

Write **A** next to the sentences with active voice verbs and **P** next to those with passive voice verbs.

_____ 1. Antarctica is not owned by any country.

_____ 2. Interested nations from around the globe have signed an agreement to preserve Antarctica as a zone of world peace.

_____ 3. Military activity, nuclear testing, and disposal of radioactive waste are prohibited in Antarctica by the Antarctic Treaty.

_____ 4. Constantly chattering penguins bellyride down icy slopes and dive into the placid waters of Antarctica.

_____ 5. The Atlantic, Pacific, and Indian Oceans surround Antarctica.

_____ 6. Antarctica is surrounded by parts of the Atlantic, Pacific, and Indian Oceans.

_____ 7. When doing business in England, use the term *British* rather than *English*— except for referring to the language.

_____ 8. A great many jobs now involve interactions with people living in various countries.

_____ 9. Importers and exporters constantly move merchandise from one country to another.

_____ 10. Some knowledge of geography, history, and foreign languages is needed for advancement in today's global market place.

_____ 11. Companies such as Avon Products and the Fuller Brush Company used to employ sales representatives who sold products door-to-door.

_____ 12. In today's economy and culture, few products can be sold that way.

_____ 13. Many people who can afford to buy are at work, and some others won't open the door to a salesperson because of fear of crime.

_____ 14. The plants were watered every day during your vacation.

_____ 15. All freight charges must be verified before they are paid.

_____ 16. He misspelled "Mississippi" in every paragraph.

_____ 17. "Mississippi" was misspelled in every paragraph.

_____ 18. These tools are manufactured in Toronto.

_____ 19. Networking engineers take care of problems day or night.

_____ 20. She sold all her stock during a bear market.

Check your answers on page 463.

READ 62   AVOIDING DANGLERS

Another problem to look for when revising and proofreading your work is known in grammar as the **dangling verbal.**

A verbal is not a verb; it looks like a verb but isn't functioning as a verb. A dangling verbal is a phrase containing a verbal that hangs loosely, or dangles, in a sentence.

A verbal may be one of the following:

- **An infinitive:** *to* plus a verb, such as *to work, to go, to eat*
- **A past participle:** *worked, gone, eaten*
- **A present participle:** *working, going, eating*
- **A combination:** *having worked, to have gone, to be eating*

A dangling verbal phrase usually—but not always—opens a sentence, and a clause follows it. If the word group in question has a real verb, the word group is not dangling.

Sentences with Danglers

The subject of the clause following a verbal phrase must tell who does the action referred to in the verbal phrase.

If the subject doesn't tell who does the action of the verbal, the verbal phrase is dangling. The resulting sentence may amuse, confuse, or distract the reader.

Dangler   To get the most out of our time, the session will include discussion of our day-to-day problems.

The verbal is *To get*. It looks like a verb, but it isn't because it can't have a subject: You wouldn't say, "I to get the most out of our time." It would have to be "I **want** to get . . ." with *want* as the verb. After noting that the sentence begins with a phrase containing a verbal, find the subject of the clause that follows the phrase; the subject is *session*. Then ask, "Is the **session** to get the most out of our time?" No, it's **we** who want to get the most out of our time. Therefore, the verbal phrase is dangling. To stop the dangling, the subject must identify **who** is to get the most out of our time:

Correct   To get the most out of our time, we will include in the session a discussion of our day-to-day problems.

Dangler   Having made too many errors on the test, the personnel director did not hire Joe.

Since it was not the personnel director who made the errors, the opening phrase is dangling. Save the verbal (having made) from dangling by changing the subject to the one who did make the errors.

Correct	Having made too many errors on the test, **Joe** did not get the job.

Having made is a verbal—not a verb—because you can't give it a subject.

Also correct	Because Joe made too many errors on the test, he did not get the job.
Dangler	While flying over the jungle at an altitude of 2,000 feet, the villagers could be seen hunting and fishing.

The opening phrase includes the **verbal** "flying." Notice that *flying* can't be a verb unless a helping verb precedes it. You can't say, "They flying over the jungle." The **subject** following the phrases is **villagers**. To decide whether the opener is dangling, ask, "Are the villagers flying over the jungle?" Since the answer is "no," correct the sentence so that the subject tells who is flying:

Correct	While we were flying over the jungle at an altitude of 2,000 feet, we could see the villagers hunting and fishing.
Dangler	After looking at the cars for a while, the salesperson approached me.

After looking at the cars for a while is dangling. Was the salesperson looking at the cars? To make this sentence clear and avoid a dangler, the **subject** must be the one doing the looking:

Correct	After looking at the cars for a while, I was approached by the salesperson.

RECAP	Rewrite this sentence so that the verbal doesn't dangle. [Make the **subject** of the **independent clause** do the verbal's action; for example, the subject could be *you* or *I*.]

Dangler	While strolling along the beach, unusual shells and pebbles can be found.
Correct	_____

Check your answer on page 463.

Another way to correct a dangling verbal is to change it to a subject and verb—that is, a clause; clauses don't dangle.

Dangler	While swimming in a river near his farm, his clothes were stolen.

Since his clothes were not swimming in the river, change the dangling verbal phrase to a dependent clause; that is, a dependent conjunction (*While*) followed by a subject and a verb. Then the second clause does not have to be changed.

Correct	While **he was swimming** in a river near his farm, his clothes were stolen.

Do not try to correct a dangler by merely moving the beginning of the sentence to another place. The result is often a dangler in the middle or at the end of the sentence instead of at the beginning:

Dangler   His clothes were stolen while swimming in a river near his farm.

The sentence still reads as though his clothes were swimming in the river, but the verbal is now midsentence.

Dangler   Having been sick for two weeks, Enrique's father took him to the doctor.

Father is the subject; *Enrique's* is a possessive noun. Father was not sick for two weeks. Therefore, *having been sick for two weeks* is dangling. The correction below changes the opener to a dependent clause.

Correct   After Enrique had been sick for two weeks, his father took him to the doctor.

Dangler   Driving too fast through the busy intersection, the brake was applied quickly.

Correct   After driving too fast through the busy intersection, I applied the brake quickly.

                After I had driven too fast through the busy intersection, a police officer stopped me. [Verbal is changed to a dependent clause.]

RECAP   Use the methods described here to rewrite these sentences so that the verbals are no longer dangling.

---

1. **Dangler**   Being one of our most discriminating customers, we invite you to attend this private showing. [*we* are not our own customer]

   Correct   _____

                 _____

2. **Dangler**   Turning the corner, the new building was right in front of him.

   Correct   _____

3. **Dangler**   While using the computer, the cursor became stuck in the middle of the screen.

   Correct   _____

4. **Dangler**   Unlike many others who became millionaires in the 1990s, her talents in fine art and classical music resulted in her financial success.

   Correct   _____

                 _____

5. **Dangler**   Before having dinner with the woman he met through Ultimate Encounters Online Dating, his table manners need improvement.

   Correct   _____

                 _____

Check your answers against possible solutions on page 463.

REPLAY 62

If the sentence has a dangler, underline it and write **D** in the blank. Otherwise, write **C** for correct.

_____ 1. Having typed just half the report, the phone began ringing insistently.

_____ 2. On examining the goods, we found them to be defective.

_____ 3. Like many people living in Alaska, the summer months are our favorites.

_____ 4. Having recovered from his illness, his mother took him to Israel.

_____ 5. To keep the machine running in perfect condition, we oiled it once a month.

_____ 6. Before going to lunch, this report must be typed.

_____ 7. This report must be typed before going to lunch.

_____ 8. Walking quickly down the aisle, her skirt caught on a nail.

_____ 9. While doing the daily chores, a fire started in the farmer's barn.

_____ 10. Handing me the $50,000 order, his face broke into a broad smile.

_____ 11. Having produced a printout, the text was stored on the CD.

_____ 12. After looking the cars over for a while, a saleswoman approached me.

_____ 13. Looking marvelously glamorous in a midnight blue gown, Mr. Martinez accompanied Stella Glitter to the performance.

_____ 14. Upon landing in Dallas, his assistant picked him up at the airport.

_____ 15. Good communication skills and interpersonal effectiveness are qualities employers look for when interviewing job candidates.

_____ 16. When looking up a word in the dictionary, notice its pronunciation as well as definitions.

_____ 17. Being in dilapidated condition, she bought the building cheaply.

_____ 18. If invited to dinner at a colleague's home, chocolates or flowers are a suitable gift for the hosts.

_____ 19. If you decide to give flowers, avoid white lilies as they suggest death.

_____ 20. To be a serious student of business, you should understand advertising, promotion, and marketing.

_____ 21. Confused by crowds rushing around the campus, a new student welcomes a familiar face with a sigh of relief.

_____ 22. After standing and repeating the pledge, the meeting began.

_____ 23. While walking home, a hundred dollar bill suddenly appeared before me.

_____ 24. While I was walking home, a hundred dollar bill suddenly appeared before me.

_____ 25. It began to rain after being on vacation for two hours, and it didn't stop for two weeks.

Check your answers on page 464. Then take the Pop Quiz on page 317.

CONCEPT REVIEW & SKILL-BUILDING APPLICATIONS

Checkpoint

Overcoming common sentence faults is a major step toward improving your workplace writing and increasing your opportunities for a successful career. Place a check in the blank next to each item when you can recognize and correct the following sentence faults.

_____ run-on sentences   _____ comma splices

_____ fragments   _____ too many short, simple or long, complex sentences

_____ unclear pronouns   _____ misplaced words

_____ nonparallel construction _____ gobbledygook

_____ dangling verbals   _____ active and passive voice

Special Assignments

A. Writing That Works

In 100 to 150 words write an explanation of how to do something while imagining that your reader does not know how to do the task. The explanation must be clear enough that your reader could perform the task by following your written instructions. Choose something that you understand very well; for example, sewing on a button, changing a tire, filling up your tank at a self-service gas station, making a favorite snack or meal, or answering a business telephone and taking a message. Use complete sentences with smooth transitions. Vary your writing style—the length and structure of your sentences—and make sure sentences are clear, concise, logical, and grammatically correct.

Sample Opening Sentence

Sewing a button on a shirt is easy if you have the right tools and follow these steps:

Date to submit this assignment: _____

B. Write What You Mean

Rewrite these ads so that they say what they mean and mean what they say:

■ Wanted: Student to deliver fish and oysters with good references.

■ Now you can buy six different products to protect your car from your ExxonMobil dealer.

■ Wanted: Someone to take care of horses who can speak German.

■ Now on the market: a Norco Shaver for women with three heads.

Date to submit this assignment: _____

Proofreading for Careers

A well-written article has been altered to provide practice in correcting word and sentence errors based on the principles you have mastered so far. Correct the printed copy using proofreading symbols or go online to correct the document electronically.

The Power of Creative Thinking

Much of what we call progress in the world, it come from seeing old ideas from new perspectives. The New World would not have been discovered by the explorers in the fifteenth century If they had held to the widely accepted belief that the world was flat. If no one had of challenged the notion that only men are smart enough to vote; women would still be without this basic right.

Creative thinkers'examine information and are looking at data from all sides! They ask "What if?" How about if I tried this? "How can that be?" and wonder if that works, maybe I could try this.

Creative thinker's trust their instincts. Do you sometimes just "have a hunch." Do you feel that something is right or wrong A feeling that seems to come from within, are called your natural instinct. The dictionary defines instinct as a natural aptitude. Don't negotiate your way on natural instincts alone, The world is far too complex. Don't forget creativity springs from internal "hunches". Combine hunches with a solid knowledge base. For example, creative artists often base their subject matter on real life creating a work of art for others to appreciate by relying on shared experiences expressed through the medium of their chosen art form and similarly, great actors often rely on instinct to interpret a role They still follows the rules of the stage when performing. The lesson is this instincts, combined with intellectual knowledge and skill, is a powerful combination.

Practice Quiz

Take the Practice Quiz as though it were a real test—don't look back through the chapter.

I. Write the appropriate letter and number in the blank according to these instructions:

A Properly constructed sentence

B (1) Fragment or (2) Unclear pronoun

C (1) Run-on or (2) Comma splice

D (1) Lacks parallel parts (2) Has too many short, simple sentences (3) Has a dangling verbal

E (1) Misplaced words or (2) Gobbledygook

_____ **1.** Marianne is smart. She likes to study. She also likes her job.
_____ **2.** The new drug has proved to be highly effective it has no side effects.

_____ 3. Mara heard Beth talking to her boyfriend on the phone.

_____ 4. He is an extremely capable worker, however, he lacks seniority.

_____ 5. The angry manager began stamping his foot and to pound the desk.

_____ 6. Managers tend to promote people who can make decisions even at the risk of being wrong.

_____ 7. He is very much interested in science, which he acquired from his cousin who is a chemist.

_____ 8. Working accurately is more important than to work fast.

_____ 9. The main problem for people who grow African violets is that they stop blooming.

_____ 10. When completing the invoice, one item was omitted.

_____ 11. After voting on several issues, the meeting was adjourned.

_____ 12. The bank approves loans to reliable individuals of any size.

_____ 13. Even though Shirley's project is in shambles.

_____ 14. The steps for making peanut butter are picking the nuts, roasting the nuts, and to squeeze the oil from the nuts.

_____ 15. Learning to fly is challenging and a thrill.

_____ 16. This is a beautiful sentiment from _The Diary of Anne Frank_: "Think of all the beauty still left in and around you, and be happy."

_____ 17. Market research and analysis is assuredly and definitely a specialized field of endeavor, and especially excellent career opportunities for being productive exist in these fields of productivity for human beings who seek to be gainfully employed.

_____ 18. To get the most from your employees, it is important to be sympathetic.

_____ 19. While going over the work more carefully, more errors were discovered.

_____ 20. A symbol of life, wealth, and fertility since ancient times, rice sustains half the world.

II. Write **A** if the verb is in the active voice and **P** if it is in the passive voice.

_____ 21. The people of Scotland are called _Scots,_ not _Scotch._

_____ 22. They named the alcoholic beverage _Scotch._

_____ 23. Scots speak _Scottish_, not _Scotch._

_____ 24. "Cheese" should be said by everyone who wants to be in the picture.

_____ 25. Allegiance to the flag is pledged by me.

Self-Study Practice and Tutorials

Vocabulary and Spelling for Careers
For additional practice go to Appendix B, page 321.

Replay Drills
For additional practice go to Appendix C, page 401.

Companion Web Site: www.prenhall.com/smith
Go to the companion Web site to test your knowledge on self-grading quizzes and for links to other helpful online resources.

MyWritingLab
Use this online learning system for an assessment of your progress on topics covered in this chapter and progressive exercises that fit your individual needs.

13 Writing Workplace Communications

After completing Chapter 13, you will be able to do the following:

- Write workplace communications using a friendly tone, appropriate to your audience.

- Follow the process of planning, drafting, revising, and proofreading written communications.

- Compose and format the standard parts of emails, interoffice memos, and letters.

READ 63 WRITING STYLE

Today's workplace thrives on written information. While much of it is still communicated on paper, email has replaced the need for many printed written communications—particularly interoffice memos and letters on routine business matters. **Written communications**—both print and electronic—provide a record for both sender and receiver. Unlike telephone calls, arrival of written communications doesn't interrupt the receiver.

Employees and entrepreneurs who are effective communicators are vital to an organization's success and are often rewarded by career advancement.

Knowing how to write and format professionally prepared written communications—emails, interoffice memorandums, and letters—is essential. We will begin with the process of planning and drafting your writing.

Planning

Whether you are writing a routine email message or a complex letter or report, planning is essential to clear and concise communication.

Planning involves three key steps:

Define Your Purpose

Know what your purpose is and do not stray from it. Use separate communications to deal with different subjects to make it easier for your reader to respond. Make notes or develop an outline to structure the organization of your message. Move topics around until you are sure the order is logical and will be clear to your reader.

Know Your Reader

Target your message or the information you include in a longer document to the needs of your reader. The more complex your subject, the more you will need to think about exactly how much detail is needed. Know exactly what you want from the reader, and be explicit in your message if a specific action is being requested.

Gather Quality Information

Make sure your content is correct and is adequate to achieve your purpose. Double-check numerical data, calendar dates, dollar amounts, spelling of names, and other such factual information, no matter how routine the communication might be.

Drafting

Begin writing with the idea that you will revise. Even the most experienced business writers make changes on their first drafts. Your thoughts will flow more smoothly if you write quickly and get all your thoughts down without stopping to make changes or reorganize.

Develop Paragraphs

Paragraphing is based on the key points you want to cover. Breaking content into paragraphs provides a structure for the information, which aids reading and understanding. Each paragraph needs an opening sentence that introduces the main idea, followed by supporting statements that provide details. Keep in mind that readers don't like to be confronted with long blocks of text. In the revision stage you will review each paragraph and look for places to break up long blocks of text.

As you draft, try to develop an **opening**, a **body** (the main content), and a **closing**. Opening and closing paragraphs are often short—sometimes just one or two sentences is enough. A brief and clear opening tells the reader what the letter is about and is followed by the main message. A closing sentence or short paragraph might briefly summarize key points, express appreciation, or directly state what you want the reader to do. For example:

Dear Mr. Goldman:

The three dozen gold charms you ordered January 3, Order No. 268, were shipped overnight today. The attached order form provides details and the UPS tracking number for the package. We apologize for the delay, but believe you'll be pleased with the rapid turnover of these delicately engraved charms.

We appreciate your business and look forward to continuing the relationship. Our sales representative, Kim Silverstein, will be in to see you soon to show you our newest sterling bracelets—designed by Pagliano, the famous Italian silversmith. She will contact you within the next week to make an appointment.

It is a pleasure doing business with you.

Sincerely,

There is no "right" or "wrong" way to separate content into paragraphs—only good or poor judgment. Avoid a "chopped-up" look of too many short paragraphs one after the other. Long paragraphs, however, look hard to read and discourage busy people from concentrating on the message. The logical organization of your subject will determine the number and length of paragraphs.

RECAP   Write **T** for true or **F** for false beside each statement.

_____ 1. Good writers follow specific paragraphing rules.

_____ 2. The first and last paragraphs of written communications are often the shortest.

_____ 3. Most communications written in the workplace don't require any planning.

_____ 4. For the sake of time, try to write only one draft whenever possible.

_____ 5. Even routine communications require fact checking.

Check your answers on page 464.

Use a Friendly Tone

The majority of written workplace communications involve sending or requesting information, providing directions or instructions, transmitting or acknowledging receipt of something, and confirming plans and agreements. All of these communications have a secondary purpose: To build rapport with the recipient, who may be a colleague, a customer, a client, or a professional acquaintance with whom you wish to establish a working relationship. Given this underlying purpose for writing, all communications should aim to make the reader feel that a warm human being wrote the message, not an impersonal corporation or a computer.

Say It in Plain English

Often business writers go out of their way to use words that will make them seem "businesslike"; this is exactly the opposite of good workplace writing. Using words with many syllables and attempting to sound impressive or adopting a stiff, formal tone makes writing come across as pretentious and makes the writer look insecure. Instead, select words that deliver your message clearly and completely, and that help build a good relationship between you (and your company) and the reader. Plain (but correct) English can boost productivity, improve customer relations, and reduce costs caused by misunderstandings.

Compose emails, letters, and memos in a friendly, conversational tone—but use complete, clear sentences and Standard English.

Business communications shouldn't look like you wrote them for an antique collection (see the letter that follows) nor as though "you ain't seen no schools."

Here is the "antique" version of a business letter to a client:

Dear Sir and Madam:

Enclosed herewith please find your life insurance policy; we trust it is in order. If our company can be of any further service toward fulfilling your insurance needs, kindly feel free to advise us. Please do not hesitate to contact us in the event that you have any questions.

Respectfully yours,

Now read an updated version of the same letter:

Dear Mr. and Mrs. Marvin:

We are pleased to enclose your new life insurance policy with Westbrook Mutual. Please call us at 800.345.6789 if you have any questions about this policy or if we may help you with any other insurance matters.

I have enclosed some information on our Mutual Fund Investment and Retirement Annuity Programs. It is never too early to start planning for a secure retirement in which you can enjoy the lifestyle of your choice.

I enjoyed meeting you both and wish you a happy holiday season.

Sincerely,

Here are some additional examples that will give you a feel for avoiding stiff writing and adopting a friendly tone:

NO This company sincerely regrets any inconvenience caused you by our inadvertently miscalculating the amounts on our invoice to you.

YES We're sorry about the error on our Invoice No. 2482.

NO This letter is to advise you that the merchandise you ordered is out of stock. We regret to inform you, therefore, that we cannot fulfill your requested order at this time, but it will remain pending until we are able to make shipment on the anticipated date of March 1.

YES Thank you for your order for one dozen gold birthday charms. Although we are temporarily out of the charms, we expect them from our factory the first week in March. We'll rush them to you as soon as they arrive.

Writing for Your Career

Avoid out-of-date jargon: We/I trust, aforementioned, aforesaid, herein, hereto, herewith, in due course of time, for your perusal . . . This will acknowledge your request for . . . I am writing to inform you . . . This is to advise you . . .

Modern style experts advise taking the "just say it" approach: Attached are . . . Enclosed is . . . In response to your request we are . . . We have reviewed your proposal . . . Thank you for . . .

RECAP Rewrite the following sentences to sound friendly, conversational, and clear.

1. I am writing to inform you that I have received the book that you sent me, and I sincerely appreciate your kindness. _____

2. In accordance with your request, we are herewith enclosing the price list. _____
_____

Check your answers against possible solutions on page 464.

Revising

After finishing the draft, read it and make improvements on screen; then print and reread it. You will usually think of additional changes to further improve your communication. Follow this procedure for all written documents, including emails that are important to your work.

Check for faults based on all of the principles you have learned in Chapters 1 to 12. The following are a few more pitfalls that are common to workplace writing. Knowing how to find these faults will help you polish your writing even further.

Wordy Expressions

Writing that uses too many words will turn off your reader. Wordy writing results when you attempt to "sound official" instead of using simple, everyday language. Always aim for clarity and conciseness by editing wordy phrases. Here are a few examples of expressions to avoid—along with suggestions for writing concisely and clearly without sacrificing courtesy.

AVOID	USE
allow me to introduce myself	I am [OR state business without introduction when information is available in the letterhead and closing signature]
I am writing to OR This letter will inform you	[omit and state specifics]
at an early date, in the near future	soon [OR a specific date]
at your earliest convenience	[omit, be specific, or give approximate time]
please do not hesitate to call OR please feel free to call	please call
we regret to inform you that	we're sorry that
allow me to state that	[omit; just go ahead and say it]
may I take the liberty of	[omit or just do it]
we are in receipt of	we received OR thank you for
attached please find	here is/are, enclosed is/are, attached is/are
reached the conclusion	concluded
for the purpose of	to, for
in a satisfactory manner	satisfactorily
utilize	use
in the event that	if

It takes time and careful proofreading to cut excess verbiage from business communications and academic writing, such as term papers.

Word to the Wise

Blaise Pascal, an eminent 17th-century French philosopher and mathematician (for whom Pascal computer language was named), ended a letter to a colleague with these words: "I have made this letter so long only because I have not had the time to make it shorter."

Emphasize the Positive

People respond best to positive ideas. Even if you have something negative to write about, you can often find a positive way to express it.

Try to write about what you or your company *can* do, not what you *can't* do.

Negative	We cannot conduct this seminar with fewer than ten students.
Positive	We can conduct this seminar with ten or more students.
Negative	We're sorry we can't extend more than $3,000 credit to you.
Positive	We are pleased to extend to you a $3,000 credit line.
Negative	We do not give refunds without a receipt.
Positive	Merchandise may be returned for a full refund when accompanied by a receipt.

RECAP   Use a positive tone to rewrite these negatively expressed sentences.

1. We hope you will not be disappointed. _____

   _____

2. We are not open after 8 p.m. on weekdays or on weekends after five. _____

   _____

3. You can't have a refund. We only give gift cards on returned merchandise. _____

   _____

Check your answers against possible solutions on page 465.

Don't Be Redundant

Purposeless repetition is called *redundancy*. Concise writing means each word contributes to the purpose of the message. The text of a document is **redundant** if it includes unnecessary, repeated words and ideas. Conciseness is essential to convey a desired meaning and tone.

Unless repetition is for special effect, express an idea just once.

REDUNDANT	CONCISE
advance planning	planning
all throughout	throughout
cooperate together	cooperate
final outcome	outcome
free gift	gift
my personal opinion is	my opinion is OR I believe
new innovation	innovation
past history	history
repeat again	repeat
return back	return
round in shape	round
true facts	facts
visible to the eye	visible
whole entire	whole OR entire [never both]
the color yellow	yellow

NO   It is absolutely essential that each and every widget be round in shape.

YES   Each widget must be round.

NO   The consensus of opinion is that although the object is 4 feet long in size, we can see it visually from a distance of 50 feet.

YES   We believe that although the object is 4 feet long, we can see it from 50 feet.

NO   We requested final completion of the project by the year 2009.

YES   We requested completion of the project by 2009.

> ## RECAP
> Rewrite these sentences to eliminate the redundancies.

1. We want to suggest to you that first and foremost you pack each and every basic essential. _____

2. Final completion of the research investigation revealed and showed that the UFO is small in size, triangular in shape, and purple in color. _____
   _____

Check your answers against possible solutions on page 465.

REPLAY 63

A. Write **T** (true) or **F** (false) in each blank.

_____ 1. Long, businesslike words give readers the impression you are well educated.

_____ 2. Conversational-style writing should be avoided in business communications.

_____ 3. In workplace writing, it is more important to get to the point than to spend time worrying about relationships.

_____ 4. Business writing today is more informal than it used to be.

_____ 5. To be sure a message states your policy clearly, stress what your company cannot do.

B. Improve the following sentences according to Read 63 suggestions.

1. About half the flowers in my garden have died. _____
   _____

2. This letter is to advise you that the parts you ordered were shipped today via overnight air by FedEx. _____

3. We believe you won't have any trouble with our newly designed products. _____
   _____

4. We have forwarded the price list to you by fax. If you have any questions about any of the items, please do not hesitate to contact us at your earliest convenience.
   _____

5. Upon investigation, it has come to our attention that we didn't receive your check in the amount of $6,453.00 to pay your bill. _____
   _____

6. I am of the opinion that the event is well attended whenever it is held during the month of December. _____

7. I would like to request that you please repeat the instructions again. _____
   _____

8. You can't have a cash refund. We only give a store gift card. _____
   _____

9. We are unable to fulfill your order for the Desk Master gift set until you remit payment in full in the amount of $165.08, plus shipping in the amount of $7.95 by check, money order, or credit card as indicated on the attached order form.

_____

_____

10. I am writing to let you know that we are in receipt of your letter of application and that we appreciate your interest in working for GreenCities.com. _____

_____

Check your answers against possible solutions on page 465.

READ 64   EMAIL AND MEMOS

In today's workplace, email often substitutes for "snail mail" (the fond name for our postal service); thus, some letters are printed on stationery and placed in envelopes, while others are typed into an email template or typed on letterhead and sent as an email attachment. Emails have also replaced printed interoffice memorandums to a great extent, although printed memos are still used for internal business communications. Memos on preprinted forms may be sent in an interoffice mailer or attached to an email.

A first consideration in effective communication in all of these formats is to be sure the correspondence contains the standard parts; the second is to format these elements in the standard business style.

Email

Email has a built-in template.

Templates vary somewhat, depending on the system you are using, but a typical email template contains the standard parts shown in Figure 13.1. Following are guidelines that will help you follow business standards for emails.

The "To" Window

Make sure email addresses are correct.

Some systems automatically insert names from the address book based on typing only a few letters; thus, names that are the same or similar might be selected in error.

Copy/Blind Copy

It is courteous to let the recipient(s) know who is being copied on an email.

Send blind copies only when you have an important reason for doing so. For large mailings, you can use the blind copy window to protect the privacy of recipients' email addresses when appropriate.

Subject

The subject line tells the recipient precisely why you are writing.

Use only a few words that explicitly describe the subject:

Agenda for May 1 Planning Meeting

Request for Budget Information

Are you free for lunch?

Your Monthly Report is Past Due

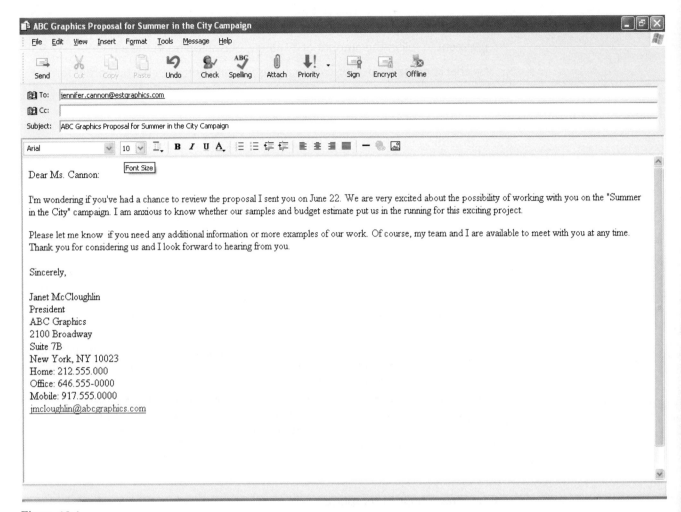

Figure 13.1
Microsoft product screen shot reprinted with permission from Microsoft Corporation.

Limit each email you write to one subject. This makes it easier for recipients to respond, and makes it easier to archive or file copies that will need to be retrieved for future reference or retained for company records.

Salutation

A formal salutation such as "Dear Evelyn:" is optional in email messages that are exchanged in the normal course of business. Most people, however, do include an informal salutation when communicating with business colleagues.

A salutation is essential when writing to someone you don't know well.

Unless you are already on a first-name basis with the correspondent, use your judgment as to how the person should be addressed. The world of electronic communication is a lot less formal than traditional correspondence, and people often address complete strangers informally.

A formal salutation ends with a colon; an informal salutation ends with a comma.

Informal	Hi Doreen,	Doreen,
Formal	Dear Ms. Lieberman:	Dear Joseph:

In a case such as the example in Figure 13.1, where the writer is applying for a job, a formal salutation is essential if no prior relationship exists. Always consider your reader and how he or she would expect to be addressed. Err on the side of formality.

Body

Follow exactly the same rules of Standard English usage and writing style recommended in this book for all other forms of workplace writing. Stick to the main subject of the email and structure your message so that the main ideas can be broken into paragraphs for ease of reading, comprehension, and future reference.

Closing

A courtesy closing is warranted in any type of email, but when you are using electronic communication in place of a traditional letter, always use an appropriate closing followed by a comma, such as "Sincerely," "Sincerely yours," "Cordially," "Regards." When you know the person well, an informal closing such as "Thanks," "Best," or "Cheers" is appropriate, or the closing may be omitted.

Signature

Sign off with your first name only or first and last name, depending on your relationship with the recipient. Include a signature block with your full name, business title, company name, and contact information: address, telephone number(s), and email address. Include the email address because many email systems display the sender's full name, not the address.

Word to the Wise

Email DOs and DON'Ts

DO
- Provide a meaningful subject line for your reader.
- Double-check your message for grammar and spelling accuracy.
- Prepare email messages that make you appear efficient and courteous.
- Respond to emails as quickly as possible or let the recipient know you will need more time.

DO NOT
- Write emails with all capital letters.
- Write emails in anger.
- Use email and instant message shorthand in business emails.
- Send confidential messages via email.
- Write anything you wouldn't want made public or forwarded to others.

RECAP   Write **T** (true) or **F** (false) in each blank.

_____ 1. Writing emails in the workplace requires using the same standards of English usage applied to other written communications.

_____ 2. In the workplace, it is customary to address all email recipients formally in the salutation.

_____ 3. Make email subject lines as long as necessary to communicate the purpose of your message.

Check your answers on page 465.

Interoffice Memos

Memorandums are principally for communicating within an organization.

Some interoffice *memos* (also called memorandums) are formal communications to employees and others are informal. Occasionally, memos are sent to people outside of an organization, usually in the case of ongoing projects between companies because of speed of preparation. Memos can be important to career progress. Your colleagues or superiors who receive yours judge you, perhaps subconsciously, on the content and on the way you express yourself in writing.

Memos have a preset format, and most companies have preprinted memo forms with the company name and logo. If not, you have the option of using a word processing template. Regardless of how the form is produced, a memorandum is designed to be typed and formatted quickly. The preprinted words at the top of the form (**Date To, From, Subject**) are called **guide words.** Formatting is shown in Figure 13.2.

PACIFIC IMPORTS, INC.

MEMO

DATE: June 30, 2009

TO: Sharon Alexander, Accounting Associate

CC: Yasmin Salazar, Director, Accounting Services

FROM: Ronald Leland, Director, Human Resources *RL*

SUBJECT: Welcome to Pacific Imports, Inc.

We are pleased to have you join our staff and hope you'll find your employment here enjoyable and personally rewarding. Because we are currently reprinting our official Employee Manual, I have summarized a few key policies to help you understand our operation and the importance of your job:

Security: Please wear your identification card at all times when on the company premises. Security guards at the main points of entry are required to check the identification of all employees.

Attendance: Employees are expected to be in their assigned departments and ready to begin work at 8:30 a.m. If you are unable to come to work, please call your department manager no later than 9 a.m. Please contact my office in the event of any extended absence from work.

Smoking: Employees are permitted to smoke on the terrace outside the cafeteria—and nowhere else in the building or on the grounds.

If you have any questions, please see my assistant Jim Harrison or me. Stop by my office at any time. I look forward to working with you.

Figure 13.2

Formatting for Memos

1. Align text following the guide words two spaces after the longest guide word.
2. Align the left margin of the message with the guide words.
3. Double space after the "Subject" line and between paragraphs.
4. Do not place a signature at the bottom. Sign your name or initials next to the typed name at the top if you wish.

Optional Memo Notations

Three types of notations might be included at the end of a memo: typist's initials, copy notations, and enclosure notations. The format for these is the same for both memos and letters. See Read 65 on letters.

RECAP   Write **T** (true) or **F** (false) in each blank.

_____ 1. Interoffice memos are never sent outside the office.

_____ 2. The preprinted words *Date, To, From, Subject* at the top of a memo form are called guide words.

_____ 3. It isn't necessary to sign your name on an interoffice memo.

Check your answers on page 466.

REPLAY 64

Write **T** (true) or **F** (false) in each blank.

_____ 1. It isn't necessary to let the recipient(s) know who is being copied on correspondence.

_____ 2. Sign off emails with your first name only.

_____ 3. You have no control over whether an email you send is forwarded to others.

_____ 4. A signature block in an email should contain your full name and complete contact information.

_____ 5. Sending blind copies is a way to protect the privacy of email addresses on large mailings.

_____ 6. Interoffice memos are used only for formal communications to employees.

_____ 7. Templates are electronic forms for formatting memos.

_____ 8. It is best to use blind copies only when you have an important reason for doing so.

_____ 9. It would not be appropriate to send a letter typed on letterhead as an email attachment.

_____ 10. Emails have largely replaced the use of printed interoffice memos.

Check your answers on page 466.

READ 65   LETTERS

Business letter formats can vary slightly, but all have essentially the same parts. In this section you will learn how to format the individual parts of the most commonly used style, which is called **block letter format**. Examples of other styles can be found in Appendix D.

Standard Letter Parts

The standard parts of business letters from top to bottom are listed below. See how these parts are formatted in Figure 13.3 on page 275.

Date

Type the date (the day the letter is being sent) two or three lines below the printed letterhead. Always spell out the complete word for the month; do not use *nd, th, rd,* or *st* after the figure for the day.

American style	June 2, 2009
International and military style	2 June 2009 [no comma]

Inside Address

The inside address is the name and address of the person and/or company to receive the letter.

Type the inside address single spaced, beginning the first line four spaces below the date. If your letter is very short, you can space down as many as ten lines to help balance the letter in the center of the page.

> Professor Mary Rowe
> Miami Dade Community College
> 11380 NW 27 Avenue
> Miami, FL 33179

- Spell out personal titles, except for *Ms., Mr.,* and *Dr.* In workplace correspondence, indicating a woman's marital status (Mrs. or Miss) is unnecessary and out of date.

- Write the organization name exactly as it is written by the company. If you don't know, look it up in a directory or consult the organization's letterhead or Web site. Spell out street names and designations such as *Avenue, Street,* and *Court.*

- Spell out state names or use the postal service two-letter abbreviations (see Appendix D).

Salutation

The salutation of a letter always begins with "Dear."

Begin typing two line spaces after the inside address. Precede the name with a professional title such as *Dr., Captain, Father, Rabbi, Senator, Professor,* etc.; or with a personal title, *Mr.* or *Ms.,* and punctuate the salutation with a colon.

Dear Professor Rowe: Dear Bob: Dear Ms. O'Rourke:

If no professional title is known and you don't know whether you're addressing a man or a woman, use the complete name in the address and the salutation.

Dear Chris O'Brien:

Body

The body of the letter is the message.

Begin it two line spaces below the salutation. Single-space the body, but double-space between paragraphs.

Leaving a blank line between paragraphs eliminates the need to indent the first line. While it isn't wrong to indent paragraphs, this style is infrequently used today (it was useful when correspondence was handwritten.) See Figure 13.3.

Complimentary Close

The complimentary close signals the end of the message.

Type the closing two line spaces below the last line of the body, and capitalize only the first word.

Traditional complimentary closes used frequently today include the following:

Sincerely,   Sincerely yours,

Regards,   Best regards,   Cordially,

Respectfully is inappropriate for ordinary business letters but may close a letter to a judge or high-ranking government, school, or church official. Closings such as *Very truly yours*, and *Yours truly*, are considered outdated.

Signature

The signature includes the writer's name and position title, department name, and handwritten signature.

In the signature block, type the writer's name and official job title or department four spaces below the complimentary close, thus leaving space for the signature. If the writer's job title fits on the same line as the name or department, it is optional to type it this way, separated with a comma.

Sincerely,   Regards,

Larry Lutsky   *JoAnn R. Michels*

Larry Lutsky   JoAnn R. Michels
Vice President   Manager, Accounts Payable
Real Estate Holdings

With a pen that writes blue or black, sign in the space after the complimentary close. Do not use a title (Mr., Mrs., Ms., Dr.) with your signature in business letters.

The writer's address, phone number, and email address are normally preprinted on business stationery. If you're not using stationery, you can create a letterhead with a word processing template or type an inside address (see the following section on optional letter parts).

Writing for Your Career

Use Appropriate Stationery for Letters

Type business letters on good quality 8½ by 11-inch letterhead stationery and mail in a matching envelope. Smaller stationery is used in some professional-level and executive offices. White or off-white paper is standard. The company name (and logo) are always at the top. The address, phone number, and so on may be at the top or at the bottom.

Some business letters you write deal with your personal transactions, not those of your employer. For example, you might write to your insurance company, the motor vehicle department about your license, an employer about applying for a job, a department store about billing errors still uncorrected after your phone calls, and so on. Create personal letterhead from a word processing template or use plain paper for such letters—do not use company letterhead.

Identification Initials

Identification initials indicate that someone other than the author typed the letter.

Type the initials in lowercase letters at the left margin, a double space below the name and title or department name.

> Betty Van Meter
>
> *Betty Van Meter*
>
> Manager
> Business Skills Center
>
> lrs

Enclosure Notation

An enclosure notation is used when you send something with a letter.

This notation tells the reader to look for an enclosure and serves to remind the writer to include it. Type "Enclosure" (singular or plural) at the left margin a double space below the title/department of the sender of the letter or the typist's initials, followed by a colon and a brief description of the item. The description does not have to be included when the item is described in the body of the letter.

> Enclosure: Check No. 268   OR   Enc.

Copy Notation

A copy notation tells the recipient that others are receiving copies of the letter.

Type the notation at the left margin a double space below the typed signature line (either *c:* or *cc:* is correct).

> cc: Professor Nina Nixon

If you don't want the addressee to know you've sent copies, type *bc* (for blind copy) only on the copy or copies being sent to others (and your file copy)—not the original—followed by the name/s of those to receive a copy.

> bc: Professor Foster

Eric Smith FINANCIAL SERVICES
4464 Fremont Avenue No. • Seattle, WA 98103 • (206)632-3337

(1)   September 18, 2009

(2)   Professor Adell Shay
      Los Angeles Harbor College
      1111 Figueroa Place
      Wilmington, CA 90744

(3)   Dear Professor Shay:

(4)   Joe Santona gave us your name as someone who likes to see profit, good
      business practices, protection of the environment, and social responsibility
      all working hand in hand.

      Joe thinks you'll be interested in learning more about how you can have a
      healthy profit, growth, and safety while investing wisely in activities you believe
      in. Few had even heard of socially responsible investing in 1986 when we began
      to develop SRI programs. Individuals like you, small businesses, and large
      pension funds are now benefiting from our experience in the social investment
      field.

      We invite you to a complimentary initial consultation during which we'll discuss
      your present needs and financial goals. We'll determine whether we can help
      you meet your objectives for short-term profit, long-term growth, and safety
      through socially responsible solutions. A brochure is enclosed that shows how
      we help our clients achieve peace of mind while their money works for them.

      To arrange a no-obligation appointment, please fill out the enclosed card and
      return it to us.

(5)   Sincerely,

      Eric A. Smith

(6)   Eric A. Smith
(7)   Certified Financial Planner

(8)   lrs

(9)   Enclosure

(10) bc Joseph Santona

SIPC

Member National Association of Securities Dealers, Inc.

1. Date	**6.** Writer's name
2. Inside address	**7.** Writer's title
3. Salutation	**8.** Typist's initials
4. Body	**9.** Enclosure notation
5. Complimentary close	**10.** Copy notation

Figure 13.3

Writing for Your Career

Salutations *Dear Sirs, To Whom It May Concern,* and *Dear Sir or Madam* are considered old fashioned. If you don't know the individual's name, use an appropriate official title, such as *Dear Sales Manager, Dear Lacy's Linens, Dear Credit Department, Ladies and Gentlemen* (but not *Dear Ladies and Gentlemen*).

Signatures Do not include a personal title in the signature or the typed name. To indicate whether the writer is male or female, spell out names such as Chris to Christine or Christopher, or Pat to Patrick or Patricia, and then sign the shortened name. Another possibility is to include the writer's middle name—Whitney Dawn Blake or W. Dawn Blake. These devices let the reader know whether to use Mr. or Ms. when responding. Using only initials before your last name (E. J. Anderson) is inconsiderate and appears pompous unless that is the official way you spell your name.

Optional Letter Parts

Inside Address

If you don't use printed letterhead, include your address at the top of the page.

Do not include your name because it will appear in the signature position at the end of the letter. Single space your street address, city, state, and ZIP.

Begin typing the address about one to two inches from the top of the page. The date follows two lines below, and other letter parts are the same as a letter on letterhead stationery.

2166 Clinton Avenue
Bronx, NY 10406

May 31, 20xx

Mr. Joseph Andrews
Attorney at Law
302 E. 84th Street
New York, NY 10021

Dear Mr. Andrews:

Special Notations

Special notations include CONFIDENTIAL, BY MESSENGER, REGISTERED or other mailing notations.

Type special notations a double space below the date.

January 2, 2009
PERSONAL

These might include the following:

Subject or Reference Line

A subject or reference line may be used to state the letter's main topic and serve as a heading for the message.

Type it between the salutation and the body, or it may replace the salutation.

Dear Mr. Wallace:

JOB PLACEMENT OF GRADUATES

The five graduates listed below had high scores on our employment test and . . .

Some letters require a name or transaction number. Type the word *Reference* below the inside address.

> Reference: Policy No. 26382

Company Name (at End of Letter)

The name of the organization sending the letter is sometimes typed in all capital letters a double space below the complimentary close.

Then leave three or four blank lines before the name and title (if any) of the person who will sign the letter in the blank space. In some cases, the company name replaces an individual's name.

Sincerely,

SNYDER COMMUNICATIONS, INC.

Handwritten signature here

Joshua Snyder, Personnel Director

Postscript (PS)

If a postscript is included, it is the final item on the page.

The abbreviation *PS* is correct, but not required, before the message. Avoid using a postscript for something you forgot to include in the letter. Instead, insert the information where it belongs within the letter. Use a postscript for emphasis (particularly in sales letters), occasionally for a personal message, or for information on a topic different from the rest of the letter.

> PS Please fill out the enclosed reply card and return it today. [for emphasis in a sales letter]

> PS Have a great time on your Trinidad trip. [personal message added to a letter to a client]

REPLAY 65

Write **T** (true) or **F** (false) in each blank.

_____ 1. Spell out the word *copy* in the copy notation of a letter.

_____ 2. It is courteous to let the recipient(s) know who is being copied on correspondence.

_____ 3. The typist's initials should be in capital letters.

_____ 4. Mail sent through the US postal system is known as "snail mail."

_____ 5. A personal title should be used before the letter writer's name.

_____ 6. A *bc* notation should not appear on the original of a letter.

_____ 7. One correct way to type the date in a business letter is 6 June 2009.

_____ 8. The letters *PS* are not required before a sentence that is a postscript.

_____ 9. If a subject line is used in a letter, type it a double space after the salutation.

_____ 10. The company name is not required as part of the closing information.

_____ 11. When typing the number for the day in the date of a letter, always include *st, nd, rd,* and *th.*

_____ 12. Today's knowledgeable business letter writers always include a subject line.

_____ 13. If the inside address begins *Mr. Peter Settle*, use *Dear Sir* as the salutation.

_____ 14. The purpose of a postscript (PS) is to add information you forgot to put in the body of a letter.

_____ 15. When writing a personal business letter, put your address below the date.

Check your answers on page 466; then take the Pop Quiz on page 319.

Writing for Your Career

Before signing, proofread letters and other documents, not only to detect and correct errors but also to improve writing style.

After initially proofreading on your computer screen, print the document on draft paper and proofread the printout. You will often find an error you missed or a way to improve the communication. If so, make the change, proofread again, and then print the final copy. If possible, proofread correspondence a final time before inserting it in the envelope.

Sign letters with a pen, never a pencil.

CONCEPT REVIEW & SKILL-BUILDING APPLICATIONS

Checkpoint

Chapter 13 provides you with technical skills to compose and format business communications, whether transmitted electronically or manually. Place a check in the blank next to each item when you understand it, and know where and how to apply it to communications on the job.

_____ Apply the writing process—the planning, drafting, revising, and proofreading stages—when preparing workplace communications.

_____ Compose workplace communications using a conversational style and positive tone appropriate to your audience and purpose.

_____ Improve readability of communications by using concise language, avoiding repetition, and organizing ideas in logical paragraphs.

Use Standard Guidelines For:

_____ Filling in the email template and guide words of an interoffice memo.

_____ Composing the salutation, body, and closing for an email, memo, or letter.

_____ Formatting standard and optional parts of business letters: Inside address, salutation, subject line (optional), body, signature, company name (optional), and notations.

Special Assignment

A. Draw a line through the redundant words in the following expressions:

1. free gift

2. at the hour of 3 p.m.

3. square in shape

4. at the present time

5. each and every

6. enclosed herewith

7. few in number

8. in the state of Missouri

9. we want to thank you for

B. Replace these expressions with a single word:

10. a large number of _____

11. are of the opinion that _____

12. in the event that _____

13. at the present time _____

14. made the announcement that _____

15. are in a position to _____

Date to submit this assignment: _____

Proofreading for Careers

If you have worked your way through most of the material in this book and much of the extra practice as well, you have a done a distinguished job of learning—and applying what you have learned. We have tried to make grammar more interesting than your past experiences with it and even tried to introduce a little bit of fun now and then. In that spirit, we want you to have fun with this last Proofreading for Careers exercise. It is an absurd letter that would never be sent, but it's fun to read. Proofread and correct the format, punctuation, and other errors. Correct the printed copy using proofreading symbols and then retype the letter in block style, or go online to correct and reformat the document.

Steve Gates
Vice President
Computers Intn'l
103 Null St
New York NY, 10015

Dear Mr. Gates

Thank you for your letter of March 7th. after careful consideration I regret to inform you that I am unable to accept your refusal to offer me employment. This year, I have been particularly fortunate in receiving an unusual large number of rejection letters. Wth such a varied and promising field of candidates it is impossible for me to accept all refusals. Despite Computer Internationals outstanding qualifications and previous experience in rejecting applicants I find your rejection, does not meet my needs at the present time, therefore I will initiate employment with your firm immediately following graduation I look forward to seeing you then.

Sincerely

Bill Jobs

Practice Quiz

Write **T** (true) or **F** (false) next to each sentence.

_____ 1. Leave four spaces between the closing and the writer's typed name for a handwritten signature at the end of the letter.

_____ 2. The recommended place for a subject line is below the salutation.

_____ 3. It isn't always necessary to include a salutation in an email.

_____ 4. *25 September 2009* is the military and international style for the date in a letter.

_____ 5. If the first line of a letter's inside address is TurboTax Video, Inc., a correct salutation could be *Ladies and Gentlemen*.

_____ 6. *Very truly yours* is currently the preferred complimentary close.

_____ 7. "Let's meet at 4 p.m. in the afternoon" is an example of redundancy.

_____ 8. The first paragraph of a business letter should usually be the longest.

_____ 9. When possible use a personal title in the signature of a letter.

_____ 10. Good business writers use more formal language than was used in the past.

_____ 11. "To keep your good credit rating, send your check for $843 today" is an example of emphasizing the positive in workplace writing.

_____ 12. Try to keep all paragraphs in business letters about the same length.

_____ 13. Use "To Whom It May Concern" as a salutation if you don't know the name of the person to whom you must write.

_____ 14. "We are herewith enclosing the price list" is an example of good language style for a business letter.

_____ 15. After typing a business letter, proofread it first on the screen/monitor before you print. After printing a copy, proofread again from the printed copy.

Self-Study Practice and Tutorials

 Vocabulary and Spelling for Careers

For additional practice go to Appendix B, page 321.

 Replay Drills

For additional practice go to Appendix C, page 406.

 Companion Web Site: www.prenhall.com/smith

Go to the companion Web site to test your knowledge on self-grading quizzes and for links to other helpful online resources.

 **MyWritingLab**

Use this online learning system for an assessment of your progress on topics covered in this chapter and progressive exercises that fit your individual needs.

14 Writing for Multimedia

After completing Chapter 14, you will be able to do the following:

- Identify the steps necessary to plan and write an oral presentation.
- Plan an oral presentation with visuals.
- Explain the differences between writing for print and multimedia.
- Identify important features of text written for publication on a Web site.

READ 66 — MAKING ORAL PRESENTATIONS

Congratulations! You have come a long way and absorbed a lot of information that will make you a competent, and possibly, a superior communicator. Much of what you have learned about Standard English is applicable to speaking *and* writing. In the case of oral presentations, the two skills must work in tandem.

Planning a Successful Presentation

Do you know the reason so many people become frightened at the thought of standing before an audience and speaking? It's simple. To imagine yourself giving a speech in the abstract is scary. How will you know what to say? To whom will you be speaking? Will they be interested? How long will you have to speak? It's no wonder that the idea of public speaking is frightening when you don't have answers to all of these questions. This is where preparation comes in and where practice follows.

Confidence comes with carefully thinking through every aspect of a presentation; then scripting it and practicing it. You still might not feel comfortable and you might be anxious until it's over, but preparation will eliminate a big reason for being fearful.

A successful presentation requires you to write a first draft in which you do the following: Determine your precise objectives, outline the content—introduction, ideas, supporting facts, and specific examples—and conclude with a summary and action plan, where appropriate.

Define Your Objective

Write out your objective; that is, what you want to accomplish as a result of the presentation.

Here is an example:

> My objective is to convince supervisors and managers that the company should purchase QXR Software because it will save the company money and time and increase productivity.

Your objective should be concise. If it can't be stated in one sentence, your thinking might not be clear. Work on it until you can boil your thoughts down to their essence and make one clear statement of what you want to do.

Plan Your Presentation

Everything you say during the presentation must help you meet your objective.

Plan what the presentation will include and how you will deliver it. Will you use note cards or a script? Either one can be used to list key points and key words that will trigger what you want to say. If you are doing a multimedia presentation, prepare your points and visuals as an integrated package that uses the visual medium to maximum effect.

In planning how you will develop and present your content, think about where you will make the presentation and what equipment and handouts you will need. Consider such details as whether you will be standing or sitting. Will there be a podium? Are you a member of a panel? If you will need equipment, such as a microphone, practice using it as you practice giving your speech aloud.

Know how much time you have and prepare and practice to ensure that you stay within the allotted time.

If you intend to provide handouts to your audience, make their development a part of your planning process. Some presenters use a printout of their slides as their handout.

Prepare the Content

To prepare your content, follow the traditional advice for structuring a speech:

Tell them what you're going to tell them (introduction), tell them (body), and tell them what you told them (conclusion).

Here is how it might work using the QXR Software presentation as an example:

Introduction   If you feel comfortable, begin with a story or joke relating to the subject. Then summarize the key points that you will be making, but don't go into detail.

- Last week I spent 10 minutes on what should have been a 15-second task: trying to retrieve a customer's lost file.
- I had to keep the customer on hold, which could have resulted in lost business.
- I did some research and discovered that a new, relatively inexpensive software package could eliminate this problem.

Body   Get down to business and tell them. Provide supporting facts that explain what the software is, how it works, and how it will save the company money and time and make their jobs easier. Each fact you state must support your objective. Use visuals if possible, and give specific examples of what this software will do. Speak at a level that is appropriate to your audience. Avoid jargon, details, and vocabulary some listeners may not understand. Explain and simplify as needed, without making listeners feel foolish. Prepare handouts if they will help.

- What QXR software is: how it works; examples (with visuals).
- Its reputation; testimonials/success stories from users.
- Cost/benefits for us: money, time, productivity.
- Backup data verifying potential outcomes.

Conclusion   Tell them what you've told them. Summarize what you explained and make specific recommendations. Avoid introducing new ideas in the conclusion!

- Why QXR is the best choice for our needs (review key points from the "body").
- Action plan: suggested timeline for implementation—purchase, installation, and training.
- Questions from the audience.

Delivering Your Presentation

Practice, practice, practice. During the first round of practice, focus on fitting your content into the amount of time you have without rushing or leaving a void. Look for a balance of time and content that allows you to speak at a normal, conversational rate of speed and connect with your audience. If you tend to speak too fast, especially when you're nervous, practice deep breathing and slowing down.

Next, focus on practicing techniques for building rapport with your audience. If you are not going to be using a microphone, practice speaking clearly, and loudly enough to be heard in the back of the room. Plan to make direct eye contact with as many listeners as possible, dress appropriately, have good posture, and vary your tone of voice and volume appropriately for the content. Above all, speak clearly, distinctly, and enthusiastically.

Decide whether or not you feel comfortable taking questions during your talk. If you worry that questions will make you run overtime or sidetrack your thinking, ask the audience to hold their questions until the end.

Finally, put it all together—practice your delivery, timing, and techniques until you feel comfortable and confident.

Using Presentation Slides

PowerPoint is a slide presentation software program used in many work settings. If you are going to prepare an oral presentation supplemented with slides, consider using this program or a similar one. Slide presentation software provides pre-designed templates and wizards that make it easy for you to develop a presentation simply by "filling in the blanks."

Slides Supplement Your Words

Audiences expect slides to provide short bites of information that are augmented by the speaker. Therefore, the text you put on slides should hit key points—it should not be a script for your oral presentation. Your script should be typed in large type on white paper or written on note cards if you feel comfortable speaking from memory while looking at notes as a guide. Avoid reading a presentation word for word from a script. Looking down at a written speech makes it extremely hard to achieve a high level of audience rapport. It is important to look at your audience, speak in a natural tone and rhythm, and work to make a connection with your listener. With practice, you will be able to speak without relying on reading.

You can outline your presentation on the slide template, using a blank black and white slide while making notes on paper. This will help you decide what you are going to say and what points you want to highlight on the slides. The key is to use as few words as possible on the screen—you don't want to overload your audience or encourage them to read the slides at the expense of listening to you. You might also opt to create a storyboard.

A storyboard is a method of writing in two columns, one for graphics and one for the points about each image.

	Script Notes	Slide Text
Slide 1	■ Develop a fitness plan that fits your needs and interests. ■ Make it enjoyable and part of your lifestyle. ■ Don't use exercise as a quick fix.	*IMPORTANT CONSIDERATIONS* ■ Have you been active or sedentary? ■ What activities do you like? ■ What is your fitness level?

This is an excellent way to avoid having the slide show become a "script" of your spoken message. Notice in the example how the points to be covered in the "script" column relate to the questions on the slide, but they do not duplicate each other.

The speaker will discuss the three general points and augment each point with a question that personalizes the content for the audience. The speaker can opt to have the questions "build" on the slide; that is, appear one after the other on the same slide. Another option would be to put each question on a different slide with images.

A rule of thumb for the amount of text per slide is one key point for each line of text; not more than 6 to 8 words per line; and no more than 6 lines per slide.

Color and Design

Slide presentation templates provide pre-designed background color combinations and attractive graphics. Unless you are a design "wizard" yourself, rely on these to make an attractive presentation. Select type colors that provide sharp contrast for reading and that are appropriately conservative or "jazzy," depending on the purpose of your presentation and the audience's expectations. Use visual aids that include images such as photographs or clip art that are appropriate for the audience and subject matter. Do not use images for purely decorative or entertainment purposes in a business setting.

Once you settle on font (style, colors, and sizes) and background, use them for all of the slides. Some variations in format can make the presentation more interesting, but consistency is important for visual attention and understanding. For example, if you are using a headline at the top and bullet points, don't switch to paragraphs with no headline.

Writing for Your Career

- Print the slides and proofread them for spelling, consistency, style, language usage, punctuation, and capitalization.
- Follow the rule of parallel structure for items listed in a series.
- Avoid using all-capital letters for emphasis; instead, use a larger or different style font.
- Avoid fancy fonts that are hard to read.
- Limit lines of text on each slide to no more than six.

REPLAY 66

Write **T** (true) or **F** (false) in each blank.

_____ 1. Use your slides as a script for your presentation.

_____ 2. Never begin a presentation with a joke; if your boss doesn't think it's funny, you'll probably get fired.

_____ 3. The most comfortable presenters are those who can speak extemporaneously—in other words, "just wing it."

_____ 4. Colorful slides with lots of pizzazz are not necessarily the best way to hold an audience's attention.

_____ 5. Don't waste paper and time preparing handouts before giving a presentation.

_____ 6. So that you'll sound natural and be more relaxed, practice your timing and techniques before making a presentation to your colleagues.

_____ 7. Avoid direct eye contact with your audience as you might encourage them to start asking questions.

_____ 8. If you have a new idea for improving sales of your company's products, tell the audience about it in your conclusion.

_____ 9. Making a good presentation to supervisors and coworkers can improve your chances for promotion.

_____10. This is the hardest Replay in the whole course.

Check your answers on page 466.

READ 67   WRITING FOR THE WEB

Multimedia communication enables businesspeople to provide information effectively in electronic format.

In this format, your readers view your words on a screen, and they use the information in different ways.

In most workplaces, trained professionals with technical skills prepare and publish information for the company's Web site. You might become one of those specialists or you might be like many regular employees who are called upon from time to time to contribute written information for the company Web site. This might include articles, press releases, company facts, product descriptions, or service information. This section provides techniques for the nontechnical person writing for the Web.

Understand the Purpose

When preparing written information for a Web site, the first consideration is how it will be presented. Will it be accompanied by images, animation, banners, or other design elements or will it be designed primarily for reading? Knowing how the written text will fit in with other elements on the screen is the first step in planning your writing.

The second step is to clearly understand the purpose for which you are writing. Will the text be used to inform, to sell, to entertain? The tone and approach you take will depend on the purpose of the Web site as a whole, as well as the particular section that will contain your written material.

Writing Style

Writing for traditional media—letters, memos, and reports—is arranged in paragraphs and sentences, with sections broken with headings that reflect the overall organization. Written text for the Web might be similar in structure, but it also has some distinct differences based on how the information is received by the user.

Words written on paper are held in the reader's hands. The recipient reads the documents at his or her own pace from beginning to end. On a Web site writing is usually read on the computer screen. The user typically expects to take as little time as possible, often scanning just to find some specific piece of information located on the Web site. Users are accustomed to scrolling with the mouse from point to point and using **links**—the menus, buttons, graphics, and underlined words that Web sites provide—as tools for getting them to the needed information quickly. Users expect to find information presented concisely and in small bites; for that reason, brief sentences, paragraphs, and columns of text are preferred.

Planning Your Writing

As with any quality business communication, you need to decide what you want to say, why you want to say it, and with whom you wish to communicate. Begin by defining your audience. Are you writing for your company's **intranet**, a Web site accessed by employees within the organization, or for the **Internet**, aiming for the audience that is the consumer of your specialized product, service, or information?

Follow these steps to plan your writing:

- **Summarize the goal of your writing in one or two paragraphs.** If you can't do this, think about it more.

- **Describe your audience in one or two sentences.** Are you trying to reach a certain age or demographic group or a specific business clientele or customer base? Get to know your audience well; this information will influence your writing style.

- **Gather your information and ideas.** Structure information in logical order and group related topics together. If you are writing for a Web site that is already established, review the writing style and format, and try to match it. If you are creating a new Web site, you may want to draw a chart, mapping out what information will be on your **home page** (the main page of your site) and where links from your home page will go. Model your Web site on others that have a purpose similar to yours.

- **Understand how Web sites work.** Be familiar with the **navigational tools** users rely on to find information and move around the site: menus, buttons, graphics, and underlined words that provide links or connections between Web pages.

Preparing Your Text

After planning and deciding on content, prepare a rough draft. Then leave it for a while, and come back later to edit and revise. If possible, have someone review it with you. Ask yourself these questions:

- Does it flow in a clear, organized way?

- Is it accurate? (Your credibility is at stake.)

- Are spelling, grammar, and punctuation correct? Any inaccuracy reflects poorly upon the professionalism of your entire effort.

- Is it concise, yet complete?

- Is the tone and level appropriate for the subject matter and audience—that is, formal versus informal, humorous versus serious, introductory versus advanced, objective versus persuasive?

- If information is from another source, did you credit the source? If not, you may have committed **plagiarism**, which is the unlawful use of copyrighted work. Always identify the title and author of your source.

- Proofread carefully, using the same rules applied to print.

Word Power

When writing copy for the Web, you are competing for attention with other Internet sources that are at the user's fingertips. Engage the user with active words and tone as well as short sentences and phrases.

Boring	Learn How to Cook Chinese Food
Better	Create Chinese Cuisine
Boring	Find Out about Mexico
Better	Explore Mexico
Boring	A message is best conveyed with carefully chosen and effectively applied words.
Better	Choose the right words to convey your message.
Boring	When writing, always try to tailor your business presentation for your specific audience.
Better	Write for your audience.

Create Strong Visual Impact

Use words as graphic elements. The amount of text, arrangement of text, font choices (style, size, and color), movement (animation), and sound all affect your audience—and therefore your message.

Amount of Text

Avoid crowding words. On a screen, a bundle of words can be time-consuming and hard to view and comprehend. Long words and sentences take more time to digest than short words and sentences or phrases. A large, blocky chunk of text is not inviting to a viewer. Keep sentences and paragraphs short.

Arrangement of Text

Leave space between lines. Make use of bullets and text boxes. The placement of words affects their importance and tells viewers where to look first. Blank space provides impact too. Use open space—or "negative space"— for balance or a dramatic effect.

Type Font Choices

It is your job as a business writer to capture and keep the viewer's attention with brightly composed, effectively displayed text with emphasis where needed. *The style, size, and color of type font you use* **affects the viewers and their mood**. The font **size** affects the importance of the **words**. We generally notice **bigger** text before smaller text. The color of text also affects the viewer. Choose aesthetically pleasing **colors**. Other techniques for emphasis include **boldface,** *italics,* underlining, changing portions **of text** to **different** fonts, putting text in boxes, and text that moves—animation. Be careful not to **overuse** *emphasis* techniques. Choose what you use carefully, or your multimedia effort will look meSSy and unprofessiOnal. A little goes a l o n g way.

Special Considerations

When you publish a book, it's finished. But when you publish a Web site, you've just begun to write! Plan to update your Web site regularly—monthly, weekly, or even daily—to keep visitors coming back.

When you read the front page of a newspaper, the most important headlines are "above the fold"—to use newspaper jargon. Web pages rely on a scroll bar. When you plan a Web page, therefore, be sure your most important and interesting information is "above the fold" or at the top of the Web page. This means the viewer doesn't have to scroll down the page to see it. The less important the information, the farther down the page you can put it. Also remember that lines may break differently on different users' screens. Your Web content won't always look just the way you formatted it, so observe the age-old advice: keep it simple.

Don't crowd too much text in one place. Viewers mustn't feel lost, confused, irritated, or bored trying to use your Web site. Control the value of your visitors' experience through the quality, organization, and appearance of your content.

REPLAY 67

A. Write **T** (true) or **F** (false) in each blank.

_____ 1. In multimedia writing, briefer is better.

_____ 2. With an Internet Web site, your audience is the world.

_____ 3. Visitors to a Web site bring no expectations.

_____ 4. Web site users are affected by their first impression of a Web page.

_____ 5. "Negative space" should be avoided in multimedia writing.

_____ 6. Always use as many emphasis techniques as possible.

_____ 7. The experience of visitors to your Web site depends on the quality and organization of your written content.

B. List six ways to emphasize text.

1. _____   4. _____

2. _____   5. _____

3. _____   6. _____

Check your answers on page 466; then take the Pop Quiz on page 320.

CONCEPT REVIEW & SKILL-BUILDING APPLICATIONS

Checkpoint

Chapter 14 provides you with some basic knowledge about writing for electronic media and using both oral and written communications skills to connect with an audience. Place a check in the blank next to each item when you understand it, and know where and how to apply it to communications on the job.

_____ Confidence comes with carefully thinking through every aspect of a presentation; then developing it and practicing it. You still might not feel comfortable, and you might be anxious until it's over, but preparation will eliminate a big reason for being fearful.

_____ A well-tested formula for a successful presentation is tell them what you're going to tell them (introduction), tell them (body), and tell them what you've told them (conclusion).

_____ For a successful presentation, you should know the surroundings and arrange for equipment and handouts, in addition to preparing the content.

_____ Audiences expect slides to augment the speaker's presentation. Therefore, the text you put on slides should hit key points—it should not be a script for your oral presentation.

_____ Outlining your presentation will help you decide what you are going to say and what points you want to highlight on the slides.

_____ Use only key words and phrases on the slides; your script in the form of notes will guide what you say as each slide is shown.

_____ When delivering your presentation, speak clearly, distinctly, and enthusiastically. Speak loudly enough to be heard in the back of the room if there is no microphone. Make direct eye contact, dress appropriately, have good posture, and vary your tone of voice and volume appropriately for the content.

_____ When preparing written information for a Web site, consider the ways in which Web site users' expectations are different from users of printed material.

_____ When developing content for the Web, consider graphics, amount and arrangement of text, font choices (style, size, and color), movement (animation), and sound.

_____ Draft, revise, and proofread text prepared for the Web using the same standards you would use for any other written communication. Remember that Web site users expect information to be kept up to date.

  ## Special Assignment

Using the example of how to prepare a storyboard in Read 66, prepare a two- to five-minute oral presentation on a topic of your choice; for example, a "how to" on one of your favorite hobbies or recipes, an overview of your chosen career field, or how to prepare for a job interview. Prepare your storyboard at the computer or use pen and paper. Draft, edit, and revise the text that will appear on slides, making sure the length is within the guidelines suggested in this chapter. Practice speaking from your script, which may be in the form of notes or sentences. Time your presentation and be ready to share it with your class at your instructor's request.

Date to submit this assignment: _____

Proofreading for Careers

Identify the two errors in Slide 1 and the four errors in Slide 2. Write your corrections in the blanks next to the slide.

Slide 1 1. Change _____ to _____ 2. Change _____ to _____	<u>Five-Year Sales Growth</u> ■ 1985-90 0.35% ■ 1991-85 −0.25% ■ 1996-00 .18% ■ 2001-05 0.23%
Slide 2 3. Change _____ to _____ 4. Change _____ to _____ 5. Change _____ to _____ 6. Change _____ to _____	**Best Selling Diet Book** **1. Hollywood Wieghtlost Secrets** **2. You Are Not What You Eat** **3. The Malibu Beech Diet** **4. The Swim to Be Slime Diet**

Practice Quiz

Write **T** (true) or **F** (false) next to each sentence.

_____ **1.** In writing for multimedia presentations, content (words) is less important than graphics.

_____ **2.** Words are the least important component of a Web site or slide show.

_____ **3.** Include as many words as possible on each slide in a slide show.

_____ **4.** When making an oral presentation to your colleagues at work, you'll impress them by using as many technical terms as possible.

_____ **5.** Place your most important information "above the fold" on a Web page.

_____ **6.** Using visual aids that support your message will keep your audience's attention.

_____ **7.** When making an oral presentation to colleagues at work, avoid repeating your ideas; once is enough.

_____ **8.** Audience members should always be allowed to ask questions as they come up during a speech.

_____ **9.** Eye contact isn't so important in oral presentations since you want your listeners to focus on reading the slides.

_____ **10.** Although regular employees might prepare text for a Web site, many companies employ technical specialists to design and write online content.

Self-Study Practice and Tutorials

Vocabulary and Spelling for Careers

For additional practice go to Appendix B, page 321.

Replay Drills

For additional practice go to Appendix C, page 408.

Companion Web Site: www.prenhall.com/smith

Go to the companion Web site to test your knowledge on self-grading quizzes and for links to other helpful online resources.

MyWritingLab

Use this online learning system for an assessment of your progress on topics covered in this chapter and progressive exercises that fit your individual needs.

Score Sheet for _____
Student's Name

Chapter	Read No.	Page No.	Date Completed	Total Questions	No. Right
1	1–4	294			
2	6–8	296			
3	11–13	297			
3	14–15	299			
4	16–17	300			
4	18–21	301			
5	22–23	302			
6	24–30	303			
7	31–37	304			
8	38–40	306			
8	41–43	307			
9	44–46	308			
9	47–49	310			
10	50–51	311			
10	52–53	312			
11	54–55	313			
11	56–57	315			
12	58	316			
12	59–62	317			
13	63–65	319			
14	66–67	320			

POP QUIZ FOR Reads AND Replays 1–4 (CHAPTER 1)

1. What is the name of your dictionary? _____

2. What is a lexicographer? _____

3. Dictionaries *describe* how English is used. They don't *prescribe* how to use English.
   (a) true _____ (b) false _____

4. To interpret the abbreviations used in your dictionary, look in the _____.

5. If you're having difficulty thinking of just the right word for something you're writing, look up a related word in a _____.

6. If you need help with writing business documents a business _____ will help you.

7. *Abstract* is used as what parts of speech? _____

8. The treasurer dis__rsed (pe or bu?) all the funds. _____

9. What does the abbreviation ILGWU mean? _____

10. Like *Webster* in dictionaries, the famous name in thesauruses is _____

11. What do you find in a thesaurus? _____

12. Which syllable has the primary accent in the preferred pronunciation of *incomparable:* first, second, third, fourth, fifth? _____

13. Using a college dictionary or a thesaurus, find a synonym (word with a similar meaning) for *incomparable.* _____

14. What was the nationality of the poet and playwright Dante? _____

15. Is a college dictionary abridged or unabridged? _____

16. *Disinterested* and *uninterested* mean the same. (a) true _____ (b) false _____ (c) maybe _____

Referring to your dictionary, divide these words into syllables by rewriting the word and drawing a diagonal (/) at the end of each syllable. For a one-syllable word, draw the diagonal at the end.

17. worked _____

18. getting _____

19. contagion _____

20. beetle _____

21. fullness _____

22. Write a brief definition obtained from your dictionary for:
    a. prepotent _____
    b. pisciculture _____
    c. effusive _____
    d. primavera _____

Answers will vary somewhat depending on the dictionary used and how the definition is condensed.

23. Correctly pronounce No. 22 b, c, and d.

24. What does it mean if a word <u>doesn't</u> have a usage label? _____

_____

25. What is the definition in your dictionary for *bombed,* and what is the slang or colloquial meaning for *bomb*? _____

_____

26. In which decade of the 1900s was the word *cybernation* first used? _____

27. What do we call words that mean almost the same? _____

28. Why is it important to recognize the etymology in your dictionary? _____

_____

Name: _____ Date: _____

Number right: _____ out of 28

POP QUIZ FOR READS AND REPLAYS 6–8 (CHAPTER 2)

A. Please insert nouns that make sense in the blanks.

1. The _____ interviews all the _____.

2. The _____ in Lake _____ is extremely deep.

3. _____ wants a new red _____.

4. _____ was a conscientious _____.

5. Our _____ is closed on _____.

B. Please insert pronouns that make sense in the blanks.

6. Paralegals _____ are word processing experts get the best jobs.

7. Thank _____ for faxing _____ resume.

8. _____ wrote to us about _____.

9. When _____ goes wrong with _____, we'll blame _____.

10. Give _____ to _____ _____ take _____.

C. Please insert verbs that make sense in the blanks.

11. Many Americans _____ another language in addition to English.

12. Vince _____ the letter and then _____ it.

13. In Sweden don't _____ your beverage until the host _____ "Skoal."

14. Diablo Valley students _____ the float that _____ the prize.

15. The IRS _____ our tax return and _____ for a refund.

D. Please insert suitable adjectives in the blanks.

16. Our _____ copier is _____ to use.

17. Please make _____ reservations for a _____ show.

18. Professor Taylor had an _____ plan for teaching the Vietnamese language.

19. The _____ chairs and the _____ desk look _____ in your _____ office.

20. Write a _____ report outlining your _____ plan.

E. Please convert these adjectives to adverbs.

21. happy _____   24. busy _____

22. joyful _____   25. generous _____

23. real _____

Name: _____ Date: _____

Number right: _____ out of 25

POP QUIZ FOR READS AND REPLAYS 11–13 (CHAPTER 3)

A. Write **T** (true) or **F** (false).

1. To be a sentence, a group of words requires identity, action, and independence. _____

2. The identity requirement of a sentence means every sentence must have a verb. _____

3. An independent clause can stand alone as a complete sentence. _____

4. If a dependent clause is joined to an independent clause, the result is a comma splice. _____

5. A clause is a word group with a subject and a verb. _____

B. Fill in the blanks.

6. A noun or pronoun that tells who or what a sentence is about is called the _____.

7. A word that tells what the subject does, is, or has is what part of speech? _____

8. A word group beginning with a preposition that has no subject or verb is called a

   _____.

9. A clause beginning with a dependent conjunction is called a _____.

10. A comma between the independent clauses of a run-on creates a _____.

11. Two independent clauses joined with a semicolon can create a _____.

C. Write **F** for fragment, **S** for sentence, and **CS** for comma splice.

12. A boxer, which is a very friendly dog. _____

13. A boxer is a very friendly dog. _____

14. Because of the establishment of this law. _____

15. The hanging of greens, such as holly and ivy, is a British winter tradition that originated before the Christian era. _____

16. Since Austria's contribution to Christmas is the beloved carol, "Silent Night." _____

17. During the weeks preceding Christmas, the windows of Parisian department stores contain fabulous displays of animated figures. _____

18. Although in Mexico the home is decorated and ready to receive guests by December 16, the beginning of the Mexican posadas. _____

19. Japanese businesspeople who understand English say it is often difficult for them when Americans speak too fast. _____

20. Thanking you for your attention to this problem. _____

21. While she is the purchasing manager and he is the assistant manager. _____

22. Hoping to hear from you soon. _____

23. She is the purchasing manager, he is the assistant manager. _____

D. Replace incorrectly used commas with periods, and capitalize the first word of each sentence. If a comma does not create a comma splice, leave it alone.

24–27. When working at the computer, take frequent breaks before you get too tired. Do desk work for no more than 30 minutes at a time then take a mini-holiday of one to two minutes use that time for physical activity like getting up to look out the window, juggling two or more balls, running up a flight of steps, or organizing items on a high shelf.

28–33. In the international marketplace, wearing certain clothing or colors may offend the business-people of another country americans tend to let others know who they are by the way they dress some styles are inappropriate when you are with people of another country, it is wise to wear conservative clothes in quiet colors for your business meetings.

Name: _____ Date: _____

Number right: _____ out of 33

POP QUIZ FOR READS AND REPLAYS 14–15 (CHAPTER 3)

A. Correct the comma splices with a semicolon and transitional word, or phrase or with a comma and coordinating conjunction.

1. When appointments are made in China, a 30-minute "courtesy time" is often understood however, businesspeople are usually punctual.

2. Mike likes Lotus for spreadsheets, I prefer Excel.

3. Katie and Art arrive today Ron won't arrive until Friday.

4. The 90-minute lecture starts at noon, we can't meet you until 1:30.

5. The computers are down this morning; I'll do some filing.

B. In the blanks, write **CS** for a comma splice, **R** for a run-on, or **C** for a correct sentence; make needed corrections.

6. Many US firms trade with the EU therefore, they have large phone bills. _____

7. Many US firms trade with the EU, consequently, they have large phone bills. _____

8. Many US firms trade with the EU. They have large phone bills. _____

9. Since many US firms trade with the EU, they have large phone bills. _____

10. Many US firms trade with the EU, they have large phone bills. _____

C. Correct the five comma splices in Part A (previously) by making one clause dependent. Use a different dependent conjunction for each one. For number 15 use the informal, conversational, two-letter coordinating conjunction.

11. _____
_____

12. _____
_____

13. _____
_____

14. _____
_____

15. _____
_____

Name: _____ Date: _____

Number right: _____ out of 15

POP QUIZ FOR Reads AND Replays 16–17 (CHAPTER 4)

Spell the plurals of these nouns. If a word has more than one correct plural, show both. When in doubt, use your dictionary.

1. inventory _____

2. bricklayer _____

3. memento _____

4. genius _____

5. editor in chief _____

6. premises _____

7. zero _____

8. Flores _____

9. diagnosis _____

10. phenomenon _____

11. hero _____

12. entry _____

13. proxy _____

14. wolf _____

15. attorney _____

16. notary public _____

17. alto _____

18. chassis _____

19. Vietnamese _____

20. formula _____

21. medium _____

22. curriculum _____

23. scarf _____

24. index _____

Name: _____ Date: _____

Number right: _____ out of 24

POP QUIZ FOR READS AND REPLAYS 18–21 (CHAPTER 4)

A. Draw a line through the incorrect words in parentheses.

1. Many (companies/companys/companyies) don't allow smoking in the workplace.

2. Statistics (is/are) a difficult subject for many people.

3. These statistics (is/are) hard to understand.

4. Why (are/is) the clothes always all over the floor?

5. The recipe calls for two (cupfuls/cupsful/cups ful) of oat bran.

6. Two (notaries public/notarys publics/notary publics) are available. [Choose preferred form.]

7. Did you order the new (check book/check-book/checkbook)?

B. Write **S** and/or **P** in the blank to show whether these nouns are singular, plural, or used for both.

8. diagnosis _____   11. criteria _____

9. data _____   12. analysis _____

10. hypotheses _____

C. Correct the noun errors in the following sentences. Write **C** beside the three correct sentences.

13. Did you know that my Uncle was the owner of his Company?_____

14. He became a General at the age of 27. _____

15. Please send the merchandise to our receiving department. _____

16. I was born in the east, but now I am a westerner. _____

17. They were runners-up in the contest. _____

18. We need several good Nurses to work at this Hospital. _____

19. We drove North last Summer until we reached Kansas City. _____

20. The plaintiff's attorney was disbarred. _____

21. The company's recruiter is looking for an assistant who likes textbooks. _____

D. Spell the plural of each of the following words.

22. sister-in-law _____   28. addendum _____

23. memento _____   29. proxy _____

24. itinerary _____   30. solo _____

25. corps _____   31. appendix _____

26. chassis _____   32. diagnosis _____

27. proceeds (noun) _____   33. deer _____

Name: _____ Date: _____

Number right: _____ out of 33

POP QUIZ FOR READS AND REPLAYS 22–23 (CHAPTER 5)

Circle the correct noun in the following sentences.

1. The (secretary's, secretaries) flowers sat on her desk.

2. The (men's, mens, mens') conference is scheduled for two o'clock.

3. The (bosses', bosses) are planning to leave early today.

4. The (Booth's, Booths') party will be next Sunday.

5. Our computer (repairman's, repairmans) truck just pulled up.

6. The busy (clerks, clerks') hurried to fill the orders.

7. This new (employee's, employees') first day was very hectic, and she was tired.

8. Our (company's, companies') annual picnic will be in September.

9. The (freshman's, freshmans') composition was read aloud by the instructor.

10. The (professor's, professors') lecture was presented on the satellite.

11. She went to her (mother-in-law's, mother-in-laws') house for dinner.

12. The (congresswoman's, congresswomans') vote enabled the passage of the new highway bill.

13. The (child's, childs') tooth was under his pillow.

14. Several new (member's, members', members) were introduced into the society.

15. Do you know the (Williams', Williamses)?

16. The two (actresses', actresses) were sisters in the play.

17. The (tenants', tenants) rights had been violated by the landlord.

18. Two (month's, months') construction delay caused the college to open late.

19. Both (director's, directors) presented their ideas to the review board.

20. Today's, Todays') weather forecast is for sunny skies and mild temperatures.

Name: _____ Date: _____

Number right: _____ out of 20

POP QUIZ FOR **R**EADS AND **R**EPLAYS 24–30 (CHAPTER 6)

Underline the preferred wording for written English.

1. Someone left their books here./Someone left his or her books here./Someone's books were left here.

2. We may hire a credit manager (whom/who) Bloomingdale's just laid off.

3. (Who/Whom) do you believe will lead the training session?

4. From (who/whom) did you buy the accounting software system?

5. (Who/Whom) do you think we should hire as the Web site manager?

6. Did he say (who/whom) he wants to work with?

7. The program was designed by Barbara Moran (who/whom) we all know to be an excellent writer.

8. We don't know (who/whom) is to blame.

9. Marg said (everyone/every one) of her students did well on the test.

10. Each person took (their/his or her) place in line.

11. All (who/whom) were eligible took (their/his or her) places in the queue.

12. We all respect the man to (who/whom) we dedicated this building.

13. Today we met President Gina Hector (whom/who) had not been here before.

14. (Every body/Everybody) in this district is being asked to donate blood.

15. Each employee is to indicate when he or she wishes to take their vacation./All employees are to indicate when they wish to take their vacation.

16. Every student should improve their grammar so that he or she can communicate correctly at work./Students should improve their grammar so that they can communicate correctly at work.

17. Each department has (its'/it's/its) own methods of dealing with absenteeism.

18. Please send the proceeds to (whoever/whomever) made most of the payments.

19. Each student was eager to see (his or her/their) test results.

20. (Whom/Who) do you think will be the next president of Disneyland?

21. The committee members finally made (its/their/his or her) decisions.

22. Nordstrom has kept (its/it's/their) headquarters in Seattle, Washington.

23. Rosenberg, Sica, & McDaniel, Inc., filed (its/it's/their) case last week.

24. The one who deserves the prize is (she/her).

25. The guilty one appeared to be (him/he/himself).

Name: _____ Date: _____

Number right: _____ out of 25

POP QUIZ FOR READS AND REPLAYS 31–37 (CHAPTER 7)

A. Circle the verb errors in the following sentences. Write the correct replacement verbs in the blanks.

1. One of the messages were on my voice mail. _____

2. Neither of these two proposals are acceptable. _____

3. The lecture series were a great success. _____

4. If he was a better interviewer, he would have hired her. _____

5. A person with many skills and talents are fortunate. _____

6. All the accountants except Evan works on receivables. _____

7. They seen the Broadway show and then drove home. _____

8. They have ran a business in the past. _____

9. I use to drive race cars in Indianapolis. _____

10. A carton of books have been there since last week. _____

11. Xerox manufacture and sell electronic equipment. _____

12. Good grammar and spelling is important in workplace email. _____

13. Neither Charles nor Dolores leave at 5 p.m. on Fridays. _____

14. Each man and woman need an application form. _____

15. Many a young boy hope to be a professional baseball player. _____

16. Ann, along with her sisters, have a court reporting agency. _____

17. Where's your roller blades? _____

B. Underline the collective noun and the correct verb choice in each of the following sentences.

18. The staff (attend/attends) training sessions on Mondays at 8 a.m.

19. The law firm of Graham & James (have/has) been chosen to represent us.

20. Each summer my family (takes/take) its vacation in Kona, Hawaii.

C. In the blanks write the present participle of the following verbs:

21. forget _____

22. cost _____

23. pay _____

D. In the blanks write the simple past participle of the following verbs:

24. fall _____

25. pay _____

26. freeze _____

E. In the blanks write the past participle of the following verbs:

27. shake _____

28. cost _____

29. forget _____

F. Correct the verb form in the following sentence:

30. The child had fell down. _____

G. Please insert appropriate verb forms in the blanks.

EXAMPLE Those students ___should study___ more assiduously. (Where's the dictionary?)

31. Many Americans _____ another language in addition to English.

32. Vince _____ the letter before he _____ the call.

33. In Sweden you _____ your beverage after the host _____ "Skoal."

34. Diablo Valley students _____ the float that _____ the prize.

35. The IRS _____ our tax return and then _____ for more money.

36. The headquarters _____ headquartered in Dallas. (*was* or *were?*)

37. The jury _____ sequestered by the judge. (*was* or *were?*)

Name: _____ Date: _____

Number right: _____ out of 37

POP QUIZ FOR **R**EADS AND **R**EPLAYS 38–40 (CHAPTER 8)

A. For 1–5 write the four pointing adjectives and one three-letter article; follow each by the noun *kind* or *kinds*.

1. _____

2. _____

3. _____

4. _____

5. _____

B. Write *a* or *an* in the blank.

6. _____ union member

7. _____ one-inch line

8. _____ hairline fracture

9. _____ honest job

10. _____ heir

C. Use proofreading marks to correct verb, adjective, or adverb errors. If the sentence is correct, write **C** in the blank.

_____ 11. He is angryer than I have ever saw him.

_____ 12. The most safest rule is to drive within the speed limit.

_____ 13. Rex Bishop plays real good golf.

_____ 14. Dr. Hellwig looks different today.

_____ 15. Between drinking and smoking, which is the least of the two evils?

_____ 16. The accountant's report is more better than the manager's.

_____ 17. Ms. Pearl prepared the invoices as careful as possible under the circumstances.

_____ 18. The food tasted really greasy and smelled even worse than at the old restaurant.

_____ 19. The mashed potatoes taste badly too.

_____ 20. He writes more clearly than his supervisor.

_____ 21. Those kind of apples is sweet.

_____ 22. Which is the most beautiful city, Tampa or Miami?

_____ 23. When you ski faster, you negotiate turns easier.

_____ 24. She hasn't gone nowhere yet.

_____ 25. We don't want to do business with them anyway.

Name: _____ Date: _____

Number right: _____ out of 25

POP QUIZ FOR **R**EADS AND **R**EPLAYS **41–43** (CHAPTER 8)

A. Underline the adjectives and circle the adverbs in the following sentences. In the blank write the word that each one modifies. See No. 1 as an example.

1. Early radio focused (mostly) on music and news. (adjective) ___radio___ (adverb) ___focused___

2. Adventure-mystery dramas targeted adolescents chiefly. (adjective) _____ (adverb) _____

3. Television was commercially introduced to the United States in the early 1940s.
   (adjective) _____ (adjective) _____ (adverb) _____

4. The Clampetts of the 1960s television show lived—uneasily at times— in a Beverly Hills mansion.
   (adjective) _____ (adjective) _____ (adjective) _____ (adverb) _____

5. What old television shows did your parents see regularly when they were young children?
   (adjective) _____ (adjective) _____ (adverb) _____

B. Most of the following sentences have adjective or adverb errors. Cross out the incorrect word and show corrections in the blanks, or write **C** beside correct sentences. Complete 16 and 17.

6. The children sat as quiet as possible through the movie. _____

7. She dresses too casual for this office. _____

8. Them junior staffers are always competing for promotions. _____

9. Natasha is the prettiest of my sister's two daughters. _____

10. She is unhappy about Andy's behavior. _____

11. She hasn't gone nowhere yet. _____

12. When you ski faster, you negotiate turns easier. _____

13. We are real unhappy about his behavior. _____

14. These mashed potatoes taste good. _____

15. He must learn to speak and write more clearly than he does now. _____

16. The four kinds of adjectives are _____.

17. Adverbs modify _____.

18. Many adverbs are formed by simply adding *ly* to the end of an adjective. _____

C. Turn these adjectives into adverbs.

19. happy _____   23. real _____

20. joyful _____   24. smart _____

21. busy _____   25. most _____

22. generous _____

Name: _____ Date: _____

Number right: _____ out of 25

POP QUIZ FOR Reads and Replays 44–46 (CHAPTER 9)

Insert commas as needed. Write **C** beside the correct sentences.

_____ 1. A letter of transmittal for a report may include background information, supplementary information, or confidential information.

_____ 2. Personality conflicts at work are upsetting and cause serious drops in productivity.

_____ 3. According to a *Wall Street Journal* article misplaced commas are the most common error in business writing.

_____ 4. Some important morale factors are satisfaction with the job itself opportunity to learn and compatibility with coworkers.

_____ 5. A human resources department is responsible for activities concerning employees and it advises other departments and management regarding personnel matters.

_____ 6. If these ideas are interesting to you perhaps you could take courses in management human relations or industrial psychology.

_____ 7. You might discover that you have a career interest in such a position as human resources director industrial psychologist or human relations consultant.

_____ 8. Formal business management courses alone will not make you effective but they will enable you to learn about supervision and management.

_____ 9. If becoming a supervisor sounds interesting to you start to prepare now.

_____ 10. Some decisions may seem trivial to you but the quality of each decision is important to a department's success.

_____ 11. Yes you will need to talk with your most intelligent and loyal employees on many subjects.

_____ 12. A supervisor must learn how to conduct group meetings to discipline and terminate employees and to be a good member of the management team.

_____ 13. My sister's friend manages a small elegant specialty shop in Hartford Connecticut.

_____ 14. Six months ago Michael and Rachel were assigned stores to manage.

_____ 15. The four words in the English language that end with *dous* are tremendous horrendous stupendous and hazardous.

_____ 16. Yesterday Austin Silver decided he wanted to get into the management field.

_____ 17. He may not know everything about motivating others but he is willing to learn.

_____ 18. Should you move into a supervisory job from a technical one you must quickly become a people-oriented individual.

_____ 19. Whenever you can take some management courses do so.

_____ 20. Mangement requires training, not just good instincts.

_____ 21. Some top executives ask their staff managers to be alert to employee gripes and try to correct the causes if possible.

_____ 22. Only those who aim high can possibly find how high they can go.

_____ 23. Develop career goals and adjust them as you go along.

_____ 24. To be a high achiever, you must be self-motivated.

_____ 25. I'm not sure, but I believe he has potential.

Name: _____ Date: _____

Number right: _____ out of 25

POP QUIZ FOR **R**EADS AND **R**EPLAYS **47–49** (CHAPTER 9)

Insert commas as needed.

_____ 1. First he typed the letter, which had been sitting all day and then he replied to the emails.

_____ 2. They lived at 40536 Picket Fence Road, Levittown Pennsylvania in an older home that was in very good condition.

_____ 3. Visitors to the United States need to be aware that dinner which is usually between 7 and 9 p.m. is the main meal of the day.

_____ 4. It was the expense of the work not its difficulty that caused us to refuse to begin the project.

_____ 5. Allen Yoshimoto PhD will conduct the research for a fee of $52,000.

_____ 6. It is I am pleased to report an idea that the CEO finds promising.

_____ 7. "It's a good strategy to take the high road" the trainer advised "when you're involved in a disagreement."

_____ 8. Nonessential words however should be enclosed in commas.

_____ 9. The train left from Richmond Virginia and traveled to Montreal Canada.

_____ 10. Purchasing a $40000 car seems extravagant for a recent college grad.

_____ 11. The award ceremony on August 25 2010 was televised nationally.

_____ 12. We are pleased Mr. Jefferson that you have decided to accept our offer.

_____ 13. "Be careful what you wish for" she cautioned.

_____ 14. Send the package to Mr. William McIntyre 1050 W. 72nd Street New York, NY 10023 as soon as possible.

_____ 15. We expected sales to increase by 8000 to 10000 units within the next year.

Name: _____ Date: _____

Number right: _____ out of 15

POP QUIZ FOR READS AND REPLAYS 50–51 (CHAPTER 10)

Correct semicolon, colon, and comma errors in these sentences.

1. Our campaign to increase sales is ready The salespeople are trained their morale is good our product is excellent and we have an ample supply.

2. Campers must take these items tents pillows sleeping bags cooking utensils bottled water and food.

3. Our prices are competitive for example $4.99 for a ream of laser paper $3.49 for 500 envelopes and $1.59 for a glue stick.

4. Get a good education then you can compete for better jobs and earn more money.

5. We have four requirements for the job reliability common sense courtesy and accuracy.

6. Each king in a deck of playing cards represents a great ruler from history spades King David clubs Alexander the Great hearts Charlemagne and diamonds Julius Caesar.

7. Originally there were four flavors of Jell-O strawberry raspberry orange and lemon.

8. Consumer demand can be changed you can be influenced to select one item over another.

9. The judges at the canine show rejected all but two of the dogs a cocker spaniel and a bulldog.

10. His phenomenal success is due to one thing hard work.

11. Karen will survey customers in Oakland California The Bronx New York and Tampa Florida.

12. The following hotels have rooms for conference attendees Hyatt Regency 208 Barton Road Embassy Suites 300 South Street and Four Seasons 98 Rodeo Drive.

13. Some people get a great deal of work done on rainy days however when it's sunny they take the day off.

14. Michael has an overpowering ambition namely to propose to Kim atop the Empire State Building.

15. During the tour we shall visit four points of interest in Washington the Library of Congress White House Capitol and Smithsonian Institute.

Name: _____ Date: _____

Number Right: _____ out of 15

POP QUIZ FOR READS AND REPLAYS 52–53 (CHAPTER 10)

A. Correct ending punctuation and comma errors in these sentences. Write **C** beside the correct sentences.

_____ 1. The name of the book is *The Encyclopedic Dictionary of Business Terms.*

_____ 2. Will you please send us your check today.

_____ 3. Would you be able to send the report to my nephew Alex who moved to Toronto Canada last year?

_____ 4. We recommend that business travelers ask the concierge at their hotel for advice on tipping in that country.

_____ 5. May we please have your response by December 15.

_____ 6. Would you please let us know if you can't make the payment in July.

_____ 7. Is Adam pleased with his lateral transfer and Maria with her management job

_____ 8. Did you know that Hofstra University had a 1.3 million-volume library

_____ 9. Thats amazing

_____ 11. Please realign the columns of figures

_____ 12. Today as indicated above most people are employed in service or information industries thus making production increases more difficult to measure

_____ 13. The average wage earner in 1914 worked 12 hours a day for about $800 a year.

_____ 14. Is it true that you have worked as a hair stylist bartender and masseuse

_____ 15. Would you please give me a call as soon as possible

D. Insert dashes or parentheses where required or useful for emphasis or de-emphasis.

21. Sales last year the best year in our history were well over 10 million dollars.

22. The president who was once penniless was always generous to her staff.

23. American men own an average of three coats an overcoat, a topcoat, and a raincoat and five pairs of trousers.

24. A CPU, keyboard, monitor, and printer these were all essential parts of a computer system until laptops came along.

25. Our profits see chart, page 3 were the highest in the history of this company.

Name: _____ Date: _____

Number right: _____ out of 25

POP QUIZ FOR READS AND REPLAYS 54–55 (CHAPTER 11)

A. Apply Chapter 11 rules for quotation marks and punctuation, italics/underlining (underline in handwriting; use italics on the computer), and hyphens. Add a capital letter if it is essential to begin a new sentence. Write **C** to the left of items that are already correct.

_____ 1. The president of a major corporation said, to get to the top, it takes a sense of urgency about getting things done."

_____ 2. The officer asked, "Are these the boys who stole the bicycles?"

_____ 3. The boys said to the police, "No, we didn't do it."

_____ 4. Brad Pitt was named Sexiest Man Alive by People magazine.

_____ 5. Why should parents buy school age kids the latest styles in school clothes when uniforms are less expensive and easier to manage?

_____ 6. "Do you really believe that?" she asked.

_____ 7. A Confederate soldier wrote the bugle melody we call "Taps."

_____ 8. During the 1990s I saw ex-president Ford at a pre-Christmas sale at Macy's Department Store.

_____ 9. Do not use hyperbole; not one writer in a million can use it effectively, wrote Dr. Alan Dundes. [Look up hyperbole—meaning and pronunciation.]

_____ 10. "A semicolon," said the anatomy expert, "is not part of the small intestines; it is the mark that may be placed between independent clauses instead of a period."

_____ 11. English for Careers is more fun to learn from than most other textbooks.

_____ 12. The invitation said, "If you can't make it in July, please visit us in August."

_____ 13. The president's wife said, "This is an off-the-record comment."

_____ 14. He likes to eat in first class restaurants in far off places.

_____ 15. "No," he shouted angrily. "No, I didn't!"

_____ 16. The manager said, "You won the million dollar lottery!"

_____ 17. In a corporation having several thousand employees, top-level managers seldom know more than a small fraction of those on the payroll.

_____ 18. Excerpts from the article How to Become a Perfect Speller are in the chapter called Writing on the Job in the book Communication and Career Success.

_____ 19. My financial consulting business is just a small scale operation.

_____ 20. Then he added, "The difficulty is visualizing a tool or technique to double the productivity of a chef, an artist, or a teacher."

B. Draw a line (|) to show where these words may be divided at the end of a line. If a word shouldn't be divided at all, place the line at the end. Use your dictionary. Example: expen|sive

21. referred

22. preferred

23. permitting

24. catches

25. conjunction

Name: _____ Date: _____

Number right: _____ out of 25

POP QUIZ FOR READS AND REPLAYS 56–57 (CHAPTER 11)

A. Fill in the blanks with the correct forms of the nouns or pronouns in parentheses. Some nouns in parentheses are already correct. Write **C** in the blank if no correction is required.

1. From Mr. (Saunders) letter we learned that prices have advanced 11 percent since Ms. (James) article was published. _____ _____

2. If Ms. (Schultz) gets the layout into Mr. (Austerlitz) hands today, the advertisement will be run on time. _____ _____

3. The signature on the contract is my (brother-in-law). _____

4. Has (Mr. Fingles) committee reached (its) quota of contributions in the (PTA) annual fund-raising campaign? _____ _____ _____

5. A business must consider all its (customers) (needs). _____ _____

6. (Girls) (jeans) are selling fast at (Macys). _____ _____ _____

7. My (mother-in-law) will was probated by (Atlanta) most famous (attorneys). _____ _____ _____

8. This is a (weeks) supply of (groceries). _____ _____

9. (Mens) clothing is on the first floor, (womens) on the second, and (girls) on the third. _____ _____ _____

10. Both his (daughters-in-laws) (offices) are on Fifth Avenue in Manhattan. _____ _____

B. Insert apostrophes and *s* where needed. If no apostrophe is needed, write **C** to the left of the number.

_____ 11. Why isnt there ever enough time to get everything done?

_____ 12. The casting agent wouldnt choose him for that part.

_____ 13. I was surprised to see five As on my transcript.

_____ 14. Bostons average winter temperature is in the 40s.

_____ 15. They told me the staff already had two MBAs from Harvards class of '01.

_____ 16. The childrens teacher gave them each two Bs on their report cards.

_____ 17. Mr. Perkins wore the bosss hat; thats Matt Perkins were writing about.

_____ 18. We received two brochures in todays mail.

_____ 19. General Motors president read all of Aristophanes plays.

_____ 20. Moses is discussed in *Exodus,* one of the books of the Bible.

_____ 21. The president was happy with Congresss action regarding Medicare.

_____ 22. We think Vitexs sales force was very effective during last years heat wave.

_____ 23. Garlic and onion plants make Ms. Forbis farm very smelly.

_____ 24. Do *yours, hers,* and *ours* require any apostrophes?

_____ 25. He won the sweepstakes and scored 25 points two years ago.

Name: _____ Date: _____

Number right: _____ out of 25

POP QUIZ FOR READ AND REPLAY 58 (CHAPTER 12)

A. Review Chapter 12, "Polishing Your Writing," if necessary, so that you readily identify the following word groups as *fragment, comma splice, run-on,* or *correct*. Write **F** for fragment, **R** for run-on, **CS** for comma splice, or **C** for correct.

_____ 1. If it looks like a duck, talks like a duck, and quacks like a duck.

_____ 2. "Ace in the hole," "blue chip," "feed the kitty," and "follow suit" are examples of gambling slang.

_____ 3. Noah Webster, who is still considered the dean of American dictionary makers.

_____ 4. In British English a period at the end of a sentence is called a *full stop.*

_____ 5. Avoid word mix-ups, use words in proper context.

_____ 6. Your decision will not be easy several capable applicants want the job.

_____ 7. If Professor Lundin will attend the convention.

_____ 8. Professor Lundin will present a paper, she will also conduct a workshop.

_____ 9. We often identify people by their work; for example, we might introduce someone as a lawyer.

_____ 10. Some of our business students are majoring in management, others are more interested in accounting.

_____ 11. "Fear is that little darkroom where negatives are developed."—Michael Pritchard

_____ 12. "We can do no great things, only small things with great love."—Mother Teresa

_____ 13. "Shared joy is double joy, shared sorrow is half sorrow."—Swedish proverb

_____ 14. Love is not blind, it sees less.

_____ 15. "Life is either a daring adventure or nothing, security is mostly a superstition."—Helen Keller

_____ 16. A complete sentence has a subject, a verb, and independence.

_____ 17. He thought carefully about the move, then he discussed it with his family.

_____ 18. This session will begin at 2 p.m. however, our guest speaker may be late.

_____ 19. "Experience is not what happens to you, it is what you do with what happens to you."—Aldus Huxley

_____ 20. He thought carefully about the move; then he discussed it with his family.

Name: _____ Date: _____
Number right: _____ out of 20

B. On a separate sheet of paper, rewrite the **F, R,** and **CS** items in Part A so that they are correct sentences.

POP QUIZ FOR READS AND REPLAYS 59–62 (CHAPTER 12)

A. Identify sentences with the following faults, and write the appropriate letters in the blanks: (SS) short, simple, (LPC) lacks parallel construction, (G) gobbledygook, (M) misplaced words, (VP) vague pronoun usage, (F) fragment, (C) correct sentence, (CS) comma splice.

_____ 1. Christine Lundin is attending the convention for the purposes of presenting a paper and to hear the keynote address.

_____ 2. The agenda includes introducing new officers and discussing the prospectus.

_____ 3. Our bank approves loans to reliable people of any size.

_____ 4. Professionals must keep their skills up-to-date. They must take classes. They need to network.

_____ 5. In the parade will be 300 children carrying flags and the governors of several states.

_____ 6. Sometimes we must choose between giving up our ideals or to remain faithful to them.

_____ 7. Not long after the beginning of the 17th century, which means the early 1600s, a game of long times past with the common appellation of ninepins commenced to be an activity engaged in for recreation.

_____ 8. Charlene told Ms. Seefer that she needs to go to Concord.

_____ 9. The plan for the next meeting includes:

    (a) introduce new officers

    (b) reviewing current budget

    (c) to decide agenda for annual meeting

_____ 10. Carlos is not only an expert swimmer but is also an excellent cook.

_____ 11. Because when you write, you should avoid using long words as much as possible.

_____ 12. To express your meaning clearly, use precise language, avoid gobbledygook, and choose short words over long ones.

_____ 13. Enclosed are several carpeting samples. Each of which will be on sale next week.

_____ 14. Our new catalog is in the mail, it should reach you by the end of the week.

B. On a separate sheet of paper or on a computer, rewrite the sentences in Part A, correcting the sentence faults.

C. Change these passive voice sentences to active voice. In the blank, rewrite the sentence adding any missing information needed for the sentence to make sense.

15. The contracts were signed by all the college presidents. _____

_____

16. The depositions were taken by Tricia yesterday. _____

17. The package was mailed by my assistant yesterday. _____

18. Marcia Stranix's name was added to the contract by my secretary. _____
_____

19. New multinational markets will be developed by many companies within the next year.
_____

F. Change these active voice sentences to passive voice.

20. The tycoon purchased the emerald and diamond necklace for $500,000. _____
_____

21. Lorraine visited several other Ohio campuses last year. _____
_____

22. Several managers expressed approval of the new software. _____
_____

23. One member of our sales staff has sold almost 1,000 BMW leases in six months.
_____

24. Schroeder predicted a daily attendance of about 3,000 at the Houston convention.
_____

C. Write **D** in the blank if the sentence has a dangler. Otherwise, write **C** for correct.

_____ 25. Walking down Marietta Street in Atlanta, a statue of the famous editor Henry Grady caught the tourists' attention.—Error example from *SPELL Handbook*

_____ 26. Having been on the phone for three hours, her father took it away from her.

_____ 27. Her car was stolen while watching the beautiful sunset.

_____ 28. While watching the beautiful sunset, her car was stolen.

_____ 29. While they were watching the beautiful sunset, her car was stolen.

_____ 30. While watching the beautiful sunset, someone stole her car.

_____ 31. Since we were young and foolish, the partying went on all night.

_____ 32. Being young and foolish, the partying went on all night.

_____ 33. To be well baked, you should leave the potatoes in the oven for an hour.

_____ 34. If the potatoes are to be well baked, leave them in the oven for an hour.

_____ 35. If you can think of a short word to express your meaning, choose it over a long one.

Name: _____ Date: _____

Number right: _____ out of 35

POP QUIZ FOR READS AND REPLAYS 63–65 (CHAPTER 13)

Write **T** (true) or **F** (false) in the blank.

_____ 1. One correct way to express the date in a business letter is June 21st, 2006.

_____ 2. All the following are correct as salutations:
Dear Billy,   Dear Mr. Crystal: Dear Mr. Crystal

_____ 3. All the following are correct as complimentary clauses:
Sincerely   Sincerely,   Sincerely;

_____ 4. It doesn't matter whether you send copies or blind copies of emails.

_____ 5. The only way to send a letter is by "snail mail."

_____ 6. Attention lines should rarely be used in business letters.

_____ 7. It's advisable to type emails in all capital letters.

_____ 8. Style and tone don't matter when you send emails to colleagues at work.

_____ 9. Avoid using a conversational tone in important business letters.

_____ 10. Interoffice memos are used as frequently in the workplace today as emails.

_____ 11. Avoid using a conversational tone when writing an interoffice memo.

_____ 12. A concisely written letter might be very long or very short.

_____ 13. Always include a meaningful subject line in an email message.

_____ 14. Including contact information in an email is unimportant since the recipient can easily reply.

_____ 15. Even if you know the person, avoid using informal salutations like "Hi, Joe" in business communications.

Write the answer in the blanks for each of the following questions.

20. Name in order at least 10 parts that might be included in a typical business letter.

_____

_____

_____

21. What is the principal advantage of attaching a letter to an email message rather than mailing it?

_____

22. A signature block should contain: _____

_____

Name: _____   Date: _____

Number right: _____ out of 22

POP QUIZ FOR READS AND REPLAYS 66–67 (CHAPTER 14)

A. Write your answers in the blanks.

1. What are some differences between traditional and multimedia writing? _____
   _____
   _____
   _____
   _____

2. Name five ways to emphasize text in a slide show. _____
   _____

3. Copying text from a Web site without saying where you obtained it is _____.

B. Answer **T** (true) or **F** (false).

_____ 4. When you prepare to make an oral presentation to your coworkers and/or superiors, the first step should be to practice your presentation.

_____ 5. The content of your presentation should consist of an introduction, a body, and a conclusion.

_____ 6. When you make an oral presentation, avoid specific recommendations.

_____ 7. It is hard to develop rapport with your audience when you read a presentation word for word from a printed script.

_____ 8. When making an oral presentation, it's a good idea to begin with a story or joke.

_____ 9. It's advisable to introduce a few new ideas in the conclusion of an oral presentation to coworkers and supervisors.

_____ 10. A good technique is to use your slides as a script for a presentation and read them verbatim.

_____ 11. Everything you plan to do or say during your presentation should be expressed in a way that helps you meet your objective.

_____ 12. Make the concluding portion of your presentation interesting by urging the audience members to take action on your recommendations.

_____ 13. An intranet is a Web site used by people outside of the company.

_____ 14. Paying attention to the time allowed is an important aspect of planning a presentation.

_____ 15. When developing slides, use as many bells and whistles as you can to make your presentation come alive.

Name: _____   Date: _____

Number right: _____ out of 25

APPENDIX B VOCABULARY AND SPELLING FOR CAREERS READ AND REPLAY

Score Sheet for _____
Student's Name

Read	Replay	Page No.	Date Completed	Total Questions	No. Right
1	1	323			
2	2	325			
3	3	327			
4	4	329			
5	5	331			
6	6	333			
7	7	335			
8	8	338			
9	9	340			
10	10	342			
11	11	345			
12	12	348			
13	13	349			
14	14	351			

How to Use This Appendix

This appendix is designed to give you "word power." It contains a vocabulary and spelling **Read** and **Replay** for you to do after you complete each of the 14 chapters in this book. By taking the time to improve your spelling and build a larger vocabulary, you will enhance your chances for future success. An extensive vocabulary pays off in job and social success, as well as in managing personal affairs. Chances are your career and even your specific job might have its own vocabulary that you have to learn, but no matter what career you choose, you will benefit from being familiar with the words defined here.

Vocabulary

The vocabulary words are related to business, professional, and technical careers (and "real life"). For your convenience in furthering your knowledge by using your dictionary, the word lists are in alphabetical order by Read; however, the expert speller lists are not alphabetized in order to give you the opportunity to practice using the dictionary guide words. Each Read is followed by a Replay exercise. Answers to these exercises begin on page 431 in this appendix.

In addition to their general use in business, professional, and technical careers, the terms defined here will help you make decisions about such matters as banking, investments, home ownership, insurance, attorneys' services, credit, and government. You will find it easier to understand information and advice about these matters when you have command of the appropriate vocabulary.

You probably already know many of the words covered here. In that case, make sure you spell and pronounce them correctly. If some words are new to you, become sufficiently familiar with them that you'll understand them in print or conversation. For some of the words, not all definitions are provided. For example, look up *audit*. You'll find several definitions in your dictionary besides the one given here. The idea is to work your way through these word lists over time as you complete this course, and then continue to increase your workplace vocabulary through reading business and technical news in the newspaper, a weekly news magazine, and information from the Internet. Working with a group is also a fun and effective way to build your vocabulary. You'll increase your vocabulary, and you'll have fun with some new words.

- Form a small group with people who are interested in vocabulary growth and speaking expertise.

- When necessary, verify pronunciation with your instructor or with a dictionary.

- Divide the list of words among the group members, who will write sentences showing they understand the meaning of the assigned words. You'll probably find words that are new to you.

- Finally, check one another's sentences for spelling and correct usage.

Spelling

Using your computer's spell checker decreases the likelihood of spelling errors; however, the spell checker is not always available. For example, when filling out a job application at a work site, your opportunity for a good job may be ruined by a single spelling error. Surveys and interviews of managers reveal that in many occupations accurate spelling is essential to getting the job, succeeding at it, and becoming eligible for promotion. Not only are electronic spell checkers often unavailable, but they are not always used correctly. To use the checker correctly, keep these points in mind:

Remember that it is not a college dictionary; it recognizes a limited number of words and, of course, doesn't include all proper nouns.

- A spell checker will highlight as incorrect a perfectly spelled word that doesn't happen to be in its "dictionary."

- If you can add words, add your work-related terms, including proper nouns not already listed.

- Carefully proofread each document both before and after activating the spell checker. The checker does not eliminate the need to proofread. In fact, it may give a false sense of security resulting in uncorrected errors. If you use the spell checker without proofreading, a document might be left with errors such as *a line* for *align, affect* for *effect,* or *thorough* for *through*.

Using the Expert Speller Lists

At the end of each Read and Replay is a list of commonly misspelled words for you to master. Be sure you know the meaning of each word as well as the pronunciation. The **1–3–2–1 Plan** is an efficient method for mastering correct spelling of an entire list of words. Here's how:

1 Ask someone to dictate the words. After writing or typing them **once,** note those you misspelled or were unsure of.

3 Correctly say and spell aloud each misspelled word. Then write or type the misspelled words **three** times each. Use the dictionary if in doubt about pronunciation.

2 Next, write correctly each previously misspelled word **twice.**

1 Now use an audiotape or ask someone to dictate the originally misspelled words to you, and write each one **once.** After checking the spelling of each word, list any words you misspelled or felt unsure of. Practice these, using the **1–3–2–1 Plan** again.

Follow the same procedure with the other lists.

READ 1 ACCOUNT EXECUTIVE THROUGH BROKERAGE

1. **account executive** Person who manages a customer's account in a service business such as an advertising agency or a financial services organization.
2. **affidavit** Written statement sworn to before a **notary public**—a person authorized by law to administer oaths.
3. **amalgamation** Joining of two or more businesses into a single body; also called a **merger.**
4. **AMEX (American Stock Exchange)** Second largest stock exchange in the United States, (after the New York Stock Exchange (NYSE); located in New York City.
5. **annual report** Annual message to stockholders providing information about the financial status and progress of a corporation. Reports are usually published in print and on the organization's Web site.
6. **antitrust legislation** Laws against monopoly-type business practices that result in a business making unfair profits.
7. **appreciate** To increase in value.
8. **APR** Annual percentage rate—what a borrower must pay in interest.
9. **arbitration** A third party appointed to settle a dispute between two groups.
10. **arrears** An amount overdue and still unpaid is "in arrears."
11. **attachment** Court order authorizing seizure of property for failure to meet obligations.
12. **audit** Examination of financial records of a business to determine correctness; such an examination is made by an **auditor.**
13. **balance sheet** Statement of assets, liabilities, and net worth as of a certain date.
14. **bar code** A code, imprinted on consumer goods and mail, that can be read by a computerized scanner designed for that purpose.

15. (a) **bear market** The stock market when prices are declining, and many stockholders are selling their stock because they think prices will continue to decrease. These sellers are called *bears*.

    (b) **bull market** The stock market when prices are increasing, and many stockholders are buying stock because they expect prices to continue to increase. These buyers are called *bulls*.

16. **beneficiary** A person designated to receive benefits from an insurance policy, a will, or a trust fund.

17. **bid** An offer to buy or sell services or goods at a certain price.

18. **bill of lading** A form made out by a transportation company and issued to the shipper as a receipt listing goods to be shipped.

19. **blogger** Someone who writes or edits a **blog**.

20. **brokerage** A business that buys and sells stocks and bonds for its clients.

REPLAY 1

Insert the appropriate number in the blank.

1. account executive	2. affidavit	3. amalgamation
4. AMEX	5. annual report	6. antitrust legislation
7. appreciate	8. APR	9. arbitration
10. arrears	11. attachment	12. audit
13. balance sheet	14. bar code	15. bear market
16. beneficiary	17. bid	18. bill of lading
19. blogger	20. brokerage	21. bull market

a. _____ The form made out by a shipping company listing goods to be shipped.

b. _____ This code is imprinted on consumer goods and mail; it is read by a computerized scanner.

c. _____ A pessimistic stock market. Stock prices are declining, and stockholders are selling.

d. _____ Percentage of interest to be paid on one's debts.

e. _____ A court order authorizing seizure of property for failure to meet obligations.

f. _____ Second largest stock market in the United States.

g. _____ To increase in value.

h. _____ A written statement sworn to before a person authorized to administer oaths.

i. _____ A debt that is overdue and still unpaid.

j. _____ Laws against monopoly-type business practices.

k. _____ A third party appointed to settle a dispute.

l. _____ One who receives benefits from an insurance policy, a will, or a trust fund.

m. _____ Examination of business records to determine their correctness.

n. _____ Statement of assets, liabilities, and net worth as of a certain date.

o. _____ Joining two or more organizations into a single group.

p. _____ Someone who writes or edits a blog.

q. _____ Person who manages a customer's account in an advertising agency or a financial services organization.

r. _____ Business that buys and sell stocks and bonds for its clients.

s. _____ Annual message to stockholders about the corporation's progress.

t. _____ An offer to buy or sell services at a certain price.

u. _____ Stock market prices are increasing; stockbrokers are buying and expect prices to continue to increase.

Check your answers on page 487.

CHAPTER 1: EXPERT SPELLER LIST

Circle the words that are unfamiliar to you, and then look up the meaning and practice spelling them.

abbreviate	acquire	apparatus	amateur
absence	appearance	adjournment	analysis
absurd	admissible	align	amendment
acquaintance	aggressive	allotment	accessible
ambiguous	accommodate	allotted	advantageous
announcement	acceptance	altogether	approximately
ambassador			

READ 2 — CERTIFICATE OF DEPOSIT THROUGH ETHICS

21. **(CD) certificate of deposit** A written message from a bank to a depositor showing the percentage of interest to be paid during a specified time period.

22. **certified check** Personal or company check drawn on funds made available by the depositor and therefore guaranteed by the bank to be valid.

23. **COLA** Cost-of-living adjustment for wages or Social Security payments.

24. **collateral** Borrower's property held by a lender as security for payment of a loan.

25. **concierge** (pronounced *con.SYERJH*) A person employed at a hotel or an apartment building to help the residents in various ways.

26. **consumer price index (CPI)** A monthly survey of changes in consumer prices; it is used to measure inflation.

27. **copyright** Legal protection of documents, computer software, films, and other creative works of authors, composers, artists, and so on.

28. **corporation** A body formed to act as a single person although constituted by one or more persons, operating under a charter granted by a state and authorized to do business under its own name.

29. **cyberlaw** Laws relating to computers, information systems, and networks.

30. **deficit** Shortage of money; the opposite of **surplus**.

31. **depreciation** Decline in value of property because of wear and age; the opposite of **appreciation**.

32. **direct mail** Advertisements mailed directly to homes or businesses.

33. **diversification** To expand a commercial organization and make it more varied by engaging in additional or different areas of business.

34. **dividend** A payment to a stockholder of a portion of the corporation's profits.

35. **dotgov** A way of expressing a URL (Internet address) that ends in ".gov"—such as www.whitehouse.gov.

36. **Dow Jones Industrial Average** (also called simply "the Dow or Dow Jones") The daily average of the closing prices of specific stocks on the New York Stock Exchange. This figure is widely publicized and indicates current stock market trends.

37. **down time** Time during which equipment is unable to be used until it has been adjusted or repaired; also used generally to refer to time when one is not busy or not engaged in work.

38. **e-blocker** Employer who uses special software to prevent employees from visiting certain Web sites while at work.

39. **e-signature** Electronic signature.

40. **ethics** Moral principles—such as the loyalty, honesty, and integrity required of employees in business and professions.

REPLAY 2

Insert the appropriate number in the blank.

21. CD—certificate of deposit	22. certified check
23. COLA	24. collateral
25. concierge	26. CPI
27. copyright	28. corporation
29. cyberlaw	30. deficit
31. depreciation	32. direct mail
33. diversification	34. dividend
35. dotgov	36. Dow Jones
37. down time	38. e-blocker
39. e-signature	40. ethics

a. _____ Written acknowledgment to a depositor showing the interest the bank will pay.

b. _____ Check guaranteed by a bank to be worth the amount for which the depositor wrote it.

c. _____ Legal protection of creative work produced by authors, composers, artists, and so on.

d. _____ Shortage of money; opposite of surplus.

e. _____ Special software preventing employees from visiting certain Web sites while at work.

f. _____ Cost-of-living adjustment for salaries and Social Security payments.

g. _____ Electronic signature.

h. _____ Money paid by a company to a stockholder.

i. _____ Moral principles required of business and professional employees.

j. _____ Decline in value of property.

k. _____ Time during which equipment cannot be used because it needs repair.

l. _____ Daily average of closing prices of 30 stocks traded on the New York Stock Exchange.

m. _____ Consumer price index.

n. _____ Advertisements mailed directly to homes or businesses.

o. _____ Laws relating to computers and information systems.

p. _____ Borrower's property held by a lender until debt is paid.

q. _____ "Artificial person" created by law and acting under a state-granted charter.

r. _____ A hotel employee who helps guests in a variety of ways.

s. _____ A business organization that engages in various areas of business.

t. _____ A way of expressing a URL (Internet address) that ends in ".gov"—such as www.whitehouse.gov.

Check your answers on page 487.

CHAPTER 2: EXPERT SPELLER LIST

Circle the words that are unfamiliar to you, and then look up the meaning and practice spelling them.

beginning	bargain	bouquet
battalion	basically	brilliant
belligerent	bazaar	bachelor
belief	believe	beneficial
bankruptcy	bookkeeping	broccoli
balloon	boundary	buoyant

READ 3 — *EURO* THROUGH *LIABILITIES*

41. **euro** The currency unit used in many of the European Union countries.

42. **exchange rate** Price of one country's money in relation to the price of another's; for example, the rate at which pesos, euros, francs, yen, rupees, and so on, can be exchanged for dollars.

43. **exemption** A specified amount of money not subject to taxation, such as money used to support a dependent.

44. **FAQ** Frequently asked questions.

45. **FDIC** Federal Deposit Insurance Corporation A U.S. government corporation that protects bank deposits that are payable in the United States up to a limited amount that was changed in 2008 from $100,000 to $250,000.

46. **financial planner** A specially trained and licensed professional who advises clients how to handle their financial assets in the most effective manner.

47. **fiscal year** A period of 12 months between one annual balancing of accounts and another.

48. **foreclosure** A lender taking over property when a debtor is not making payments on the mortgage.

49. **401k** A retirement plan for employees.

50. **fringe benefits or benefits** Paid vacations, insurance coverage, pension plans, part-time college tuition fees, and so on, given to employees in addition to salary or wages.

51. **Fannie Mae** (Federal National Mortgage Association) A government-sponsored enterprise authorized to make loans and loan guarantees.

52. **glass ceiling** Perceived or actual invisible barrier that prevents career advancement beyond a certain level for reasons of gender, age, race, ethnicity, or sexual orientation.

53. **graphics** Visual display of data such as graphs, charts, and diagrams.

54. **gross** The total, such as gross income, gross profit, gross weight; 12 dozen.

55. **hacker** A person who infiltrates other people's computer data.

56. **infomercial** A long TV commercial made to seem like an informative talk show (information plus commercials).

57. **insolvent** Unable to pay one's debts (**broke**—slang).

58. **intranet** A Web site with access restricted to a limited group of authorized users (such as employees of a company).

59. **itinerary** A detailed written schedule of activities, commonly used for travel and group activities.

60. **liabilities** The obligations or debts of a business or an individual.

REPLAY 3

Insert the appropriate number in the blank.

41. euro	42. exchange rate	43. exemption
44. FAQ	45. FDIC	46. financial planner
47. fiscal year	48. foreclosure	49. 401k
50. fringe benefits	51. Fannie Mae	52. glass ceiling
53. graphics	54. gross	55. hacker
56. infomercial	57. insolvent	58. intranet
59. itinerary	60. liabilities	

a. _____ Currency used in the European Union.

b. _____ Frequently asked questions.

c. _____ Sum of money not subject to taxation.

d. _____ A long TV commercial.

e. _____ Visual display of data, including graphs and charts.

f. _____ Unable to pay one's debts.

g. _____ Debts.

h. _____ Invisible barrier that usually prevents job promotions.

i. _____ Price of a country's money in relation to the price of another country's money.

j. _____ Written schedule for travel and activities.

k. _____ Debtor losing property because of inability to pay debts.

l. _____ Benefits given to employees in addition to salaries.

m. _____ The total amount.

n. _____ A retirement plan for employees.

o. _____ Federal Deposit Insurance Corporation.

p. _____ A Web site with access restricted to a limited group of authorized users.

q. _____ A government-sponsored enterprise authorized to make loans.

r. _____ Person who infiltrates other people's electronic data.

s. _____ Annual report is prepared at the end of this.

t. _____ Specially trained professional who advises clients on handling financial matters.

Check your answers on page 487.

CHAPTER 3: EXPERT SPELLER LIST

Circle the words that are unfamiliar to you, and then look up the meaning and practice spelling them.

carriage	confidently	chronic	career
commission	confidentially	condemn	cemetery
chronic	chargeable	connoisseur	collaborate
concede	candidate	conscience	curriculum
ceiling	calendar	camouflage	copyright
customary	camaraderie	campaign	compelled
commencement			

READ 4 — *LIBEL* THROUGH *PDF*

61. **libel** An untrue written statement, usually published, that injures another's reputation.

62. **lien** Claim against property preventing the owner from selling it until a debt (such as taxes) is paid.

63. **liquidate** To close the affairs of a business and sell the assets; to turn assets into cash.

64. **markup** The difference between the cost price and the selling price in a retail business.

65. **merit rating** Rating employees by measurable job performance benchmarks so that fair decisions may be made about raises, promotions, and so on.

66. **monopoly** Exclusive control of the supply of a commodity or service.

67. **mortgage** Pledge of property (real estate) as security for a loan.

68. **multinational corporation** A company with subsidiaries or branches in many nations.

69. **mutual fund** An investment in a fund that invests shareholders' money in various stocks or bonds.

70. **NASDAQ** (National Association of Securities Dealers Automated Quotations System) Average computed from prices of a number of stocks; this average is announced weekdays along with the Dow Jones Industrial Average, which is for a different group of stocks.

71. **negotiable instruments** Documents in which ownership is easily transferred to another person; for example, stock certificates or checks made out to "cash."

72. **net** Amount remaining after all deductions are made; for example, net profit is the balance after all expenses have been deducted from gross profit.

73. **New York Stock Exchange (NYSE)** Largest stock exchange in the United States; it's on Wall Street in New York City.

74. **outplacement** A company's assistance in finding jobs for its employees who have been terminated.

75. **outsource** Using outside sources for labor, parts, and various services instead of personnel and services within the company.

76. **overhead** General costs of running a business, such as taxes, rent, heating, lighting, and depreciation of equipment.

77. **per annum** In or for each year.

78. **per capita** Equally to each individual.

79. **per diem** By the day.

80. **PDF (Portable Document Format)** A method of formatting documents that allows them to be read on a computer screen or printed universally regardless of what kind of computer or printer is used; PDF files cannot be manipulated by the receiver.

REPLAY 4

Insert the appropriate number in the blanks.

61. libel	62. lien	63. liquidate
64. markup	65. merit rating	66. monopoly
67. mortgage	68. multinational corporation	69. mutual fund
70. NASDAQ	71. negotiable instruments	72. net
73. New York Stock Exchange	74. outplacement	75. outsource
76. overhead	77. per annum	78. per capita
79. per diem	80. PDF	

a. _____ An untrue written statement, usually published, that injures another's reputation.

b. _____ A claim against property that prevents the owner from selling it until a debt (such as taxes) is paid.

c. _____ Largest stock exchange in the United States.

d. _____ Difference between a retailer's cost price and the selling price.

e. _____ Turning assets into cash.

f. _____ By the day.

g. _____ National Association of Securities Dealers Automated Quotations system.

h. _____ Rating employees by their job performance.

i. _____ Using property as security for a loan.

j. _____ Amount remaining after deductions.

k. _____ Finding jobs for terminated employees.

l. _____ In or for each year.

m. _____ General costs of running a business.

n. _____ Documents easily transferred to another person or organization.

o. _____ Fund that invests shareholders' money in various stocks or bonds.

p. _____ Exclusive control of a commodity or a service.

q. _____ A company with branches in many nations.

r. _____ Use of outside sources for labor instead of the company's own employees.

s. _____ Equally to each individual.

t. _____ A method of formatting documents that allows them to be read or printed universally.

Check your answers on page 487.

CHAPTER 4: EXPERT SPELLER LIST

Circle the words that are unfamiliar to you, and then look up the meaning and practice spelling them.

debatable	deterrent	disappearance	default
disappointed	develop	disapprove	discretion
deductible	diligent	disguise	deceive
deferred	dimension	dissatisfied	dilemma
deluge	disastrous	desperate	defendant
definitely	discrepancy	deficient	dependent

READ 5 — *PROXY THROUGH WEBMASTER*

81. **proxy** A written authorization by a stockholder for someone to vote in his or her place at a stockholders' meeting.

82. **quorum** The number of members of an organization required to be present to have a formal meeting at which business is transacted.

83. **ream** 500 sheets of paper.

84. **reconciliation** Bringing into agreement a bank's records with the depositor's records of checks and deposits.

85. **requisition** A written request, made within an organization, for supplies or equipment.

86. **retainer** A fee paid to a lawyer or other professional for services to be rendered in the future.

87. **shareholder** Shareholder and stockholder have the same meaning—one who owns stock (or shares) in a corporation.

88. **slander** Untrue *spoken* remarks about someone that harm the person's reputation. (**Libel** refers to untrue *written* remarks.)

89. **solvent** Having the funds necessary to pay all debts.

90. **spyware** Software installed on a hard disk without the user's knowledge; it can be used to relay encoded information.

91. **start-up** A new company that is just beginning to operate as a business.

92. **stock** Investment in a corporation; stockholders are entitled to vote on various corporate matters and to share in the company's profits—based on the amount of stock they possess.

93. **tariff** A tax, called a **duty**, on imported items.

94. **turnaround time** Time elapsed between starting a task and completing it.

95. **turnover** Change in employees because of people being terminated or quitting; also refers to sale of products that are then replaced by additional merchandise.

96. **URL** (Uniform Resource Locator) The global address of documents and other resources on the World Wide Web.

97. **voice recognition** Ability of a computer program to accept speech and translate it.

98. **World Wide Web** (or **Web**) A way of transmitting and accessing information over the medium of the Internet through the use of graphics and documents that are connected by hyperlinks.

99. **Wikipedia** An online encyclopedia written collaboratively by its users and originators (www.wikipedia.org).

100. **Webmaster** One who organizes or updates information on a Web site.

REPLAY 5

Insert the appropriate number in the blank.

81. proxy	82. quorum	83. ream
84. reconciliation	85. requisition	86. retainer
87. shareholder	88. slander	89. solvent
90. spywear	91. start-up	92. stock
93. tariff	94. turnaround time	95. turnover
96. URL	97. voice recognition	98. World Wide Web
99. Wikipedia	100. Webmaster	

a. _____ A means for transmitting and accessing information over the medium of the Internet.

b. _____ Untrue spoken remarks about someone that harm the person's reputation.

c. _____ Written authorization by a stockholder for someone else to vote in his or her place.

d. _____ One who owns shares in a corporation.

e. _____ 500 sheets of paper.

f. _____ Fee paid to a lawyer or other professional for services to be rendered in the future.

g. _____ The number of members who must be present in order to have a formal meeting.

h. _____ One who organizes or updates information on a Web site.

i. _____ Time elapsed between starting and completing a task.

j. _____ Having funds needed to pay all debts.

k. _____ An online encyclopedia written collaboratively.

l. _____ Investment in a corporation entitling the investor to vote and to share in profits.

m. _____ A new company.

n. _____ Replacement of employees or sale of merchandise to be replaced by additional employees or items.

o. _____ Computer program enabling the user to translate speech into meaningful code.

p. _____ Tax, often called a *duty,* on imported items.

q. _____ Written request for supplies made within an organization.

r. _____ Determining that a bank's records agree with the depositor's records.

s. _____ Software that can be used illegally and without the user's knowledge.

t. _____ The global address of documents and other resources on the World Wide Web.

Check your answers on page 488.

CHAPTER 5: EXPERT SPELLER LIST

Circle the words that are unfamiliar to you and then look up the meaning and practice spelling them.

especially	eligible	enforceable	environment
eerie	eliminate	enormous	equipped
economics	emphasize	en route	erroneous
effervescent	encouragement	enthusiastically	especially
efficiency	endorsement	enumerate	espionage
eighth	embarrass		

READ 6 WORD POWER REVIEW

According to the *Microsoft Encarta College Dictionary,* a maven is an "expert or a knowledgeable enthusiast of something." Be a word maven by reading the following sentences to increase your familiarity with the meaning, spelling, and pronunciation of words highlighted in Appendix B, Reads 1–5. If you're unsure of a pronunciation, look it up in your dictionary.

1. Beginning in 2000, 13 **stocks** on the **NYSE** and **AMEX** began to be traded in decimals instead of fractions; that is, if a stock was listed in the newspaper as selling for 14¼, it would now appear as 14.25, meaning $14.25 a share.

2. Our bank's **FDIC** insured account is ideal as an income **CD.**

3. **COLA** and **NASDAQ** are acronyms.

4. The **annual report** provides details about our **amalgamation** with the June Company Department Stores.

5. We bought the stock because we expect it to **appreciate,** not **depreciate.**

6. We have a **deficit** because of all the **down time** on the new equipment.

7. The **balance sheet** had already been **audited** before the **exchange rate** changed.

8. His grandsons are the **beneficiaries** of the **mutual funds.**

9. This **corporation** is very sensitive to **cyberlaw.**

10. The **exchange rate** is affected by the value of the **euro.**

11. The advice of a **financial planner** would have prevented the **foreclosure** of his home.

12. The **balance sheet** shows the **liabilities** as well as the assets.

13. The **concierge** can provide a guest with an iternerary.

14. He used a **certified check** and a **CD** as **collateral.**

15. One of his **fringe benefits** is a **401k,** and another is a low-interest **mortgage.**

16. **Outplacement** is often helpful when a business is about to be **liquidated.**

17. A **multinational corporation** usually has many **shareholders,** and some may engage in **slander** and even **libel** from time to time.

18. A **bill of lading** and an **affidavit** are attached to the **beneficiary's itinerary.**

19. **Antitrust legislation** prohibits most **monopolies,** but **amalgamation** is often legal.

20. This **start-up** will not be successful because of the rapid **turnover** of employees, slow **turnaround time** for production, **spyware** installed by a dishonest competitor, and failure of its **Webmaster** to keep the Web site updated.

21. Pepsi Cola and Nissan Motors are **multinational corporations** doing business within the **European Union** and are always watchful of the **euro's exchange rate.**

22. The **hacker** was showing off by infiltrating a **financial planner's** records.

23. Because we don't have a **quorum,** the **ream** of costly paper we **requisitioned** isn't needed.

24. The lawyer was given a **retainer** and will file suit for **slander** against the **Webmaster** who holds the **mortgage** on the property.

25. He was also guilty of **libel** for claiming the **financial planner** is a **hacker.**

REPLAY 6

A. In the blanks write the correct spelling of the following incorrectly spelled words without using a dictionary.

1. amalgemation _____   2. depreciate _____

3. dificet _____   4. balence sheet _____

5. benificiarys _____   6. uro _____
7. forclosure _____   8. slandar _____
9. lible _____   10. morgage _____

Check your answers on page 488.

CHAPTER 6: EXPERT SPELLER LIST

Circle the words that are unfamiliar to you, and then look up the meaning and practice spelling them.

forfeit	fundamentally	fortunately	forehead
fiscal	foreseeable	freight	fascism
fluorescent	foreign	fulfill	fraudulent
forth (forward)	flexible	February	furor
fourth (after third)	feasible	forty	FAQ
fictitious	frieze	feint	

READ 7   HOMOPHONES

English has hundreds of **homophones** (soundalikes, such as *right, write, rite*). Only careful proofreading catches most homophone errors because computer programs overlook words that are spelled correctly but used incorrectly in a sentence. The following are some common homophones that often cause embarrassing errors.

accept	agree to receive
except	excluding, as in *everyone except me*
access	ability to enter, obtain, or use something
excess	more than is needed or wanted
ad	short for advertisement; one *d* like advertisement
add	to join; two *d's* as in addition
affect	verb meaning to change, to influence, to pretend (His limited education will affect his ability to do the job.)
effect	verb meaning to bring about or to result in (We can effect no changes without your approval.)
effect	a noun that means result (We all know the effect would be disastrous.)
alot— **no such word**	Do not write this "nonword"! Your spell checker will alert you to this error.
allot	with two *l's*, the word is correct when it means to apportion or distribute

a lot	correctly written as two words; use this expression only in conversation or informal writing; instead use *a great deal, very much,* or *many.* Of course, *a lot* also refers to a small piece of land.
alright	avoid this spelling
all right	this spelling is preferred: two *l's;* two words
alter	change (The groom said, "Don't try to alter me after we leave the altar.")
altar	a place for sacred rituals
bazaar	a sale or marketplace (note three *a's*)
bizarre	odd; grotesque; strange (note two *r's*)
capital	wealth; a city that is the capital of a state; an uppercase letter; execution, as in *capital punishment*
capitol	a building where legislators make laws
cite	summon to court; to honor; to quote
sight	ability to see; a thing regarded as worth seeing; something ludicrous or disorderly in appearance
site	noun meaning a location
coarse	rough; of poor quality; crude
course	school subject; portion of meal; place where golf is played; a direction taken
counsel	lawyer; advice or to give advice
council	group that meets to discuss, plan, or decide action
die, dying	to pass from life
dye, dyeing	to change a color, such as fabric or hair
dissent	disagreement
descent	a downward movement; the verb is *descend*
here	at this place
hear	ear is in hear; proofread carefully to avoid careless here/hear errors
heir	person who inherits (A female who inherits is an heiress.)
air	referring to atmosphere; pronounced like heir
illicit	not legal; prohibited; improper
elicit	to draw forth or to bring out
principle	a rule; a fundamental truth; a law
principal	main or most important; the chief administrator of a school

REPLAY 7

Write the correct word in the blank without looking at the definitions.

accept/except   1. We'll _____ deliveries every
                 2. day _____ Sunday.

ad/add	3. We'll _____ the figures before 4. we place the _____ in the newspaper.
dyeing/dying	5. I'm _____ to hear what he'll say after finding out 6. that I've been _____ my hair.
descent/dissent	7. Peaceful _____ should be encouraged. 8. The _____ from Mt. Baldy will be difficult.
bazaar/bizarre	9. His behavior was so _____ 10. that she left him at the _____ .
coarse/course	11. Her _____ manners were distasteful to him, but the 12. professor, of _____ , couldn't exclude her from the course.
site/sight/cite	13. A magnificent _____ was selected for the new theater. 14. We could _____ several examples of unfair taxation. 15. What a _____ he was with his torn clothing!
council/counsel	16. Richard is the _____ for the defense. 17. The City _____ meets every Friday morning.
access/excess	18. Do you have _____ 19. to the _____ funds?
affect/effect	20. How does the hot weather _____ you? 21. What _____ does the heat have on you?
capital/capitol	22. Is the _____ in 23. the downtown section of the _____?
a lot/allot	24. We cannot _____ any funds for the company 25. to purchase _____ for the new parking structure because it will cost a great deal of money.
principle/principal	26. An important _____ for students to remember is to be 27. respectful to the _____ .
elicit/illicit	28. We are trying to _____ the full details concerning 29. the _____ business deal.

Check your answers on page 488.

CHAPTER 7: EXPERT SPELLER LIST

Circle the words that are unfamiliar to you, and then look up the meaning and practice spelling them.

generalize	guarantee	grammar	gigantic
government	genealogy	granddaughter	grievous
grandeur	government	grieve	guaranty
grateful	governor	guardian	guesstimate
grievance	graffiti	guidance	
guitar	gnash		

READ 8   COMMONLY CONFUSED WORDS

Although the following pairs of words on the left are similar in appearance, spelling, and pronunciation, they differ greatly. Be sure to observe the distinctions in your reading, writing, and speech.

beside	by the side of; near; next to
besides	in addition to
choose	present tense; pronounce the *oo* as in *pool*
chose	past tense of *choose*; pronounce the *o* like the alphabet sound of *o*
compliment	to praise
complement	something that completes
conscience	the part of us that hurts when we do wrong
conscious	alert; awake; aware
defer	to put off or to postpone (accent on the second syllable)
differ	disagree
desert	accent on first syllable—where camels hang out
desert	accent on second syllable—to leave behind or to abandon
dessert	last course of a meal (Taking seconds on dessert is the memory hook for spelling this word with two *s's*.)
device	a machine, tool, or method to achieve or do something (rhymes with rice)
devise	to plan or figure out (rhymes with rise)
eligible	have the qualifications to participate
illegible	not readable or difficult to read
eminent	well known for accomplishments; outstanding; famous
imminent	about to happen
envelope	paper container for sending mail
envelop	to wrap or surround
irregardless	NOT a word. Do NOT say it or write it! Instead use *regardless*.
regardless	no matter what else happens
fiscal	pertaining to financial affairs
physical	pertaining to the body
guise	a false outward appearance
guys	informal word for men or boys
it's	with the apostrophe—contraction for it is
its	no apostrophe—shows possession; for example, *Its wings were flapping.*
led	past tense of lead, as in *He led the parade.*
lead	to guide; to direct operations or activity, as in *He'll lead it again tomorrow.*
minor	under 18; unimportant
miner	worker in a mine

REPLAY 8

Write the correct word in the blank.

eminent/imminent

1. A storm is _____.
2. The _____ statesman Winston Churchill is admired for his eloquent use of the English language.

regardless/irregardless

3. He plans to attend _____ of the weather. (Do not say or write *irregardless;* don't even *think* about using it.)

eligible/illegible

4. He is not _____ to play soccer this semester
5. because his handwriting is _____.

devise/device

6. Can you _____
7. a _____ that is less expensive?

desert/dessert

8. Will you join me for _____ when we meet
9. in the _____,
10. but don't _____ me.

choose/chose

11. Did you _____ the same books
12. that I _____?

defer/differ

13. I will always _____ to your wishes.
14. I do not _____ with you on any subject.

conscience/conscious

15. My _____ is clear.
16. He was _____ but not in pain.

beside/besides

17. No one _____ Ms. Muffet sits on tuffets.
18. However, a spider did come along and sit down _____ her.

envelop/envelope

19. When I see him, I'll _____ him in my arms.
20. He'll carry an _____ with a great deal of money in it.

fiscal/physical

21. During this _____ year, we won't have the funds to
22. construct a _____ education building at the high school.

compliment/complement

23. She _____ me on the quality of my work.
24. The fabric and color of the curtains _____ the new sofa.

guys/guise

25. She hid her true self under the _____ of friendliness.
26. That girl likes _____ [informal word] who are intelligent.

Check your answers on page 488.

CHAPTER 8: EXPERT SPELLER LIST

Circle the words that are unfamiliar to you, and then look up the meaning and practice spelling them.

harass	hierarchy	happiness	Hawaii
hazardous	handful	hoping	headhunter

hesitant	hygiene	humorous	healthful
hindrance	habeas corpus	hemorrhage	hence
hypocrite	handkerchief	handicapped	hesitant
hoax	haphazard	hindsight	

READ 9   MORE COMMONLY CONFUSED WORDS

Hasty proofreading can cause errors—especially with the following words that are easily mistaken for each other. Carefully check your writing for these kinds of "quiet mistakes."

lose	to misplace or leave something behind
loose	not tight or not fastened
moral	a concept of right behavior
morale	spirit; sense of common purpose
perquisite	a privilege, a benefit, a payment, or a profit in addition to salary; this word is usually used in the abbreviated form **perk** or the plural **perks**
prerequisite	something required beforehand, such as taking a beginning class before being permitted to enroll in the advanced class
persecute	to mistreat or injure, often because of a belief or a way of life
prosecute	to take legal action against someone accused of a crime
personnel	employees of a particular company or others who make up a group
personal	private
perspective	ability to see objects in terms of their relative distance from one another or to consider ideas in terms of their relative importance to one another
prospective	expected; likely to happen in the future
proceed	to go ahead, advance, or continue
precede	to go before; to be earlier
proceeds	the money or profits derived from a business transaction; pronounced PRO.ceeds
quit	cease; give up employment; admit defeat
quite	positively; completely
quiet	without noise
reality	what is real or true
realty	real estate; property
reason is because	avoid this phrase; it is non-Standard English
reason is that	use *reason is that* or simply *because* without the word *reason*
respectfully	with respect

Note: do not use *respectfully* as a closing for typical business letters—unless a letter is to someone warranting an unusual degree of respect, such as a high-ranking official or religious leader. |
respectively	in the order named
rye	a grain or seeds used for making flour or whiskey
wry	twisted; perverse; ironic (read the dictionary entry for wry)

suit	clothing consisting of a matched outfit; a legal action (in business writing use the complete word *lawsuit*).
suite	group of items forming a unit, such as matched furniture, or a group of adjoining rooms or offices
then	at that time; next
than	used in comparisons such as better than, rather than, more than, and so on
through	across or from one side to another
thorough	with attention to detail; complete
were **we're** **where**	When writing, be careful (avoid carelessness) to make appropriate distinctions among these three words.
whether	indicates a choice
weather	climate condition

REPLAY 9

Select the appropriate word for each blank without looking at the definitions.

personal/personnel
1. Don't open an envelope marked _____ unless it is addressed to you.

lose/loose
2. The lamp broke because the wires were _____.

than/then
3. His work is usually better _____ anyone else's.

thorough/through
suit/suite
4. She is doing a _____ job of redesigning the executive _____.

weather/whether
suit/suite
5. _____ the _____ is cold or hot, men are required to wear a _____ to work every day except Friday.

prosecute/persecute
6. Mr. Chandra would be the best attorney to _____ this case.

that/because
7. The reason Sarah was promoted is _____ she now has an MBA.

weather/whether
8. Do you know _____ the _____ will change tonight?

proceeds/proceed
rye/wry
9. With the _____ from the sale, we'll buy a dozen loaves of _____ bread.

we're/were
quite/quiet
10. _____ _____ sure he receives many perks.

proceed/proceeds
moral/morale
personal/personnel
11. Are you going to _____ with evaluation of the _____ of our _____?

prospective/perspective
perquisite/prerequisite
wry/rye
personal/personnel
12. The _____ instructor wanted the _____ that only full professors receive, but the _____ grin of the university's _____ director indicated refusal.

moral/morale
13. The _____ is good in this company because the executives make _____ decisions.

where/wear we're/were	14. _____ are you when _____ doing all the work?
perspective/prospective	15. Seen in _____, the incident was not too serious.
respectfully/respectively quit/quite/quiet	16. I _____ disagree with your decision to _____ your job
we're/were weather/whether thorough/through	17. _____ wondering _____ we'll ever get _____ with this job.
persecuted/prosecuted	18. They were _____ because of their beliefs.
moral/morale personal/personnel	19. _____ is good in this department because the _____ are all well trained.
proceed/precede suit/suite	20. The attorney was asked to _____ with the meeting in the executive _____.
wry/rye lose/loose	21. He expressed himself with _____ humor when told he would _____ his job.
personal/personnel	22. Job interviewers must be cautious about asking _____ questions of applicants.
We're/were/ where/ware	23. _____ going _____ the jobs are.
then/than	24. _____ he said that I look better _____ ever.
that/because realty/reality	25. The reason is _____ he works in the _____ business.

See answers on page 489.

CHAPTER 9: EXPERT SPELLER LIST

Circle the words that are unfamiliar to you, and then look up the meaning and practice spelling them.

impromptu	intangible	idiosyncrasy	inoculation
improvement	interpretation	illegal	interference
incidentally	intolerable	imaginary	irrational
indispensable	irrelevant	immediately	innuendo
initiative	itemize	inaccurate	incredible
insistence	itinerary		

READ 10   HOMONYMS AND HOMOPHONES

Avoid embarrassing errors in your writing by remembering the different meanings of these **homonyms** (spelled similarly) and **homophones** (soundalikes). You'll also find useful words for vocabulary growth. Keep your dictionary handy for further information.

appraise	to estimate the value of an item
apprise	to inform

bloc	a group of persons or countries combined to achieve a purpose
block	a large solid piece of a heavy material; see dictionary for multiple meanings
canvas	coarse cloth
canvass	to ask for votes, opinions, information
everyday	ordinary
every day	each day
foreword	an introduction to a written work
forward	toward the front
halve	verb meaning to reduce to half
half	one of the two equal parts of something
have	possess
key	a device used for unlocking; an instrumental or deciding factor
quay	(pronounced the same as key) concrete or stone waterfront structure
lesson	something to learn
lessen	decrease
marquee	a rooflike projecting structure over an entrance
marquis	(*quis* pronounced *key*) royalty ranking above a count
marquise	(pronounced *keez*) wife or widow of a marquis
naval	referring to a navy
navel	small scar in the abdomen; a kind of orange
ode	a dignified poem
owed	responsibility to repay
peak	the top
peek	a brief or concealed look at something
pique	to be annoyed
reign	royal power
rain	water from the sky
rein	means of controlling an animal
serge	a strong fabric
surge	a sudden, strong increase, as in power or water
stationery	writing paper
stationary	unmovable
taught	past tense for teach
taut	tightly pulled or stretched
their	belonging to them
there	at that place
they're	contraction of they are
throes	spasm or pangs of pain
throws	tosses

vise	a device for holding an object so that it can be worked on
vice	an evil action or habit
waive	to give up or postpone
wave	to signal by moving a hand or an arm
wary	cautious
wear and tear	business term for loss and damage as a result of using a product

REPLAY 10

Write the correct word in the blank without looking at the definitions.

appraise/apprise

1. After we _____ you of the cost, you can decide whether you want Mr. Gold to _____ the ring.

bloc/block

2. The European _____ wants to _____ further action. (See number 3 for additional use of *block*.)

canvass/canvas

3. We hope to _____ the neighborhood to get the majority opinion regarding the _____ tent for the block party.

every day/everyday

4. I wear my _____ clothes _____.

foreword/forward

5. Read the _____, and then tell the members about going _____ with the project.

halve/half/have

6. To _____ a smaller cake, simply _____ the ingredients. Then serve the cake with coffee and hope only _____ the people stay to eat.

key/quay

7. You don't need a _____ until you arrive at the _____.

lesson/lessen

8. A _____ is something we sometimes learn the hard way. If we try to do the right thing, perhaps we'll _____ the consequences.

marquis/marquise/marquee

9. The actors who play the _____ and the _____ will have their names on the theater _____.

navel/naval

10. It isn't advisable to wear clothing that exposes one's _____ when attending a party at a _____ base.

ode/owed

11. Did you know that an _____ is a lovely poem expressing romantic emotion? After her bad behavior at the prom, she _____ him one.

proceed/precede

12. His speech will _____ our arrival. When he finishes speaking, we will _____ to the refreshment tables.

rain/reign/rein

13. He needs to _____ in his horse and return to the stable because of the _____. Long may he _____.

peek/pique/peak

14. The mountain _____ will _____ your attention but you must not _____ until you reach the top.

surge/serge	15.	I don't know anyone else who still wears unfashionable _____ clothing. You may experience a _____ of anger at hearing this.
stationery/stationary	16.	We have a large supply of _____ in the desk that is _____; that is, fastened to the floor.
taut/taught	17.	I was _____ that one of the meanings of _____ is emotionally tense.
vise/vice	18.	A _____ is closed with a screw or a lever and holds the object being worked on. It is totally different from a _____, which is a negative activity.
wary/wear and tear	19.	Be _____ of the _____ on your new tools when you lend them to friends with limited experience in using such tools.
waive/wave	20.	If you _____ your right to be first at the buffet, you might as well _____ good-bye to the best appetizers.

Check your answers on page 489.

CHAPTER 10: EXPERT SPELLER LIST

Circle the words that are unfamiliar to you, and then look up the meaning and practice spelling them.

jeopardize	jack-of-all-trades	jell	jester
jewelry	jackpot	java	jetliner
judgment	jagged	Jaycee	jettison
justifiable	joystick	jaywalk	jicama
jealous	jargon	jeep	jillion
journal	job lot	jeer	jitney

READ 11 SIMILAR WORD PAIRS

The following pairs of words often cause confusion; some are similar in meaning and others differ considerably.

anxious	worry or fear
eager	looking forward to something
disinterested	impartial; one who listens to all sides of an issue; can also mean uninterested
uninterested	not interested or lacking enthusiasm
enthuse/enthused	Avoid using these words; they are not Standard English.
enthusiastic/enthusiasm	strong excitement

emigrate	to move out of a country
immigrate	to move into a country
explicit	clearly expressed
implicit	not stated, but understood—"between the lines"
flammable/inflammable	These two words mean the same: can burn.
nonflammable	cannot burn; the opposite of flammable and inflammable
farther	refers to actual distance
further	refers to figurative distance, e.g., to a greater degree
indigenous	people, wildlife, plants, and culture, native to a particular area
indigent	poor or needy
less	a more limited number or amount that can't be counted; of lower rank, degree, or importance; of reduced size, extent, or degree
fewer	a smaller number or amount that *can* be counted
imply	the speaker or writer "implies" something by what is said, done, or written
infer	the listener or reader "infers" a meaning from another's words or actions
lesson	something to learn
lessen	decrease
per annum	by the year, annually (Latin) or a yearly salary
per diem	by the day (Latin) or a daily salary (These terms refer to wages.)
rsvp	French abbreviation for *Respond if you please* or *Please respond.*
please rsvp	Do not use this expression: it's redundant (saying the same thing twice).
simple	easy-to-understand
simplistic	using poor judgment by making complex ideas sound deceptively easy
thought	the action or process of thinking; something that is thought (an idea)
through	across or from one side to another
throrough	with attention to detail; complete

REPLAY 11

Insert the appropriate Read 11 word in each blank. Use your dictionary when needed. Have fun with this "romp" through a number of interesting words.

anxious/eager   1. We are _____ to see you but are _____ about your health.

disinterested/uninterested	2. Although he is a _____ observer, he is not _____ in the outcome.
enthuse/enthused enthusiastic/enthusiasm	3. We are _____ about this new project, and our _____ shows.
implicit/explicit	4. _____ orders were not given; however, there was_____ acceptance of the orders by the entire staff.
per annum/per diem	5. His _____ is enormous, but her _____ is low.
flammable	6. _____ blankets are illegal in this city's hospitals.
inflammable/nonflammable	7. Only _____ blankets may be used.
farther/further	8. To succeed _____ in your career, you must go _____ in your studies.
indigenous/indigent	9. _____ food is available for the _____ workers and their families.
emigrate/immigrate	10. To _____ is to leave a country, while to _____ means to move to another country.
less/fewer	11. We bought _____ apples than planned and made_____ applesauce.
infer/imply	12. The speaker _____, the listener _____.
thorough/through/thought	13. We _____ we did a _____ job of going _____ the test items.
simple/simplistic	14. The problem is not _____ to solve and his _____ solution will make it worse.
please rsvp/rsvp	15. We hope you will _____ by September 1 to let us know whether you can attend.
proceed/proceeds	16. Let's _____ with the rehearsal.
	17. The _____ from admission to the performance will be divided equally.

Check your answers on pages 489.

CHAPTER 11: EXPERT SPELLER LIST

Circle the words that are unfamiliar to you, and then look up the meaning and practice spelling them.

khaki	kopek	laboratory	liaison
kaleidoscope	kibitz	launch	liqueur
knowledgeable	kleptomaniac	legitimate	luscious

kumquat	knead	lucrative	leisure
kung fu	kinesiology	likelihood	larceny
kook (slang)	knuckleball	library	length

READ 12   PRONUNCIATION PRACTICE

Avoid "behind your back" criticism. These words are frequently mispronounced. To increase confidence in your communication ability, practice saying them correctly.

accessories—ak SES uh rees

affluence—AF loo ens

affluent—AF loo ent

asked—askt (never: ast)

debris—de BREE

Des Moines—de MOYN

genuine—JEN u in

grievous—GREEV us

height—HITE

Illinois—ill e NOY

incomparable—in COMP er uh bul

irrelevant—ir REL a vint

irrevocable—ir REV uh kuh bul

Italian—i TAL yin

jewelry—JOO el ree

library—LI brer ee

mischievous—MIS chiv us

naive—ni EEV

nuclear—NOO cle er

pageant—PĂJ nt

picnic—PIK nik

picture—PIK cher

preface—PRE fis

preferable—PREF er uh bul

probably—PROB ub lee

realtor—REE ul tor

realty—REE ul tee

recognize—REC og nize

similar—SIM i ler

statistics—sta TIS tiks

subtle—SUH tl

superfluous—su PER floo us

REPLAY 12

Fill in the blank with the correct word from vocabulary learned in words highlighted in Appendix B, Reads 7–11.

1. We cannot _____ any more funds to this project. (alot/allot/a lot)

2. The _____ professor prepared the _____. (eminent/imminent, bibliography/biographical)

3. Yesterday we _____ to _____ the legal action. (choose/chose, differ/defer)

4. Even though his writing is _____, he is _____ to win the prize. (eligible/illegible)

5. _____ going to _____ to _____ home before the _____ begins. (We're/Were/Where, proceed/precede, there/their, reign/rein/rain)

6. She _____ the company for a _____ tent, which had been _____for more than $1,000. (ode/owed, canvas/canvass, appraised/apprised)

7. _____ a fundamental _____ that when you tour the _____ building, you don't try to _____ or lobby our officials about your pet project. (It's/Its, principle/principal, capital/capitol, elicit/illicit)

8. _____ doing a _____ job of refurbishing the _____. (Were/We're/Where, through/though/thorough, suit/suite)

9. With a _____ grin, he asked what the _____ would have been if he had concealed his true character with a _____ of friendliness. (rye/wry, perks or perquisites/prerequisites, guys/guise)

10. He _____ the coal _____ to the building where the _____ is stored in _____ bags. (led/lead, minor/miner, canvas/canvass)

11. _____ of the company's _____ situation, we cannot in good _____ encourage _____ irresponsibility. (Regardless/Irregardless, fiscal/physical, conscious/conscience)

12. During the next _____ year, we cannot _____ funds to rebuild the historic _____ in the _____ city. (physical/fiscal, allot/alot, alter/altar, capitol/capital)

13. Your _____ is needed at this time. (advice advise)

14. We worked _____ the night to do a _____ job of taking inventory before the start of the sale. (through/thorough)

15. I know you are _____ in the results of this survey, but would you please randomly select ten _____ parties to complete the questionnaire. (uninterested/disinterested)

Check Answers on page 490.

CHAPTER 12: EXPERT SPELLER LIST

Circle the words that are unfamiliar to you, and then look up the meaning and practice spelling them.

manageable	mediator	notable
management	messenger	naïve
media	memorize	necessary
maneuver	mortgage	ninety
miscellaneous	mischievous	noticeable
marriage	misspelling	nuclear
maintenance	Mediterranean	
neighbor	medieval	
ninth	millennium	

READ 13   AVOIDING GENDER BIAS

When communicating in the workplace, choose language that is without gender identification unless it is relevant. Many terms that include the word *man* can be expressed in neutral gender without sounding clumsy. If an expression sounds awkward, rephrase it.

Avoid	Use
mankind	human beings, society, human race, humanity
manmade	synthetic, artificial, constructed, factory-made, plastic
manpower	workers, employees, crew, laborers, staff, workforce, etc.
workmen's compensation	workers' compensation
businessmen	business workers, businesspersons, business people, professionals, executives, managers
cameraman	photographer, cinematographer
chairman	chairperson, chair, leader, moderator, coordinator, facilitator
clergyman	member of the clergy, minister (or term specific to the religion; rabbi, priest, imam, reverend, and so on)
congressmen	congressmen and congresswomen, congressperson/s, representatives, legislators
husband/wife	spouse
boyfriend/girlfriend	partner
fireman	firefighter
girls (when referring to adults)	women
insurance man	insurance agent
mailman	mail carrier, letter carrier, postal worker
male nurse	nurse
male secretary	secretary
policeman	police officer

Avoid attaching *ess* or *ette* to a noun to create a feminine word for historically masculine roles:

actress [still often appropriate]	actor [preferred by some females]
poetess, authoress	poet, author
proprietress	proprietor
stewardess	flight attendant or steward (on a ship)
waitress/waiter	server

REPLAY 13

Correct the language in these sentences to eliminate gender-biased terms.

1. Mankind can rejoice when a way is found to settle conflicts without war.

2. The stewardess is bringing drinks now.

3. Ask the men from our office if they wish to play golf during the convention.

4. The chairman needs a good understanding of parliamentary procedure.

5. The president invited the managers and their wives to a formal dinner.

6. The common man wants peace.

7. Several lady policemen are guarding against intruders.

8. Please ask our waitress to come to our table.

9. Cameramen love taking pictures of Angelina Jolie.

10. The girls in my office go to lunch at 12.

11. Wednesday is National Secretary's Day so invite all the girls for lunch.

12. She is doing a man sized job.

13. My husband is a male nurse.

14. We prefer garments made of natural rather than manmade fabrics.

15. Can you recommend a good insurance man ?

Check your answers on page 490.

CHAPTER 13: EXPERT SPELLER LIST

Circle the words that are unfamiliar to you, and then look up the meaning and practice spelling them.

occasionally	observant	ozone	plausible
occupation	omitted	oppression	perceptible
odyssey	opponent	pamphlet	prominent
occurrence	optimistic	participant	quota
omission	outrageous	perceive	questionnaire
occurred	override	per annum	queue

READ 14   SPEAKING WITH CONFIDENCE

Being sure that you are pronouncing words correctly increases your confidence in the workplace. Some mispronounced words give the impression that the speaker is undereducated, uneducated, or even ignorant. Whether you are speaking formally or informally use words correctly and be aware of your pronunciation. If you are not a native speaker of English, listeners will be understanding if you mispronounce a word; native English-speakers, however, are subject to being judged more harshly.

The frequently mispronounced words following are spelled to show correct pronunciation; the syllable receiving the most emphasis is capitalized.

The common mispronunciations are in parentheses AFTER the sample sentence.

accessories	ak SES uh rees—The interior designer recommended that the accessories be selected last. (uh SES a rees)
affluence **affluent**	AF loo ens/AF loo ent—Palm Beach, Florida, and Beverly Hills, California, are examples of affluent communities. (a FLOO ens, a FLOO ent)

applicable	AP lik uhbul—This information is not applicable to our dilemma. (uh PLIK uhbul)
asked	askt—He asked the four questions. (ast or axt)
athletics	ath LET iks—Participation in athletics contributes to good health. (ath uh LET iks)
debris	de BREE—After the storm, debris was everywhere. (Dee BREE)
debut	day bYOO—She made her debut in a British film. (DEB yoot)
Des Moines	de MOYN—The site for our new factory is in Des Moines. (des MOYNS)
entrée	ON tray—The interviewer ordered the cheapest entrée on the menu. (EN tree)
etcetera	et SET e ra or et SET ra (usually abbreviated as etc.)—The king of Siam was fond of saying "etcetera, etcetera, etcetera." (ek SET era)
February	FEB ru er ee—Valentine's Day is February 14. (FEB u airy)
genuine	JEN u in—The stock certificates are genuine. (JEN u wine)
gourmet	goor MAY—A diet of burgers and fries doesn't qualify one as a gourmet. (goorMET)
grievous	GREEV us—A grievous crime has been committed. (greev e us)
height	HITE—The height of the new building has not been decided. (hithe)
hostile	HOS til—His hostile attitude made us uncomfortable. (HOS tile)
Illinois	ill e NOY—The salesman's territory is the entire state of Illinois. (ILL i noys)
incomparable	in COMP er uh bul—Our products are incomparable. (in com PARE able)
irrelevant	ir REL a vint—The course is irrelevant to my major but is related to my hobby. (ir REV a lint)
irrevocable	i REV uh kuh bul—An irrevocable decision cannot be revoked. (i ree VOKE a ble)
Italian	i TAL yin—If you move to Rome, you'll need to learn Italian. (eye TAL yin)
jewelry	JOO el ree—Many jewelry manufacturers are still on 45th Street. (JOO lcr ce)
lackadasical	LAK uh DAY zuh kul—Employers don't hire applicants who appear lackadasical. (lax uh DAY zuh kul)
library	LI brer ee—Be sure to pronounce both r's in library. (LI berry)
lieu	LOO— In lieu of means instead of or in place of. (LEE oo)
mischievous	MIS chiv us—Some children are mischievous on Halloween. (mis CHEEV e us)
naïve	ni EEV—He is naïve to think he will get a raise without asking for it. (NAVE)
picnic	PIK nik—I look forward to meeting your husband at the company picnic. (PIT nik)
picture	PIK cher—Pictures of past presidents hang in the gallery. (PITCH er)
preface	PRE fis—Have you read the preface to this book? (PREE face)

preferable	PREF er uh bul or PREF ra bul—I think the old equipment would be preferable to the new. (pre FER uh bul)
probably	PROB ub lee—Two baristas will probably serve coffee at the meeting. (PROB lee)
pronunciation	pro NUN see A shun—Pronounce the second syllable nun. (pro NOUN see A shun)
realty	REE ul tee—Several new realty offices opened last year in Fairbanks, Alaska. (REEL uh tee)
relevant	REL uh vint—Mr. Goldman included only relevant statistics in his report. (REV uh lint)
statistics	sta TIS tiks—The sales statistics are included in Ms. Gomez's report. (suh TIS tiks)
subpoena	suh PEE nuh—A subpoena was issued for the murder witness. (sub PEE nuh)
subtle	SUH tl—George was so subtle that Jesse didn't understand he had been fired. (SUB tl)
superfluous	su PER floo us—Those items are superfluous and should be returned. (su PERF e lus or sooper FLU us)
vehicle	VEE i kul—Do not pronounce the h in vehicle. (vee HICK el)
versatile	VER suh tl—A versatile object can be used for various purposes. A versatile person can do many different things. (VER suh tile)
visa	VEE zuh—The word VISA came into the English language from French in the early 1800s. (VEE suh)

REPLAY 14

Say each word aloud before responding to these questions.

A. How many syllables does each word have?

1. grievous _____
2. superfluous _____
3. mischievous _____
4. probably _____
5. naïve _____

B. Which letters are silent in these words?

6. Des Moines _____
7. Illinois _____
8. debris _____
9. subtle _____
10. vehicle _____

C. Write **T** (true) or **F** (false) in the blank.

_____ 11. Pronounce *affluent* with the accent on the first syllable.

_____ 12. The *i* in *versatile* is pronounced the same as the alphabet sound of *i*.

_____ 13. When saying *preferable*, the accent is on the first syllable.

_____ 14. The capital *i* in *Italian* sounds like the alphabet sound of *I*.

_____ 15. *Height* ends with a *th* sound.

_____ 16. Pronounce *jewelry JOOL e ree*.

_____ 17. *Realty* should be pronounced *reel i tee*.

_____ 18. The second syllable of *pronunciation* sounds different from the second syllable of *pronounce*.

_____ 19. The second syllable of *hostile* is pronounced like the word *tile*.

_____ 20. The first syllable of *statistics* sounds like *sis*.

_____ 21. To remember how to pronounce and spell *irrelevant* and *relevant*, notice that the *l* goes before the *v*.

_____ 22. *Picture* is pronounced the same as the word for a baseball player who pitches.

_____ 23. *Irrevocable* has the primary accent on the third syllable.

_____ 24. The second syllable of *preface* is pronounced like the word *face*.

_____ 25. When identifying the nationality of a native of Italy, the first syllable should sound like the word *eye*.

Check your answers on page 490.

CHAPTER 14: EXPERT SPELLER LIST

Circle the words that are unfamiliar to you, and then look up the meaning and practice spelling them.

relevant	silhouette	vacuum	Xerox
reference	tariff	weird	yo-yo
recurrence	tedious	wholly	yield
referred	tournament	workable	zealous
relegate	ultimately	write-off	zillionaire
subsidize	vacillate	X-rated	

APPENDIX C   REPLAY DRILLS

Score Sheet for _____
Student's Name

Chapter	Drill No.	Page No.	Date Completed	Total Questions	No. Right
1	1-A	357			
	1-B	357			
	1-C	358			
2	2-A	359			
	2-B	359			
	2-C	360			
	2-D	361			
	2-E	362			
	2-F	362			
	2-G	363			
3	3-A	364			
	3-B	365			
	3-C	366			
	3-D	367			
	3-E	368			
4	4-A	369			
	4-B	369			
	4-C	370			
	4-D	371			
	4-E	371			
5	5-A	372			
	5-B	373			
6	6-A	374			
	6-B	375			
	6-C	376			
	6-D	377			
	6-E	377			
	6-F	378			
7	7-A	379			
	7-B	379			
	7-C	380			
	7-D	381			
	7-E	382			
	7-F	383			

Chapter	Drill No.	Page No.	Date Completed	Total Questions	No. Right
8	8-A	384			
	8-B	384			
	8-C	385			
	8-D	386			
	8-E	387			
	8-F	388			
9	9-A	389			
	9-B	390			
	9-C	390			
	9-D	391			
	9-E	392			
	9-F	393			
	9-G	394			
10	10-A	395			
	10-B	396			
	10-C	397			
	10-D	397			
11	11-A	398			
	11-B	399			
	11-C	400			
	11-D	401			
12	12-A	401			
	12-B	402			
	12-C	403			
	12-D	404			
	12-E	405			
13	13-A	406			
	13-B	407			
	13-C	408			
14	14-A	408			
	14-B	409			

CHAPTER 1: MASTERING LANGUAGE: RESOURCES AND WORDS

REPLAY DRILL 1-A: DEFINITIONS

Use your dictionary and briefly state the meaning of each of the following:

1. embryology _____
2. geology _____
3. seismologist _____
4. therapeutic _____
5. hieroglyphic (noun) _____
6. egocentric _____
7. neurosis _____
8. agoraphobia _____

    _____

9. anthropology _____
10. demographics _____

Check your answers on page 467.

REPLAY DRILL 1-B: SPELLING

Rewrite the misspelled words. Write C beside the one correctly spelled word.

1. absense _____
2. accurasy _____
3. analyse _____
4. attendence _____
5. britian _____
6. cemetary _____
7. changable _____
8. changeing _____
9. comeing _____
10. defered _____
11. dineing _____

12. excelince _____

13. existance _____

14. fourty _____

15. grammer _____

16. grievious _____

17. inevitable _____

18. lonliness _____

19. ninty _____

20. omited _____

Check your answers on page 467.

REPLAY DRILL 1-C: DICTIONARY CODE

Draw vertical lines to show where the syllables are divided. In the blank write the number of syllables in each word.

1. September _____

2. wonderful _____

3. merriment _____

4. methodology _____

5. totality _____

Write the part or parts of speech for each word.

6. motor _____

7. metal _____

8. facility _____

9. grandeur _____

10. make _____

Pronounce each word and then check your answers.

11. maudlin _____

12. nuclear _____

13. literature _____

14. spastic _____

15. bastion _____

Find the language or languages of derivation and write them in the blanks.

16. fanatic _____

17. syllogism _____

18. phonetic _____

19. oration _____

20. milieu _____

Check your answers on page 467.

CHAPTER 2: GETTING TO KNOW THE PARTS OF SPEECH

REPLAY DRILL 2-A: NOUNS

Underline the nouns in the following sentences. The number of nouns is in parentheses.

Example: The <u>secretary</u> greeted each <u>visitor</u> who entered the <u>building</u>. (3)

1. Shenita handed Mark his textbook (3)
2. Some students drive more than 20 miles to school each day. (4)
3. The assignments were due in two weeks. (2)
4. The syllabi contain all the information for each subject . (3)
5. Tina and Rose sent in their applications for a student loan. (4)
6. Will was embarrassed when his stomach growled during math class. (3)
7. Correct your errors before sending emails. (2)
8. The instructor announced the examination schedule for next week. (3)
9. Larry rearranged the textbooks, notebooks, and papers in his backpack. (5)
10. The classroom contained 20 computers and 5 printers. (3)

Check your answers on page 468.

REPLAY DRILL 2-B: PRONOUNS

Underline the pronouns in the following sentences. The number of pronouns is in parentheses.

Example: <u>We</u> gave <u>them</u> directions to the party. (2)

1. She announced that anyone could attend the seminar. (2)
2. Your insurance will cover his hospital bills. (2)
3. John and I received their application in the mail. (2)
4. Who will accept the award for him ? (2)

5. Something was missing from the top of her bureau. (2)

6. I worked twelve hours on this. (2)

7. Everyone in the audience clapped loudly after their presentation. (2)

8. He tried to unscramble the puzzle, but nothing made sense. (2)

9. You must learn the home keys on the keyboard. (1)

10. Those of you who were absent must turn in your assignments. (4)

11. Whomever you select as chairperson will choose the new committee members. (2)

12. The girl curled her hair this morning. (1)

13. The panel members asked the judge for her decision. (1)

14. Somebody in the audience dropped his or her wallet on the floor. (3)

15. Since everyone was anxious to leave, no one heard the teacher give the assignment. (2)

16. The class knew that she had won the contest. (1)

17. I thought the eraser was mine, but Betty said it was hers. (4)

18. We are renting a truck and moving ourselves to our new home. (3)

19. The child sat between his mother and me on the bus. (2)

20. Everything in the store will be discontinued at the annual sidewalk sale. (1)

Check your answers on page 468.

REPLAY DRILL 2-C: VERBS

Underline the complete verb in the following sentences. Remember to include any helping verbs as part of the complete verb.

Example: Melissa <u>was elected</u> to the Activities Board.

1. The Admissions Director welcomed each student.

2. Martha will be attending the orientation program on Monday.

3. Bill was eager to see his new class schedule.

4. The counselor has handed each new student a college catalog.

5. The admissions office required a high school transcript.

6. Stacey will be a student for the first time in ten years.

7. The butterflies were jumping in Maria's stomach on the first day of class.

8. The professor's friendly smile brightened the student's entire day.

9. The young man's laughter echoed throughout the Student Union.

10. The new students were looking forward to the first day of the semester.

Check your answers on page 468.

REPLAY DRILL 2-D: ADJECTIVES

Part 1: Underline the descriptive adjectives in the following sentences. The number of descriptive adjectives is in parentheses.

Example: The <u>pepperoni</u> pizza tasted <u>delicious</u>. (2)

1. The irritating caller harassed the busy receptionist. (2)
2. The tired and thirsty workmen appreciated the cold lemonade. (3)
3. The noisy water pipes rattled throughout the law offices. (3)
4. The slippery tape slid off the wooden desk. (2)
5. The efficient assistant typed the ten-page report. (2)
6. Mr. Thomas had a magnificent view of the inner harbor from his office window. (3)
7. The elegant executive greeted the new clients with a firm handshake. (3)
8. The pages in that old book are faded and torn. (3)
9. The heavier paper jammed the laser printer. (2)
10. The grouchy administrator needed a fresh cup of brewed coffee. (3)

Check your answers on page 468.

Part 2: Underline the one limiting adjective in each sentence.

Example: The sale brought <u>many</u> new customers to the store.

11. Several people rushed into the classroom as the bell rang.
12. Do you have enough time to complete the test?
13. Twenty-five new students enrolled in the course.
14. Her paper contained no errors.
15. The teacher gave Keith a few ideas for his speech.

Check your answers on page 468.

Part 3: Underline the one pointing adjective and the one article in each of the following sentences.

16. These checks include the annual bonus.
17. A special delivery letter arrived this morning.
18. The accounting manager requested that software program.
19. An angry customer returned those broken file cabinets.
20. This reference book has an excellent chapter on economics.

Check your answers on page 468.

REPLAY DRILL 2-E: ADVERBS

Underline the one adverb in the following sentences.

Example: Amy types <u>quickly</u>.

1. Ron finally proposed to Mary.
2. Jonas worked diligently on his homework.
3. The report is due immediately.
4. The new computer is very expensive.
5. Turner worked well with the other employees.
6. Mr. Jones really wanted a raise.
7. Cynthia was an extremely talented singer.
8. Michael almost lost her contract.
9. The job applicant was dressed appropriately.
10. These figures are added accurately.
11. Many products are cheaply manufactured.
12. Mr. Johnson never arrives on time.
13. The clerk was working hard on the filing project.
14. The most outstanding employee of the year received an award today.
15. The paper was too messy to read.
16. Her voice is exceptionally loud on the telephone.
17. The computer rapidly produced the results of the survey.
18. John's new haircut is so stylish.
19. Mr. Perkins frequently attends the opera.
20. The supervisor demanded his resignation now.

Check your answers on page 469.

REPLAY DRILL 2-F: CONJUNCTIONS AND PREPOSITIONS

Part 1: Underline the conjunctions in the following sentences.

Example: Brenda <u>and</u> Barbara were late for work.

1. Although Andy attended the conference, he didn't see me.
2. Shannon left class when the teacher was finished lecturing.
3. They waited under the tree until the rain stopped.

4. Ryan studied hard so that he would pass the test.

5. The supervisor requested that James or Linda stay after work.

6. The couple wanted to go to the movies, but it was too late.

7. The crowd waited in the lobby while the elevator was being repaired.

8. Al and Jeremy hurried to the office since the meeting was about to begin.

9. The employees didn't know if they had received a raise.

10. The instructor praised the students whenever they answered correctly.

Check your answers on page 469.

Part 2: Underline the prepositional phrases in the following sentences.

Example: Carol went <u>with me</u>.

11. Please put the laptop on the desk.

12. The secretary put the papers in the folder.

13. The sun broke through the clouds.

14. The flowers were blooming along the path.

15. The store owners lived above the business.

16. The clerk bumped into the file cabinet.

17. Louise moved her car across the street.

18. Everyone except Luther will be going on the business trip.

19. Several people were talking during the lecture.

20. We found the birth certificate beneath the other papers.

Check your answers on page 469.

REPLAY DRILL 2-G: IDENTIFYING THE PARTS OF SPEECH

Identify the underlined words as either nouns, verbs, or adjectives.

Example: He signed up to take <u>dance</u> lessons. <u>(adjective)</u>

1. She put her money in the <u>bank</u>. _____

2. Jim was training to be a <u>bank</u> teller. _____

3. The store's motto was, "You can <u>bank</u> on us!" _____

4. In what <u>time</u> zone do you live? _____

5. I will <u>time</u> the runners. _____

6. Do you have the <u>time</u> to read this assignment? _____

7. The baseball game's final <u>score</u> was 7 to 5. _____

8. Lincoln <u>scored</u> the winning touchdown. _____

9. The caddie kept the <u>score</u> card during the golf match. _____

10. The <u>swim</u> coach taught Darla the backstroke. _____

11. He will <u>swim</u> each morning to keep in shape. _____

12. The long <u>swim</u> across the lake was exhausting. _____

13. Martin <u>shops</u> for bargains. _____

14. The <u>shop</u> manager retired after 30 years. _____

15. That new <u>shop</u> has good bargains. _____

16. Mrs. Brown's <u>garden</u> contains more than one hundred flowers. _____

17. The <u>garden</u> furniture needs painting. _____

18. Mother said she will <u>garden</u> after breakfast. _____

19. The cashier could not read the amount on the <u>price</u> tag. _____

20. We must <u>price</u> the furniture at several stores. _____

Check your answers on page 469.

CHAPTER 3: WRITING COMPLETE SENTENCES

REPLAY DRILL 3-A: RECOGNIZING COMPLETE SENTENCES AND FRAGMENTS

Place a (C) at the end of the following word groups that are complete sentences and an (F) if they are fragments (incomplete thoughts).

Example: When the bell rang for class. __F__

1. The payroll clerk computed the salaries. _____

2. While the payroll clerk computed the salaries. _____

3. Provided you can begin the job Monday. _____

4. You can begin the job on Monday. _____

5. The instructor's lecture lasted the whole hour. _____

6. Since the instructor's lecture lasted the whole hour. _____

7. The boss handed George his paycheck. _____

8. Unless the boss handed George his paycheck. _____

9. The employees left the office at 5 o'clock. _____

10. After the employees left the office at 5 o'clock. _____

11. As Mr. Harrison accepted the award. _____

12. Mr. Harrison accepted the award. _____

13. The president read all the reports in two hours. _____

14. Although the president read all the reports in two hours. _____

15. Because Mr. Schaffer handed in his resignation. _____

16. Mr. Schaffer handed in his resignation. _____

17. All the class members passed the final exam. _____

18. Until all the class members passed the final exam. _____

19. Marsha spoke with the new professor. _____

20. If Marsha spoke with the new professor. _____

Check your answers on page 469.

REPLAY DRILL 3-B: CORRECTING COMMA SPLICES AND RUN-ONS

Identify the following word groups as either a complete sentence (C), a comma splice (CS), or a run-on (R).

Example: Mom baked some cookies they tasted delicious. R

1. The secretary handed the report to the supervisor, he read it quickly. _____

2. When the secretary handed the report to the supervisor, he read it quickly. _____

3. The secretary handed the report to the supervisor he read it quickly. _____

4. While the lawyer prepared the case, her assistant checked the reference sheets. _____

5. The lawyer prepared the case her assistant checked the reference sheets. _____

6. The lawyer prepared the case, her assistant checked the reference sheets. _____

7. The corporation expanded its holdings; it now oversees $2 billion a year. _____

8. Since the corporation expanded its holdings, it now oversees $2 billion a year. _____

9. The corporation expanded its holdings, it now oversees $2 billion a year. _____

10. The corporation expanded its holdings it now oversees $2 billion a year. _____

11. The reporter wrote the award-winning story it was published in over two hundred newspapers. _____

12. The reporter wrote the award-winning story; it was published in over two hundred newspapers. _____

13. The reporter wrote the award-winning story, it was published in over two hundred newspapers. _____

14. The company jet flow to London, all the major executives were abroad. _____

15. When the company jet flew to London, all the major executives were aboard. _____

16. The company jet flew to London all the major executives were aboard. _____

17. When the mayor spoke to the council, all the members listened. _____

18. The mayor spoke to the council, all the members listened. _____

19. The mayor spoke to the council all the members listened. _____

20. The mayor spoke to the council; all the members listened. _____

Check your answers on page 470.

REPLAY DRILL 3-C: TRANSITIONAL WORDS

Part 1: Underline the transitional words in the following sentences.

Example: I hurried to work, <u>yet</u> I was late.

1. Barbara did not study for her test; therefore, she was happy to see the barely passing grade.

2. Ron worked hard to get good grades; for example, he reviewed his class notes every night.

3. Mrs. Williams expected the best from her students; hence, they were always prepared in class.

4. Please hand in your homework; then you may begin working on the next assignment.

5. Rose did not hear the alarm; consequently, she was late arriving for English class.

6. Twenty-five percent of the class received an "A"; furthermore, all the students passed the test.

7. Please sign in if you are late; otherwise, you will be marked absent.

8. Laura lost her wallet in class; however, someone turned it in to the office.

9. The instructor handed out the course outline; in fact, she explained every assignment.

10. The copy machine broke down; nevertheless, the teacher had the test ready for class.

11. Each student needs to rent a locker in the Student Union Building; also, he or she must purchase a new lock.

12. The graduation ceremony is Saturday night; in addition, the practice will be Thursday morning.

13. The instructor gave a reading assignment; moreover, she also assigned a three-page composition.

14. Stephanie had completed the assignment at home; thus, she had time to work on the next assignment in class.

15. The director introduced the speaker; that is, he gave a summary of the speaker's qualifications.

Check your answers on page 470.

Part 2: Underline the conjunction that joins the independent clauses in the following sentences.

Example: Edna typed the report, <u>and</u> she left it on Mr. Brown's desk.

16. Sandra decided to attend business college, for she wanted to increase her job skills.

17. Greg found his wallet, but his money was missing.

18. The sun is shining, yet the rain is beginning to pour down.

19. You cannot pay by check, nor can you charge the purchase to your account.

20. Richard will speak on Thursday, or he will send a replacement.

Check your answers on page 470.

REPLAY DRILL 3-D: DEPENDENT CLAUSES

Underline the dependent clause in each sentence.

1. After the workers finished the project, they all received bonuses.

2. The sun was shining brightly until the clouds moved in.

3. Because the biscuits were hard, the family refused to eat them.

4. Since Susan left town, there is not a great swimmer on the team.

5. When salespeople are successful, the company reaches its goal.

6. Although we had a wet spring, the water table is still low.

7. Esther and David are planning to get married soon even though they have no money.

8. John F. Kennedy delivered many great speeches when he was president.

9. Even though his supervisor gave clear directions, Mark still made several mistakes on his report.

10. Since wrong answers will be subtracted from the total number of correct responses, do not guess.

Check your answers on page 470.

REPLAY DRILL 3-E: DEPENDENT AND INDEPENDENT CLAUSES

Edit the following sentences to make one of the clauses a dependent clause and connect it to an independent clause.

1. John is an excellent student. John gets good grades. _____
   _____

2. The manager of the store trains the employees very well. The store has the highest sales in the district. _____
   _____

3. The short story was very dramatic. The students in the English Composition class responded enthusiastically. _____
   _____

4. Modern psychologists do not all agree with Sigmund Freud's theories. Freud was a pioneer in the field of psychology. _____
   _____

5. Political activist C. Delores Tucker attacked the moral standards of Hip-Hop music in the 1990s. The public had mixed views on the subject. _____
   _____
   _____

6. Bobby Flay prepared six different pork belly dishes. He is one of the Food Network's "Iron Chefs." _____
   _____

7. The Accounting Department will issue new expense forms this week. Many people are confused about how to tabulate mileage reports. _____
   _____
   _____

8. American Indians were stereotyped in films of the 1940s and 1950s. Very few sympathetic portrayals were presented. _____
   _____

9. We cannot issue paychecks on the 15th of this month. Our checks are late coming from the home office. _____
   _____

10. Bob and Art are sitting on the fence. They will need to make a bid on the house by close of business tomorrow. _____
    _____

Check your answers on pages 470–471.

CHAPTER 4: MASTERING NOUNS: PLURALS AND CAPITALS

REPLAY DRILL 4-A: REGULAR NOUN PLURALS

Make the following singular nouns plural.

Example: writer ___writers___

	Singular	Plural
1.	baby	_____
2.	alloy	_____
3.	daisy	_____
4.	play	_____
5.	rally	_____
6.	country	_____
7.	church	_____
8.	tax	_____
9.	wish	_____
10.	glass	_____
11.	veto	_____
12.	echo	_____
13.	radio	_____
14.	alto	_____
15.	leaf	_____
16.	roof	_____
17.	shelf	_____
18.	wife	_____
19.	chief	_____
20.	dwarf	_____

Check your answers on page 471.

REPLAY DRILL 4-B: IRREGULAR NOUN PLURALS

Part 1: Write the plural of the following nouns. Use a dictionary if needed. If two plurals are acceptable, write both.

Example: basis ___bases___

	Singular	Plural
1.	thesis	_____

	Singular	Plural
2.	bacteria	_____
3.	analysis	_____
4.	stimulus	_____
5.	alga	_____
6.	sheep	_____
7.	hypothesis	_____
8.	curriculum	_____
9.	memorandum	_____
10.	fungus	_____
11.	antenna	_____
12.	appendix	_____
13.	syllabus	_____
14.	crisis	_____

Check your answers on page 471.

Part 2: Decide if the following words are singular (S), plural (P), or if they can be both.

Example: fungi ___P___

15. data _____
16. crisis _____
17. media _____
18. alumni _____
19. algae _____
20. bacteria _____

Check your answers on page 471.

REPLAY DRILL 4-C: RECOGNIZING SINGULAR AND PLURAL NOUNS

Write (S) or (P) to indicate if the following nouns are usually singular or plural.

Example: trousers ___S___

1. economics _____
2. statistics _____
3. news _____
4. goods _____
5. thanks _____
6. scissors _____

7. civics _____

8. measles _____

9. proceeds _____

10. mathematics _____

Check your answers on page 471.

REPLAY DRILL 4-D: PLURALS OF PROPER NOUNS

Write the plurals of the following proper nouns.

Example: Anderson ___Andersons___

	Singular	Plural
1.	Bush	_____
2.	Kelly	_____
3.	Jones	_____
4.	Hartman	_____
5.	James	_____
6.	Rodriguez	_____
7.	Chen	_____
8.	Williams	_____
9.	Booth	_____
10.	Morgenthau	_____

Check your answers on page 472.

REPLAY DRILL 4-E: PLURALS OF COMPOUND NOUNS

Part 1: Write the plural form of the following compound nouns.

Example: police chief ___police chiefs___

	Singular	Plural
1.	get-together	_____
2.	post office	_____
3.	runner-up	_____
4.	cupful	_____
5.	son-in-law	_____
6.	nurses aide	_____

7.	photocopy	_____
8.	hand-me-down	_____
9.	chairperson	_____
10.	letter of recommendation	_____

Check your answers on page 472.

Part 2: Underline any nouns in the following sentences that should be capitalized. Write (C) for the one sentence that is correct as is.

Example: On our vacation we went to <u>England</u>.

11. Ann is studying german and accounting.

12. The building will be closed memorial day weekend.

13. My father retired from united airlines.

14. The new schedule will begin on april 1.

15. A letter of reference was signed by commander John Enrico.

16. Your application will be sent to the human resources department.

17. Marvin will be taking statistics 101 next fall.

18. He signed the letter John L. Smith, purchasing agent.

19. After high school he drove from california to the east coast.

20. Mayor Cook was the youngest man ever elected mayor of our city.

Check your answers on page 472.

CHAPTER 5: MASTERING NOUNS: POSSESSIVES

REPLAY DRILL 5-A: POSSESSIVE NOUNS

Underline the noun that is the possessor of the other noun in the following word groups and place the missing apostrophe either before or after the *s*.

Example: the <u>author's</u> new book

1. the childs hungry friends

2. the little engines whistle

3. a very angry customers complaints

4. an honorable judges decisions

5. a hazy afternoons shower

6. the two factories contracts

7. the gossipy secretaries whispers

8. a months interest

9. a sale on childrens clothes

10. Virginias improving economy

11. two mens derby hats

12. our companys insurance policy

13. the five accountants calculations

14. a six months postponement

15. a years worth of interest

16. the tired womans shopping bag

17. the happy employees pay raise

18. the Europeans accent

19. the singing waiters song

20. the honor students grade point average

Check your answers on page 472.

REPLAY DRILL 5-B: SINGULAR AND PLURAL POSSESSIVES

Indicate in the first blank whether each word underlined in 5-A is singular (S) or plural (P) and write the possessive form in the second blank. Note that four of the items could be singular or plural.

Example: authors___S___ ___author's___

	Singular		Possessive or Plural
1.	childs	_____	_____
2.	engines	_____	_____
3.	customers	_____	_____
4.	judges	_____	_____
5.	afternoons	_____	_____
6.	factories	_____	_____
7.	secretaries	_____	_____
8.	months	_____	_____
9.	childrens	_____	_____
10.	Virginias	_____	_____

11.	mens	____	_____
12.	companys	____	_____
13.	accountants	____	_____
14.	months	____	_____
15.	years	____	_____
16.	womans	____	_____
17.	employees	____	_____
18.	Europeans	____	_____
19.	waiters	____	_____
20.	students	____	_____

Check your answers on page 472.

CHAPTER 6: MASTERING PRONOUNS

REPLAY DRILL 6-A: PRONOUN CASE

Underline the correct pronoun for each sentence.

Example: Please give (I, <u>me</u>) your answer.

1. Bob and (I, me) went to the movies.
2. Give (we, us) the new course outlines.
3. (They, Them) worked hard to complete their assignments.
4. Please pass the test papers to (I, me).
5. (We, Us) teachers are looking forward to vacation.
6. The secretary handed (he, him) the messages.
7. It was (they, them) who were late for class.
8. Bring your baked goods to (we, us) on Saturday morning.
9. Give your answer to (I, me) by this afternoon.
10. (He, Him) will be attending the conference in Atlanta.
11. Mr. Johnson presented the award to (she, her).
12. John sat behind (we, us) at the football game.
13. It was (she, her) who answered the telephone.
14. Jerry sat between George and (I, me) on the bus.
15. The speakers will be Mr. Benjamin and (I, me).
16. The teacher introduced Tracey as well as (I, me) to the class.

17. Everyone stayed after class except Holly and (she, her).

18. (We, Us) graduates will proceed down the aisle when the music begins.

19. The ballots were given out to (we, us) students during first period class.

20. His friend and (he, him) left class before dismissal time.

Check your answers on page 473.

REPLAY DRILL 6-B: PRONOUN REFERENCE

Part 1: Underline the correct pronoun to complete the following sentences.

Example: John gave (hisself, himself) a raise.

1. The manager and (he, him, himself) waited for the paychecks to arrive from the Payroll Department.

2. No one works harder in class than Michael and (she, her, herself).

3. The student council members (themselves, theirselves) made all the food for the bake sale.

4. She arrived in class earlier than (he, him).

5. Please send the downloaded files to (me, myself).

6. Barry is just as good a student as (he, him).

7. The other workers left earlier than (I, me, myself).

8. The barber gave (hisself, himself) a haircut.

9. The committee members (theirselves, themselves) decided to have another meeting in two weeks.

10. We gave (ourselves, ourself) tests on speaking Spanish.

Check your answers on page 473.

Part 2: Six of the following ten sentences contain an error in pronoun usage and four are correct. Correct the error in the sentences that are incorrect, and write (C) for the sentences that are correct.

11. The author himself autographed the novel.

12. Salinda does not type as fast as myself.

13. Mr. Cone has spoken to the trainees more often than him.

14. I myself worked till the project was completed.

15. The executives may be finding theirselves working overtime this weekend.

16. John granted hisself a leave of absence from the office.

17. No other student completed the test as quickly as she.

18. It was him who welcomed us to the conference.

19. Tina hurt herself during the fire drill.

20. Ann knows her legal terminology better than me.

Check your answers on page 473.

Replay Drill 6-C: Possessive Pronouns

Underline the correct pronoun in each sentence.

Example: The house is (<u>theirs</u>, there's).

1. The dog buried (its, it's) bone in the backyard.

2. Do you know (whose, who's) book is on the desk?

3. Is (you're, your) mother coming to graduation?

4. (No ones, No one's) project received a grade lower than a "B."

5. Is (yours, your's) the one that has been graded already?

6. (Whose, Who's) going to attend the seminar this afternoon?

7. Almost (everyones, everyone's) job was threatened by the strike.

8. (Their, They're) going with us to the retreat.

9. The encyclopedia is (mines, mine).

10. The newly renovated building on Third Street is (our's, ours).

11. (Its, It's) too late to begin the project now.

12. (Who's, Whose) working overtime tonight?

13. If (you're, your) running out of paper, you can use some of mine.

14. (Somebodys, Somebody's) child was crying in the lobby.

15. I hope (your's, yours) is the one selected by the judge.

16. Are you the one (whose, who's) car is double-parked?

17. Is this (anyone's, anyones) jacket under the desk?

18. We will be going to (they're, their) house after the show is over.

19. (My, Mine) children will be in high school next fall.

20. The cat knocked over (it's, its) water bowl.

Check your answers on page 473.

REPLAY DRILL 6-D: WHO AND WHOM

Select either <u>who</u> or <u>whom</u> to complete each of the following sentences.

Example: The man (who, <u>whom</u>) you just met is my father.

1. Mr. Brooks, (who, whom) is a technical support manager, received a promotion.
2. Do you know (who, whom) is working overtime?
3. The man (who, whom) the police arrested stole Frank's car.
4. Give the extra food to (whoever, whomever) can use it.
5. Dr. Holley, (who, whom) was elected mayor last week, is also my dentist.
6. (Who, Whom) will you ask to speak to the class?
7. Mr. Harris, (who, whom) I mentioned in my letter, will be arriving next week.
8. The young man, (who, whom) is getting married today, works in Richard's office.
9. The contest winner, (who, whom) will be chosen today, will win a trip to Europe.
10. (Who, Whom) spoke to Mr. Anderson before he left?
11. The baseball manager, (who, whom) the umpire threw out of the game, complained to the team.
12. Give the receipt to (whoever, whomever) paid for the package.
13. The new stock analyst, (who, whom) was just hired, will start next week.
14. The new city manager, (who, whom) no one has met, will be in the office this afternoon.
15. He is the applicant (who, whom), I am sure, you will want to meet.
16. (Whoever, Whomever) signs up first will be given the opportunity to go to the conference.
17. I am the teacher (who, whom) will be teaching the career development class next quarter.
18. (Whoever, Whomever) you choose for the position should have good computer skills.
19. I wonder (who, whom) will do my work while I am on vacation.
20. The woman (who, whom) I met on the bus is Theresa's mother.

Check your answers on page 473.

REPLAY DRILL 6-E: PRONOUN FORMS

Select the correct form of the pronoun in the following sentences.

Example: (<u>Anything</u>, Any thing) you purchase is 30 percent off.

1. (Everyone, Every one) of the students needed more time to finish the test.

2. (Someone, Some one) left his notebook in class.

3. Do you know if (anybody, any body) is planning on going to the picnic?

4. The teacher asked if (somebody, some body) would carry the textbooks to the office.

5. (Anyone, Any one) of the students' essays could be published in the literary magazine.

6. (Everything, Every thing) seems to be going wrong today.

7. The police could find (nobody, no body) who had witnessed the crime.

8. (Everyone, Every one) in the class applauded after Barbara finished her speech.

9. (Something, Some thing) made a loud crashing noise in the hall during class.

10. (Anything, Any thing) you plan for the conference will be fine with me.

11. Few of the students had (his, their) dictionaries with them.

12. Each of the teachers assigned (his or her, their) classes a project today.

13. Everyone in the cast gave (his, their, his or her) best performance.

14. Many of the customers complained about (his, their) purchases.

15. Every team member gave (his or her, their) best effort to get the job done.

16. Several speakers complimented (his, their) audience.

17. Anybody can still add (his or her, their) name to the list.

18. Someone must volunteer (his or her, their) name to the list.

19. Both my sons lost (his, their) keys on the same day.

20. Students did not raise (his or her, their) hands to answer the question.

Check your answers on page 474.

REPLAY DRILL 6-F: ITS AND THEIR

Select either <u>its</u> or <u>their</u> to complete each of the following sentences.

1. The company gave (its, their) gift to the college building fund.

2. Each group has (its, their) own type of music.

3. The team celebrated (its, their) first victory.

4. The herd of bison thundered (its, their) way across the plain.

5. The orchestra will play (its, their) first performance on Sunday.

6. The band had to change (its, their) uniforms after the game because of the muddy field.

7. The faculty angrily returned to (its, their) offices.

8. The union won (its, their) attempt to represent the employees.

9. The counseling staff disagreed about endorsing (its, their) president's position.

10. The jury pondered (its, their) verdict a long time before announcing it to the judge.

Check your answers on page 474.

CHAPTER 7: MASTERING VERBS

Replay Drill 7-A: Verb Tense

Underline the verb in the following sentences. Then identify the tense of the verb as either present, past, or future.

Example: Mike <u>helps</u> his son with his homework. ___present___

1. Dawn jogs to class every morning. _____
2. Frankie will sing in the concert on Saturday. _____
3. The baby cries when her mother leaves the room. _____
4. The audience laughed at the comedian's jokes. _____
5. Pamela married her childhood sweetheart. _____
6. We will fly to Orlando next Wednesday. _____
7. During the week, Brian stays with his uncle. _____
8. Harry and his wife saw a counselor for several months. _____
9. The children wanted their parents to buy a new car. _____
10. The contractor will paint the walls this afternoon. _____
11. Anthony takes a course in Arabic on Thursdays. _____
12. Mark needs a new suit for his interview. _____
13. Laverne oversees the Red Cross volunteers. _____
14. The band marched during the halftime show. _____
15. The out-of-stock items will arrive in two weeks. _____
16. The finance committee recommended a raise for all employees. _____
17. Christy gained ten pounds on her vacation. _____
18. John walks to work every day. _____
19. The teacher will talk with me after class. _____
20. The ivy climbs up the backyard fence. _____

Check your answers on page 474.

Replay Drill 7-B: Verb Tense

Underline the correct tense of the verbs in the following sentences.

Example: Jack (wears, <u>wore</u>) a new suit yesterday.

1. Barney has (took, taken) several courses in accounting.

2. The Vietnam Memorial (stands, stood) as a tribute to all who served in the war.

3. The judge has (spoke, spoken) to our law class twice.

4. We have (saw, seen) the view from the top of the Empire State Building.

5. The couple (ran, run) to catch the bus at the corner.

6. The sun (rises, rose) this morning at 5:45.

7. The doorbell (rang, rung) several times before Mr. Johnson came to the door.

8. The team has (went, gone) to the playoffs each year.

9. The manager (give, gave) each player a pep talk before the game.

10. Our supervisor (flew, flown) to the corporate headquarters in California.

11. Greg has (ate, eaten) pizza for dinner each night this week.

12. During the party the guests (drank, drunk) a toast to the award winner.

13. Mr. Stanko (does, do) the payroll checks each Thursday.

14. When Tiffany enrolled in college, she (chose, chosen) the medical assistant program.

15. That man has (broke, broken) every rule in the book.

16. The temperature has (began, begun) to get colder.

17. The furniture has (wore, worn) well over the years.

18. The professor had (took, taken) a leave of absence from his classes.

19. The telephone had (rang, rung) ten times before the operator picked it up.

20. The children had (drank, drunk) all the lemonade and yelled for more.

Check your answers on page 475.

REPLAY DRILL 7-C: REGULAR VERBS

Select the correct form of the verb in the following sentences.

Example: Peter (<u>broke</u>, broken) one of the dishes.

1. Mr. Yearby has (wrote, written) a letter to the editor.

2. The burglar had (threw, thrown) the furniture around the room.

3. The choir (sang, sung) three hymns during the service.

4. The passengers on the bus were (shook, shaken) by the near accident.

5. The treasure was (hid, hidden) at the end of the rainbow.

6. The water should have (froze, frozen) quickly in the new freezer.

7. Everyone had (forgot, forgotten) what time the program was scheduled to start.

8. The prices of new homes have (fell, fallen) ten percent in the last year.

9. The artist had (drew, drawn) a portrait of the couple as a wedding gift.

10. The regional managers had (came, come) to Washington for their annual meeting.

11. The strong wind (blew, blown) the clothes off the line.

12. The fish has (bit, bitten) the bait on the line.

13. The author has (wrote, written) several articles against child abuse.

14. The team's owner (threw, thrown) the first ball of the game to the pitcher.

15. We have (sang, sung) that song fifty times during rehearsal.

16. The coins (sank, sunk) to the bottom of the pond.

17. The usher had (shook, shaken) the man who had fallen asleep during the film.

18. The mothers have (hid, hidden) the Easter eggs under the bushes in the backyard.

19. The stock prices had (fell, fallen) by the end of the trading season.

20. The children had (drew, drawn) a hopscotch pattern on the sidewalk.

Check your answers on page 475.

REPLAY DRILL 7-D: BEING VERBS

Select the correct form of the verb for written English in the following sentences.

Example: I (am, is) happy about the promotion.

1. (Is, Are) you going to the meeting tomorrow morning?

2. Marissa (is, be) the new receptionist.

3. The visitors (were, was) greeted upon their arrival.

4. I (had been, been) to Radio City Music Hall when I visited New York City.

5. We (is, are) waiting for your answer.

6. (Is, Are) anybody going with me?

7. You (is, are) required to sign in when you enter the building after hours.

8. (I'd, I would) like to speak to Mr. Bryant about a salary increase.

9. The baseball team (be going, will be going) to Montreal next week.

10. Doctor Swenson (be, will be) speaking at the physician's conference in Norfolk.

11. The textbook shipment (is, are) expected next week.

12. The teachers (is, are) having help sessions after school.

13. Keith (is, are) making waffles for breakfast.

14. The proofs for the annual report (is, are) being reviewed by the editors.

15. The modular workstations (was, were) ordered last week.

16. The copy machine (will be, be) repaired by noon.

17. During the summer the children (have been, been) sleeping later than usual each morning.

18. You (was, were) chosen to represent our class at the conference.

19. The employees (has been, have been) working in the new building for more than two years.

20. (We'd, We would) like to nominate Mr. Rodriguez as the employee of the month.

Check your answers on page 475.

Replay Drill 7-E: Subjects and Verbs

Circle the subject and underline the verb in the following sentences.

Example: The child grabbed a cookie.

1. The morning sun rose at 6 a.m.

2. The hungry wolves howled throughout the valley.

3. Do you have a completed resume?

4. Gourmet cooking is Martina's favorite hobby.

5. Please answer his question immediately.

6. The daily newspaper is delivered each morning.

7. There are 25 students in the communications class.

8. Both mother and son were found safe before nightfall.

9. The job placement director sent Andrew on three job interviews.

10. Did you buy a ticket for the afternoon or evening performance?

11. Across the street from our office is our favorite restaurant.

12. Early sign-ups for Little League will be held next Sunday.

13. Across the countryside word spread about the fire.

14. Mr. Overton, along with his wife, attended the mayor's conference in San Francisco.

15. The toy manufacturer recalled the new product because of sharp edges.

16. The boy and his grandfather strolled through the city park.

17. Advancement courses are taught for all employees on Wednesday evenings.

18. Along the Outer Banks, residents were warned of the approaching hurricane.

19. In the morning Sidney will learn his test scores.

20. All during August the football team practiced in the hot sun.

Check your answers on pages 475–476.

REPLAY DRILL 7-F: SUBJECT AND VERB AGREEMENT

Select the verb that is correct in the following sentences. Locate the subject. If the subject is singular, your verb should be singular. If the subject is plural, your verb should be plural.

Example: Mrs. Smith (<u>runs</u>, run) every morning before work.

1. Kelly (writes, write) an entry in her diary every night.

2. All the students (want, wants) a good grade on the exam.

3. The executive and his two assistants (arrives, arrive) at the airport at noon.

4. Neither of us (is, are) going to the concert.

5. There (was, were) a house on Birch Street for sale.

6. The supervisor, as well as all the executives, (does, do) the job evaluations.

7. Each of the members (is, are) writing a set of bylaws.

8. The baby (cries, cry) whenever she is hungry.

9. The new answering machine (records, record) all of our messages.

10. The three pathologists (speaks, speak) to the medical classes each quarter.

11. Many a father and son (is, are) involved in Little League.

12. This is the woman who (talks, talk) during class.

13. Here (is, are) the supplies you need.

14. Either Marlin or his friends (is, are) planning to attend the word processing seminar.

15. The herd of horses (tries, try) to swim across the muddy stream.

16. Their mother, who (is, are) an optometrist, examined me for contact lenses.

17. General Electric Corporation (is, are) opening an airplane engine manufacturing plant near my home.

18. Several groups (was, were) touring the monument when the lightning struck.

19. Hartman Industries (has, have) a good profit sharing plan for the employees.

20. The lawyer (does, do) want to represent the client in this case.

Check your answers on page 476.

CHAPTER 8: MASTERING ADJECTIVES AND ADVERBS

REPLAY DRILL 8-A: POINTING ADJECTIVES

Select the correct word to complete the following sentences.

Example: Charles gave (them, <u>those</u>) children a ride home.

1. These (kind, kinds) of rumors cause marriages to break up.
2. Margaret wanted to buy (this, those) kind of candy.
3. The camp counselor wanted (them, those) boys to lead the group.
4. (Them, These) are my parents.
5. (That, Those) woman is my supervisor.
6. (Them, Those) actors are performing in the program tonight.
7. These (type, types) of situations are awkward for us.
8. (These, Them) textbooks are needed in class today.
9. Unfortunately, I make this (types, type) of error often.
10. (That, Those) sort of clothes should not be worn in the office.
11. Pedro does not like these (types, type) of shoes.
12. The company wants to close out (this, this here) business.
13. Please hand (that, that there) report to the secretary.
14. Priscilla wanted to save these (kind, kinds) of articles.
15. The supervisor wanted (them, those) employees to work overtime.
16. Those (kind, kinds) of memos must be typed before noon today.
17. (This, This here) restaurant is my favorite.
18. The teacher is looking for these (type, types) of ideas.
19. Those (kind, kinds) of remarks will not improve our customer relations.
20. (That, That there) student received an A+ on his English final.

Check your answers on page 476.

REPLAY DRILL 8-B: ARTICLES

Select the article *a* or *an* to put in front of the following words.

Example: (<u>a</u>, an) hungry teenager

1. (a, an) yellow raincoat
2. (a, an) umbrella
3. (a, an) ten-key calculator
4. (a, an) honorable gentleman
5. (a, an) IRS agent
6. (a, an) 18 percent increase
7. (a, an) FBI agent
8. (a, an) unified agreement
9. (a, an) M & M candy lover
10. (a, an) one-way street
11. (a, an) heavy package
12. (a, an) angry customer
13. (a, an) unknown author
14. (a, an) honest man
15. (a, an) USC football player
16. (a, an) early riser
17. (a, an) universal policy
18. (a, an) holiday greeting
19. (a, an) omelette
20. (a, an) one-horse town

Check your answers on page 476.

REPLAY DRILL 8-C: DOUBLE NEGATIVES

Select the correct word for each sentence. Remember to avoid two negatives in the same sentence.

Example: I do not want (no, <u>any</u>) potatoes.

1. (Nobody, Everybody) wasn't paying attention when the rules were read.
2. Mary doesn't want (no, any) chicken.
3. The store (can't, can) hardly keep those shoes in stock.
4. Stanley hasn't gone (nowhere, anywhere) in this new car.
5. I won't (never, ever) speak to Helen again.
6. Since you are on a diet, you don't need (no, any) ice cream.
7. Johnny doesn't know (nothing, anything) about Russia.

8. Mrs. French won't go (nowhere, anywhere) without her dog.

9. There was hardly (no, any) difference between the two bids on the school.

10. Linda said she wouldn't (never, ever) cheat on her diet.

11. Nobody (can, can't) leave class early today.

12. Susan hardly (ever, never) drives anymore.

13. Don't put (no, any) gravy on the potatoes.

14. Mr. Langley doesn't need (no, any) help with the proposals.

15. I shouldn't go (anywhere, nowhere) with all this work to do.

16. Bob (can't, can) barely see in the fog.

17. Mr. Bowles can't get (any, none) of his report written with all the noise.

18. The baseball player (could, couldn't) never hit the curve ball.

19. Our family doesn't (never, ever) go to that restaurant to eat.

20. That child shouldn't eat (no, any) more candy.

Check your answers on page 477.

REPLAY DRILL 8-D: COMPARATIVE FORMS OF ADJECTIVES

Select the appropriate adjective for each sentence.

Example: Mrs. Brown is the (nicer, <u>nicest</u>) teacher I know.

1. We had the (goodest, best) teacher I know.

2. Mr. Little is the (kindest, kinder) of the two gentlemen.

3. Frank is a (gooder, better) worker than his brother.

4. The Browns' new baby is the (prettiest, prettier) of the two children.

5. Alison is the (most friendliest, friendliest) person in our neighborhood.

6. Which one of all the stars do you think is shining the (brighter, brightest)?

7. Which is the (better, best) medication for these patients, Serine or Berine?

8. Who is (younger, youngest), her brother or sister?

9. Benjamin received the (worse, worst) grades.

10. Bernadette is a (better, more better) athlete.

11. Here is the (more recent, most recent) of the two photos.

12. That statue is the (less valuable, least valuable) of any in his huge collection.

13. Rich walked (farther, further) than his wife.

14. This is the (worse, worst) soup I have ever tasted.

15. Who's the (better, best) lawyer, Rosen or Chandra?

16. Raymond is the (older, oldest) of all his brothers and sisters.

17. This is the (most unusual, most unique) home I've ever seen.

18. The view from the top of the Empire State Building is the (more beautiful, most beautiful) of any in the city of New York.

19. Which is (more, most) expensive, the airfare to Spain, France, or Italy?

20. Would email or fax be (better, best) for this message?

Check your answers on page 477.

REPLAY DRILL 8-E: ADJECTIVES AND ADVERBS

Decide which is needed—an adjective or an adverb—in the following sentences. Then select the correct word from the choices given.

Example: She walked (quick, quickly) to her car.

1. She did (good, well) on the driver's test.

2. Marilyn's new dress looks (good, well) with her new shoes.

3. The decorations on the cake are (sure, very) pretty.

4. The car runs (smoother, more smoothly) than it did before.

5. He drives (more careful, more carefully) now.

6. Those cookies tasted (delicious, deliciously).

7. If you do (good, well) on the test, you'll be accepted at the college.

8. The driver felt (bad, badly) about the accident.

9. The film seemed to move (slow, slowly).

10. The band played so (loud, loudly) that we couldn't hear the sirens.

11. My sister feels (good, well, either good or well) today.

12. Edna did (good, well) in the interview.

13. He (sure, surely) didn't treat her well.

14. Can you work (quicker, more quickly)?

15. The students worked (real, really) hard on their science project.

16. Our doctor always writes his prescriptions (clear, clearly).

17. He works (neat, neatly) and fast.

18. That hat looks (good, well) on you.

19. I am (sure, surely) working hard on the project.

20. I have learned all the answers (well, good).

Check your answers on page 477.

REPLAY DRILL 8-F: ADJECTIVES AND ADVERBS

Most of the following sentences contain errors in the use of adjectives or adverbs. Make the necessary corrections. Write (C) for the correct sentences.

Example: Paula has the ~~whiter~~ ^{whitest} teeth of all the dentist's patients.

1. He writes more better than George.
2. Lauren speaks good.
3. This homemade ice cream tastes deliciously.
4. Our manager runs an efficienter office.
5. The math teacher explained the rules real good.
6. The carpenter stayed more later than anyone else.
7. These type of questions are unfair.
8. Pierre played miserable yesterday in the tennis match.
9. If the team works together, it can get the job done quicker.
10. He works quick and accurate.
11. The actor felt calmly before her performance.
12. Your new home is sure decorated attractively.
13. This fragrance is wider used than the others.
14. Since it was repaired, the car engine runs smoother.
15. Of all of the stockbrokers, he has the better reputation.
16. The lion looked angrily at the trainer.
17. Return to the office as quick as you can.
18. She dropped a umbrella and a actor picked it up.
19. The dancers performed good.
20. Be sure to dress comfortable when you work in the warehouse.

Check your answers on page 477.

CHAPTER 9: USING COMMAS CORRECTLY

REPLAY DRILL 9-A: THE SERIES COMMA

Underline the series in the following sentences. Then add the necessary commas. If no commas are needed, write (C).

Example: I bought milk, butter, and eggs.

1. Tonight Chris must study English accounting and marketing.

2. The instructor said to be organized to speak clearly and to show enthusiasm.

3. The company president the managers and the supervisor attended the conference.

4. On our vacation we traveled to Washington Philadelphia and New York City.

5. Phyllis needed to find books about child abuse single-parent families and homeless shelters.

6. The students their parents and their teachers are planning the museum trip.

7. The chefs the cooks and the waiters celebrated the opening of the new restaurant.

8. All customers must wear shoes shirts and long pants in the new nightclub.

9. Please bring a main dish vegetable and dessert to the picnic.

10. The administrative assistant's task was to type proofread and fax the reports.

11. Please do not fold bend or staple the enclosed payment form.

12. The board will be meeting October 5 November 9 and January 15.

13. Pineapples kiwis and mangos are all available in local markets.

14. Harrison had to pay his rent phone bill and electric bill.

15. Mrs. Swanson buys her meats at Super Fresh her produce at Farm Fresh and her grocery items at Food Lion.

16. The young actor's parents agent and director discussed his future.

17. The family went swimming boating and snorkeling while on vacation.

18. The police searched the streets the alleys and the buildings near the robbery.

19. The surgeon the lab technician and the radiologist discussed the patient's prognosis.

20. In August my friend will celebrate her birthday and her daughter's wedding.

Check your answers on page 478.

REPLAY DRILL 9-B: COMMAS WITH A SERIES OF ITEMS OR ADJECTIVES

Insert a comma where needed in the following sentences. You will need to put a comma in a series or between adjectives only. If no comma is needed, write (C).

Example: Mason wiped the hot, sticky sauce off his fingers.

1. The elderly residents stayed inside because of the hot humid weather.
2. They drove the old gray dump truck to the junkyard.
3. Tommy took a bite of the chocolate chewy candy bar.
4. For her recipe Barbie needed two eggs one stick of butter and two cups of flour.
5. Her father's bright cheery smile cheered up Melissa.
6. Linda longed for a day to enjoy the warm gentle ocean breezes.
7. The dentist told Sam he could not eat any hard crunchy foods.
8. The FBI accepts only intelligent competent applicants.
9. Elena wants ketchup mustard and relish on her hotdog.
10. Margaret's accurate efficient accounting skills led to her promotion.
11. Many soldiers were killed during the long fierce battle.
12. The friendly honest stranger returned my briefcase.
13. When Kerry got the cast off her foot, she wanted to run jump and dance.
14. Her mother's note told Joanie to dust the furniture peel the potatoes and iron the shirts.
15. Keith's daring competent actions during the fire were praised by the mayor.
16. His ridiculous comic behavior made everyone laugh.
17. Patricia craved the hot salty taste of the freshly roasted peanuts.
18. The owner gave the first five customers a rose a $100 gift certificate and a big smile.
19. The city's new operating system accounting procedures and auditing methods will be installed this week.
20. The novice skateboarder skinned his knee bruised his arm and broke his front tooth in the accident.

Check your answers on page 479.

REPLAY DRILL 9-C: COMMAS WITH CLAUSES

Insert any necessary commas in the following sentences. Write (C) if no comma is needed.

Example: I want to go to the movies, yet I also have to finish my essay.

1. Please give me your test paper and you may then begin reading Chapter 5.

2. Susan baked some chocolate-chip cookies and she gave some to all the people in our group.

3. We were ready to go to class but Buddy couldn't get the car started.

4. Brenda worked quickly yet the class ended before she completed the test.

5. The secretary answered the telephone but no one was on the line.

6. The baseball player hit the ball hard and he ran quickly to first base.

7. I don't want to study but I don't want to flunk the test.

8. Alex does not want to go to the meeting nor will he be ready to leave.

9. Peggy waited by the phone for the interviewer said she would call today.

10. Are you going to buy the shoes or do you want to wait until they go on sale?

11. The toddler built a sandcastle but the waves washed it away.

12. Bob gobbled down the two hamburgers and then he ate three orders of french fries.

13. Angela was on a diet yet she still managed to eat the strawberry shortcake.

14. The minister preached a good sermon but several people still fell asleep.

15. James sent in his reservation for he planned on attending the banquet.

16. The applicant was not prepared for the keyboarding test nor could she verify her keyboarding speed.

17. The young girl enjoyed her first plane ride and thanked the flight attendant and pilot.

18. William bought a ticket but did not attend the concert.

19. Catherine wanted to be a basketball player and she practiced her shooting every day.

20. My friend was angry for the hairstylist had cut her hair too short.

Check your answers on page 479.

REPLAY DRILL **9-D**: COMMAS WITH INTRODUCTORY WORDS AND EXPRESSIONS

Insert any necessary commas in the following sentences.

Example: When we were in Atlanta, we visited Stone Mountain.

1. Yes I'll give your papers back on Monday.

2. Ms. Johansson can you help me with this problem?

3. In the early morning before dawn Rich went fishing.

4. If you arrive after the play begins you must wait until the usher can seat you.

5. No I am not working overtime tonight.

6. Since you will be the first to arrive would you please set up the chairs for the meeting.

7. Mr. Bryant could you get a temporary worker for me for next Friday?

8. Before leaving for work I did the laundry and washed the dishes.

9. After the thunderstorm stopped the sun came out.

10. Since going to his reunion Jerry has renewed acquaintances with his high school buddies.

11. Once outside the man lit up a cigarette.

12. Well I am not sure if I can go with you this weekend.

13. When I attended business school I learned to use WordPerfect.

14. Underneath the chair by the door Mickey found his missing glasses.

15. Oh I can't believe it's Monday already.

16. Arriving late for work Paula rushed up the steps.

17. Mr. Olivas when is our final exam?

18. When Suzie came in the door everyone shouted at her.

19. The girls shopped for hours at the mall and then they went to the movies.

20. Curtis had a lot of work to do yet he still had time to play ball with his son.

Check your answers on page 479.

REPLAY DRILL 9-E: COMMAS WITH NONESSENTIAL EXPRESSIONS

Insert the necessary commas in the following sentences. Remember, you are looking for parenthetical expressions.

Example: Ms. Brown wants the information, however, so please give her a call.

1. My son who likes to surf is a good swimmer. (I have one son.)

2. We would like to ask you Dr. Harvey to speak at our graduation.

3. My college roommate Toni Heiser writes faithfully each month.

4. Our reference book *Guide to Business Careers* is on hold at the library.

5. Any person young or old is invited to the festivities at the park.

6. The lottery winner who is my brother-in-law will spend his earnings wisely.

7. Can you fix the jammed copier Mr. Pope?

8. The city manager Mr. Orton will meet with the area civic leagues.

9. Our math textbook *Understanding Business Mathematics* explains how to round off decimals.

10. Leave an answer either yes or no on my voice mail about attending the seminar next week.

11. The mayor who is also a dentist was re-elected last fall.

12. The Phillies my favorite baseball team have won sixteen games in a row in Philadelphia.

13. Have you made any plans for your retirement Mr. Hunting?

14. My childhood friend Janet Sturn is visiting us next week.

15. Because of your patience with children Ms. Norfleet I know you'll be a good child care worker.

16. Have you read Danielle Steel's new book *Amazing Grace*?

17. I would like now ladies and gentlemen to introduce our speaker.

18. Our French teacher who is also my aunt grew up outside of Paris.

19. The encyclopedia salesman Mr. Breeden urged my parents to buy the complete set.

20. Have you met the new president of the college Dr. Morgan?

Check your answers on page 479.

REPLAY DRILL 9-F: COMMAS WITH QUOTATIONS

Decide if the commas used in the following sentences are correct and if additional commas may be needed. If the sentences are correct, write (C). If a comma is used incorrectly, delete it; if a comma is needed, insert it.

Example: Her mother said, "No, you can't stay home from school today."

1. "Can you come to work early on Friday?" asked Mrs. Lincoln.

2. "You may go," his father said, "but be home by midnight."

3. My grandmother always told me, "Don't wish your life away; it will go by fast enough on its own."

4. "Please" the professor said, "use specific examples to prove your answers."

5. Frank shouted, "Watch out!," and ran to grab the child from the path of the oncoming car.

6. His friends yelled "Surprise" when Al came into the restaurant.

7. "Are you exempt from taking the final exam in English?" asked Mrs. Franklin.

8. Greg kept answering every question with "I don't know."

9. The supervisor instructed "Everyone must complete the questionnaire in fifteen minutes."

10. "All the students clapped after my speech!" Anna exclaimed.

11. Instead of saying he would take the job, the applicant just said, "Maybe."

12. "Thanks for tutoring me in Spanish, Mrs. Edgars," said Timothy.

13. Lana's friends yelled, "Good-bye" as her bus pulled out of the station.

14. "Who will drive the carpool van next week,?" asked Mr. Lewis.

15. "Since the bank is closing," the manager explained, "you must make an appointment for tomorrow."

16. "Can you believe this gorgeous view!" Melissa shouted.

17. Marvin asked "When will the word processing seminar begin?"

18. When Lester finished his speech, the audience yelled "Hurray!"

19. The student replied,"The word group is not a complete thought; therefore, it is a fragment."

20. When his father gave him the keys to the new car, John could only say, "Wow!"

Check your answers on page 480.

REPLAY DRILL 9-G: COMMAS WITH NAMES, DATES, AND PLACES

Insert the necessary commas in the following sentences.

Example: Our grand opening was on August, 15, 1979, in Philadelphia.

1. Jared Olansky moved to Lansing Michigan after graduation.

2. The children's museum in Washington DC has a new exhibition on safety.

3. The exchange student from Madrid Spain will live with the Kennedys.

4. Both his parents graduated on June 12 1975 from Penn State University.

5. My dentist James Kail DDS has just opened his own practice.

6. The commencement address on June 14 2010 was televised nationally.

7. My dad always says that San Francisco California is the most beautiful city in America.

8. Have you visited Disneyland in Anaheim California or Disney World in Orlando Florida?

9. James Little PhD spoke to our psychology class.

10. His birthday September 6 1974 is the same date as his uncle's birthday.

11. Did your brother live in Portsmouth New Hampshire or in Portsmouth Virginia?

12. John McGuire MD received his graduate degree from the University of Virginia.

13. On October 14 1989 the stock market suffered a severe loss in trading.

14. Will the yearly conference be in Tampa Florida or Charleston South Carolina?

15. Classes first began on Thursday September 5 1991 at this college.

16. On November 15 2001 John's father retired after thirty years with the company.

17. Both John P. Smith PhD and William R. Smith MD paid for a world cruise for their parents.

18. Our plane leaves from Pittsburgh Pennsylvania and we transfer in Denver, Colorado.

19. The conference will begin on Monday October 5 and end on Wednesday October 12.

20. Muriel Freeman MD will be the guest lecturer at the Pavillion in Longport Rhode Island.

Check your answers on page 480.

CHAPTER 10: PUNCTUATING SENTENCES PROPERLY

REPLAY DRILL 10-A: SEMICOLONS AND COLONS

Insert the semicolons, colons, and commas where needed in the following sentences.

Example: Avis is an excellent student; she studies hard.

1. Doctor Hobley who was our mayor will speak at the meeting; he is an excellent presenter.

2. Sabrina ran toward the bus then she suddenly dropped all her packages.

3. Harold was hurt in an accident therefore he missed three weeks of work.

4. The young couple saved every penny they could nevertheless it took them ten years to save for a home.

5. The public relations firm will handle the event that is location food and entertainment.

6. My mother works hard at her job then she comes home to prepare dinner.

7. The exhibit hours have been established booths open at 9 a.m. and close at 3 p.m.

8. Bessie Cambria the branch manager is coming to town please prepare for her visit.

9. Phil worked overtime for three months so he was glad to get home early.

10. Mr. Leslie has worked for our company for 30 years therefore he is eligible for retirement.

11. Three players got base hits still the team could not score any runs.

12. Angela works two different jobs also she volunteers for the literacy council.

13. The owners sold a large amount of stock thus they could afford the new office space.

14. Mr. Barrows has suggested the following summer office hours 8:00 a.m. instead of 9 a.m. Monday–Thursday 8 a.m. to 2 p.m. on Fridays.

15. Your radio publicity schedule will be in the following cities Cambridge Massachusetts Portsmouth New Hampshire and Augusta Maine.

16. Joanna wanted a raise however she was afraid to ask her supervisor.

17. Mr. Johnson completed a speech course nevertheless he was still nervous when he stood in front of the audience.

18. It is Mr. Bell's birthday his friends are planning a surprise party.

19. A heavy rainstorm is predicted for Friday therefore we are rescheduling the family day picnic.

20. Two of the panelists started arguing thus the moderator had to intervene to continue the discussion.

Check your answers on pages 480–481.

REPLAY DRILL 10-B: COLONS

Insert colons where they are needed in the following sentences. Write (C) for the three sentences that do not require a colon.

Example: We need to buy the following supplies: pens, folders, and envelopes.

1. Each set of silverware includes 12 each of these utensils salad forks, dinner forks, spoons, and knives.

2. Sunrise will be at 545 a.m. tomorrow morning.

3. Karen's goals were the following graduation, career, and marriage.

4. Peter had one thought in mind food.

5. We can schedule the banquet on February 8, February 15, or March 1.

6. Please send the following by UPS 100 reams of copy paper and four quarts of toner.

7. The following people were elected to the City Council Matthew Lawrence, Madeline Booth, and Stevie Hughes.

8. Jonathan received double-time for working three holidays Thanksgiving, Christmas, and New Year's Day.

9. Bring the following supplies with you to class plain white paper, a manila folder, and a good dictionary.

10. Benjamin Franklin wrote, "A penny saved is a penny earned."

11. Chris has to eliminate eating the following foods while on his diet candy, ice cream, and snack foods.

12. The advertising circular featured several protein specials ground beef, whole chickens, sirloin steak.

13. Three interviewees were called back for second interviews Betty Mandez, Avis Bartlett, and Dan Baker.

14. Be sure to attend our Grand Opening on the following dates April 7, 8, and 10.

15. Registration will begin at 8 p.m., and the seminar will start at 9:30.

Check your answers on page 481.

REPLAY DRILL 10-C: END-OF-SENTENCE PUNCTUATION

Insert the correct punctuation marks: a period, question mark, or exclamation point.

Example: Do you have practice tomorrow?

1. Please present your report to the committee
2. Excellent work
3. Would you please come by my office at 5 o'clock
4. Are you able to complete this work by noon
5. Great idea
6. The supervisor asked if you would be there
7. I wonder if the employees will get a raise
8. Do you know how to post a video online
9. Terrific
10. Frank asked when you would be ready to leave
11. Would you help me with this math problem
12. Thanks, John, for a job well done
13. What a fantastic report
14. Watch out
15. John wondered what time the seminar would end
16. May I have your reply by tomorrow morning
17. Martha asked if you enjoyed your new job
18. I am looking forward to working with you
19. You won
20. Would December 1 or 2 be the better date to meet

Check your answers on page 481.

REPLAY DRILL 10-D: PARENTHESES, BRACKETS, AND DASHES

Part 1: Put parentheses or brackets where needed in the following sentences.

Example: John (my sister's first husband) is coming for dinner.

1. I worked hard believe me to complete this assignment.
2. "We will go not now *sic* to whatever is necessary to get the votes," said the senator.

3. The dress cost $149 not $159.

4. The bank's Saturday hours 9 to noon will soon be changed.

5. The decimal equivalents see Figure 4, page 80 will help you with the percentages.

6. These DVD players last year's models are reduced.

7. Reverend Chamberlain our first minister is coming to Suzanne's wedding.

8. It will be Wendy not her sister who will be maid of honor.

9. The state postal abbreviations see chart, page 23 should be used on all envelopes.

10. The new Food Carnival the one near the mall has the best selection of meats.

Check your answers on page 481.

Part 2: Put dashes where they belong in the following sentences.

Example: The company party is Saturday—I can't wait!

11. Please make a donation we need your help now.

12. Happiness it's yours for the asking.

13. He won money a great deal of money by playing the lottery each week.

14. Our new refrigerator rated number one by *Consumer Reports* has an icemaker and water dispenser.

15. Our supervisor a real sweetheart gave us the afternoon off.

16. The new board members Dr. Duzeck and Ms. Swenson will meet with the press this afternoon.

17. Bottled water avoid it for the environment's sake!

18. Style, grace, and beauty the pageant winner had them all!

19. Zelika she was the winner praised her parents for their love and devotion.

20. The new product brochure in full-color and printed on heavy stock will increase sales, I'm sure.

Check your answers on page 481.

CHAPTER 11: MASTERING THE FINE POINTS OF PUNCTUATION

Rᴇᴘʟᴀʏ Dʀɪʟʟ 11-A: Qᴜᴏᴛᴀᴛɪᴏɴ Mᴀʀᴋs

Put the quotation marks where they are needed in the following sentences. If you are typing your responses, use italics where appropriate. Write (C) if the sentence does not need to be changed.

Example: When she completed her exams, Mallory exclaimed, "Hurray!"

1. Many students confuse accept with except.
2. Say I can instead of I can't.
3. Thank you, Mr. Lockner, Ryan said sincerely.
4. Look for the silver lining in every cloud.
5. Charlie yelled, We're lost!
6. Please read the chapter entitled Uses for Quotation Marks in your text.
7. What time will your plane arrive? Dale asked.
8. Martin was chosen Employee of the Year in 1990.
9. The crowd cheered, We won!
10. Did you mean eligible or illegible?
11 The article Money Management in this morning's paper gave me some good ideas.
12. His friends told the actor to break a leg.
13. Don't use ain't in formal business communications.
14. Mitch asked, Are you working overtime tonight?
15. The refrigerator magnet read, Don't Feed Me!
16. The poem Still I Rise by Maya Angelou is a good one to recite.
17. April wondered, Should I order dessert?
18. Never use irregardless in your writing: it's a non-Standard word form.
19. The umpire yelled, Play ball!
20. The surfers hoped they could catch a wave today.

Check your answers on page 482.

REPLAY DRILL 11-B: THE HYPHEN

Put the necessary hyphens in the following word groups. Write (C) for the one in which hyphens are not needed.

Example: seventy-seven students

1. an up to date weather report
2. first rate accommodations
3. my editor in chief's report
4. his lack of self respect
5. the out of stock sale item

6. a four year college

7. a ten story office building

8. a hard to find location

9. a part time position

10. a high priced antique

11. ninety nine percent of the vote

12. a mid July white sale

13. the quality of self control

14. the stressed out executive

15. six foot sections

16. my brother in law's new car

17. a kind hearted individual

18. high risk investment

19. first class postage rate

20. Larry's self taught

Check your answers on page 482.

REPLAY DRILL 11-C: POSSESSIVES

Add an apostrophe or 's where it is needed in the following word groups.

Example: Sid's scorecard

1. two weeks pay

2. Mr. Hernandez car

3. the children bike

4. the child skateboard

5. the boss memo

6. the secretaries desks

7. someone briefcase

8. Janice computer

9. a woman rights

10. the ladies purses

11. Benjamin Franklin experiments

12. James report card

13. both authors opinions

14. my mother-in-law cooking

15. three months interest

16. all the employees parking structure

17. the Prime Ministers address

18. the two companies merger

19. the Joneses party

20. the teachers lounge

Check your answers on page 482.

REPLAY DRILL 11-D: CONTRACTIONS

Insert apostrophes where needed. Write (C) if no apostrophe is needed.

1. The children carved jack-o-lanterns for Halloween.

2. John cant go to the movie tonight.

3. Most games at our school start at seven oclock.

4. Well be here today, but not tomorrow.

5. Dont you think that is a good idea?

6. Its so cold this morning that my teeth are chattering.

7. Mary is planning on investing well so that she can retire young.

8. Susan was determined to get all As in college.

9. Bob is studying the probabilities of 7s and 11s coming up on the roll of the dice.

10. Early rock music was played in the 50s and 60s era.

Check your answers on page 483.

CHAPTER 12: WRITING POWERFUL SENTENCES

REPLAY DRILL 12-A: COMPLETE SENTENCES VERSUS FRAGMENTS

Decide if the following word groups are complete sentences (C) or if they are fragments (incomplete thoughts) (F).

Example: Mr. Johnson who is our manager. F

1. The receptionist, who was away last week.
2. The receptionist returning to work today.
3. The receptionist returned to work today.
4. The board meeting, which will be held on Friday.
5. The board meeting will be held on Friday.
6. The board meeting being held on Friday.
7. The education director, who is Mr. Bryant.
8. The education director is Mr. Bryant.
9. Norfolk, being a large U.S. Navy port.
10. Norfolk, which is a large U.S. Navy port.
11. Norfolk is a large U.S. Navy port.
12. The graduate who received her diploma.
13. The graduate, while receiving her diploma.
14. The graduate received her diploma.
15. Mr. Mathews, while speaking to the business students.
16. Mr. Mathews is speaking to the business students.
17. Mr. Mathews, speaking to the business students.
18. Betsy Ross's house, which is in Philadelphia.
19. Betsy Ross's house, being in Philadelphia.
20. Betsy Ross's house is in Philadelphia.

Check your answers on page 483.

REPLAY DRILL 12-B: WRITING STYLE

Part 1: Combine these short, simple sentences into one smooth sentence.

Example: Jim likes ice cream. Chocolate is his favorite. Jim likes chocolate ice cream.

1. Ellen went to business school. She majored in Computer Information Systems. _____

_____

2. Chris plays football. He is on the junior varsity team. _____

_____

3. The shoe store at the mall had a sale. It was an end-of-summer sale. _____

_____

4. The hamburger was juicy. It was covered with onions. _____

_____

5. The clock was ticking loudly. It gave Marissa a headache. _____

_____

6. He completed his homework. Then he had a snack. _____

_____

7. Brenda read the budget report. She fell asleep while reading it. _____

_____

8. Kenneth gained 25 pounds. He decided to go on a diet. _____

_____

9. Linda and Freddie share a large office. They are on the 32nd floor. _____

_____

10. Classes will begin on September 5. That is the day after Labor Day. _____

_____

Check your answers on page 483.

Part 2: Cross out the vague pronoun and replace it with more specific wording. Edit and change verb forms if necessary. Answers may vary.

Example: ~~They~~ The management require~~s~~ customers to wear shoes and shirts.

11. Ms. Meyers trained Ellen on the new computer program, and she did a good job.
12. They say our taxes were overpaid.
13. Tiffany told her mother that they were allowed to go.
14. Helen saw Patricia talking to her daughter. (Helen's daughter)
15. Mark met Frank while he was in college. (both were in college)
16. They say you must bring a textbook, notebook paper, and a folder to class.
17. Leslie's mother is a beautiful woman, and I'm sure she'll be a beauty too.
18. Tim was a track star in high school; it was a sport he loved.
19. You are not allowed to smoke in the theater.
20. Lance's father, is a carpenter, and he will be able to build the cabinet you want.

Check your answers on page 483.

REPLAY DRILL 12-C: MISPLACED WORDS AND PARALLEL PARTS

Underline the misplaced words in the following sentences.

Example: Thelma played a hymn in church <u>by Mozart</u>.

1. Throw over the fence some hay.

2. The mother sang a lullaby with a beautiful voice.

3. The mirror was returned by the customer with the crack in the middle.

4. The ice cream was gobbled down by the children with the chocolate swirls.

5. My bike is in the garage with two flat tires.

6. The parking lot was repaved by the contractor with the speed bumps.

7. The dog buried its bone with the furry tail.

8. The student came to the school with no textbooks.

9. The rosebush was pruned by the gardener with the thorns.

10. Sally searched for her purse in the English classroom, which was misplaced this afternoon.

Check your answers on page 484.

Part 2: If the following sentences need parallel parts, write (NP). If the sentence is correct, write (C).

Example: Susan has red hair, fair skin, and is heavily built. C

11. Amanda is an attorney, spends time cooking, and she loves to ski.

12. My uncle is a chef and an ambulance driver.

13. Bob would rather travel by train or by bus.

14. The crowd was noisy and the music played loudly.

15. Laurie is an honor society member, a cheerleader, and sings in the school choral group.

16. The third baseman ran to first, slid into second, and scored the winning run.

17. Polly jogged down the street, across the boulevard, and over the bridge to her mother's house.

18. The play was entertaining, made us laugh, and was mysterious.

19. The research specialist's talk was motivating and challenged us.

20. You must write clearly and with conciseness.

Answers are on page 484.

REPLAY DRILL 12-D: ACTIVE AND PASSIVE VERBS

Decide if the following sentences are examples of active style (A) or passive style (P).

Example: Jonah typed the letter. A

1. The supervisor announced the new work schedule.

2. The compositions were corrected by the teacher.

3. The farmer collected antique tractors.

4. The man's name was mispronounced by all the speakers.

5. John threw the softball to his daughter.

6. The staff flew to Denver for the convention.

7. Her luggage was lost by the airline.

8. Richard wallpapered the bathroom.

9. The airline lost Bernadette's suitcase.

10. The telephone was answered by the department manager.

11. The cafeteria is serving your favorite dessert.

12. Too many "you knows" were used throughout the speech.

13. You should mail those contracts to the new address.

14. Last year the electric company increased rates to its residential customers.

15. The radiologist read the patient's X-ray.

16. Several mistakes were found by the editors.

17. The seminar was conducted by the personnel department.

18. The reporter presented the top news story.

19. Our company was outsold by the competition.

20. Mr. Bell coaches his son's Little League team.

Check your answers on page 484.

REPLAY DRILL 12-E: CORRECTING DANGLERS

Underline the dangler in the following sentences. If the sentence does not have a dangler write (C).

Example: While walking through the park, the wind blew my hat into the bushes.

1. Having taken too many sick days, the supervisor was forced to fire Ralph.

2. Because Ralph took too many sick days, the supervisor was forced to fire him.

3. Biting quickly on the bait, the young fisherman caught his first fish.

4. When the fish bit on the bait, the young fisherman caught his first fish.

5. The teacher read from his old textbook, which was torn around the edges.

6. Torn around the edges, the teacher read from his old textbook.

7. Sitting on the windowsill, Ms. Williams watered the geraniums.

8. Ms. Williams watered the geraniums, which were sitting on the windowsill.

9. His mother gave John, who received good grades, tickets to a rock concert.

10. Having received good grades, his mother gave John tickets to a rock concert.

11. Being on the discount table, Ms. Jefferies saved $10 on the new gloves.

12. Ms. Jefferies saved $10 on the new gloves that were on the discount table.

13. Feeling as though labor had begun, Debbie asked her husband to take her to the hospital.

14. Feeling as though labor had begun, her husband took Debbie to the hospital.

15. Jogging quickly around the block, her new shoes hurt her feet.

16. While Janice was jogging around the block, her new shoes hurt her feet.

17. Before going home, this account must be audited.

18. Before you go home, this account must be audited.

19. After browsing through the store, the clerk rang up my purchases.

20. When I finished browsing through the store, the clerk rang up my purchases.

Check your answers on page 484.

CHAPTER 13: WRITING WORKPLACE COMMUNICATIONS

REPLAY DRILL 13-A: WRITING AND FORMATTING

Place a T before true statements and an F before false ones.

1. It is best to revise and correct errors while writing a first draft. _____

2. A paragraph can be no longer than one or two sentences. _____

3. The date in a letter should reflect the day it is written whether or not it is sent the same day. _____

4. International and military style place the month before the day when writing the date. _____

5. Official state abbreviations are never used in the inside address. _____

6. Double spacing between paragraphs eliminates the need to indent the first line of each new paragraph. _____

7. Modern business writers try to learn the name of the person they are writing to instead of writing to the attention of a department. _____

8. It is inappropriate to use a friendly tone in business communications if you do not know the person well. _____

9. Since the age of word processing, it is incorrect to add postscripts except to attract attention. _____

10. A blind copy notation always appears on the original copy of the letter. _____

11. Email is used much more frequently than printed memorandums today. _____

12. "Herewith, please find" is a perfectly appropriate way to open a communication when you are sending an enclosure or attachment. _____

13. Include your company name in the signature block of a letter, whether or not it is printed on the letterhead. _____

14. The opening and closing paragraphs are often the longest ones in a letter. _____

15. Using long, sophisticated words impresses the receiver of the letter. _____

16. You have no control over whether or not an email you send is forwarded to others. _____

17. Text message shorthand is not appropriate for business email except in very informal situations. _____

18. The complimentary close is a traditional way to end letters and is no longer used today. _____

19. The official job title or department name appears directly above the writer's typed name. _____

20. When the first line of the inside address is Mr. John Brown, an appropriate salutation would usually be "Dear Sir." _____

Check your answers on page 484.

REPLAY DRILL 13-B: STYLE AND TONE IN WRITING

Find the redundant and out-of-date expressions in the following letter and rewrite it in a current style. Correct any formatting, punctuation, or usage errors you find. See the example on page 275. Answers will vary.

March 25 20xx
Mr. John Smith
Jack's Jewels
246 Elm Drive
Akron, OH, 44624

Dear Mr. Smith,
    I am writing to inform you that we are in receipt of your recent letter dated February 26 of 20xx. It is always a pleasure to hear from such a valued customer. In the aforementioned letter you stated that you were unhappy with our shipment # HN2468297 containing the 50 plain blue gift boxes that you did not order. We submit our heartfelt apology for this unfortunate error. We will make every possible effort to rectify it. Our shipping department will make every effort to send you the correct gift boxes in due course of time with

your store name embossed that you requested. I personally believe that this can be taken care of in a speedy fashion to everyone's satisfaction.

Hoping to hear from you soon, I remain,

Faithfully yours,

Robert Orderly
Sales Manager

See a possible revision on page 485; yours may vary.

REPLAY DRILL 13-C: POLISHED WRITING

Proofread and correct the following letter. Remember to proofread for sense while you correct the word and punctuation errors.

Dear Ms. Jackson:

You're Oct. issue of TODAY'S BUSINESS is now on the way to you at your new address in Brooklyn. As our way of apologizeing for the delay we are extending your subscription by 3 months without charge.

Though an over-sight your letter of 9/25 requesting us to change your address from Philadelphia, Pennsylvania to Brooklyn, New York was not properly processed. As a result your copies' of Today's Business was still being sent to Brooklyn for the passed few months.

Please let us know on the enclose card if the misaddressed copys were forwarded to you. If knot, please check the blanks showing which issue's you did'nt recieve.

Sincerely yours

See a possible revision on page 485; yours may vary.

CHAPTER 14: WRITING FOR MULTIMEDIA

REPLAY DRILL 14-A: PLANNING A PRESENTATION

List five things you consider in planning a presentation.

1. _____

2. _____

3. _____

4. _____

5. _____

What is the traditional three-part structure used to prepare the content of a speech?

6. _____

7. _____

8. _____

What are labels for these three parts?

9. _____

Summarize three things that you need to practice:

10. _____

Check your answers on page 486.

REPLAY DRILL 14-B WRITING FOR THE WEB

List four steps to planning text you will write for a Web site.

1. _____

2. _____

3. _____

4. _____

Answers are on page 486.

Change these boring statements and phrases written for Web text to active, engaging phrases:

5. A trip like none you have ever experienced before _____

6. We can offer you a service that will allow you to plan more leisure time

_____

7. If we don't have the rare book you're looking for listed here, we can find it at no cost. _____

Suggested answers are on page 486.

What are three special considerations for visitors viewing Web content?

8. _____

9. _____

10. _____

Check your answers on page 486.

APPENDIX D MINI-REFERENCE MANUAL

NUMBERS

Numbers are important to business, professional, and technical writing. Write them in figures on invoices, orders, requisitions, statistical documents, and tables within written documents. The following information—a consensus of the style used by most business writers—enables you to decide whether to spell out a number or use figures in emails, memos, letters, reports, and other workplace documents.

1. **General**

a. Use words for figures zero through ten; use figures for specific numbers over ten. If numbers under ten and over ten are used in a related way, use figures for all.

> We need **five** computer engineers in our Akron office.

> We need **5** computer engineers, **25** clerks, and **30** assemblers in our Cleveland office.

b. Spell out or use figures for approximate numbers that can be written in one or two words.

> Nearly **five thousand** employees were laid off last year due to downsizing.

> We have hired over **two hundred** new employees this year and have developed **104** new products. [It would also be correct to use figures for both numbers.]

> **BUT**

> Our estimate is that more than 250,000 people per year will visit our Web site.

c. When a number begins a sentence, spell it out if you can do so in one or two words. If more than two words are required, rephrase the sentence.

> **Six hundred** crates were shipped to you yesterday.

> Yesterday **642** crates were shipped to you.

d. To express millions or billions, combine figures with words to make reading easier.

> We produced **1.5 million** electric fans last year.

> Our gross profit last year was **$66 million.**

e. When two numbers appear together, spell out the number that can be written with fewer letters.

> Lloyd designed **twenty 16**-unit apartment buildings.
>
> Frank designed **110 sixteen**-unit apartment buildings.

2. Time

a. Use figures with **a.m.** and **p.m.** Use figures or words before *o'clock, morning, afternoon,* and similar words. Type *a.m.* and *p.m.* in lowercase letters, with no space after the first period. For time on the hour, omit the colon and zeros.

> **YES**   The teleconference will take place from **9 a.m.** through **5:30 p.m.**
>
>   We should be there at **9 o'clock** in the evening.
>
> **NO**   nine p.m.
>
>   9:00 p.m.

b. Use just one way to express time; avoid redundancy.

> **YES**   9 a.m.
>
>   9 in the morning
>
>   nine o'clock in the morning
>
> **NO**   9 a.m. in the morning

3. Dates

a. Use figures if the date follows the name of the month; do not use *th, nd, rd,* or *st* after the figure.

> The American Bankers Association will meet here again on **May 7, 2011.**

b. In military, international, and some government correspondence, write the date before the month; do not use a comma in this style date.

> The International Bankers Association will meet in Oslo on **7 May 2004.**

c. Use words or figures for centuries and decades.

> This book is about nineteenth-century poets. [or 19th-century poets]

d. Do not use an apostrophe when referring to a period of years in numbers.

> The 1990s **not** 1990's

4. Money

a. Use figures for amounts of money. The decimal point is unnecessary with even dollar amounts (no cents).

> Eduardo paid $500 to join and $25.50 a month to exercise at the gym.
>
> They need about $150,000 to remodel the gym.

b. Use a dollar sign and decimal point for cents to be consistent with other amounts used in the same context. If other amounts are not involved, use figures for the number but spell out the word *cents.*

> We sold **1,000** cookies at **$.25** each, **42** pies at **$7.80** each, and two big cakes at **$50** each.
>
> The plugs cost **8 cents** each.

c. In legal documents amounts are often spelled and then written in figures enclosed in parentheses. In ordinary correspondence, do not repeat numbers in this legal style.

The fee for use of said property is to be **Two Hundred and Fifty Dollars ($250.00)** a month.

BUT

We paid **$250** for those tickets.

5. **Addresses**

a. For numbered street names follow the exact style as written by the correspondent or municipality.

> The store is on **Sixth Street.**

> Professor Maxey of Oroville moved to **11th Avenue** in Newport.

b. Use figures for address numbers except One.

> Their new suite of offices is at **One Lake Street.**

> The Atlanta factory is at **8 Leland Avenue.**

6. **Percentages and Fractions**

a. Spell out *percent,* but use figures for the number (use the % sign in statistical and technical documents and in tables).

> The unemployment rate was **5 percent** that year.

b. Spell out a common fraction when it is the only one in the sentence. Use figures for less common fractions or when several fractions are in a sentence.

> We have received only **one-fourth** of our order.

> The specifications for the blue widgets are **3/8** of an inch and for the purple widgets, **4/5** of an inch.

c. Use figures for a mixed number (fraction and whole number).

> Our profits are **4 1/2** times those of last year.

7. **Measurements**

a. Express fractions in measurements as numerals or decimals; be consistent in each document.

> Please purchase **5 1/2** more yards of fabric. [or 5.5]

b. In business letters and reports, spell out measuring words, such as *feet, pounds,* and *inches;* use figures for the numbers.

> The boards are **5 by 6 by 2 inches.** [Use *by,* not *x.*]

> Each one weighs **6 pounds 4 ounces** and is **8 feet** long.

c. When abbreviations for measures are used, do not end them with a period.

> lbs   ft   yds

8. **Age**

Usually spell out an age expressed in years only—unless it immediately follows a person's name. Notice that no commas are needed in the third example, which illustrates age expressed in years as well as months and days.

> Mr. Weber will be **sixty-three** on the day his medal is presented.

> Carl Weber, **63,** will receive a Medal of Honor at the White House.

> The records show her age at death was **74 years 5 months and 6 days.**

9. **Books**

Use figures for numbers of pages, chapters, volumes, and so on.

> The information you need is on **page 46** in **Chapter 5.**

CAPITALIZATION

Always capitalize the first word of a sentence and proper nouns. These capitalization principles are discussed in Read 26. The following outlines additional rules.

1. General

a. Capitalize names of *specific* people, animals, places, days, months, holidays, religions, gods, documents, and historical events.

Joseph	United Airlines
Uganda	Veteran's Day
Declaration of Independence	Fabulous Forties
Wednesday	Atomic Age

b. Do not capitalize seasons.

fall   spring   winter   summer

c. Capitalize titles and headings but only the first word of an item in an outline or list. Use lowercase for short prepositions, articles, *to* in infinitives, and the conjunctions *and* or *or* unless one of these words begins the sentence.

Titles or Headings: How to Cook with Electricity

Outlines or Lists: **I.** How to cook with electricity

2. Titles of People

a. Capitalize a title that directly precedes a person's name.

Professor Washington   Reverend Juan Perez   Madame Curie

b. Do not capitalize the title if a comma separates it from the name.

Our English professor, Dolores Denova, is . . .

The captain, Patrick O'Connor, seemed . . .

c. Do not capitalize occupational titles when used generally; do capitalize them when they identify a person's job title directly after the name.

My accountant is also an attorney.

Joy Reid, Manager of Production, has been with the company for 20 years.

3. Titles of Publications and Artistic Works

a. Capitalize the first word and all principal words of titles of books, films, plays, songs, and so on. Do not capitalize short prepositions (such as *in*, *on*, *of*) or conjunctions (such as *and, but, or*) unless they have four or more letters or are the first word of a title or subtitle. Do not capitalize articles (*a, an, the*) unless they are the first word of a title or subtitle.

I saw the movie *Gone With the Wind*.

The best-selling book that year was *To Kill a Mockingbird*.

Chapter 8 is entitled "The Taming of the Apostrophe."

"The Star Spangled Banner" is the national anthem of the United States.

4. Names of Organizations

a. Capitalize names of organizations and specific government groups.

Supreme Court	Fullerton College
Palm Springs Tennis Club	Department of Motor Vehicles
Royal Canadian Air Force	Arkansas Paper Mill

b. Except in legal documents and formal communications, do not capitalize words like *company, department, college* when not part of a name.

> Melissa and Steven attend Seattle court reporting **schools**.
>
> This **company** will not issue common stock this year, but Knott **Company** will.
>
> Give the papers to the **committee** at the **college**.

c. Capitalize specific names of departments within organizations but do not capitalize general references.

> Our **Shipping Department** packed the order and shipped it via FedEx.
>
> Do not send a resume to **human resources** without a specific individual's name.

5. **Names of Places**

Capitalize official names of specific places, but do not capitalize general terms.

> Charleston   **BUT**   We're going to the **city** of Charleston for the weekend.
>
> Victory Boulevard   **BUT**   Our house is the first street after the main **boulevard**.
>
> The Atlantic Ocean   **BUT**   North America lies between two **oceans**.
>
> Yosemite National Park   **BUT**   We vacationed in a **national park** last year.

6. **Regional Names**

a. Capitalize regional names when they refer to specific geographical regions. Do not capitalize such terms when they are used to indicate general locations.

> Far East   West Coast   Midwest
>
> The sun sets in the **west**.
>
> Drive **south** along Main Street.
>
> He would like to settle in **Southern** California. [Names a specific region.]

b. Capitalize derivatives of regional names referring to people.

> I believe **Northerners** usually appreciate **Southern** hospitality.

7. **Trade Names**

Capitalize the trade name of a product; write trade names exactly as they are written by the company. Do not capitalize general references to the product when they appear with the name.

> Do you like **Pizza Hut's** pizzas?
>
> Do you like **Dunkin' Donuts** coffee?

8. **Family Relationships**

a. Capitalize a family relationship title when used as part of the name or instead of the name. Do not capitalize general references to family titles.

> Do you think **Uncle George** will retire soon?
>
> Do you think **Uncle** will retire soon?
>
> My **mother** teaches at the university.
>
> I believe my **cousin** Esther should apply for the job.

9. **Course Names and Education Degrees**

a. Capitalize official names of courses. Do not capitalize the name of a subject or course that isn't the official name—except languages, which are always capitalized.

> Professors Denova, Hixon, and Shay will teach Business 31 this year.
>
> Professor Dennison was asked to teach a business English course next year.

Do you plan to take a Spanish or business law class next year?

b. Capitalize the name of a spelled-out degree directly after a person's name—or anywhere in a sentence if abbreviated. Do not capitalize a spelled-out degree unless it immediately follows the person's name. Notice the comma before and after the degree following a name.

Sarala Chandra, **PhD**, specializes in management of nonprofit organizations.

Jonathan Waller has a **master of arts** degree in speech pathology.

Nina Chandra's **BS** is in animal husbandry.

With an associate's level degree such as an **AA** or **AS**, you can qualify for many good jobs.

Sean S. Chandra, **Doctor of Jurisprudence**, is the newest Supreme Court judge.

10. Racial and Ethnic Terms

a. Capitalize names of nationalities and religions.

Dutch   Korean   British   Catholic   Hindu   Jewish

b. Capitalize names of races except for races named by a color.

Asian   African American   Caucasian   **BUT**   black   white

ABBREVIATIONS

Spelling words out instead of abbreviating them helps create an image of thoroughness, carefulness, and accuracy; **when in doubt**, **spell it out**. In workplace letters and reports, avoid abbreviations except as shown following. Abbreviations are appropriate, however, in very informal communications, telephone messages, catalogs, statistical reports, and business forms such as invoices and orders.

1. Abbreviations in Business Letters and Reports

a. Spell out an abbreviation or acronym the first time it is used and follow it with the abbreviation in parentheses. Thereafter in the same document, use just the abbreviation or acronym.

Wide Area Information Systems (WAIS)

b. Names of well-known organizations may be abbreviated without being spelled out in all but the most formal documents. Do not, however, abbreviate unless you're sure the reader will understand. Spelling out these abbreviations (as in *a* above) may be required for international communications.

AT&T   CIA   FBI   AFL-CIO   CBS

c. Always abbreviate the following titles: *Mr., Ms., Dr., Jr., Sr., Esq., PhD, CPA,* and other academic degrees following names. In workplace writing it is customary to use *Mr.* or *Ms. Miss* and *Mrs.* to indicate marital status are considered outdated.

Ronald Rosenberg, Esq.   Ms. Sarala Waller   Dr. Spencer Blackman

Note: In the United States, *Esq.* (Esquire) is used only after an attorney's name—either male or female. In Great Britain, however, *Esq.* is a courtesy title equivalent to *Mr.* but used *after* a man's name regardless of occupation.

d. Spell out other professional, military, and religious titles in written text.

The Reverend Jonathan Flaherty

Captain Jeffrey Ortiz

Professor Mildred Murphy

e. Abbreviate references to time periods and eras.

CE and BCE are contemporary forms of AD and BC (without religious connotation). Choose one set or the other for consistency.

CE Common Era	**OR**	AD in the year of our Lord
BCE before the Common Era	**OR**	BC before Christ

Place the abbreviations after the year:

10 BC   1059 AD

f. Abbreviate parts of company names such as *Inc.*, *Co.*, or *Ltd.* when they appear in the official spelling.

Marco's Painting Co.

Turner Broadcasting Systems, Inc.

g. Spell out words used to designate parts of addresses: *Street, Avenue,* or *Boulevard* and names of cities.

h. Spell out state names in written text; abbreviate them or spell out in the inside address of letters. Use the two-letter state abbreviations on envelopes (see page 419).

2. **Commonly Used Business Abbreviations and Acronyms**

a. These abbreviations are acceptable in most workplace documents. Many are written with or without periods. The trend is to omit periods. Some of the following are acceptable in capital or lowercase; for example cod or COD (collect on delivery).

CEO	chief executive officer
CFO	chief financial officer
CFP	certified financial planner
COB	close of business
COD	collect, or cash, on delivery
CPA	certified public accountant
EEO	equal employment opportunity
e.g.	for example
etc.	and so on (preferred)
Ext., ext., or ex.	when followed by a number for a telephone extension (Ext. 32)
FAQ	frequently asked questions
FAX	facsimile copy
FOB	free on board (the point from which the customer pays shipping charges)
GDP	gross domestic product
HRD	human resources department
ID	identification
Inc., Corp., or Ltd.	when part of a company name (incorporated, corporation, limited)
IRS	Internal Revenue Service
MIS	management information systems

PO Box	Post Office Box No. 0000 (as part of a mailing address)
PR	public relations
PS	postscript
RE	regarding or concerning
R&D	research and development
RSVP	Respond (translated from French—*Répondez s'il vous plaît*)
SEC	Securities and Exchange Commission
VIP	very important person

b.   The following abbreviations are usually spelled out in the body of a business letter or in a formal report, but are often abbreviated in less formal documents.

acct.	or a/c account
amt.	amount
anon.	anonymous, nameless
ARM	adjustable rate mortgage
ASAP	as soon as possible
assn. or assoc.	association
bal.	balance
b.l., b/l, or B/L	bill of lading
BTW or btw (email only)	by the way
c/o	care of
ctn.	carton
cwt.	hundredweight
e.g.	for example
ESL	English as a second language
et al.	and others
frt.	freight
ft	foot or feet
FYI (email or memo)	for your information
g	gram
gal	gallon
GNP	gross national product
i.e.	that is
lb	pound
mfr.	manufacturer
misc.	miscellaneous
p. or pp.	page or pages
pd.	paid
PLC	public limited company (British equivalent of U.S. corporation)
rec'd	received

viz.	namely
vs.	versus
yd	yard

3. Abbreviations of Academic Degrees

Abbreviate an academic degree when it follows a person's name. The periods may be omitted. When spelled out, use lowercase letters.

His AA degree qualifies him for the job. She has a bachelor of science degree. Jose Hernandez, D.D.S., will speak on dental health.

AA	associate in arts (two-year degree)
AS	associate in science (two-year degree)
BA or AB	bachelor of arts
BBA	bachelor of business administration
BS	bachelor of science
DD	doctor of divinity
DDS	doctor of dental surgery or of dental science
EdD	doctor of education
JD	doctor of jurisprudence
JM	master of jurisprudence
LLB	bachelor of laws
MA	master of arts
MBA	master of business administration
MD	doctor of medicine
MS	master of science
PhD	doctor of philosophy

4. Two-letter State Abbreviations

Alabama	AL
Alaska	AK
Arizona	AZ
Arkansas	AR
California	CA
Colorado	CO
Connecticut	CT
Delaware	DE
District of Columbia	DC
Florida	FL
Georgia	GA
Hawaii	HI
Idaho	ID
Illinois	IL
Indiana	IN
Iowa	IA
Kansas	KS

Kentucky	KY
Louisiana	LA
Maine	ME
Maryland	MD
Massachusetts	MA
Michigan	MI
Minnesota	MN
Mississippi	MS
Missouri	MO
Montana	MT
Nebraska	NE
Nevada	NV
New Hampshire	NH
New Jersey	NJ
New Mexico	NM
New York	NY
North Carolina	NC
North Dakota	ND
Ohio	OH
Oklahoma	OK
Oregon	OR
Pennsylvania	PA
Rhode Island	RI
South Carolina	SC
South Dakota	SD
Tennessee	TN
Texas	TX
Utah	UT
Vermont	VT
Virginia	VA
Washington	WA
West Virginia	WV
Wisconsin	WI
Wyoming	WY

Territories

Canal Zone	CZ
Puerto Rico	PR
Guam	GU
Virgin Islands	VI

LETTER STYLES

Stationery

Type business letters on quality 8 1/2-by-11-inch letterhead stationery and mail them in matching envelopes (where available). White or off-white paper is most appropriate.

Letter Styles

a. **Block Letter Style—See page 275**
b. **Modified-Block Letter Style**

In the following letter, modified-block layout is used. This format is explained in the letter.

Business Training, Inc.
209 W. 66th Street
New York, NY 10023
212.000.000
www.businesstraining.xxx

March 10, 20xx

Keisha Mary Washington
Executive Assistant to the
President of the United States
The White House
Washington, DC 20500

Dear Ms Washington:

In the modified-block letter, the date and closing begin at about the horizontal center of the line. The first word of each paragraph may begin at the left margin as in this letter, or it may be indented five to ten spaces for a more conservative look. We recommend using block paragraphs for the more current look shown here. Please note that all other spacing and placement of letter elements are the same as the more widely used block letter style.

Some people prefer modified-block format because it is more conservative and traditional looking than the block style. Therefore, modified-block may suggest a more appropriate image for your fiscal policies or political philosophy.

Congratulations on being named executive assistant to the President of the United States of America. I hope this information helps you respond to the many letters your office receives from the people of America.

Respectfully,

Savannah G. Bourne

Savannah G. Bourne
President

lrs

---

c. **Summary of Letter Placement**

- Use a standard font for business letters; 12 point Times New Roman is recommended.
- Use margins of about 1 inch to 1 1/4 inches left and right. Avoid right-margin justification (all lines ending at exactly the same point).
- Leave a bottom margin of at least 1 inch.
- Type the date two or three spaces below the letterhead.
- Spell out the month in the date
- You can improve the appearance of especially short letters by adding an extra blank line or two before and/or after the date and by enlarging the margins.
- To fit long letters on one page, decrease the left and right margins to about 3/4 of an inch (0.75).
- To center short or long letters, reduce or enlarge the font size and/or change the font style to one providing either more or fewer characters to the inch.
- For letters of two or more pages, type a heading with the recipient's name, page number, and date beginning 1 inch from the top of the second (and succeeding) pages.

  Ms. Betty G. Dillard
  page 2
  January 4, 20xx

- Print second pages on plain paper (without letterhead) matching the quality and color of the letterhead stationery.

ENVELOPES

a. **Addressing Envelopes**

- Most business letters are mailed in business envelopes known as No. 9 or No. 10.
- Most organizations use envelopes with a printed return address. If you do not have preprinted envelopes, single space the sender's name and address to print in the upper left corner of the envelope.
- Single space the recipient's address; use either the envelope default placement or begin at about the center of the envelope.
- Take a moment now to look at the stationery and envelope samples on pages 423 and 424.

b. **Folding Letters**

- When folding a letter to place in an envelope, you want the top to open first. To achieve this, fold the 8 1/2- by-11-inch sheet in thirds as follows: Bring the bottom third of the letter up, and make a crease. Then fold the top of the letter down, but stop a fraction of an inch before the crease you already made. Now make the second crease. Holding the second crease, insert the letter into the envelope. The idea is to have the top of the letter unfold first.
- Take a moment now to fold a sheet of 8 1/2- by-11-inch paper.

Nintendo

Nintendo of America Inc.

4820 150th Avenue N.E.
P.O. Box 957
Redmond, Washington
98052-5111 U.S.A.
Telephone: 206 882-2040
Telex: 152933
Fax: 206 882-3585

GUESS?, INC.

NIKE

ANGELES, CALIFORNIA 90021 • PHONE (213) 765-3100
LOC ANGELES, CALIFORNIA 90079 • PHONE (213) 312-3500

One Bowerman Drive
Beaverton, OR 97005-6453

Knott's
BERRY FARM.

8039 Beach Boulevard
P.O. Box 5002
Buena Park, California 90622-5002

NIKE, Inc.
One Bowerman Drive
Beaverton, OR 97005-6453

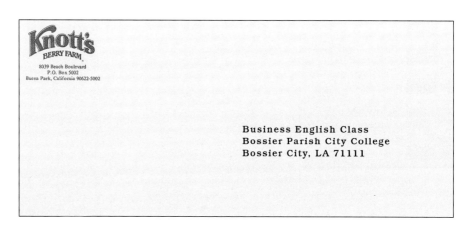

EDITING AND PROOFREADING GUIDELINES

Editing Paragraphs and Sentences

After writing and revising a drafted document to fix general problems of organization and content, review each paragraph to look for ways to improve the details of the message.

■ Does the opening paragraph capture the reader's attention?

■ Does it clearly state the purpose?

■ Does it focus on the reader's point of view?

■ Do middle paragraphs state a main point and develop it logically?

■ Do paragraphs contain sentences that form a clear organizational structure and logical flow of ideas?

■ Is the last paragraph a concise conclusion?

■ Does it leave the reader with an understanding of how to respond?

Editing Grammar and Sentence Structure

Review each sentence critically and look for the following:

- Are sentences grammatically complete? Are there run-on sentences, comma splices, or sentence fragments?
- Are phrases and clauses arranged to emphasize the most important ideas? Would some ideas come across more effectively if they were moved to the beginning or the end of the sentence?
- Are modifying words, phrases, and clauses as close as possible to the sentence elements they modify?
- Are series of elements and listed items expressed in parallel structure?
- Is there variation in sentence length and structure?
- Are there places where sentences in succession all have the same structure?
- Are sentences too long or too short?
- Is the same rhythm repeated without variety, creating a monotonous tone?
- Are most sentences in the active voice?
- Is the passive voice used appropriately for emphasis?
- Use the active voice most of the time, but not all the time.

Editing Words

Consider the individual words and ask these questions:

- Does each word contribute to clarifying the message?
- Are there "wordy" phrases that could be more concise?
- Are words in the proper order? (Sometimes word order is inadvertently changed while revising.)
- Is word usage precise and appropriate?
- Does the choice of words fit the intended tone and degree of formality?
- Are pronoun references clear? Do you need to remove a pronoun and repeat the reference, provide a missing reference, or revise a sentence to avoid pronoun confusion?
- Are there any "big words" that should be replaced with more common terminology for clarity?
- Are there any technical words, abbreviations, or business jargon that the reader might not understand?
- Are there any negative words that could be changed to make your message sound more positive?
- Do any words reflect bias or other lack of consideration for the reader?

Final Proofreading

A good technique for uncovering errors you missed in previous readings is to read each sentence out loud to yourself or with a partner. Be alert for:

- Typographical or spelling errors
- Omitted words
- Grammar, punctuation, and capitalization errors
- Word usage errors

Accuracy and consistency

■ Are figures, names, and numerical data correct and consistent?

■ Is information such as dates and times correct?

Format and appearance

■ Does the document have the standard elements required?

■ Are the elements formatted correctly?

■ Are spacing and margins correct and consistent?

This is a rehearsal for your final exam. Before you begin, review your scores on the Practice Quizzes and use the recommended Self-Study Practice and Tutorial materials where you need extra practice. Then correct the following sentences based on what you have studied in the 14 chapters of this text. Use proofreading marks to correct these errors or write C beside the sentences that are already correct.

Please don't change words because you think other words might "sound better"; correct specific errors only. Many sentences have more than one error. For sentences that may be corrected in more than one way; choose the simplest way.

_____ 1. The sidewalks of Paris are an art display in theirself.

_____ 2. The passer by throw coins to the musicians who especially pleases them.

_____ 3. One of the most spectacular sights are the light demonstration at Notre Dame.

_____ 4. *Per annum* is Latin for *by the day*.

_____ 5. An overdue amount that is unpaid is *in arrears.*

_____ 6. Donald's father-in-law, in addition to his brother-in-laws, has encourage him to train for a triathlon.

_____ 7. Watterson's student's wrote good storys about they childhood.

_____ 8. Although many students already have good English skills, and do not require this practice.

_____ 9. For some students' however, learning to use verbs according to Standard English can make a big differents in career potential.

_____ 10. Neither Ben nor he know the the names of the witnesses we subpoenaed.

_____ 11. I saw the man today whom they say will be the new CEO.

_____ 12. The smallest unit of space in a computer image is called a pixel.

_____ 13. I told Seinfeld that you done the work good and had come to work on time everyday.

_____ 14. Most business-people want their business to be insolvent.

_____ 15. If you was him, you would have axed her for a specific meeting date.

_____ 16. He dont plan to give you excess to your text book during the final exam.

_____ 17. Mathematics is important to every one but each department most choose their own coarses.

_____ 18. A chart and a photograph was in the file.

_____ 19. "A adverb describes a verb, a adjective, or another adverb," said the instructor."

_____ 20. Each one of us have succeeded.

_____ 21. The defendant has no liability; consequently you have no chance of recovering any of your losses.

_____ 22. The title page of a report include the reports title, it's author, the name of the person or organization for who the report is prepared and the date its to be submitted.

_____ 23. The plural form of *appendix* can be spelled two ways: *appendixes* or *appendices*. (Use italics if typed; quotation marks are also correct.)

_____ 24. Some reports also have a preface it comes before the introduction.

_____ 25. A reports introduction sets the stage that is, it tells readers what the report contains

_____ 26. A upper birth on a ship is less comfortable than a lower berth.

_____ 27. Do you know whose in charge of this company

_____ 28. He was using a common idiot when the said "I wouldn't touch this job with a 10 foot foot pole."

_____ 29. *Mischievous* is correctly pronounced with four syllables.

_____ 30. Their planning to expand the Teaneck New Jersey plant.

_____ 31. Of the two applicants we're considering, the first one seems best qualified.

_____ 32. He dug and hoed his little field and planted sweet potatoes.

_____ 33. "Good morning, Little Red Riding Hood," said the big bad wolf.

_____ 34. Please deliver them packages before April 1 which is her birthday.

_____ 35. Savanna replied by just saying, "Good-bye."

_____ 36. He conducts training for YMCAs all over the country.

_____ 37. *Lien* rhymes with *seen.*

_____ 38. Thank you for sending us the free gift.

_____ 39. Judging by his passed performance, he is a "gem."

_____ 40. Each one of us have succeeded.

_____ 41. My brakes suddenly stopped working while driving to the conference.

_____ 42. The senator's campaign has elicited the support of womens organizations.

_____ 43. Just to stand up in the face of lifes problems. That takes courage.

_____ 44. While opening a can of juice his hand was cut real bad.

_____ 45. The staff go on a retreat each August.

_____ 46. Many alumnus attended the home coming game and dance.

_____ 47. Three items—the bookcase, cash register, and display rack—are not for sale.

_____ 48. Because I forgot to punch the time card, the manager docked my pay.

_____ 49. While going over the work carefully, she found a major error.

_____ 50. The native food tasted strangely to the American tourists.

_____ 51. Some reports have a title page it precedes the Contents page.

_____ 52. The boss's memo said, "Please print the report, write a cover memo, and leave it on his desk.

_____ 53. The term *arrears* applies to an unpaid bill.

_____ 54. Time between starting a task and completing it is called "turnaround time."

_____ 55. I am writing to let you know that we received the packet yesterday and are indeed grateful to you for sending us the information.

_____ 56. A pledge of property as security for a loan is a mortgage.

_____ 57. Pronounce _affluent_ with the accent on the second syllable.

_____ 58. The correct pronunciation of _versatile_ is with the accent on the first syllable.

_____ 59. Use a thesaurus to find definitions when you're not sure of the meaning of a word.

_____ 60. _Etymology_ is the history of computer.

_____ 61. Diacritical marks in the dictionary show how a word is spelled.

_____ 62. Because of a misunderstanding we lost the customer and discharged one of our best sales reps.

_____ 63. If you don't know where you're going, youll probably end up somewhere else.

_____ 64. The general costs of running a business, such as taxes, rent, and heating, are called the markup.

_____ 65. A analasis of the discrepencys prooved disaterous. An analysis of the discrepancies proved disastrous.

_____ 66. The children were told to sit quiet and read his or her books.

_____ 67. After adjusting the carburetor, the car ran smooth.

_____ 68. Are all employees required to have lunch in the employees' cafeteria

_____ 69. Punctuation marks act like road signs they tell us when to slow down, and when to stop.

_____ 70. Antonyms are words with similar meanings.

_____ 71. _We, us, I, he, she, you_ are examples of personal pronouns.

_____ 72. The State and Federal governments is helping people get access to higher education.

_____ 73. Your speaking style is clear, forceful, and pleasant.

_____ 74. "Why did the peanut cross the road "asked Professor Johnson

_____ 75. "To get to the Shell station," replied the Delta students.

_____ 76. We visited a factory. It makes mobile phones.

_____ 77. Seattle is the closest of the two cities.

_____ 78. Upon what criterium did you base your opinions on?

_____ 79. The congregation were quiet while the rabbi spoke.

_____ 80. The coach trusted Leo and I to run the practice session while him and the assistant coach met with the principle.

_____ 81. Mathematics are my favorite subject.

_____ 82. The plural of alumna is alumnas.

_____ 83. Everyone must make their own decision.

_____ 84. Whos laptop computer is missing?

_____ 85. Everybodys' going to the office party.

_____ 86. Whom did you say will handle the new account?

_____ 87. Him and me will report it to whomever is in charge.

_____ 88. Ms. Hermann explained that many fine people lived in Torrance now.

_____ 89. Accuracy in figures mark the expert accountant.

_____ 90. You have broke one of the rules.

_____ 91. I politely said, "Go home now."

_____ 92. Greta writes good.

_____ 93. I feel badly about wrecking my motorcycle.

_____ 94. These kind of games are to much like gambling.

_____ 95. We would sure like to meet him.

_____ 96. The butler stood at the doorway and called the guests' names.

_____ 97. Five minutes' planning can sometimes save an hours work.

_____ 98. He likes traveling, writing and to go on long walks.

_____ 99. Business is part of our society there is no escape.

_____ 100. Thomas Carlyle referred to music as the "speech of angels."

TRUE/FALSE

_____ 101. A letter should not be sent as an attachment to an email according to modern business standards.

_____ 102. A slide presentation with animation is always desirable.

_____ 103. "You'll lose your good credit rating if you don't send your check today" is good wording to persuade your customer to pay.

_____ 104. "Can you meet me at 10 a.m. tomorrow?" is an example of redundancy.

_____ 105. Even though a letter writer's name is typed at the end of the letter, it's necessary to include his or her handwritten signature.

_____ 106. A good formula for an oral presentation is:

     a. introduction: tell them what you're going to tell them

     b. body: tell them

     c. conclusion: tell them what you've told them

_____ 107. In the body of your presentation, avoid details such as how your plan would work and how it will save the company money.

_____ 108. To make a good impression, use as many big words and job-related technical vocabulary as you can during your presentation.

_____ 109. Users of Web pages have pretty much the same reading habits as readers of documents.

_____ 110. Trying to anticipate what a user of the Web wants to find is a lost cause, so just write what you think is best.

APPENDIX F RECAP AND REPLAY ANSWERS

CHAPTER 1

REPLAY 1

1. Answers will vary.
2. unabridged
3. abridged
4. college, pocket or handheld electronic
5. True
6. False
7. Standard English
8. archaic
9. copyright page
10. lexicographers

RECAP—READ 2

1. mu/ti/pli/(ca)/tion
2. mum/bo/(jum)/bo
3. lex/i/(cog)/ra/pher
4. col/(lo)/qui/al

REPLAY 2

1. x and s
2. three
3. first
4. third
5. second
6. verb
7. second
8. Answers will vary depending on the dictionary.
9. b
10. Answers will vary depending on the dictionary.
11. A secondary school that prepares students for attending a university
12. first
13. (sub)·tle, (ra)·tion·al, (in)·fra.struc.ture
14. catalogue   catalog   noun and verb

RECAP—READ 3

1. F
2. F
3. F

REPLAY 3

A.

1. T
2. T
3. F
4. F
5. F
6. T
7. F
8. T
9. F

Circle the following: pronounciation, seperate, reccomend, congradulate, persue, bachlor. Corrected spellings are—pronunciation, separate, recommend, congratulate, pursue, bachelor

B.

1. b
2. c
3. a
4. a
5. c

C.

1. weird
2. accommodate
3. bachelor
4. privilege
5. persistent
6. congratulate
7. pronunciation
8. recommend
9. embarrassed
10. pursued

D.

1. accommodations
2. indispensable
3. judgment
4. consensus
5. recurrence
6. acknowledgment

RECAP—READ 4

1. Answers will vary. Examples: matchless, unsurpassed
2. Answers will vary. Examples: unbelievable, implausible
3. Answers will vary. Examples: unpleasant, objectionable

REPLAY 4

1. Answers will vary. Examples: enjoyable, fine, pleasurable
2. Answers will vary. Examples: careless, foolhardy, rash
3. Answers will vary. Examples: experience, expertise
4. Answers will vary. Examples: displeased, annoyed, offended
5. five thousand

6. fifty

7. 11 percent

8. We flew on American Airlines last summer with the president of Israel and the senator from Maine.

9. The judge said that the Supreme Court decision was favorable to my company.

10. I will know Chinese well enough by September to take a university course in Chinese literature.

11. Securities and Exchange Commission

12. Chief Executive Officer

CHAPTER 2

REPLAY 5

1. verb
2. adjective
3. pronoun

4. interjection
5. conjunction
6. preposition

7. adverb
8. noun

RECAP—READ 6

1. bay
2. United States
3. baby
4. business
5. interviewers, applicants, energy, competence, loyalty, skill, ambition, flexibility
6. Answers will vary.
7. Answers will vary.

REPLAY 6

A.

1. smile, situation
2. correspondence, United States, Asia, South America, Europe, Africa
3. career, people, cultures, individuals
4. slang, coworkers, English, language
5. neighborhood, classroom, workplace, United States, Canada, Great Britain, parts, world

B.

1. It
2. He

3. Who
4. She, her

5. They, her, him

RECAP—READ 7

A. action verbs: wrote, proofread, received, looked, read, invited, has, helped
pronouns: He, it, it, she, it, she, she, She, who, her

B. being verbs: is, appears, am, sounds, were, seems, was, smells, feel, remains

RECAP

(does) enjoy   (has) stayed

(had) seen   (had) not greeted

(will) select   (is) planning

REPLAY 7

A.

1. is
2. seems
3. am, are

4. were
5. are, think is the action verb
6. sounds

7. appears, being

B.

1. do work, haven't met
2. has read
3. are reading

4. has chosen
5. will be going
6. will have been working

7. might have noticed
8. does sign

C. Sample answers:

1. need, have
2. spend

3. are asking
4. is

5. spend

D. Verbs:

1. are judged
2. is
3. has
4. do call, are, is
5. was
6. were typing
7. should have completed

8. should go
9. is known
10. will ask
11. have been sent
12. know, will represent
13. rescheduled
14. should deliver

15. is
16. will mail
17. received
18. checked
19. built
20. dressed

Nouns

1. Applicants, behavior, knowledge
2. Etiquette, part, activities, job
3. data, topic
4. clients, colleagues, names, organization
5. Sheila Danielle, winner, scholarship
6. secretaries, answers, blanks
7. job, Tuesday
8. conference, Las Vegas
9. husband, manager, courtesy
10. mail
11. Southeastern Community College
12. lawyer, building
13. Kelly Clarkson, performances, Europe
14. Larry, tickets
15. drawer, computer
16. receptionist, Monday
17. Aldrich Company
18. auditors, books, accuracy
19. contractor, factory, city, coast
20. children

Pronouns

1. Their, their
2. None
3. No one
4. Their, you, it your
5. none
6. None
7. Someone
8. Who
9. his
10. He
11. These
12. They, who, me
13. None
14. you
15. It
16. Their, these
17. everything
18. Our, everyone's
19. None
20. Themselves

RECAP—READ 8

1. idea, carpet, desk, fan
2. You, Ethics, Ms. Parks
3. building

RECAP

Sample answers:

1. yesterday, today, immediately
2. well, poorly, quickly
3. carefully, recklessly, fast
4. correctly, accurately, slowly, quickly
5. always

REPLAY 8

A.

Nouns: rooms, air-conditioning, windows, office, homes, street, tri-level, attorneys, firm, year
Limiting Adjectives: any, several, Some, Ten
Pointing Adjectives: These, That, this, this, this
Article: the

B.

1. an
2. an exclusive resort
3. the beautiful
4. the crystal blue
5. the white sand
6. exquisite guest
7. Mediterranean
8. luxurious
9. The, smogless, sunny, mild
10. this

C.

1. (Some) people in (that) room have (a good) attitude.
2. (This) morning I found (two) dimes near (a red) phone.
3. (These) companies bought (a new) computer for (every) manager.

D. Sample Answers

1. away, there
2. more, less
3. rarely, seldom, never
4. really, always, never
5. elegantly, tastefully
6. extremely, very, such
7. most, least
8. not, very, sometimes
9. usually, often, always
10. much, even

RECAP—READ 9

and, but, or, nor, for, yet, so

RECAP

Dependent conjunctions—if, because; coordinating conjunctions—but, or, and, and, and; conjunctive adverb—therefore

RECAP

1. you, plane, villa, mountain

2. _Filed_ is a verb and _to attend_ is an infinitive. A prepositional phrase begins with a preposition, ends with a noun or pronoun, and never includes a verb.

REPLAY 9

A. Sample answers:

1. nor
2. but
3. and, when
4. although
5. Since, while
6. and
7. until
8. If
9. because
10. or

B.

1. into
2. By
3. to
4. Through
5. Over
6. across

C.

1. in the workplace, of kindness and consideration, toward other employees and customers
2. on the behavior, of people, on their lifestyles
3. between a dream and a goal
4. from your office, to my home
5. at producing spot announcements for their customers

REPLAY 10

A.

1. verb   2. adjective   3. noun

B.

1. noun   2. verb   3. adjective

C.

1. Ozzie is reading a report from the president.
2. Reading is my favorite activity.
3. She needs new reading glasses.

D.

1. Let's plant roses and gardenias this year.
2. In our Seattle plant, we hire many environmentalists.

E.

1. adjectives
2. Young children are probably better off in the country than in the city. Answers will vary.

CHAPTER 3

RECAP—READ 11

A.

1. We
2. Ms. Hirsch
3. You
4. crime, punishment
5. They
6. companies
7. (understood you) (understood you)
8. he, Jonathan Edwards

B.

communication, is, to the nation's productivity

REPLAY 11

A.

1. director	could have filmed
2. You	must be
3. winner	sees
4. loser	sees
5. books	were put
6. you/you	earn/learn
7. members	have
8. visitors	arrived
9. (You)	give
10. Professor Friede	found

B.

(a) Independent: 1, 4, 6, 8 Dependent: 2, 3, 5, 7, 9, 10

(b) 2. —because   3. although   5. since   7. when   9. although   10. after

(c)

1. She couldn't arrange the reports in chronological order.

2. (Because) Many organizations have similar problems with employees.

3. (Although) An information technology professional needs excellent communication skills.

4. In the workplace you may converse with many people.

5. (Since) They have limited English skill.

6. Don't laugh at someone's pronunciation or grammar error.

7. (When) The trucker arrived with the shipment.

8. It's better than I thought.

9. (Although) She prefers driving to flying.

10. (After) You've learned a few phrases in other languages.

RECAP—READ 12

1. When she dines at the college cafe, the beans taste like caviar. (Answers will vary.)
2. The beans taste like caviar when she dines at the college cafe. (Answers will vary.)

REPLAY 12

A.

1. F	3. F	5. S	7. F	9. F
2. S	4. S	6. F	8. S	10. S

B.
1. If you do a good job on the Mendocino project, you will get a salary increase after the first of the month.
2. Although most corporations use the services of an auditor to examine the books, some errors may never be found.
3. Don't ever think that you know it all.
4. Because sexual harassment is illegal and immoral, Julia filed a complaint.
5. When Mr. Lopez became general manager, he asked the staff to greet Spanish-speaking customers in Spanish.

C.

1. F	3. F	5. S	7. S	9. S
2. F	4. S	6. F	8. F	10. S

D. Sample answers
1. The man whom we met yesterday in Fullerton is the treasurer of the Cambridge Corporation.
2. Our Human Resources Department is on the third floor.
3. Keisha, believing she was right, took the matter to the Human Resources Department.
6. Lester, having been on vacation last week, was shocked by the news.
8. The team that won all the games in Oklahoma City last year will be hard to beat.

REPLAY 13

1. R	7. C	13. C
2. C	8. CS	14. C
3. CS	9. C	15. C
4. C	10. C	
5. R	11. CS	
6. R	12. CS	

RECAP—READ 14

1. Don't fill a business letter with long sentences or with words of many syllables, for it doesn't impress anyone.
2. Don't fill a business letter with long sentences or with words of many syllables; it doesn't impress anyone.
3. Don't fill a business letter with long sentences or with words of many syllables. It doesn't impress anyone.

REPLAY 14

A.

1. CS   2. CS   3. R   4. C   5. R   6. C   7. CS

B.

1. CS—quickly, yet
2. CS—errors, so
3. R—floor, but
4. CS—once, and
5. R—conference, or
6. CS—bones, but
7. C
8. C

C.

1. however, therefore, for example, also, yet, then (answers vary)
2. True
3. False
4. True

D.

1. C
2. today; then
3. rehearsals; that is,
4. C
5. sleeps; consequently,
6. C

RECAP—READ 15

Dear Professor Head:

Thank you for the time and courtesy you extended to our representative, Laura Mann, at your college last month. She enjoyed her visit with you.

At Laura's request we have sent you the new edition of *Mathematics for Business.* This was sent to you several weeks ago, and you should have it by now. We do hope you'll look it over carefully. In addition, your name has been placed on our mailing list to receive an examination copy of *Business Math: Practical Applications.* A new edition of this book by Cleaves, Hobbs, and Dudenhef is expected off the press sometime next month.

We'll send your copy just as soon as it is available. If there is any way we can be of help to you, Professor Head, please let us know. Best wishes for a happy holiday season.

Cordially,

Hal Balmer
Vice President

lrs

REPLAY 15

A.

1. R workaholic; that is,
2. C which
3. R work; they
4. C Although
5. C although
6. CS than . . . person. They
7. R person; they
8. C because
9. C Because
10. C

11. CS performers;
12. C
13. R questions; also
14. R interview; make
15. C
16. C
17. CS tasks; begin
18. C
19. R plans; it
20. C as

B.

1. C
2. since
3. Although

4. When
5. because

CHAPTER 4

RECAP—READ 16

1. allies
2. accessories

3. injuries
4. facilities

RECAP

1. tattoos
2. dominos, dominoes

3. altos
4. potatoes

RECAP

1. thieves
2. handkerchiefs

3. halves
4. safes

REPLAY 16

1. itineraries
2. portfolios
3. ferries
4. moneys or monies
5. wolves
6. zeros, zeroes
7. pianos
8. authorities
9. heroes
10. melodies
11. knives
12. tariffs
13. proxies
14. surveys
15. plaintiffs
16. wives
17. chiefs
18. cargoes, cargos
19. attorneys
20. mementos, mementoes

REPLAY 17

A.

1. corps
2. economics
3. deer
4. Georges
5. series
6. Chinese
7. Joneses
8. aircraft
9. fish
10. stepchildren
11. feet
12. Floreses

B.

1. P   2. S/P   3. S/P   4. S/P   5. S   6. S/P

C.

1. have
2. is
3. are
4. were
5. are
6. are
7. is
8. was
9. is
10. were

REPLAY 18

A.

1. formulas, formulae
2. alumni
3. bases
4. censuses
5. criteria, criterions
6. axes
7. parentheses
8. crocuses, croci
9. appendixes, appendices
10. concertos, concerti
11. indexes, indices
12. analyses
13. media, mediums
14. diagnoses

B.

1. S   2. P   3. S   4. P or S   5. P   6. P

C.

1. medium
2. vertebrae
3. criteria
4. parenthesis
5. alumni

RECAP—READ 19

brother-in-law, stock car, trade-ins, price tags, letterhead

REPLAY 19

A.

1. follow-up, follow-ups
2. textbook, textbooks
3. trade-in, trade-ins
4. editor in chief, editors in chief
5. runner-up, runners-up
6. spaceflight, spaceflights
7. headhunter, headhunters
8. bush league, bush leagues
9. chief of staff, chiefs of staff
10. volleyball, volleyballs

REPLAY 20

A.

1. The Atomic Age, Hiroshima
2. We, American Airlines, Israel, Maine
3. Eric A. Smith, CFP
4. Winston Churchill, Triumph and Tragedy, World War II
5. The, Supreme Court
6. I, Chinese, September, Chinese
7. The Atlantic and Pacific Oceans, United States
8. Use Hunt's Tomato Sauce, Tuesdays, March
9. Lalitha, Hindu, India, MD
10. The, Dear Customer, Sincerely

B.

1. general manager, Telephone, tostadas, tacos
2. business teacher
3. C
4. Spanish
5. President
6. Catholic
7. C
8. east, summer, City
9. city, state
10. C
11. Anthropology, colleges
12. company
13. C
14. C
15. Academy Award, Nobel Prize

REPLAY 21

1. businesspersons/ businesspeople
2. plaintiff
3. software
4. premises
5. editors in chief
6. cargo
7. corps
8. portfolio
9. proxy
10. proceeds
11. itinerary
12. memento
13. notaries public
14. chassis
15. write-offs

CHAPTER 5

Word Power Answer: 1

RECAP—READ 22

1. minutes' planning, hour's work, New Year's Day, Alicia's mother, Ben's father
2. "Seward's Folly," critic's foolishness, Seward's foolishness

Word to the Wise

1. noun   2. verb

REPLAY 22

1. C
2. editor's stories
3. C
4. brother-in-law's manager
5. C
6. attorneys' offices
7. South Dakota's resources
8. Men's women's clothes
9. Ms. Lopez's orders
10. industry's directors
11. crew's strength
12. California's gold mines, orange groves
13. nation's wine, raisins
14. world's manufacturers
15. Men's College
16. C
17. Tom's book
18. hours' work
19. Penney's success
20. Barbie's fame, Mattel's success

RECAP—READ 23

1. Smith's, Perkins', City's, week's   2. son-in-law's, son's

RECAP—READ 23

1. brothers', Martinezes   2. Women's, women's, men's   3. daughters-in-law's

REPLAY 23

A.

1. representative's   representatives   representatives'
2. week's   weeks   weeks'
3. witness's   witnesses   witnesses'

4. James's	Jameses	Jameses'
5. country's	countries	countries'
6. Filipino's	Filipinos	Filipinos'
7. man's	men	men's
8. Asian's	Asians	Asians'
9. wife's	wives	wives'
10. father-in-law's	fathers-in-law	fathers-in-law's
11. congresswoman's	congresswomen	congresswomen's
12. family's	families	families'
13. Webster's	Websters	Websters'
14. hour's	hours	hours'
15. Wolf's	Wolfs	Wolfs'
16. wolf's	wolves	wolves'
17. organization's	organizations	organizations'
18. boss's	bosses	bosses'
19. woman's	women	women's
20. child's	children	children's

B.

1. C
2. years'
3. person's
4. Men's fashions women's
5. minute's

6. Childress's, days
7. ladies' coats
8. Goldsteins, days
9. Brunswick's, years
10. Jenkins'

11. coaches', players'
12. Keats's
13. Hendrix's
14. brothers' films
15. guests' names

CHAPTER 6

REPLAY 24

A.

1. I, subjective case
2. him, objective case

3. I, subjective case
4. her, objective case

5. Who, subjective case

B. Answers may vary; examples are provided.

1. I believe you.
2. He admires her.
3. She respects him.

4. Who knows them?
5. I am staying with him.
6. We are starting with it.

7. He is leaving with her.
8. They are going with whom?

C.

1. no one, everyone
2. someone
3. himself

4. anything, someone/somebody
5. myself
6. Something

REPLAY 25

1. she and I	8. her	15. He and I	22. he
2. me	9. we	16. me	23. him
3. They	10. he	17. he	24. me
4. We	11. me	18. We	25. they
5. I	12. us	19. her	26. me
6. us	13. them	20. them	
7. me	14. him	21. me	

RECAP—READ 26

1. she	2. he	3. do	④ he likes

REPLAY 26

A.

1. does	2. he loves	3. does	4. you know	5. can

B.

1. C	6. C	11. I	16. themselves
2. themselves	7. I leave (or I do)	12. C	17. C
3. he (can)	8. C	13. C	18. himself
4. he	9. themselves	14. C	19. myself
5. me	10. you	15. C	20. C

REPLAY 27

1. Everybody's	5. ours, yours	9. You're	13. anyone's
2. Nobody's	6. Yours	10. you're, your	14. Who's
3. its, it's	7. hers	11. Everybody's	15. Whose
4. C	8. mine, theirs	12. No one's	

RECAP—READ 28

1. whom	4. whomever	7. whoever	10. whom
2. who	5. whoever	8. Whom	
3. whomever	6. whom	9. whom	

RECAP

1. Who	2. who	3. who	4. whom

REPLAY 28

1. whoever	10. whomever	19. whom
2. whoever	11. whom	20. whoever
3. who	12. who	21. whomever
4. who	13. whom	22. whom
5. Whom	14. whom	23. whoever
6. Whom	15. who	24. whoever
7. Who	16. whomever	25. who
8. Whom	17. who	
9. Whoever	18. who	

RECAP—READ 29

1. No one	3. his or her instead of their	5. any one
2. Every one	4. someone	

REPLAY 29

A.

1. Members of this department (or All department members) should be sure their nouns and pronouns agree in number in their written communications.
2. All the mechanics finished their work quickly. OR Each mechanic finished the work quickly.
3. Every child in the class needs a book. OR All the children in the class need their own book.
4. All applicants should write their name in the blank. OR Each applicant should write his or her name in the blank.

B.

1. Anybody	4. anyone	7. Any one	10. its
2. Every one	5. Everybody	8. no body	11. its
3. No one	6. someone	9. their	12. their

C.

1. c/b	2. a/d	3. b/d	4. b/c	5. d/b

RECAP—READ 30

1. its   2. its   3. their

REPLAY 30

A. Sample answers:

1. group   3. jury   5. staff
2. class   4. team   6. committee

B.

1. plural   8. I   15. she
2. singular   9. its   16. he
3. subject   10. its   17. I
4. its   11. its   18. they
5. it is   12. its   19. I
6. its   13. the janitorial service   20. us clerks
7. its   14. trash shouldn't be thrown

CHAPTER 7

REPLAY 31

A.

1. works   8. climbed   15. selected
2. needs   9. will/should find   16. will (or should) consider
3. moved   10. want   17. is considering
4. are sailing 11. wants   18. stay
5. waxed   12. wanted   19. watched
6. are   13. will (or would) want   20. discussed
7. looks   14. influences

B.   4. are   8. knows
1. is   5. is   9. is
2. is   6. are   10. being
3. need   7. flow

REPLAY 32

1. broken, worn
2. began (or had just begun), rang
3. chooses (or *chose*)
4. chosen (or delete *had*)
5. does, stands
6. risen (or delete *had*)
7. eaten (or delete *have*)
8. saw, did (or insert helping verbs)
9. flown (or delete *had*)
10. quit

11. run, broken (or delete both *hads*)
12. worn (or delete *had*)
13. given (or delete *had*)
14. saw, spoken (or delete *had*)
15. taken (or delete *had*)
16. wear (or *wore*)
17. saw (or *has/had seen*)
18. doesn't
19. swung
20. gave (or *had given*)

REPLAY 33

A.

1. being, was, been
2. biting, bit, bitten
3. blowing, blew, blown
4. coming, came, come
5. costing, cost, cost
6. falling, fell, fallen
7. forgetting, forgot, forgotten
8. freezing, froze, frozen

9. hiding, hid, hidden
10. leading, led, led
11. paying, paid, paid
12. shaking, shook, shaken
13. sinking, sank, sunk, or sunken
14. singing, sang, sung
15. throwing, threw, thrown

B.

1. beaten, winning
2. paid
3. broken, hidden

4. hung, forgotten
5. stayed, written

RECAP—READ 34

1. you, *finish*, (you understood) *leave*
2. Everyone, *was discharged.*
3. Lewis, Martin *told*, *sang*
4. we, *should tell*

REPLAY 34

Subjects Verbs (Helping and Main Verb):

1. you	do enjoy
2. analysts	are doing
3. she	will get
4. clothing, you	should be, select
5. you (understood), appearance, that	ask, sends, will benefit
6. women	should limit
7. diner, he, she	puts, cuts
8. knife	remains
9. advancement, employees	is, get along
10. work	turns
11. Playing	is
12. sales	have risen
13. Cleveland, women	said, do . . . want
14. Everyone	is working
15. Xerox	made
16. assistant, who	is, will . . . help
17. you	Would like
18. turnover	is
19. poverty, riches	are
20. grammar, spelling	are

RECAP—READ 35

1. seems	2. likes	3. fit
4. has	5. seem	

REPLAY 35

1. were to was	7. C	13. C
2. seem to seems	8. are to is	14. C
3. was to were	9. are to is	15. C
4. C	10. have to has	16. have to has
5. were to was	11. is to are	17. has to have
6. C	12. rides to ride	18. are to is

19. don't to doesn't
20. was to were
21. is to are
22. are to is
23. have to has
24. greets to greet

25. have to has
26. pack to packs
27. C
28. We'd to We would
29. leaves to leave
30. do to does

31. don't to doesn't
32. work to works
33. are to is
34. goes to go
35. have to has

REPLAY 36

1. was to were
2. C
3. was to were
4. C

5. was to were
6. C
7. was to were

8. were to was and weren't to wasn't
9. was to were
10. is to was

REPLAY 37

1. takes to take
2. C
3. have their to has its
4. need to needs

5. was to were
6. was to were
7. favor to favors
8. C

9. are to is and their to its
10. work to works

CHAPTER 8

REPLAY 38

1. that kind
2. Those or These
3. types
4. sorts

5. those types of people or that type of person
6. delete here
7. delete there

8. Ask these or those people. . . .
9. delete there
10. delete an

RECAP—READ 39

1. an	5. a	9. a	13. an	17. an	21. a
2. a	6. an	10. a	14. an	18. a	22. a
3. an	7. a	11. a	15. an	19. an	23. an
4. an	8. an	12. an	16. an	20. a	24. an

REPLAY 39

1. a, an
2. A, an, an
3. an, a, an
4. a, an
5. A, an

6. An, an
7. A, a, a
8. A, a, an
9. a, a, an
10. a, a, an

11. An, a
12. an, an
13. An, an
14. an, a
15. A, a, an

REPLAY 40

1. rarely or hardly ever (~~scarcely never~~)
2. anything, anybody (~~nothing~~ about it to ~~nobody~~)
3. any (~~none~~)
4. any (~~no~~)
5. C
6. anything (~~nothing~~)

7. anywhere (~~nowhere~~)
8. any (~~no~~)
9. C
10. anywhere (~~nowhere~~)
11. could (~~couldn't~~)
12. any (~~no~~)

RECAP—READ 41

wisest, wiser

REPLAY 41

A.

COMPARATIVE	SUPERLATIVE
1. farther/further	farthest/furthest
2. worse	worst
3. littler or less	littlest or least
4. more	most
5. better	best

B.

1. delete *most*
2. change *the worst* to *worse*
3. C
4. change *older* to *oldest*
5. change *best* to *better*

6. change *more heavy* to *heavier*; delete *more heavy*
7. change *recenter* to *more recent*
8. change *brightest* to *brighter*
9. delete *more*
10. change *biggest* to *bigger*

RECAP—READ 42

1. smoothly   2. beautiful   3. awfully   4. quickly

RECAP—READ 42

1. more clearly   2. writes   3. adverb

REPLAY 42

1. bad
2. clearly/correctly
3. sad
4. carefully
5. legibly
6. C
7. deeply
8. fairly
9. efficiently
10. gracefully
11. bad
12. C
13. sweet
14. quietly
15. more quietly
16. more smoothly
17. satisfactorily
18. calmer
19. C
20. louder
21. worse
22. more quietly
23. most capable
24. more concisely
25. older

RECAP—READ 43

1. well
2. well
3. either good or well
4. well
5. bad

RECAP—READ 43

1. very or extremely   2. really or especially

REPLAY 43

1. really, very
2. surely, certainly
3. logically
4. better
5. better
6. more widely
7. better
8. really well
9. most poorly
10. C
11. differently
12. bad
13. well, an
14. kinds, an
15. C

CHAPTER 9

RECAP—READ 44

1. Taiwan, Hong Kong, Singapore, and Korea
2. report, . . . accuracy, and, . . finally,
3. language, religion, politics, and
4. in, . . . at, and
5. lunch, . . . appropriately, . . . manners, . . . eat,
6. company, . . . them, and

RECAP—READ 44

1. bright, enthusiastic   2. C   3. C   4. highly paid, famous

REPLAY 44

1. A dazed, demure . . . disheveled, double-dealing
2. unique, exciting
3. why you came, what you wanted, and what you expect to do.
4. Our showroom is in a small, elegant
5. C
6. Forth Worth, Dallas, and Austin.
7. profitable, highly
8. bonus, . . . salary, and stock options.
9. Use *nd, rd, st, or th* . . . itself; for example, the 4th of May
10. settled, well-educated

RECAP—READ 45

1. Pam's work, and we   2. Rosalyn's work, and I   3. like sports, but she   4. C

REPLAY 45

1. C
2. workplace, but
3. sorority, and
4. morning, but
5. New York, but
6. October, a . . . November, a
7. today, for
8. job, nor
9. C
10. C
11. C
12. Luc, for
13. rich, but
14. available, and
15. brother, and

RECAP—READ 46

1. month, we . . . contracts, the . . . wing, and
2. C
3. train, you
4. meeting, he
5. C
6. directions, he
7. Hank, please

REPLAY 46

1. Inn, we
2. her, he
3. attractive, modern . . . room, you
4. know, real
5. igloo, kayak, moccasin, skunk, and persimmon.
6. C
7. speaker, indicate
8. C
9. salesperson, he
10. No, he
11. C
12. be, it
13. C
14. store, but
15. C

RECAP—READ 47

1. Peninsula, where . . . summers, holds
2. parts, "Job Content"
3. want, therefore, may
4. system, which . . . Department, eliminates
5. courthouse, even

Word to the wise Brad thought Ron was very generous.

RECAP—READ 47

1. C
2. honored because
3. student must . . . rooms without a chaperone approved by the principal or her

REPLAY 47

1. stockholders, often . . . family, and
2. C
3. C
4. C
5. C
6. C
7. Internet, the . . . communications, that
8. loudest, however, is
9. costs, as . . . know, are
10. administrator, Goria Rojas, telephoned
11. Room No. 103, is
12. Office, which is on the third floor, is
13. Simon, the auditor, found
14. C
15. C
16. C
17. worth, which
18. C
19. booklet, which . . . information, for
20. C
21. idea, it has been said, comes
22. attending, "Career Networking in Cyberspace," begins
23. C
24. service, which . . . yesterday, suddenly
25. C

REPLAY 48

1. March 2, 2010, we
2. C
3. Smith, PhD, will
4. Long Beach, New York, nightclub
5. Friday, January 4, 8:30 a.m., in my office
6. shop, and
7. Little Rock, Arkansas, was
8. Albuquerque, New Mexico, store
9. Edinburgh, Scotland, on
10. C

REPLAY 49

A. Sample answers:

1. Jeff told the students, "Use last names in the workplace unless you're sure first names are appropriate."
2. "I emailed the price list two weeks ago," said Ms. Kato.
3. The instructor said, "The more public speaking you do, the more comfortable you will become," and then gave each student a chance to practice.
4. "It is important to look at your audience," he said, "and that means direct eye contact."
5. "I'm shocked!" shouted Jeff.
6. Procrastinators do not believe in the adage "never put off until tomorrow what you can do today."

B.

1. (1) Use commas for direct address. (2) Use commas to separate the parts of an address that are in sentence form. (3) Do not use a comma between state and ZIP.

2. Use a comma before a coordinating conjunction that joins independent clauses.

3. (1) Enclose elements of dates within commas. (2) In the US style date, enclose the year in commas when it follows the day. (3) A comma may be used in four-digit figures if the number refers to quantity.

4. (1) Use a comma after direct address. (2) Use a comma after an introductory expression that has a verb.

5. (1) When needed for clarity, use a comma after an introductory phrase. (2) Insert commas between items of a series.

CHAPTER 10

RECAP—READ 50

1. more; now
2. high, your
3. money; they are, however,
4. C
5. employer, Mr. Anton, was . . . criticism; and

6. Banks, he explained, . . . accounts; but
7. a raise; that is, each
8. C
9. City Council; the vote
10. limited, keep

REPLAY 50

A.

1. acronym; that is, it's . . . word; the.
2. Lance Armstrong, winner . . . times, did
3. show, December, that . . . you; every
4. you; every
5. Louise Fuller, president; Sandra Hall, vice president; and . . . Ginn Hecht, treasurer
6. ambition; namely, to
7. about; for example, he
8. C
9. understand; it
10. applicants, his . . . good; however, they
11. dividend; that is, a sum
12. history, I
13. C
14. harder, I
15. believe, therefore, that

B. Charles the First walked and talked; half an hour after, his head was cut off.

REPLAY 51

A.

1. following: two
2. C
3. life: revenge
4. life: It
5. cities: Winston Salem

6. shoplifting: place
7. community: Nearby
8. about: A
9. duty: protect
10. following: "Appearance

Word Power: No. 1

REPLAY 52

1. I wonder whether he uses voice recognition software.
2. The pizza is good, but where's the pepperoni?
3. Would you please send these items overnight mail to us.
4. A winner says he fell; a loser says somebody pushed him. OR A winner says he fell. A loser says somebody pushed him.
5. Management makes important policies and decisions. We just carry them out.
6. Do you know what subprime mortgage is?
7. Would Thursday be more convenient for you?
8. Take advantage of this deal today!
9. Would you please fax this report before you go to lunch.
10. That's wonderful!

Word Power: No. 1

REPLAY 53

1. The new board members—Dr. Duzeck and Ms. Swenson—will meet with the press this afternoon.
2. Charmaine—the scholarship recipient—praised her parents for their love and devotion.
3. The officers of this corporation (the president, the vice president, the treasurer, and the secretary) are all graduates of the same university.
4. The decimal equivalents (see Figure 4, page 80) will help you with the percentages.
5. Harbor Office Supply Company (I'll check the address) has ordered three photocopiers.
6. *Roget's Thesaurus*—a treasury of synonyms, antonyms, parallel words, and related words—was first published in 1852 by Peter Mark Roget (look up pronunciation of Roget).

7. The 7-11 chain—which featured spoon straws for Slurpees, plastic straws for sodas, and reusable straws for car cups—added straws that change color as a drink changes temperature.

8. Money, beauty, intelligence, and charm—Stella Glitter has them all.

9. The "soap" star has money, beauty, intelligence, and charm.

10. She has all the attributes of a star—beauty, intelligence, and charm—but has not made a film in five years.

11. We must see him at once—not tomorrow.

12. His check for $152 (not $156) was returned by the bank.

13. Roosevelt Island was described as "New York City's ideal place to live—a crime-free, auto-free, dog-free new [*sic*] island in the East River."

14. The report indicates that "the majority of new jobs created in America today [2005] are in small companies" (fewer than one hundred employees).

15. The three departments of the United States government—the executive, the legislative, and the judicial—derive their authority from the Constitution.

CHAPTER 11

REPLAY 54

A.

1. He shouted, "Your house is on fire!"

2. "Your house is on fire!" he shouted.

3. Alonzo whispered, "Are you sure you have the right data?"

4. "Are you positive the numbers are correct?" he whispered again.

5. Do you know whether Jessica said, "Reserve a rental car?"

6. If you use words like "ain't" and "theirselves," in some places you will be considered uneducated.

7. My classmate pointed out that many professionals use sloppy language all the time.

8. What does the phrase "negotiable instrument" mean?

9. He faxed us as follows: "We depart from O'Hare on American Flight 23 at 8 a.m. and arrive at Kennedy at 10:30 p.m."

10. Was it Mr. Higgins, the character in <u>My Fair Lady</u>, who said, "Results are what count"?

11. "We need more tacos for the company party!" Jim yelled.

12. "This shipment," the manager said, "will arrive in time for your January sale."

13. "Are you all right?" asked Ann. "Yes," groaned her dad, as he lifted <u>Merriam-Webster's Unabridged Dictionary</u>.

14. Bach's "Suite No. 2 in B Minor" is first on the program at the concert.

15. University of South Carolina Professor Benjamin Franklin is tired of people asking him, "Why aren't you out flying your kite?"

RECAP—READ 55

1. brother-in-law
2. vice president
3. semisweet
4. up-to-date
5. off-limits
6. de-escalate
7. ex-boyfriend
8. rediscover

RECAP—READ 55

1. back-to-school, Windows-based
2. C
3. part-time, never-to-be-forgotten
4. seven-foot-tall, problem-solving
5. state-of-the-art, built-in, self-cleaning
6. C

REPLAY 55

A.

1. I work in a 100-story building.
2. Do you need a 10- or a 20-foot ladder to do the repairs?
3. My father is a hard-working man.
4. The case against the Dallas-based company was handled in Seattle.

B.

5. re-creation
6. C
7. C
8. C
9. father-in-law
10. self-made
11. self-sufficient
12. C
13. twenty-five
14. Johnny-come-lately
15. anti-intellectual

C.

func/tion	thou/sands	inter/rupt
be/lieve	punctu/ation	syl/lables
hori/zontal	aligned/	stopped/
wouldn't/	impos/sible	guess/work

REPLAY 56

1. representative's, assistant's
2. Hill's
3. women's, girls'
4. Gary's, money's, retailer's
5. Watkins', year's
6. Germany's, America's
7. weekend's
8. wife's, New York's
9. Lopezes
10. Dr. Lopez's husband

REPLAY 57

1. couldn't, o'clock
2. i's, t's, you'd
3. C
4. C
5. CFO's, 2007
6. Don't
7. C
8. it's, yds, lbs.
9. '90s, workers
10. C
11. t's
12. Won't
13. A's
14. C
15. Couldn't

CHAPTER 12

RECAP—READ 58

1. S   2. F   3. F   4. S   5. S

RECAP—READ 58

Sample answers:

1. R (explanation. You)
2. CS (service. Therefore,)
3. R (service; therefore,)
4. C
5. C
6. R (marketing. It)
7. CS (marketing; it)
8. C

REPLAY 58

A.

Your instructor will provide the solution.

B.

1. downtown;
2. it;
3. map;
4. C
5. working; flow."
6. C
7. agree,
8. eat; example, whole lobster, pasta, or
9. C
10. first; hungry,

C.

1. CS rings, and   2. C   3. CS sounding, but   4. C   5. C

RECAP—READ 59

1. He finished dinner and returned to work. OR After finishing dinner, he returned to work.
2. If you go to China on a business trip, don't give your hosts expensive gifts; they might be embarrassed or even refuse to accept them.
3. When you dine in China, hold the rice bowl close to your mouth and sample every dish offered.

REPLAY 59

Sample answers:

1. The beautiful movie star smashed a bottle of champagne over the stern as the ship slid gracefully into the sea.
2. We got up at 6 o'clock and had a quick breakfast.
3. A college pennant and a Monet painting are on the wall of the student's room.
4. A house in need of painting sits far back among the trees.
5. Dennis and Mike spent all afternoon walking to the telephone, gas, and electric company offices to pay their bills.
6. An animal that appeared to be a hyena paced restlessly back and forth in the cage.
7. We realize travelers choose an airline based on the quality of its service, and we're sorry we let you down.
8. Enclosed is our check for $635.23 in payment of your May statement.
9. I missed the final examination because I had been out late the night before. Nevertheless, the instructor and the dean refused to change my F grade to "Incomplete" or "Withdrew."
10. For those of you who didn't know it, we have a nursery downstairs for small children.
11. Because Mr. Anderson is so busy, we don't recommend that Mr. Nguyen go to his office.
12. Despite our repeated reminders about nonpayment of your long overdue account, we have not received your check.

RECAP—READ 60

1. We sat there in awed silence listening to his singing.
2. Ms. Grigg worked for CNN's Headline News Department during her vacation.
3. Genevive Astor died at the age of 96 in the home in which she had been born.
4. The fire department brought the fire under control before much damage was done.

RECAP—READ 60

A.

1. With the new software we hope to improve response time, reduce input errors, and identify systems problems more readily.
2. Typing accurately can be more important than typing fast.
3. Linda is a full-time securities analyst, and her husband is a part-time insurance agent.
4. We would appreciate learning your views on how to introduce change, control quality, and motivate employees.
5. Ophthalmologists and optometrists may examine eyes and may also issue prescriptions for glasses or contact lenses.

Word to the Wise misplaced words

REPLAY 60

1. M	5. P	9. P	13. P	17. P
2. M	6. P	10. C	14. M	18. C
3. P	7. P	11. M	15. P	19. P
4. M	8. P	12. C	16. C	20. M

REPLAY 61

1. P	5. A	9. A	13. A	17. P
2. A	6. P	10. P	14. P	18. P
3. P	7. A	11. A	15. P	19. A
4. A	8. A	12. P	16. A	20. A

RECAP—READ 62

Possible Answer: While strolling along the beach, you can find unusual shells and pebbles.

RECAP—READ 62

1. Because you are one of our most discriminating customers, we invite you to attend this private showing.
2. When he turned the corner, the new building was right in front of him.
3. While I was using the computer, the cursor became stuck in the middle of the screen.
4. Unlike many others who became millionaires in the 1990s, she became financially successful through her talents in fine art and classical music.
5. Before he has dinner with the woman he met through Ultimate Encounters Online Dating, he needs to improve his table manners.

REPLAY 62

1. D Having typed just half the report,
2. D On examining the goods,
3. D Like many people living in Alaska,
4. D Having recovered from his illness,
5. C
6. D Before going to lunch,
7. D before going to lunch.
8. D Walking quickly down the aisle,
9. D While doing the daily chores,
10. D Handing me the $50,000 order,
11. D Having produced a printout,
12. D After looking the cars over for a while,
13. D Looking marvelously glamorous in a midnight blue gown,
14. D Upon landing in Dallas,
15. C
16. C
17. D Being in dilapidated condition,
18. D If invited to dinner at a British home,
19. C
20. C
21. C
22. D After standing and repeating the pledge,
23. D While walking home,
24. C While I was walking home,
25. D after being on vacation for two hours,

CHAPTER 13

RECAP—READ 63

1. F   2. T   3. F   4. F   5. T

RECAP—READ 63

Sample answers:
1. Thank you for sending *Writing Better Letters.*
2. Enclosed is the price list you requested.

RECAP—READ 63

Sample answers:

1. We hope you will be pleased.
2. We are open from 10 a.m. until 8 p.m. on weekdays and until 5 p.m. on weekends.
3. We'll be glad to give you a gift card that you can use for any other item in the store.

RECAP—READ 63

Sample answers:

1. We suggest you pack the essentials first.
2. The investigation revealed a small, triangular purple UFO.

REPLAY 63

A.

1. F	2. F	3. F	4. T	5. F

B.

1. About half the flowers in my garden are blooming.
2. The parts you ordered were shipped today via overnight FedEx.
3. Our newly designed products have been carefully tested.
4. We faxed the price list to you yesterday. Let us know if you have any questions.
5. Please send your payment of $6,453 in the enclosed envelope today.
6. I believe attendance is high when the event is held in December.
7. Please repeat the instructions.
8. We'll be glad to give you a gift card that you can use for any other item in the store.
9. Your order for the Desk Master gift set will be filled promptly upon receipt of $173.03 (cost + shipping). We accept checks, money orders, and credit card payments (see attached order form).
10. Thank you for your interest in working for GreenCities.com. (It's obvious the letter was received since the writer is answering it.)

RECAP—READ 64

Write T (true) or F (false) in each blank.

1. T	2. F	3. F

RECAP—READ 64

Write T (true) or F (false) in each blank.

1. F	2. T	3. T

REPLAY 64

Write T (true) or F (false) in each blank.

1. F	3. T	5. T	7. T	9. F
2. F	4. T	6. F	8. T	10. T

REPLAY 65

Write T (true) or F (false) in each blank.

1. F	4. T	7. T	10. T	13. F
2. T	5. F	8. T	11. F	14. F
3. F	6. T	9. T	12. F	15. F

CHAPTER 14

REPLAY 66

1. F	3. F	5. F	7. F	9. T
2. F	4. T	6. T	8. F	10. F

REPLAY 67

A.

1. T	3. F	5. F	7. T
2. T	4. T	6. F	

B.

1. underline, negative space
2. italics, animation
3. color, bullets
4. bold, text boxes
5. large font size
6. font style, sound

REPLAY DRILL ANSWERS

CHAPTER 1

REPLAY DRILL 1-A

1. branch of biology dealing with embryos
2. science that deals with history of the earth and its life, especially rocks
3. scientist who deals with earthquakes and with artificially produced vibrations of the earth
4. of or relating to the treatment of disease or disorders by remedial agents or methods
5. picture script of the ancient Egyptian priesthood
6. concerned with the individual rather than society
7. mental and emotional disorder that affects only part of the personality
8. abnormal fear of being helpless in an embarrassing or inescapable situation, characterized especially by the avoidance of open or public spaces
9. the science of human beings
10. statistical characteristics of human populations

REPLAY DRILL 1-B

1. absence
2. accuracy
3. analyze
4. attendance
5. Britain
6. cemetery
7. changeable
8. changing
9. coming
10. deferred
11. dining
12. excellence
13. existence
14. forty
15. grammar
16. grievous
17. C
18. loneliness
19. ninety
20. omitted

REPLAY DRILL 1-C

1. Sep|tem|ber 3
2. won|der|ful 3
3. mer|ri|ment 3
4. meth|od|ol|o|gy 5
5. to|tal|i|ty 4
6. motor: noun, verb, adjective
7. metal: noun, adjective
8. facility: noun
9. grandeur: noun
10. make: noun, verb
11. maudlin/MAWD len
12. nuclear/NEW klee er
13. literature/LIT er uh chur
14. spastic/SPAS tik
15. bastion/BAS chun
16. fanatic – Latin
17. syllogism—Middle English, from Anglo-French, from Latin, from Greek
18. phonetic—New Latin from Greek
19. oration—Latin
20. milieu—French from Old French

CHAPTER 2

REPLAY DRILL 2-A

1. Shenita, Mark, textbook
2. students, miles, school, day
3. assignments, weeks
4. syllabi, information, subject
5. Tina, Rose, applications, loan
6. Will, stomach, class
7. errors, emails
8. instructor, schedule, week
9. Larry, textbooks, notebooks, papers, backpack
10. classroom, computers, printers

REPLAY DRILL 2-B

1. She, anyone
2. Your, his
3. I, their
4. Who, him
5. Something, her
6. I, this
7. Everyone, their
8. He, nothing
9. You
10. Those, you who, your
11. Whomever, you
12. her
13. her
14. Somebody, his, her
15. everyone, no one
16. she
17. I, mine, it, hers
18. We, ourselves, our
19. his, me
20. Everything

REPLAY DRILL 2-C

1. welcomed
2. will be attending
3. was
4. has handed
5. required
6. will be
7. were jumping
8. brightened
9. echoed
10. were looking

REPLAY DRILL 2-D

Part 1
1. irritating, busy
2. tired, thirsty, cold
3. noisy, water, law
4. slippery, wooden
5. efficient, ten-page
6. magnificent, inner, office
7. elegant, new, firm
8. old, faded, torn
9. heavier, laser
10. grouchy, fresh, brewed

Part 2
11. Several
12. enough
13. Twenty-five
14. no
15. few

Part 3
16. These, the
17. A, this
18. The, that
19. An, those
20. This, an

REPLAY DRILL 2-E

1. finally
2. diligently
3. immediately
4. very
5. well
6. really
7. extremely

8. almost
9. appropriately
10. accurately
11. cheaply
12. never
13. hard
14. today

15. too
16. exceptionally
17. rapidly
18. so
19. frequently
20. now

REPLAY DRILL 2-F

Part 1
1. Although
2. when
3. until
4. so that
5. that, or
6. but
7. while

8. and, since
9. if
10. whenever
Part 2
11. on the desk
12. in the folder
13. through the clouds
14. along the path

15. above the business
16. into the file cabinet
17. across the street
18. except Luther, on the business trip
19. during the lecture
20. beneath the other papers

REPLAY DRILL 2-G

1. noun
2. adjective
3. verb
4. adjective
5. verb

6. noun
7. noun
8. verb
9. adjective
10. adjective

11. verb
12. noun
13. verb
14. adjective
15. noun

16. noun
17. adjective
18. verb
19. adjective
20. verb

CHAPTER 3

REPLAY DRILL 3-A

1. C
2. F
3. F
4. C
5. C

6. F
7. C
8. F
9. C
10. F

11. F
12. C
13. C
14. F
15. F

16. C
17. C
18. F
19. C
20. F

REPLAY DRILL 3-B

1. CS	5. R	9. CS	13. CS	17. C
2. C	6. CS	10. R	14. CS	18. CS
3. R	7. C	11. R	15. C	19. R
4. C	8. C	12. C	16. R	20. C

REPLAY DRILL 3-C

Part 1
1. therefore
2. for example
3. hence
4. then
5. consequently
6. furthermore
7. otherwise
8. however
9. in fact
10. nevertheless
11. also
12. in addition
13. moreover
14. thus
15. that is
16. for
17. but
18. yet
19. nor
20. or

Part 2
16. for

REPLAY DRILL 3-D

1. After the workers finished the project
2. until the clouds moved in
3. Because the biscuits were hard
4. Since Susan left town
5. When salespeople are successful
6. Although we had a wet spring
7. even though they have no money
8. when he was president
9. Even though his supervisor gave clear directions
10. Since wrong answers will be subtracted from the total number of correct responses

REPLAY DRILL 3-E

Possible answers.

1. Because John is an excellent student, he gets good grades
2. The store has the highest sales in the district because the manager of the store trains the employees very well.
3. Since the short story was very dramatic, the students in the English Composition class responded enthusiastically.
4. Although Sigmund Freud was a pioneer in the field of psychology, modern psychologists do not all agree with his theories.

5. Political activist C. Delores Tucker attacked the moral standards of Hip-Hop music in the 1990s, but the public had mixed views on the subject.
6. Bobby Flay, one of the Food Network's "Iron Chefs," prepared six different pork belly dishes.
7. The Accounting Department will issue new expense forms this week because many people are confused about how to tabulate mileage reports.
8. American Indians were stereotyped in films of the 1940s and 1950s, when very few sympathetic portrayals were presented.
9. We cannot issue paychecks on the 15th of this month because our checks are late coming from the home office.
10. Bob and Art are sitting on the fence, but they will need to make a bid on the house by close of business tomorrow.

CHAPTER 4

REPLAY DRILL 4-A

1. babies
2. alloys
3. daisies
4. plays
5. rallies
6. countries
7. churches
8. taxes
9. wishes
10. glasses
11. vetoes
12. echoes
13. radios
14. altos
15. leaves
16. roofs
17. shelves
18. wives
19. chiefs
20. dwarfs

REPLAY DRILL 4-B

Part 1
1. theses
2. bacteria
3. analyses
4. stimuli
5. algae
6. sheep
7. hypotheses
8. curricula/curriculums
9. memoranda/memorandums
10. fungi
11. antennae
12. appendixes/appendices
13. syllabi/syllabuses
14. crises

Part 2
15. data (P), (S)
16. crisis (S)
17. media (P)
18. alumni (P)
19. algae (P)
20. bacteria (P), (S)

REPLAY DRILL 4-C

Write S or P to indicate if the following nouns are usually singular or plural.

Example: trousers (S)

1. economics (S)
2. statistics (P)
3. news (S)
4. goods (P)
5. thanks (S)
6. scissors (S)
7. civics (S)
8. measles (S)
9. proceeds (P)
10. mathematics (S)

REPLAY DRILL 4-D

1. Bushes
2. Kellys
3. Joneses
4. Hartmans
5. Jameses
6. Rodrguezes
7. Chens
8. Williamses
9. Booths
10. Morganthaus

REPLAY DRILL 4-E

Part 1
1. get-togethers
2. post offices
3. runners-up
4. cupfuls
5. sons-in-law
6. nurses aides
7. photocopies
8. hand-me-downs
9. chairpersons
10. letters of recommendation

Part 2
11. German
12. Memorial Day
13. United Airlines
14. April
15. Commander
16. Human Resources Department
17. Statistics
18. Purchasing Agent
19. California/East Coast
20. C

CHAPTER 5

REPLAY DRILL 5-A

1. child's
2. engine's
3. customer's
4. judge's
5. afternoon's
6. factories'
7. secretaries'
8. month's
9. children's
10. Virginia's
11. men's
12. company's
13. accountants'
14. months'
15. year's
16. woman's
17. employee's or employees'
18. European's or Europeans'
19. waiter's or waiters'
20. student's or students'

REPLAY DRILL 5-B

1. S/child's
2. S/engine's
3. S/customer's
4. S/judge's
5. S/afternoon's
6. P/factories'
7. P/secretaries'
8. S/month's
9. P/children's
10. S/Virginia's
11. P/men's
12. S/company's
13. P/accountants'
14. P/ months'
15. S/year's
16. S/woman's
17. S/P/employee's/employees'
18. S/P/European's/Europeans'
19. S/P/waiter's/waiters'
20. S/P/student's/students'

CHAPTER 6

REPLAY DRILL 6-A

1. I	6. him	11. her	16. me
2. us	7. they	12. us	17. her
3. They	8. us	13. she	18. We
4. me	9. me	14. me	19. us
5. We	10. He	15. I	20. he

REPLAY DRILL 6-B

Part 1	6. he	**Part 2**	16. himself
1. he	7. I	11. C	17. C
2. she	8. himself	12. I	18. he
3. themselves	9. themselves	13. he	19. C
4. he	10. ourselves	14. C	20. I
5. me		15. themselves	

REPLAY DRILL 6-C

1. its	6. Who's	11. It's	16. whose
2. whose	7. everyone's	12. Who's	17. anyone's
3. your	8. They're	13. you're	18. their
4. No one's	9. mine	14. Somebody's	19. My
5. yours	10. ours	15. yours	20. its

REPLAY DRILL 6-D

1. who	6. Whom	11. whom	16. Whoever
2. who	7. whom	12. whomever	17. who
3. whom	8. who	13. who	18. Whomever
4. whomever	9. who	14. whom	19. who
5. who	10. Who	15. whom	20. whom

REPLAY DRILL 6-E

1. Every one
2. Someone
3. anybody
4. somebody
5. Any one
6. Everything
7. nobody
8. Everyone
9. Something
10. Anything
11. their
12. his or her
13. his or her
14. their
15. his or her
16. their
17. his or her
18. his or her
19. their
20. their

REPLAY DRILL 6-F

1. its
2. its
3. its
4. its
5. its
6. their
7. their
8. its
9. their
10. its

CHAPTER 7

REPLAY DRILL 7-A

1. jogs — present
2. will sing — future
3. cries; leaves — present
4. laughed — past
5. married — past
6. will fly — future
7. stays — present
8. saw — past
9. wanted — past
10. will paint — future
11. takes — present
12. needs — present
13. oversees — present
14. marched — past
15. will arrive — future
16. recommended — past
17. gained — past
18. walks — present
19. will talk — future
20. climbs — present

REPLAY DRILL 7-B

1. taken
2. stands
3. spoken
4. seen
5. ran
6. rose
7. rang
8. gone
9. gave
10. flew
11. eaten
12. drank
13. does
14. chose
15. broken
16. begun
17. worn
18. taken
19. rung
20. drunk

REPLAY DRILL 7-C

1. written
2. thrown
3. sang
4. shaken
5. hidden
6. frozen
7. forgotten
8. fallen
9. drawn
10. come
11. blew
12. bitten
13. written
14. threw
15. sung
16. sank
17. shaken
18. hidden
19. fallen
20. drawn

REPLAY DRILL 7-D

1. Are
2. is
3. were
4. had been
5. are
6. Is
7. are
8. I would
9. will be going
10. will be
11. is
12. are
13. is
14. are
15. were
16. will be
17. have been
18. were
19. have been
20. We would

REPLAY DRILL 7-E

Subject	Verb
1. sun	rose
2. wolves	howled
3. you	do have
4. cooking	is
5. (you)	answer
6. newspaper	is delivered
7. students	are
8. mother, son	were found
9. director	sent
10. you	did buy

11. restaurant	is
12. sign-ups	will be held
13. word	spread
14. Mr. Overton, wife	attended
15. manufacturer	recalled
16. boy, grandfather	strolled
17. courses	are taught
18. residents	were warned
19. Sidney	will learn
20. team	practiced

REPLAY DRILL 7-F

1. writes	6. does	11. are	16. is
2. want	7. is	12. talks	17. is
3. arrive	8. cries	13. are	18. were
4. is	9. records	14. are	19. has
5. was	10. speak	15. tries	20. does

CHAPTER 8

REPLAY DRILL 8-A

1. kinds	6. Those	11. types	16. kinds
2. this	7. types	12. this	17. This
3. those	8. These	13. that	18. types
4. These	9. type	14. kinds	19. kinds
5. That	10. That	15. those	20. That

REPLAY DRILL 8-B

1. a	6. an	11. a	16. an
2. an	7. an	12. an	17. a
3. a	8. a	13. an	18. a
4. an	9. an	14. an	19. an
5. an	10. a	15. a	20. a

REPLAY DRILL 8-C

1. Everybody
2. any
3. can
4. anywhere
5. ever

6. any
7. anything
8. anywhere
9. any
10. ever

11. can
12. ever
13. any
14. any
15. anywhere

16. can
17. any
18. could
19. ever
20. any

REPLAY DRILL 8-D

1. best
2. kinder
3. better
4. prettier
5. friendliest

6. brightest
7. better
8. younger
9. worst
10. better

11. more recent
12. least valuable
13. farther
14. worst
15. better

16. oldest
17. most unusual
18. most beautiful
19. most
20. better

REPLAY DRILL 8-E

1. well
2. good
3. very
4. more smoothly
5. more carefully

6. delicious
7. well
8. bad
9. slowly
10. loudly

11. either good or well
12. well
13. surely
14. more quickly
15. really

16. clearly
17. neatly
18. good
19. sure
20. well

REPLAY DRILL 8-F

1. change more better to better
2. change good to well
3. change deliciously to delicious
4. change efficienter to a more efficient
5. change real good to really well
6. change more later to later
7. change type to types
8. change miserable to miserably

9. change <u>quicker</u> to <u>quickly</u> or <u>more quickly</u>

10. change <u>quick, accurate</u> to <u>quickly and accurately</u>

11. change <u>calmly</u> to <u>calm</u>

12. change <u>sure</u> to <u>really</u>

13. change <u>wider</u> to <u>more widely</u>

14. change <u>smoother</u> to <u>more smoothly</u>

15. change <u>better</u> to <u>best</u>

16. C

17. change <u>quick</u> to <u>quickly</u>

18. change <u>a, a</u> to <u>an, an</u>

19. change <u>good</u> to <u>well</u>

20. change <u>comfortable</u> to <u>comfortably</u>

CHAPTER 9

REPLAY DRILL 9-A

1. English, accounting, and marketing
2. to be organized, to speak clearly, and to show enthusiasm
3. president, the managers, and the supervisor
4. Washington, Philadelphia, and New York City
5. child abuse, single-parent families, and homeless shelters
6. The students, their parents, and their teachers
7. The chefs, the cooks, and the waiters
8. shoes, shirts, and long pants
9. main dish, vegetable, and dessert
10. to type, proofread, and fax the reports
11. fold, bend, or staple
12. October 5, November 9, and January 15
13. Pineapples, kiwis, and mangos
14. rent, phone bill, and electric bill
15. her meats at Super Fresh, her produce at Farm Fresh, and her grocery items at Food Lion
16. parents, agent, and director
17. swimming, boating, and snorkeling
18. the streets, the alleys, and the buildings
19. The surgeon, the lab technician, and the radiologist
20. C

REPLAY DRILL 9-B

1. hot, humid
2. C
3. chocolate, chewy
4. two eggs, one stick of butter, and two cups of flour
5. bright, cheery
6. warm, gentle
7. hard, crunchy
8. intelligent, competent
9. ketchup, mustard, and relish
10. accurate, efficient
11. long, fierce
12. friendly, honest
13. run, jump, and dance
14. dust the furniture, peel the potatoes, and iron the shirts
15. daring, competent
16. ridiculous, comic
17. hot, salty
18. a rose, a $100 gift certificate, and a big smile
19. operating system, accounting procedures, and an auditing methods
20. skinned his knee, bruised his arm, and broke his front tooth

REPLAY DRILL 9-C

1. ,and
2. ,and
3. ,but
4. ,yet
5. ,but
6. ,and
7. ,but
8. ,nor
9. ,for
10. ,or
11. ,but
12. ,and
13. ,yet
14. ,but
15. ,for
16. ,nor
17. C
18. C
19. ,and
20. ,for

REPLAY DRILL 9-D

1. Yes,
2. Ms. Johansson,
3. morning, dawn,
4. begins,
5. No,
6. arrive,
7. Byrant,
8. work,
9. stopped,
10. reunion,
11. outside,
12. Well,
13. school,
14. door,
15. Oh,
16. work,
17. Olivas,
18. door,
19. mall,
20. do,

REPLAY DRILL 9-E

1. ,who likes to surf,
2. ,Dr. Harvey,
3. ,Toni Heiser,
4. ,*Guide to Business Careers*,
5. ,young or old,
6. ,who is my brother-in-law,
7. ,Mr. Pope?
8. ,Mr. Orton,
9. ,*Understanding Business Mathematics*,
10. ,either yes or no,
11. ,who is also a dentist,

12. ,my favorite baseball team,
13. ,Mr. Hunting?
14. ,Janet Sturn,

15. ,Ms. Norfleet,
16. ,*Amazing Grace*?
17. ,ladies and gentlemen,

18. ,who is also my aunt,
19. ,Mr. Breeden,
20. ,Dr. Morgan?

REPLAY DRILL 9-F

1. C
2. C
3. C
4. "Please,"
5. "Watch out!"
6. C
7. C

8. C
9. instructed,
10. C
11. C
12. C
13. yelled "Good-bye"
14. week?"

15. C
16. C
17. Marvin asked,
18. C
19. C
20. say "Wow!"

REPLAY DRILL 9-G

1. Lansing, Michigan,
2. Washington, DC,
3. Madrid, Spain,
4. June 12, 1975,
5. ,James Kail, DDS,
6. on June 14, 2010,
7. San Francisco, California,
8. Anaheim, California, Orlando, Florida?
9. ,PhD,
10. ,September 6, 1974,
11. Portsmouth, New Hampshire, Portsmouth Virginia?
12. ,MD,

13. October 14, 1989,
14. Tampa, Florida, Charleston, South Carolina?
15. Thursday, September 5, 1991,
16. November 15, 2001,
17. ,PhD, . . . MD,
18. Pittsburg, Pennsylvania, Denver, Colorado
19. Monday, October 5, . . . Wednesday, October 12.
20. ,MD, Longport, Rhode Island

CHAPTER 10

REPLAY DRILL 10-A

1. Hobley, mayor,
2. bus; then
3. accident; therefore,
4. could; nevertheless,
5. event; that is, location, food,
6. job; then

7. established:
8. Cambria, manager, town;
9. months, so
10. years; therefore,
11. hits; still
12. jobs; also

13. stock; thus,
14. hours: 8:00 a.m. instead of 9 a.m., Monday–Thursday; 8 a.m
15. cities: Cambridge, Massachusetts; Portsmouth, New Hampshire; and Augusta, Maine
16. raise; however,
17. course; nevertheless,
18. birthday; his
19. Friday; therefore,
20. arguing; thus,

REPLAY DRILL 10-B

1. utensils:
2. 5:45
3. the following:
4. mind:
5. C
6. UPS:
7. Council:
8. holidays:
9. class:
10. C
11. diet:
12. specials:
13. interviews:
14. dates:
15. C

REPLAY DRILL 10-C

1. period
2. exclamation mark
3. period
4. question mark
5. exclamation mark
6. period
7. period
8. question mark
9. exclamation mark
10. period
11. question mark
12. period
13. exclamation mark
14. exclamation mark
15. period
16. period
17. period
18. period
19. exclamation mark
20. question mark

REPLAY DRILL 10-D

Part 1
1. (believe me)
2. [*sic*]
3. (not $159)
4. (9 to noon)
5. (see Figure 4, page 80)
6. (last year's models)
7. (our first minister)
8. (not her sister)
9. (see chart, page 23)
10. (the one near the mall)

Part 2
11. donation—we
12. Happiness—it's
13. money—a great deal of money—by
14. refrigerator—rated number one by *Consumer Reports*—has
15. supervisor—a real sweetheart—gave
16. members—Dr. Duzeck and Ms. Swenson—will
17. Bottled water—avoid
18. beauty—the
19. Zelika—she was the winner—praised
20. brochure—in full-color and printed on heavy stock—will

CHAPTER 11

REPLAY DRILL 11-A

1. "accept" "except" or use italics
2. "I can" "I can't" or use italics
3. "Thank you, Mr. Lockner,"
4. C
5. "We're lost!"
6. "Uses for Quotation Marks"
7. "What time will your plane arrive?"
8. "Employee of the Year"
9. "We won!"
10. "eligible" "illegible?" or use italics
11. "Money Management"
12. "break a leg."
13. "ain't" or use italics
14. asked, "Are you working overtime tonight?"
15. "Don't Feed Me!"
16. "I Still Rise"
17. "Should I order dessert?"
18. "irregardless" or use italics
19. yelled, "Play ball!"
20. "catch a wave"

REPLAY DRILL 11-B

1. up-to-date
2. first-rate
3. C
4. self-respect
5. out-of-stock
6. four-year
7. ten-story
8. hard-to-find
9. part-time
10. high-priced
11. ninety-nine
12. mid-July
13. self-control
14. stressed-out
15. six-foot
16. brother-in-law's
17. kind-hearted
18. high-risk
19. first-class
20. self-taught

REPLAY DRILL 11-C

1. weeks'
2. Mr. Hernandez's
3. children's
4. child's
5. boss's
6. secretaries'
7. someone's
8. Janice's
9. woman's
10. ladies'
11. Franklin's
12. James's
13. authors'
14. mother-in-law's
15. months'
16. employees'
17. Minister's
18. companies'
19. Joneses'
20. teachers'

REPLAY DRILL 11-D

1. C	3. o'clock	5. Don't	7. C	9. C
2. can't	4. We'll	6. It's	8. A's	10. C

CHAPTER 12

REPLAY DRILL 12-A

1. F	5. C	9. F	13. F	17. F
2. F	6. F	10. F	14. C	18. F
3. C	7. F	11. C	15. F	19. F
4. F	8. C	12. F	16. C	20. C

REPLAY DRILL 12-B

Part 1

1. Ellen majored in Computer Information Systems at business school.
2. Chris plays football on the junior varsity team.
3. The shoe store at the mall had an end-of-summer sale.
4. The juicy hamburger was covered with onions.
5. The loud ticking of the clock gave Marissa a headache.
6. After he completed his homework, he had a snack.
7. While reading the budget report, Brenda fell asleep.
8. Kenneth decided to go on a diet because he gained 25 pounds.
9. Linda and Freddie share a large office on the 32nd floor.
10. Classes will begin on September 5, the day after Labor Day.

Part 2

11. Ms. Meyers trained Ellen on the new computer program, and Ellen did a good job.
12. The IRS says our taxes were overpaid.
13. Tiffany told her mother that the students were allowed to go.
14. Helen saw her daughter talking to Patricia. [Helen's daughter]
15. Mark met Frank while they were in college. [both were in college]
16. The professor says you must bring a textbook, notebook paper, and a folder to class.
17. Leslie's mother is a beautiful woman, and I'm sure Leslie will be a beauty too.
18. Tim was a track star in high school; sprinting was a sport he loved.
19. Customers are not allowed to smoke in the theater.
20. Lance's father, who is a carpenter, will be able to build the cabinet you want.

REPLAY DRILL 12-C

Part 1
1. some hay
2. with beautiful voice
3. with the crack in the middle
4. with the chocolate swirls
5. with two flat tires
6. with the speed bumps
7. with the furry tail
8. with no textbooks
9. with the thorns
10. which was misplaced this morning

Part 2
11. NP
12. C
13. C
14. C
15. NP
16. C
17. C
18. NP
19. NP
20. NP

REPLAY DRILL 12-D

1. A	5. A	9. A	13. A	17. P
2. P	6. A	10. P	14. A	18. A
3. A	7. P	11. A	15. A	19. P
4. P	8. A	12. P	16. P	20. A

REPLAY DRILL 12-E

1. Having taken too many sick days,
2. C
3. Biting quickly on the bait,
4. C
5. C
6. Torn around the edges,
7. Sitting on the windowsill,
8. C
9. C
10. Having received good grades,
11. Being on the discount table,
12. C
13. C
14. Feeling as though labor had begun,
15. Jogging quickly around the block,
16. C
17. Before going home,
18. C
19. After browsing through the store,
20. C

CHAPTER 13

REPLAY DRILL 13-A

1. F	5. F	9. T	13. F	17. T
2. F	6. T	10. F	14. F	18. F
3. F	7. T	11. T	15. F	19. F
4. F	8. F	12. F	16. T	20. F

REPLAY DRILL 13-B

March 25, 20xx

Mr. John Smith
Jack's Jewels
246 Elm Drive
Akron, OH 44624

Dear Mr. Smith:

We apologize for the error in your recent order, #HN2468297, for 250 gift boxes embossed with your store name. We are having your boxes printed immediately and will ship the corrected order within the next 48 hours.

We value your business and will do everything in our power to ensure that no such problems occur in the future. I expect the new shipment to leave our warehouse on March 27 and to be in your hands the next day.

Thank you for your patience, and we look forward to serving you in the future.

Sincerely yours,

Robert Orderly

Sales Manager

REPLAY DRILL 13-C

Dear Ms. Jackson:

Your October issue of *Today's Business* is now on the way to you at your new address in Brooklyn. As our way of apologizing for the delay, we are extending your subscription by three months without charge.

Through an oversight, your letter of September 25 asking us to change your address from Philadelphia, Pennsylvania, to Brooklyn, New York, was not properly processed. As a result your copies of *Today's Business* were still being sent to Philadelphia for the past few months.

Would you please let us know on the enclosed card if the misaddressed copies were forwarded to you. If not, please check the blanks showing which issues you didn't receive so that we can send them to you.

Sincerely yours,

CHAPTER 14

REPLAY DRILL 14-A: PLANNING A PRESENTATION

1. Your objective: what you want to accomplish
2. What the presentation will include
3. The circumstances in which you will deliver the presentation
4. What equipment and handouts you will need
5. How much time you will need
6. Tell them what you're going to tell them
7. Tell them
8. Tell them what you told them
9. Introduction, body, and conclusion
10. Delivery, timing, and techniques

REPLAY DRILL 14-B

1. Summarize the goal of your writing in one or two paragraphs.
2. Describe your audience in one or two sentences.
3. Gather your information and ideas.
4. Understand how Web sites work.
5. A once-in-a-lifetime travel experience
6. Let us put leisure time on your agenda
7. Free rare book search! If we don't have it, we'll find it.
8. How frequently you need to update content
9. How the visitor will view information on the screen
10. Viewers' feelings about the content—the quality, organization, and appearance

VOCABULARY AND SPELLING REPLAY ANSWERS

CHAPTER 1 REPLAY

a. 18	f. 4	k. 9	p. 19	u. 21
b. 14	g. 7	l. 16	q. 1	
c. 15	h. 2	m. 12	r. 20	
d. 8	i. 10	n. 13	s. 5	
e. 11	j. 6	o. 3	t. 17	

CHAPTER 2 REPLAY

a. 21	e. 38	i. 40	m. 26	q. 28
b. 22	f. 23	j. 31	n. 32	r. 25
c. 27	g. 39	k. 37	o. 29	s. 33
d. 30	h. 34	l. 36	p. 24	t. 35

CHAPTER 3 REPLAY

a. 41	e. 53	i. 42	m. 54	q. 51
b. 44	f. 57	j. 59	n. 49	r. 55
c. 43	g. 60	k. 48	o. 45	s. 47
d. 56	h. 52	l. 50	p. 58	t. 46

CHAPTER 4 REPLAY

a. 61	e. 63	i. 67	m. 76	q. 68
b. 62	f. 79	j. 72	n. 71	r. 75
c. 73	g. 70	k. 74	o. 69	s. 78
d. 64	h. 65	l. 77	p. 66	t. 80

CHAPTER 5 REPLAY

a. 98	e. 83	i. 94	m. 91	q. 85
b. 88	f. 86	j. 89	n. 95	r. 84
c. 81	g. 82	k. 99	o. 97	s. 90
d. 87	h. 100	l. 92	p. 93	t. 96

CHAPTER 6 REPLAY

1. amalgamation
2. depreciate
3. deficit
4. balance sheet
5. beneficiaries
6. euro
7. foreclosure
8. slander
9. libel
10. mortgage

CHAPTER 7 REPLAY

1. accept
2. except
3. add
4. ad
5. dying
6. dyeing
7. dissent
8. descent
9. bizarre
10. bazaar
11. coarse
12. course
13. site
14. cite
15. sight
16. counsel
17. Council
18. access
19. excess
20. affect
21. effect
22. capitol
23. capital
24. allot
25. a lot
26. principle
27. principal
28. elicit
29. illicit

CHAPTER 8 REPLAY

1. imminent
2. eminent
3. regardless
4. eligible
5. illegible
6. devise
7. device
8. dessert
9. desert
10. desert
11. choose
12. chose
13. defer
14. differ
15. conscience
16. conscious
17. besides
18. beside
19. envelop
20. envelope
21. fiscal
22. physical
23. complimented
24. complemented
25. guise
26. guys

CHAPTER 9 REPLAY

1. personal
2. loose
3. than
4. thorough, suite
5. Whether, weather, suit
6. prosecute
7. that
8. whether, weather
9. proceeds, rye
10. We're, quite
11. proceed, morale, personnel
12. prospective, perks, wry, personnel
13. morale, moral
14. Where, we're
15. perspective
16. respectfully, quit
17. We're, whether, through
18. persecuted
19. Morale, personnel
20. proceed, suite
21. wry, lose
22. personal
23. We're, where
24. Then, than
25. that, realty

CHAPTER 10 REPLAY

1. apprise, appraise
2. bloc, block
3. canvass, canvas
4. everyday
5. foreword, forward
6. have, halve, half
7. key, quay
8. lesson, lessen
9. marquis, marquise, marquee
10. navel, naval
11. ode, owed
12. precede, proceed
13. rein, rain, reign
14. peak, pique, peek
15. serge, surge
16. stationery, stationary
17. taught, taut
18. vise, vice
19. wary, wear and tear
20. waive, wave

CHAPTER 11 REPLAY

1. eager, anxious
2. disinterested, uninterested
3. enthusiastic, enthusiasm
4. Explicit, implicit
5. per annum, per diem
6. Flammable, inflammable
7. nonflammable
8. further, farther
9. Indigenous, indigent
10. emigrate, immigrate
11. fewer, less
12. implies, infers
13. thought, thorough, through
14. simple, simplistic
15. RSVP
16. proceed
17. proceeds

CHAPTER 12 REPLAY

1. allot
2. eminent, bibliography
3. chose, defer
4. illegible, eligible
5. We're, proceed, their, rain
6. owed, canvas, appraised
7. It's, principle, capitol, elicit
8. We're, thorough, suite
9. wry, perks, guise
10. led, miner, lead, canvas
11. Regardless, fiscal, conscience, fiscal
12. fiscal, allot, altar, capital
13. advice
14. through, thorough
15. uninterested, disinterested

CHAPTER 13 REPLAY

1. Mankind—Society or Humanity
2. stewardess—flight attendant
3. men—staff members or men and women
4. chairman—chairperson
5. wives—spouses
6. common man—average person
7. lady policemen—police officers
8. waitress—server
9. Cameramen—Photographers or Camera operators
10. girls—women
11. girls—secretaries
12. man-size—excellent, good, huge
13. omit male
14. manmade—synthetic
15. man—agent

CHAPTER 14 REPLAY

A.
1. 2
2. 4
3. 3
4. 3
5. 2

B.
6. s, es
7. s
8. s
9. b, e
10. h, e

C.
11. T
12. F
13. T
14. F
15. F
16. F
17. F
18. T
19. F
20. F
21. T
22. F
23. F
24. F
25. F

INDEX

A

a, an, 161–164
Abbreviations, 416–420
  business, 417
  commas, 195
  plural, 230–231
  possessive, 231
Abridged dictionaries, 3
Academic degrees
  abbreviations in, 419
Accent marks, 7
Acronyms, 163, 417–419
Action verbs, 29, 30, 142, 163
Action words, 24
Addresses, 195, 199, 272
  numbers in, 413
Adjectives, 24, 33–35, 36, 46, 158–182
  absolute, 168
  articles, 34
  being verb, 126, 168
  comma, 184–186
  comparisons, 165–167, 170–175
  compound, 224, 225
  descriptive, 33–34, 159, 165–167
  irregular, 168
  limiting, 34, 159
  ly words, 169
  pointing, 34, 159–161
  three degrees, 177
  tips/hints, 169–170, 177–178
  types, 159
Adverbs, 24, 35–36, 46, 158–182
  bad, badly, 159, 169
  comparative, 170
  comparisons, 170–175
  conjunctive, 39–40
  good, well, 159, 173
  ly words, 159, 169
  recognition, 36
  superlative, 170
  three degrees, 177
  tips/hints, 169–170, 177–178
Age
  numbers in, 413
alright, all right, 10
American Dictionary of the English Language, 2
American English, 10, 161
and, 146
Anderson, Marian, 220
Antonyms, 13
any one/anyone, 120
anyway, 176

Apostrophe

Apostrophe
  compound plural possessives, 99
  compound singular nouns, 98
  contractions, 116, 229–230
  plural abbreviations, 231
  plural nouns, 77, 79, 97, 99
  plural numbers and words, 228
  possessive abbreviations, 231
  possessive nouns, 94, 95–96, 97–98, 116, 228–229
  pronouns, 116, 230
  singular nouns, 97–98
  special cases, 99–100
Articles, 34, 161–164
Auxillary verbs, 30

B

Back matter, 3, 6
bad, badly, 171, 173–1174
Being verb, 29–30, 126–127, 133, 142, 171
Bernstein, Theodore, 127
between, 111
Books
  numbers in, 413
Brackets, 213–214
British English, 10, 161
Business letters, 272–278. *See also Written communication*
  abbreviations in, 416–417, 418
  basic parts, 272–276
  body, 269, 273
  closing, 269
  company name (at end of letter), 277
  complimentary close, 68, 273
  confidential/personal, 276
  copy notation, 274
  date, 272
  enclosure notation, 274
  handwritten signature, 68, 273, 278
  identification initials, 274
  inside address, 272, 276
  letter placement, 422
  letterhead, 274
  numbers in, 411–413
  optional parts, 276–277
  postscript (PS), 277
  proofreading, 274, 278
  salutation, 68, 272–273, 276
  signature, 269, 273, 276, 278
  stationary, 274, 421
  styles, 421
  subject/reference line, 276
  writer's name, title, department name, 68

NOTES

NOTES